ECONOMIC APPROACHES TO INTELLECTUAL PROPERTY POLICY, LITIGATION, AND MANAGEMENT

ECONOMIC APPROACHES TO INTELLECTUAL PROPERTY POLICY, LITIGATION, AND MANAGEMENT

Edited by
Gregory K. Leonard
Lauren J. Stiroh

NERA ECONOMIC CONSULTING

National Economic Research Associates, Inc.
50 Main Street, 14th Floor
White Plains, NY 10606
www.nera.com

Printed in the United States of America.

Leonard, Gregory K., 1963–
Stiroh, Lauren J., 1968–
Economic Approaches to Intellectual Property Policy,
Litigation, and Management;
edited by Dr. Gregory K. Leonard and Dr. Lauren J. Stiroh,
with a foreword by Dr. Victor P. Goldberg.
Includes index.
ISBN 0-9748788-1-2 (pb)
1. Economic Approaches--Intellectual Property 2. Policy
3. Litigation 4. Portfolio Management
I. Title

Library of Congress Control Number: 2005930350

Contents

Foreword, *Victor P. Goldberg* • *ix*

Preface • *xi*

Acknowledgments • *xv*

I.   A Survey of Economic Knowledge Regarding Intellectual Property

1.   Uncertainty in the Economics of Knowledge and Information, *Lauren J. Stiroh* • 3

2.   The Economics of Patent Policy: A Review of Recent Empirical Studies, *John H. Johnson* • 13

II.   The Basics of Intellectual Property Damages

3.   A Practical Guide to Damages, *Gregory K. Leonard and Lauren J. Stiroh* • 27

4.   The Evolution of the Courts' Thinking on Damages, *Phillip A. Beutel and Bryan Ray* • 69

5.   A Critique of Noneconomic Methods of Reasonable Royalty Calculation, *Christine Meyer and Bryan Ray* • 83

6.   Valuation of Nonpatent Intellectual Property: Common Themes and Notable Differences, *Phillip A. Beutel* • 95

III.   Advanced Topics in Economic Analysis in Intellectual Property Litigation and Damages

7.   Applying Merger Simulation Techniques to Estimate Lost Profits Damages in Intellectual Property Litigation, *Gregory K. Leonard* • 111

8. The Use of Surveys in Intellectual Property Disputes,
    Eugene P. Ericksen and Sarah M. Butler • 1 2 5

9. Hedonic Characteristics in the Valuation of Intellectual
    Property, *Joseph P. Cook* • 1 4 1

10. The Use of Event Studies in Intellectual Property Litigation,
    John H. Johnson and Vinita M. Juneja • 1 5 3

11. Interest and Discount Rates in Intellectual Property Damages,
    Jesse David and Christine Meyer • 1 6 9

12. Avoiding Misidentified Incremental Costs, *Alyssa Lutz and
    Paola Maria Valenti* • 1 8 5

13. Commercial Success: Economic Principles Applied to Patent
    Litigation, *Jesse David and Marion B. Stewart* • 1 9 5

14. Preliminary Injunction Motions and the Economics of
    Irreparable Harm in Pharmaceutical Patent Infringement Cases,
    Jason Zeitler • 2 0 9

IV. The Intersection of Antitrust and Intellectual Property

15. Standard Setting and Market Power, *Richard T. Rapp and
    Lauren J. Stiroh* • 2 2 3

16. Essential Issues in the Competitive Analysis of Patent Pools,
    Lawrence Wu and Thomas R. McCarthy • 2 3 3

17. Antitrust Implications of Pharmaceutical Patent Litigation
    Settlements, *Gregory K. Leonard and Rika Onishi Mortimer* • 2 5 1

18. A Comparison of Market Tests for Evaluating Patent Damages
    Claims and Antitrust Counterclaims, *Joseph P. Cook, Susan C.S.
    Lee, and Ramsey Shehadeh* • 2 6 7

V. Intellectual Property Rights Protection in Japan and China

19. When East Meets West, *Christian Dippon and Noriko Kakihara* • *277*

20. Intellectual Property Rights Protection in China: Litigation, Economic Damages, and Case Strategies, *Alan Cox and Kristina Sepetys* • *293*

VI. Issues in the Management of Intellectual Property Portfolios

21. Using the Real Option Method to Value Intellectual Property, *George G. Korenko* • *317*

22. Transfer Pricing Issues Affecting the Value of Intangible Property in Multinational Companies, *George G. Korenko* • *335*

23. Finding Patent Litigation Strategies That Make Economic Sense, *Phillip A. Beutel* • *359*

Contributors • *369*

Index • *381*

Foreword

The central features of a modern economic system, as Joseph A. Schumpeter reminded us in the middle of the last century, are innovation and change. Information is, of course, a "public good" in the economist's sense—once it is produced, the marginal social cost of using it is zero. Governments often play a crucial role in this process, producing, disseminating, and even financing technological change. Lawmakers also set the ground rules for the private sector, which can lead to tension between innovation and competition, with consumers often caught in the middle. This conflict has been brought to light in recent years by the legal battles over the use of digital content via the Internet, and in the ongoing patent disputes over pharmaceutical products.

Without some form of intellectual property (IP) protection, innovators have little incentive to innovate. Protection takes a number of different forms—patents, copyrights, trademarks, and trade secrets, to name a few. Western nations have traditionally been the most aggressive in protecting and defending IP rights, but in recent years Japan and China have made efforts to strengthen the rights of those who seek to commercialize their intangible assets. With varying policies and legal standards throughout the world, measures to protect and enhance IP rights are increasingly complex.

Economists at NERA devote a great deal of time and effort to exploring "real world" IP issues, as well as to searching for solutions to the economic questions on which these debates often turn. How should the owner of IP rights be compensated for violation of those rights? What role should antitrust and competition policy play in intellectual property matters? How can companies that rely on innovation more accurately value their R&D investments and strategies? Should emerging economic powers implement and enforce more stringent intellectual property rights? If so, how? This collection of thinking on current IP matters by NERA economists illustrates the extent to which the application of economic concepts has become more and more ingrained into legal systems, policy decisions, and portfolio management strategies worldwide.

I have been associated with NERA for more than a decade. As economists, it is our job to effectively communicate the results of our economic analysis to noneconomists. It is this ability to communicate—in conjunction with the quality of the analysis—that makes this volume so useful. In tackling complex and often controversial IP issues, the authors examine a wide array of IP topics. The result is a thoughtful blend of principles and practical application which clarifies and illuminates the underlying economic issues. It should prove to be a useful tool for anyone who wrestles with the implications of innovation in an academic, business, or legal setting.

VICTOR P. GOLDBERG
Thomas Macioce Professor of Law
Co-director, Center for Law and Economic Studies
Columbia University School of Law

Preface

At the beginning of the twentieth century, the smokestack industries producing tangible products such as steel, paper, and textiles were the engine of economic growth in the United States. By the close of the century, however, a significant shift had occurred. As a driver of economic growth, the manufacturing of tangible products had been replaced by intangible products—technology and ideas that are collectively called intellectual property (IP). Today, IP is a crucial component of many of the products and services sold by companies in the U.S. and around the world, from computer systems to medical devices to cell phones.

Innovation is the process by which IP is developed. A system of IP rights protection, such as the U.S. patent system, must balance two conflicting concerns. Strong IP rights (such as a lengthy patent life) give inventors an incentive to engage in innovation, which has a substantial positive effect on social welfare. However, strong IP rights, by allowing the exclusion of competitors, may also create deadweight loss in the short run that has a negative effect on social welfare. To resolve these conflicting concerns, the U.S. patent system gives a patent owner the right to sue to exclude potential infringers, but only for a fixed period of time. In return for the patent right, the inventor must describe his or her invention in the patent claims. This helps potential future inventors to build upon previously patented inventions.

The U.S. federal court system provides the forum in which IP owners can seek to enforce their IP rights and recover damages for past infringement of those rights. For the incentives provided by the patent system to operate properly and generate good economic outcomes, it is necessary that the courts produce sound legal outcomes, including making IP owners whole with respect to violation of their IP rights and, where warranted, imposing penalties on violators to deter willful infringement.

Economic principles provide useful guidance concerning a number of IP issues, including how to design IP rights policies, how to determine the appropriate level of damages to award in IP litigation, and how to manage an IP portfolio. We and our colleagues at NERA Economic Consulting have spent a good deal of time thinking about these issues. This book is the result of these efforts.

The book consists of 23 chapters organized into six sections. The first section of the book concerns the state of economic knowledge about the innovative process and its relation to the legal framework of IP rights protection. Chapter 1 discusses the role that uncertainty plays in the economics of knowledge and innovation and how the uncertainty that is inherent in the process of innovation shapes the questions analyzed by economists. Chapter 2 surveys recent economic studies that investigate how to measure the amount of innovative activity and the effects of IP policy on innovation.

Section II addresses the basics of calculating compensatory damages in IP litigation. Chapter 3 provides a primer on the economics of patent damages calculations. Chapter 4 reviews the evolution of the case law and shows how the legal approaches to damages calculation have increasingly incorporated economic concepts. Chapter 5 offers the economists' view on the flaws arising in noneconomic methods of damages calculation commonly used by the courts. Chapter 6 expands the discussion to other, nonpatent, forms of IP, including trademarks, trade names, and copyrights.

Advanced topics in damages calculation are the subject of Section III. Chapter 7 demonstrates how techniques used in the competitive analysis of mergers have application in calculating IP damages. Chapter 8 discusses the use of surveys in IP disputes. Chapter 9 explains how hedonic price models and discrete choice models of consumer demand can be used to value patented technology. Chapter 10 explores the application of event study methodology, which is frequently used in economics to analyze stock price movements, to IP litigation. Chapter 11 addresses how to calculate appropriate discount and prejudgment interest rates for use in IP damages calculations. Chapter 12 discusses some issues that arise when determining incremental costs in a lost profits calculation. Chapter 13 considers how an economist might help assess whether a patented invention was a commercial success, a prerequisite for patent validity. And Chapter 14 discusses preliminary injunction motions and the economics of irreparable harm.

Issues at the intersection of antitrust and IP are the focus of Section V. Chapter 15 analyzes the relationship between standard setting and the market power of a patent owner whose IP is incorporated into a standardized technology. Chapter 16 discusses patent pools and specifically when they are procompetitive and when they are anticompetitive. Chapter 17 addresses the competitive implications of patent litigation settlements, particularly settlements in the pharmaceutical industry that have been characterized by so-called reverse payments. Chapter 18 contrasts the issues that arise in determining relevant markets for IP claims as compared to antitrust counterclaims and demonstrates that there need not be a tension between claims made in the lost profits analysis in a patent infringement case and the claimed relevant market in an antitrust counterclaim.

Section V of the book takes a look at emerging IP issues in Japan (Chapter 19) and China (Chapter 20). The nature of IP rights protection and the associated legal framework in these countries differs in significant respects from those in the U.S. Given the current and future importance of Japan and China to the U.S. economy, these chapters are timely.

The final section of the book treats topics of interest to research and development managers and IP portfolio managers. Chapter 21 shows how taking into account option value can provide superior assessments of R&D projects as compared to standard present discounted value analysis. Chapter 22 explains the tax issues that arise when a company transfers IP from one subsidiary to another subsidiary located in another country.

The book covers a great deal of ground. We hope you find it informative and thought-provoking.

DR. GREGORY K. LEONARD
DR. LAUREN J. STIROH
September 2005

Acknowledgments

Our task as co-editors was made substantially easier by the dedication of the Board of Editors. This group of NERA economists served along side us as the first-line reviewers for each chapter in this book. As such, they deserve to share in the credit for the quality of the end product. The Board of Editors consisted of:

Jesse David
Chris Dippon
John Johnson
Ken Serwin
Jason Zeitler

In addition to the Board of Editors, others at NERA served as reviewers of various chapters. Their willingness to volunteer for such duty was much appreciated and the book benefited from their insights. They include Phil Beutel, Tim Daniel, Dick Rapp, Steve Schwartz, Marion Stewart, and Paola Valenti. We would also like to thank Lawrence Wu for his valuable advice and insight throughout the process of creating this book.

We are grateful for the contributions of all of our authors and their willingness to adhere to our occasionally unreasonable deadlines. It is due to their enthusiasm, insight, and keen interest in the subject matter that allowed us to achieve coverage of the breadth of topics we had envisioned for the book.

The crucial behind-the-scenes functions of putting a book together—design, production, and marketing—were undertaken by Christine Creager-Kepko, Jack Morris, Jake George, Sarah Lukachko, Risa Uchida, Bernadette Carr, Anne Noyes, Constance Barich, and Kristina Sepetys with great aplomb and expertise. We also especially want to thank Winnie Wong for her help in managing the editing process and the multiple drafts generated by 26 authors and seven editors.

Lastly, we would like to thank Marion Stewart and Dick Rapp for their encouragement and support of the book.

I

A Survey of Economic Knowledge Regarding Intellectual Property

1

Uncertainty in the Economics of Knowledge and Information

Lauren J. Stiroh

The primary purpose of this book is to provide insight into the economics of intellectual property. It is useful to begin, however, by acknowledging that there is much that remains unknown about the primary ingredient in intellectual property: innovation. The research and development (R&D) process involves a high degree of uncertainty, which plays a significant role in both our understanding and analysis of innovation and technology markets.

To paraphrase Donald Rumsfeld, lack of information comes in three flavors: *known unknowns, unknown unknowns,* and *unknowable unknowns.*[1] In spite of decades of economic research and an accumulating wealth of data, there is much about R&D and innovation markets that still falls into these three categories.

The benefits of the innovative process are well-known: faster techno-logical progress, higher productivity, and improved standards of living. The best method or appropriate policy for achieving these outcomes, however, remains an important question at the intersection of the economics of antitrust and intellectual property. Does intellectual property protection encourage faster innovation or slow the adoption of new and beneficial technologies throughout the economy? What is the proper role of antitrust policy in innovation and technology markets in order to enhance techno-

---

[1] Defense Department Daily Briefing, 22 February 2002: "Reports that say that some-thing hasn't happened are always interesting to me, because as we know, there are known knowns; there are things we know we know. We also know there are known unknowns; that is to say we know there are some things we do not know. But there are also unknown unknowns—the ones we don't know we don't know."

logical progress?[2] Does competition in R&D lead to more or less innovation? How can we tell if innovation is strengthened or lessened?

The reality is that very little is known, or generally accepted among economists, about how competition in R&D affects the rate of innovation, how the rate and level of innovation affects technological progress and consumer welfare, or even how to distinguish economically efficient R&D from socially wasteful R&D. The high degree of uncertainty and debate concerning the appropriate policy governing information markets stems from uncertainty and heterogeneity inherent in the innovation process itself. An innovation, by definition, is something new and heretofore unseen or unthought-of. The very uniqueness of an invention that renders it patentable also renders its impact on the economy difficult to predict with precision. The goal of this chapter is to separate fact from rhetoric and to acknowledge the role that unknowable unknowns must play in our analysis of knowledge and information markets.

The Facts

Let us begin with what is known. Between 1970 and 2004 the number of patents granted per year in the U.S. almost tripled. Roughly 120,000 more patents were granted in 2004 than were granted in 1970 (Figure 1).[3] Not surprisingly, this tremendous growth in innovative output is matched by growth in the inputs to the innovative process. There has been significant growth in the U.S. both in the number of scientists and engineers working in research and development and in the amount of overall R&D spending (Figures 2 and 3). In real terms, more than twice is spent on R&D today than was spent 30 years ago. The output of this research is measurable by the corresponding increase in the number of patentable inventions. Yet, in spite of this surge in innovation, no obvious increase in trend GDP growth can be observed by charting the annual growth rate of the economy over the last three decades (Figure 4). This begs the question, where are the benefits of all of this research?

---

2   An innovation market is the market that arises prior to the realization of an invention. It is the market of trial and error in which R&D dollars are spent in the quest for knowledge. A technology market is the market that arises after the realization of an invention. It is the market in which intellectual property rights, or know-how, is traded.

3   United States Patent and Trademark Office annual reports.

Figure 1. Growth in Innovative Activity

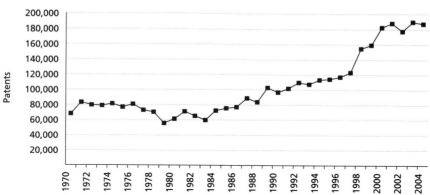

Sources: *United States Patent and Trademark Office Annual Reports (www.uspto.gov/web/offices/com/annual/index.html)*
and table of issue years and patent numbers (for years 1970 to 1975)
(www.uspto.gov/web/offices/ac/ido/oeip/taf/issuyear.htm).

Figure 2. Growth in the Search for Innovations

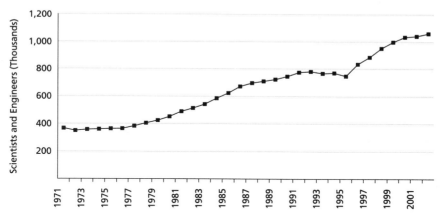

Source: *National Science Foundation (www.nsf.gov).*

Note: *As a result of a new sample design, statistics for 1988–91 have been revised since originally published, and statistics for
1991 and later years are not directly comparable with statistics for 1990 and earlier years.*

Figure 3. Growth in Real R&D Expenditures

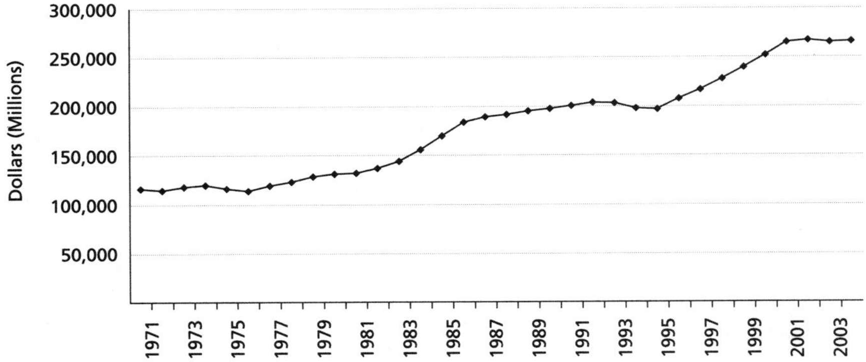

Source: U.S. Department of Labor, Bureau of Labor Statistics (www.bls.gov/cpi/home.htm).

Notes: R&D expenditures have been converted to real expenditures using a CPI conversion factor
(base year=1967) for each year.

Economic theory tells us that more investment in R&D should lead to
more innovation and more innovation should fuel GDP growth.[4] We see
more investment in R&D, we see more innovation, but GDP appears to be
growing much as it always has. Moreover, in a series of studies in 1995,
economist Charles Jones empirically tested and rejected the predictions
of economic models linking an increase in R&D to faster GDP growth.[5]

Why do we care? Among the topics of concern in intellectual property
economics is the role that antitrust policy should play in technology and
innovation markets. Does antitrust scrutiny, such as in cases like *Rambus*

---

4 See, for example, Paul M. Romer, "Endogenous Technological Change," *Journal of
Political Economy* 98, no. 5 (October 1990); Gene M. Grossman and Elhanan Helpman,
Innovation and Growth in the Global Economy (Cambridge, MA: MIT Press, 1991); Gene
M. Grossman and Elhanan Helpman, "Quality Ladders in the Theory of Growth,"
Review of Economic Studies 58 (January 1991); and Phillipe Aghion and Peter Howitt,
"A Model of Growth through Creative Destruction," *Econometrica* 60 (March 1992).

5 Charles Jones empirically tests and rejects the predictions of the economic models of
Romer, Grossman and Helpman, and Aghion and Howitt. See Charles I. Jones, "Time
Series Tests of Endogenous Growth Models," *Quarterly Journal of Economics* (1995);
and Charles I. Jones, "R&D-Based Models of Economic Growth," *Journal of Political
Economy* 103, no. 4 (1995).

Figure 4. GDP Growth Rate

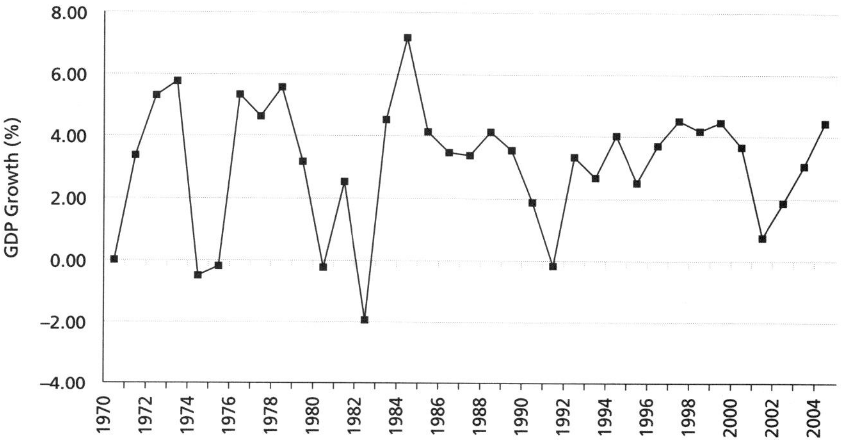

Source: Bureau of Economic Analysis at the U.S. Department of Commerce (www.bea.doc.gov)
Notes: Based on chained 2000 dollars.

or *Genzyme,* enhance or retard innovation?[6] What will happen to the rate of innovation if investments in R&D are subject to antitrust regulation or if a patent owner's use of his intellectual property draws increased antitrust attention? The concern, rooted in well-founded economic theory, is that if antitrust policy limits the rewards that technology owners receive for their inventions, that will reduce incentives to invest in R&D, leading to fewer innovations and a slower rate of technological progress, potentially harming future consumer welfare. But is this really a concern, given our experience to date?

The Uncertainty

There are potentially many reasons why we do not see the link in the data between innovation and faster GDP growth. Chief among them is that perhaps we are using the wrong instruments to measure the impact of innovation. As discussed further and in the next chapter, the number of patents granted may be a poor measure of the level of innovation in an

---

[6] See *In the Matter of Rambus Inc.,* F.T.C. Dkt. No. 9302; and *In the matter of Genzyme Corp./Novazyme Pharmaceuticals Inc.,* File No. 021 0026.

economy. Approximately 80 percent of patents granted represent improvements to products already in existence as opposed to inventions of wholly new products.[7] While some product improvements no doubt do improve consumer welfare, one cannot tell by counting patent grants which patents represent insignificant technological advances and which ones represent major technological breakthroughs.

Moreover, while Figure 4 may appear to yield no discernible trend in GDP growth since 1970, in fact, economic analysis has shown that 1995 marked the beginning of an increased pace of productivity growth.[8] This phenomenon has been referred to as the "new economy," and the higher rate of growth is attributed to technological progress, particularly in the computer-intensive sectors of the economy.[9] Prior studies failing to find a link between productivity growth and R&D may simply have been looking at a period when growth was slow for other reasons.

Even if economists were secure in the prediction that greater innovation leads to faster productivity growth and eventually to higher standards of living, we would still be left with uncertainty as to the best way to encourage greater innovation and what the appropriate antitrust and intellectual property policies should be.

Uncertainty regarding appropriate policy begins in the innovation market, where R&D is conducted in the search for patentable inventions. For innovation markets (e.g., *Genzyme*), there is uncertainty regarding whether competition in R&D (which means more firms focusing on the same research problem) leads to more or less innovation.[10] If it is a winner-take-all innovation market, such as those we see in the pharmaceutical industry, does the prospect of coming in second and having nothing that rewards the investment in R&D limit a firm's willingness to invest?

---

7   Nathan Rosenberg, "Uncertainty and Technological Change," in *Technology and Growth,* ed. J. C. Fuhrer and J. S. Little (Boston: Federal Reserve Bank of Boston, 1996), 96.

8   GDP is a measure of the output of an economy, whereas productivity measures output per hour worked. All else being equal, higher productivity growth means faster GDP growth.

9   See Kevin Stiroh, "Growth and Innovation in the New Economy," in *New Economy Handbook,* ed. Derek C. Jones (San Diego, CA: Academic Press, 2003), 723-751; and Dale W. Jorgenson, Mun S. Ho, and Kevin Stiroh, "Will the U.S. Productivity Resurgence Continue?" *Current Issues in Economics and Finance* 10, no. 13 (December 2004).

10 See, for example, Xiangkang Yin and Ehud Zuscovitch, "Is Firm Size Conducive to R&D Choice? A Strategic Analysis of Product and Process Innovations," *Journal of Economic Behavior and Organization* 35, no. 2 (April 1998); and Luis Cabral, "Bias in Market R&D Portfolios," *International Journal of Industrial Organization* 12, no. 4 (December 1994).

Or does competition spur firms to invest more and innovate faster to gain a competitive edge?

There is also uncertainty as to whether competition in R&D leads to economically *efficient* innovation.[11] Does competition lead to duplicative efforts and inefficiently spent research dollars? In other words, would the same invention be discovered more cheaply if only one firm or a government entity were running the necessary lab experiments and clinical trials?

Uncertainty continues past the innovation market stage and into the technology market—the market that arises after the patent has been granted. If antitrust regulation of technology markets lowers the return to innovation, we expect a reduction in the incentive to invest, but we do not know how that will affect the rate of growth of the economy. If investment is reduced, we do not know if firms will continue to invest in "important" inventions and scrap only research in "marginal" inventions. Moreover, there is uncertainty at the outset in determining what is an "important" investment and likely to lead to faster GDP growth and improve consumer welfare and what is a "marginal" investment likely to have little or no impact on technological progress. Ex ante we do not know which is which.

Uncertainty is inherent in the very process of inventing. One of the reasons that we may not see an obvious connection in historical data whereby more innovation leads to faster technological progress is simply that some inventions matter and some do not. The late professor Zvi Griliches declared patents a "shrinking yardstick" for measuring innovation. Adam Jaffe and Josh Lerner blame the patent system for granting too many patents on trivial, useless, or redundant inventions.[12] According to the authors, "the patent system—intended to foster and protect innovation—is generating waste and uncertainty that hinders and threatens the innovative process" by "increasing the costs of bringing new products and processes to market."[13]

While the invention of a watch that clocks time in dog years rather than human years[14] may be generally acknowledged to be of questionable economic value, it is not always immediately apparent which innovations

---

[11] Kotar Suzumara, "Cooperative and Noncooperative R&D in the Presence and Absence of Spillover Effects," *American Economic Review* 82, no. 5 (December 1992).

[12] Adam B. Jaffe and Josh Lerner, *Innovation and Its Discontents: How Our Broken Patent System Is Endangering Innovation and Progress, and What to Do About It* (Princeton, NJ: Princeton University Press, 2004).

[13] Id., 2.

[14] U.S. Patent 5,023,850, issued 11 June 1991.

contribute to the social welfare and which innovations serve only as a drain on the patent examiner's time and represent a larger opportunity cost for society.

Uncertainty does not end when the invention is patented. Predicting the long run effects of an invention is as uncertain as predicting when and how your R&D will yield results. In 1943 the Chairman of IBM predicted that there was a world market for about five computers.[15] More than 30 years later the president of Digital Equipment Corporation fearlessly declared, "There is no reason for any individual to have a computer in their home."[16] These industry leaders were clearly wrong in their initial predictions. Identifying which inventions will spur growth and which will amount to a lot of noise and fury signifying nothing is no easy task. Even the executives who led the computer industry into its current age did not foresee the impact that technological progress in computers would have on productivity in the workplace and everyday life.

Clearly, some innovations will fuel technological progress, but one cannot predict with certainty which innovations those will be. On the one hand, computers and the associated technology achieved success far beyond initial expectations. On the other hand, there are inventions like the Segway (Figure 5). This top-secret invention, unveiled on national television in 2001, was hailed as a world-changing creation that would eventually replace cars in congested areas, causing no harm to the environment and costing less than five cents per day to operate.[17] *Time* magazine praised the invention, claiming, among other things, that it was impossible to fall off the vehicle.[18]

These predictions have, thus far, proven false. Sales of the Segway had only reached 6 percent of first-year forecasts when the Consumer Products Safety Commission recalled the device to correct a software problem that was causing riders to fall off.[19] The invention, while undoubtedly remarkable in its own right, has yet to have a significant impact on day-to-day life, productivity, or the growth rate of the economy, in spite of initial forecasts to the contrary.

---

[15] Ernst R. Berndt, *The Practice of Econometrics: Classic and Contemporary* (Reading, MA: Addison-Wesley Publishing Company, 1991), 1.

[16] Id.

[17] Andy Sullivan, "Mysterious 'It' Invention Is a Motor Scooter, says *Time*," *Ottawa Citizen*, sec. A2, 3 December 2001.

[18] Id.

[19] David Armstrong, "The Segway: Bright Idea, Wobbly Business," *The Wall Street Journal*, sec. B1, 12 February 2004.

Figure 5. Segway

Source: Getty Images

There are other storied examples of our "inability to anticipate the future impact of...innovations, even after their technical feasibility has been established."[20] The inventor of the radio anticipated that it would be used only for ship-to-shore communications and not as an instrument for mass broadcast,[21] and Bell labs initially hesitated to apply for a patent

---

[20] Nathan Rosenberg, "Uncertainty and Technological Change," 91.
[21] Id., 94.

on the laser because the device had no apparent immediate relevance to the telephone industry.[22]

Famous failures are equally abundant. DuPont spent over $250 million to develop its synthetic leather, "Corfam," and showcased it as a miracle fabric at the 1964 world's fair. DuPont withdrew the product after seven years on the market because it failed to live up to initial expectations.[23] RJ Reynolds' smokeless cigarette was also a technical success but a commercial failure. After seven years in development and $325 million in R&D costs, the product was withdrawn after only four months on the market.[24]

Conclusion

The hallmark of the inventive process is uncertainty. We rarely know with certainty whether the research underway will yield a significant patent or a marginal one, whether an invention will have far reaching implications, or even whether a significant technological breakthrough will achieve market acceptance. These questions remain at the heart of the economics of knowledge and information and affect the way we think about the economics of intellectual property.

---

[22] Id., 93.
[23] Lee Neville, "A Synonym for Failure," *U.S. News & World Report,* 24 February 1997, 15.
[24] Id.

2

The Economics of Patent Policy: A Review of Recent Empirical Studies

John H. Johnson

Policy makers, company executives, and economists recognize that innovation is a fundamental source of economic growth and efficiency. Yet, the exact mechanism through which innovation accomplishes this feat is still not well understood. The study of patents and patent policy among economists is therefore well justified—intellectual property is a tangible link between innovative behavior and economic growth. Economists are exploring a number of issues related to patents. How valuable are patents? Is the number of patents a useful measure of innovative activity? How have changes in patent policy affected patenting behavior? What patents are most likely to be challenged in court? In this chapter, I highlight a sample of recent economic research papers that reflect the cutting edge of the economic analysis of patent policy.[1]

The Distribution of Patent Value
Economists routinely turn to market-based evidence when they attempt to value products, goods, and services, but valuing a patent presents particular challenges. In goods markets, value is measured by the price a product commands. Patents, though, are frequently not traded on markets, and therefore the "price" of the patent is often not observable. Moreover, while some patents may be licensed, the terms of licensing agreements are often not made public or are affected by factors other than

---

[1] This review does not, however, address any papers using theoretical research techniques, such as modeling economic behavior to determine optimal patent policy. My focus on empirical papers in no way implies that theoretical analysis has not been important or useful for understanding patent issues; these studies are excluded only because they are beyond this chapter's scope. All of the papers in this chapter were selected from refereed economics journals, and most of them have been published in the last five years.

the value of the patent at issue (such as the costs and risks of litigation). Even when arm's-length licensing terms are publicly available, whole portfolios of patents are often licensed under one royalty rate or licensing fee, making it difficult to separate out the payments attributable to a specific patent in the portfolio.

In principle, a patent could be valued by measuring the incremental profits the patented technology creates for products based on that technology. However, this approach is useful only once the patented technology has been used to create a marketed product. Moreover, if we are interested in the distribution of patent values, we would have to evaluate the market impact of a large number of patents, which would be a daunting task.

In two seminal papers, Ariel Pakes and Mark Schankerman describe an innovative method for estimating the private value of patents.[2] They base their approach on patent renewal data from France, Germany, and the United Kingdom, which require patent owners to pay a fee each year to maintain the enforceability of their patent rights. Because owners of patents in these countries must pay to renew their rights, the decision by a patent owner to renew (or not to renew) a patent provides information about the owner's private valuation of the patent.[3] The authors develop an econometric model of the renewal decision that can be used to derive an empirical distribution of patent values. This distribution is highly skewed, as shown in Figure 1.

Jean Lanjouw's study using West German patent data and Schankerman's paper using French patent data are two examples of more recent studies showing that the mean and median values of patents vary widely by technology group.[4] These studies, like the earlier work by Pakes and Schankerman, also illustrate that the distribution of returns from patented inventions is highly skewed—indicating that many patented inventions have relatively low values, while a few patented inventions

---

2   Ariel Pakes and Mark Schankerman, "Estimates of the Value of Patent Rights in European Countries During the Post 1950 Period," *Economic Journal* (December 1986): 1052-1076; and Ariel Pakes, "Patents as Options: Some Estimates of the Value of Holding European Patent Stocks," *Econometrica* 54 (July 1986): 755-784.

3   The "private valuation" of a patent reflects the value an owner of a patent places on owning the exclusive rights to an invention, as opposed to any valuation of patents that attempts to measure the social benefits from a patent or the patent system in aggregate.

4   Jean Olson Lanjouw, "Patent Protection in the Shadow of Infringement: Simulation Estimations of Patent Value," *The Review of Economic Studies* 65 (1998): 671-710; and Mark Schankerman, "How Valuable Is Patent Protection? Estimates by Technology Field," *The Rand Journal of Economics* 29, no. 1 (Spring 1998): 77-107.

Figure 1. Distribution of the Value of Patent Rights Across Countries in 1970

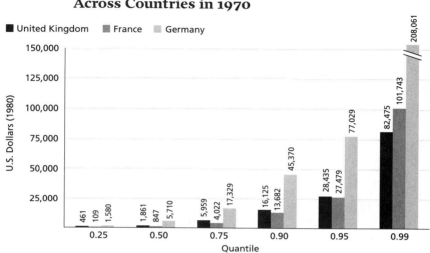

Source: Ariel Pakes and Mark Schankerman, "Estimates of the Value of Patent Rights in European Countries During the Post-1950 Period," Economic Journal (December 1986): 1052-1076.

have extremely high values. Lanjouw finds that pharmaceutical patents generate the highest mean value when compared to patents in the textile, computer, and engine industries. In contrast, Schankerman, looking at somewhat different industries, finds that on average, patents in the electronics industry have higher value than patents in the pharmaceutical, chemical, and mechanical industries.

To illustrate the skewed distribution of patent values across industries, Figure 2 shows the percentile distribution of private value for electronics patents and other technology fields in Schankerman's study. The 25th percentile of patent values is $1,450, meaning that if all of the patents in the electronics industry are rank-ordered by value, the first 25 percent of them have values of $1,450 or less, and the latter 75 percent have values above $1,450 dollars.[5] Schankerman and Lanjouw use their empirical results to measure how much value is derived from patent protection by calculating the subsidy to companies engaged in research and development (R&D) that would be required to yield the same level of R&D

---

5   Schankerman, "How Valuable Is Patent Protection?" 94, table 5.

Figure 2. Distribution of the Value of Patent Rights in France Across Technology Fields in 1970

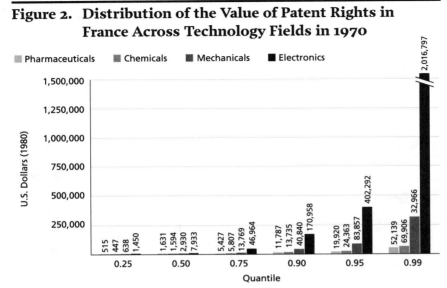

Source: Mark Schankerman, "How Valuable is Patent Protection? Estimates by Technology Field," The Rand Journal of Economics 29, no. 1 (Spring 1998): 77-107.

in a world without patent protection. This "equivalent subsidy rate" is calculated as the ratio of the value of patent rights to R&D expenditure. Schankerman finds subsidy rates of about 15.6 percent using total R&D.[6] Lanjouw's figures are slightly lower, in the range of 10 percent to 15 percent. These rates imply that if all patent protection were eliminated, the government would need to subsidize innovators by approximately 10 percent to 15 percent of their current R&D spending to ensure that the same level of investment in R&D occurred.[7]

Measures of Innovation

There is no single generally accepted way to measure the amount of "innovation" that has occurred in an industry. One potential measure is the number of patents that have been issued. However, using patent counts as a measure of innovation is controversial.

The main advantages of patent count data are that they are readily available and expansive in scope with respect to both time and industry

---

[6] Id., 95.
[7] Lanjouw, "Patent Protection in the Shadow," 699.

coverage. The key disadvantage is that not all patents are equal in value. As indicated above, the mean value of patents varies by time, cohort, and industry, and the distribution of patent value is highly skewed.[8] Thus, a simple patent count is an imperfect measure of the value of the innovations they represent. Moreover, some important innovations are never patented and therefore are not "counted" in this method. As a result, using raw patent counts as a measure of innovation can grossly overstate or understate the amount of true underlying innovation in the sector.

Lanjouw, Pakes, and Jonathan Putnam describe a methodology for improving the common practice of using patent counts as measures of innovation.[9] They use both the age of the patent and the number of countries in which the patent was filed as bases for analyses. The authors apply weights to the patent count using econometric models of patent value by cohort and by country of filing to derive a value index for each patent.[10] Not surprisingly, their study suggests that older patents should be given greater weight in measures of innovation than newer patents (recall that older patents are the ones that owners have chosen to renew year after year). Similarly, the study suggests that patents that are filed in multiple countries should also be given more weight in valuation measures than those filed in fewer countries. While this method represents an improvement over a simple patent count as a measure of innovative activity, the method can only be used in countries that have a meaningful patent renewal fee.[11]

Another potential measure of innovation that can be used with U.S. data is the number of patent citations (i.e., the number of times a particular patent is cited in applications for other patents). Adam Jaffe, Michael

---

[8] The term *cohort* refers to the patents granted in the same year.
[9] Jean O. Lanjouw, Ariel Pakes, and Jonathan Putnam, "How to Count Patents and Value Intellectual Property: The Uses of Patent Renewal and Application Data," *The Journal of Industrial Economics,* 46, no. 4 (December 1998): 405-432.
[10] Id., 414.
[11] The U.S. did not require renewal fees until 1982. See Pakes, "Patents as Options," U.S. patent holders also do not have to pay renewal fees on an annual basis; they pay $900 after 3.5 years, $2,300 after 7.5 years, and $3,800 after 11.5 years, while "small entity" patent holders pay $450, $1,150, and $1,900. Currently, holders of French patents pay an annual fee from the second through the twentieth year of a patent's life, with the fee increasing from $33 to $695 (based on the average Euro-USD exchange rate from January through March 2005). Holders of German patents pay an annual fee from the third year of the patent's life through the twentieth year, beginning at $92 and increasing to $2,544 (also based on the average Euro-USD exchange rate from January through March 2005). Holders of British patents pay an annual fee from the fifth year to the twentieth, beginning at $95 and increasing to $756 (based on the average Pound-USD exchange rate from January through March 2005).

Fogarty, and Bruce Bands explain that patent citations identify the "technological antecedents" of a given invention and thus can allow economists to trace the knowledge spillovers that flow from a given technology.[12] A patent that is cited frequently in other patent applications arguably represents a greater innovation than a patent for an invention that is never cited. From a practical standpoint, detailed data on patent citations is publicly available and machine readable, giving economists access to a broad range of data. In their case study, Jaffe et al. use an extensive database of patents and patent citations from NASA to investigate the effectiveness of publicly funded scientific research and the resulting knowledge spillovers to the economy. Among other interesting findings, Jaffe et al. illustrate that the upward trend in the 1980s in the number of patents per R&D dollar (i.e., the propensity to patent), which was coincident with an increased emphasis on a commercial orientation of government research. They also find that NASA patents were "more important" and "more general" in nature than a random sample of patents through the 1970s, but that this difference disappeared during the 1980s.[13]

The patent citation approach to innovation measurement is not without difficulties. Studies by Jaffe et al. used qualitative evidence, interviews, and surveys to gather additional information on the nature of patent citations. In the aforementioned NASA study, Jaffe et al. conducted a series of interviews with NASA scientists to learn more about patent citations referenced in the patents issued to their research center. A striking finding is that approximately one-fourth of the patent citations appear to be "essentially noise"; however, once these spurious patents are excluded, they find evidence that roughly two-thirds of citations represent true knowledge spillovers.[14] Another preliminary study, by Jaffe, Manuel Trajtenberg, and Fogarty, surveyed inventors about citations made in prior patents and about citations to subsequent patents.[15] They find that approximately one-half of citations had no correlation to true spillover.

---

12 Adam B. Jaffe, Michael S. Fogarty, and Bruce A. Bands, "Evidence from Patents and Patent Citations on the Impact of NASA and other Federal Labs on Commercial Innovation," *The Journal of Industrial Economics* 46, no. 2 (June 1998): 183-205. A knowledge spillover occurs when a given innovation builds upon the technology or knowledge developed in a prior innovation.

13 Id., 192.

14 Id., 202.

15 Adam B. Jaffe, Manuel Trajtenberg, and Michael S. Fogarty, "Knowledge Spillovers and Patent Citations: Evidence from a Survey of Inventors," *AEA Papers and Proceedings* 90, no. 2 (May 2000): 215-218.

While economists have proposed and refined measures of innovation which have proven useful, the fundamental question of how to measure innovation remains less than fully resolved.

Patent Policy and Patenting Behavior

U.S. patent protection has strengthened over the last quarter century in terms of the period of protection, legal remedies against infringers, and the scope of patentable inventions.[16] The most notable change, as described in Bronwyn Hall and Rosemarie Ziedonis's study of patent behavior in the semi-conductor industry, was the establishment of the United States Court of Appeals for the Federal Circuit (CAFC) in 1982, which is "widely credited with unifying and strengthening the judicial treatment of patent rights in the United States."[17] Since 1995, patent application filings have increased almost 60 percent in the United States, with approximately 367,000 applications filed in 2003.[18]

Numerous studies have attempted to measure the effects of changes in U.S. "regulatory" regimes on patent behavior.[19] In a recent study focusing on the semiconductor industry, Hall and Ziedonis combine qualitative and quantitative evidence to try to rectify the apparent "patent paradox" of the 1980s—the observation that firms' propensity to patent increased dramatically, but that they also did not "rely heavily on patents to appropriate returns to R&D."[20] Their study explores whether or not a causal link can be established between the upsurge in patent activity during the 1980s and the contemporaneous changes in the regulatory regime.[21]

Hall and Ziedonis develop two main hypotheses. The "strategic response" hypothesis is that the firms most vulnerable to "holdups" from infringement suits expand their portfolios of patents in response to more rigorous patent enforcement regimes. Firms whose products are likely to be covered by the patents of other firms and have sunk large costs in expensive manufacturing equipment have a strategic incentive to obtain

---

[16] Nancy T. Gallini, "The Economics of Patents: Lessons from Recent U.S. Patent Reform," *Journal of Economic Perspectives* 16, no. 2 (Spring 2002): 131-154.

[17] Bronwyn H. Hall and Rosemarie Ham Ziedonis, "The Patent Paradox Revisited: An Empirical Study of Patenting in the U.S. Semiconductor Industry, 1979-1995," *The Rand Journal of Economics* 31, no. 1 (Spring 2001): 101-128.

[18] United States Patent and Trademark Office, "Statistical Reports Available for Viewing, Calendar Year Patent Statistics," no. 744

[19] See, for example, Gallini, "The Economics of Patents," for a comprehensive list of such studies.

[20] Hall and Ziedonis, "The Patent Paradox Revisited," 102.

[21] Id., 104.

patents themselves in order to have a counter-threat against those other firms in the event of a patent dispute.[22] The "specialization" hypothesis is that the "emergence of more patent-intensive design firms" contributed to the patent surge of the 1980s.[23] The authors interviewed business personnel directly responsible for shaping patent strategy at a sample of semiconductor firms. From these interviews, they identified two major judicial events that influenced those firms' patenting strategies. The first event was Polaroid's $1 billion damage award from Kodak and the injunction barring Kodak from competing in the instant-film camera business. The second event was Texas Instruments' successful challenge against patent infringers with respect to its integrated circuits.

The authors test the hypothesis that firms use patents as strategic responses by conducting an econometric study of firm-level data on the patent holdings of publicly traded U.S.-owned firms in the semiconductor business. They estimate a standard innovation production function relating the expected number of patents to R&D spending, firm size, the capital intensity of the firm, the type of firm (i.e., whether it is a design firm or a manufacturing firm[24]), and the age of the firm.[25] They find that capital intensity has an "important effect on the propensity to patent" and view this fact as consistent with this strategic response hypothesis, as increases in capital intensity would increase a firm's vulnerability to being "held up" by other firms' patents.[26] Interestingly, the evidence suggests that spikes in patent intensity in the semiconductor industry are more closely associated with the Kodak-Polaroid case in 1986 than with the 1982 shift in the regulatory regime.

The authors test their second hypothesis by separating the firms into two types: manufacturing firms and design firms. When they estimate their model separately for each type of firm, they find that capital intensity was much more important for manufacturing firms than for design firms and that design firms were far more responsive to the regulatory change of 1982. This finding is consistent with the view that "patent rights are required to secure venture capital and other financing for entry as a specialized semiconductor design firm."[27]

---

[22] Id.
[23] Id.
[24] The authors define a manufacturing firm as one with large-scale production facilities, whereas a design firm tends to specialize in niche products.
[25] Hall and Ziedonis, "The Patent Paradox Revisited," 115.
[26] Id.
[27] Id., 120.

Hall and Ziedonis's study provides convincing evidence that changes in U.S. patent policy and judicial views led to changes in patenting behavior by firms during the 1990s. Firms appear to respond to both the incentives created by intellectual property policy reforms and the legal institutions enforcing those policies.

What Patents Are Most Likely to be Challenged in Court?

Concurrent with the upward trend in the number of patent applications and filings has been an upward trend in the number of patent lawsuits. Since 1998, the total number of patent lawsuits has increased 26.87 percent, from 2,218 cases in 1998 to 2,814 cases in 2003.[28] Litigation involving all types of intellectual property (i.e., copyrights, patents, and trademarks) has increased 15.31 percent since 1998, from 7,748 cases in 1998 to 8,934 cases in 2003.[29] Several high-profile patent cases have garnered considerable publicity, including Research in Motion's recent $450 million settlement with NTP Inc. over alleged patent infringement of the technology used in handheld personal digital assistant devices.[30]

Lanjouw and Schankerman[31] provide the most comprehensive study to date on the characteristics of patent litigation, and they find that "the burden of enforcing property rights is more severe for certain types of patentees."[32] Their study uses a unique data set for the years 1980 to 1984, which they constructed by combining case filings on U.S. patent suits with detailed information found in the patents to segment the patents by various characteristics. The authors then calculate the number of cases filed per 1,000 patents for each of those segments. Several interesting facts emerge. First, patents owned domestically are far more frequently involved in litigation. Second, litigation rates vary substantially across technology fields. The highest litigation rates are found in the pharmaceutical and health industries.[33] Third, litigation rates for individual patent owners are 16 percent higher than for corporate patent owners

---

[28] Table 2.2. U.S. District Courts. Civil Cases Filed by Nature of Suit, in *Judicial Facts and Figures*, Judgeship Analysis Staff, March 2005, www.uscourts.gov/judicialfactsfigures/contents.html.

[29] Id.

[30] See Associated Press, "Research in Motion to Settle Patent Suit," 16 March 2005, www.msnbc.msn.com/id/7205748/.

[31] Jean O. Lanjouw and Mark Schankerman, "Characteristics of Patent Litigation: A Window on Competition," *The Rand Journal of Economics* 32, no. 1 (Spring 2001): 129-151.

[32] Id., 130.

[33] Id., 136.

from the same country; one explanation for this difference that the authors provide is that corporations may have an advantage in reaching settlement agreements.[34]

Using a regression analysis, the authors find that the probability that a given patent is involved in litigation rises with both the number of patent claims and the forward citations per claim.[35] A "claim" is the portion of the patent that delineates the novel and detailed features of the patent. The term "forward citation" refers to a given patent being cited in later patents as a technological antecedent, whereas "backward citation" refers to the citations that a given patent itself makes. The authors find that both forward citation and forward self-citation (i.e., a patent being cited by its inventor in a later patent) increase the probability of a patent being litigated, while both backward citation and backward self-citation (i.e., a patent citing its inventor's past patents) reduces the probability of a patent being litigated. In other words, patents that are cited later by other patents are relatively more likely to be litigated, but patents referring to prior patents are relatively less likely to be litigated. The results also imply that the more similar a patent is to another patent, measured by the overlap among the patents' citations according to the similarity of their four-digit International Patent Classification assignments, the more likely that patent is to be litigated.

Conclusion

What are the main lessons learned from economic studies of patents and patent policy? First, the value of patents varies widely. The vast majority of patents are worth relatively little, but a few are incredibly valuable. Second, the skewed distribution of patent values makes patent counts an imperfect measure of innovation; however, patent-renewal data can be used to weight the more valuable patents to help reduce the measurement error. Survey data and other methods can also be developed to improve the precision of patent counts as a measure of innovation. Third, the policy reforms of the 1980s affected the propensity to patent, and the evidence suggests that increasing the strength of patents encouraged innovation. Fourth, the empirical evidence suggests firms respond to the

---

34 This figure excludes Japan from the sample. Japanese individual patent owners, startlingly, have three times as high a litigation rate as Japanese corporations.
35 Lanjouw and Schankerman, "Characteristics of Patent Litigation," 144. A "claim" is the number of different line items on a patent; a "citation" is a reference to other patents or innovations made on a given patent.

incentives created by patent policy. And last, some patents exhibit identifiable traits that make them more likely to be involved in litigation. The innovations in economic thinking I describe above are essential knowledge for those concerned with patent policy.

II

The Basics of Intellectual Property Damages

3

A Practical Guide to Damages

Gregory K. Leonard and Lauren J. Stiroh

A patent owner who is the victim of infringement is entitled to some compensation for the use of his patent by an unauthorized entity. The statutory floor for patent damages is a *reasonable royalty*.[1] The patent owner is entitled to recover more—the *lost profits* it sustained as a result of the infringement—if these lost profits exceed the reasonable royalty.[2] Properly calculated, damages in intellectual property disputes are guided by fundamental economic principles governing the value of the intellectual property at issue.[3] In this chapter, we outline the basic economic principles that guide the determination of reasonable royalties or lost profits in intellectual property disputes. These principles provide the foundation for the remainder of this book. Many of the issues touched on here will be addressed in greater detail in later chapters.

Lost Profits Damages: Elements of Lost Profits

Lost profits are defined as the difference between the profits the plaintiff would have made *but for* the infringement and the profits the plaintiff actually made. Determining the profits that the plaintiff would have made but for the infringement requires an assessment of the economic outcomes that would have occurred absent the infringement. This exercise has aptly been termed constructing a *but-for world*, i.e., the world that would have existed absent the infringement.[4] Constructing the but-for world is essentially equivalent to undoing the effects of the infringement.

---

[1] 35 U.S.C. § 284 (2004).

[2] Id.

[3] This discussion will primarily be placed in the context of patent infringement litigation. Economic and legal principles governing trademark or copyright infringement are discussed in Chapter 6.

[4] See, e.g., *Grain Processing Corp. v. American Maize-Products Co.*, 185 F.3d 1341 (Fed. Cir. 1999).

The profits that the plaintiff would have made absent the infringe-ment comprise three primary elements: (1) the quantity of sales that the plaintiff would have made absent infringement *(but-for quantity)*, (2) the price at which the plaintiff would have sold this quantity *(but-for price)*, and (3) the costs that the plaintiff would have incurred producing and selling the but-for quantity *(but-for cost)*. Each of these variables might have been different in the but-for world than in the actual world. Damages arise due to these differences.

Consider a hypothetical version of the market for DVD players at the time when the technology was first commercially introduced. For the pur-poses of this example, we assume that there were two companies, DigiDisc and InfrCorp, selling DVD players, with each company basing its player on its own proprietary format (much like the early days of the VCR market when the BetaMax and VHS formats competed with each other).[5]

Suppose that DigiDisc owns a patent covering the technology used in its DVD player that it believes is being infringed by InfrCorp's DVD player. Accordingly, DigiDisc brings a patent infringement suit against InfrCorp in which it is determined that InfrCorp's DVD player does, in fact, infringe DigiDisc's patent. Suppose it is further determined that InfrCorp had no feasible way of offering a noninfringing version of its DVD player. Thus, in the but-for world—the world where InfrCorp does not infringe DigiDisc's patent—InfrCorp would have had no product at all to offer to customers, and therefore DigiDisc would have been the only seller in the market.

Would it necessarily be reasonable to assume that in the but-for world DigiDisc would have made all of InfrCorp's infringing sales of DVD players? The answer is no, for several reasons. First, the DigiDisc and InfrCorp DVD players are *differentiated products*. This means that they were not perfectly interchangeable in the minds of purchasers. At least some purchasers of the InfrCorp DVD player would not automatically have purchased a DigiDisc DVD player if the InfrCorp DVD player were not available. One of the reasons for this is that (in our example) the cat-alogs of movies available on DVD during the period in question differed somewhat across the two formats—while both companies offered a good

---

5   In this regard, our example does not correspond with the actual history of the DVD
    player market because the DVD manufacturers, in fact, standardized on a single for-
    mat. However, the assumption of different formats facilitates the illustration of the
    key economic principles discussed below.

selection of general interest films, InfrCorp offered foreign and art films that were not offered by DigiDisc. Thus, some consumers who purchased an InfrCorp DVD player because of the foreign and art films available on that format may not have been willing to purchase a DigiDisc DVD player had the InfrCorp product not been available. They might have chosen to continue using their VHS tape players instead. Second, because of competition between DigiDisc and InfrCorp, the price of the DigiDisc DVD player might have been lower following infringement than it would have been in a world where DigiDisc did not face competition from InfrCorp. With a higher but-for price, overall consumer demand for DVD players would have been lower than it actually was.

To analyze what would have happened in the but-for world, we start by looking at the *demand curve* for the DigiDisc DVD player when InfrCorp was infringing. This demand curve, shown in Figure 1, reflects customers' demand for the DigiDisc product as a function of its price.

It is a fundamental principle in economics that demand curves slope downward: the higher the price, the lower the quantity demanded, and vice versa. The rate at which quantity demanded decreases when price increases depends on the price-sensitivity of consumers. The slope of the demand curve is an indication of that price-sensitivity. A steeper demand curve indicates less price-sensitivity (quantity demanded does not move

---

Figure 1. DigiDisc Demand Curve

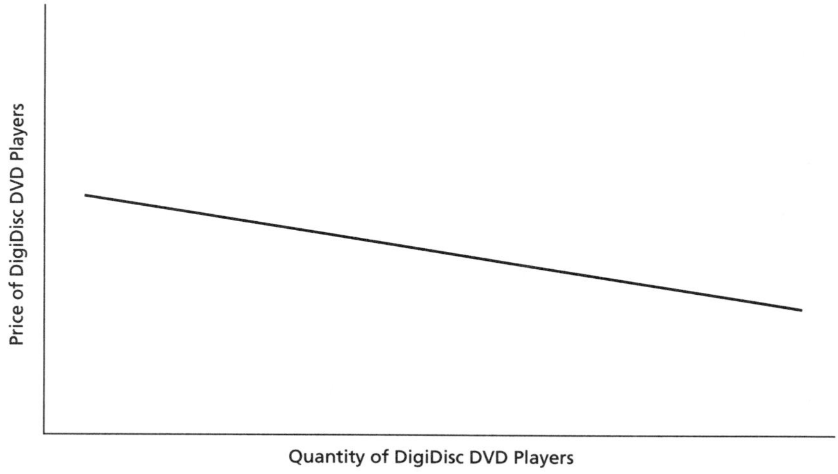

Price of DigiDisc DVD Players

Quantity of DigiDisc DVD Players

very much for a given price change), and a flatter demand curve indicates greater price-sensitivity (quantity demanded moves a lot for a given price change). Price-sensitivity, in turn, reflects in part the extent to which consumers view the DigiDisc product and the InfrCorp product as substitutes. Closer substitutability leads to greater price-sensitivity for DigiDisc because more consumers would be willing to switch to the InfrCorp DVD player in response to a price increase in the DigiDisc product.

When DigiDisc competed with InfrCorp for sales, DigiDisc would have chosen its price so as to maximize its profits given the demand curve in Figure 1. This is the demand curve "with infringement" (the demand curve faced by DigiDisc when InfrCorp infringed its patent). To find the profit-maximizing price, we add two curves to Figure 1 (see Figure 2). The first curve, that showing the marginal revenue (represented by the dotted line labeled MR), indicates the amount of additional revenue that DigiDisc would gain from selling an additional DVD player. Note that DigiDisc does not gain revenue equal to the price by selling an additional unit. This is because DigiDisc was already selling as many DVD players as customers wanted to buy at the old price and would have to lower its price to sell an additional unit. As a result, the marginal revenue curve lies below the demand curve and is also downward sloping. The second curve is the marginal cost curve, labeled MC. It shows the amount of additional cost DigiDisc would incur in order to sell an additional unit. This curve is horizontal which means that, in this example, the additional cost of producing one more unit is always the same no matter how many DVD players DigiDisc is already producing.[6] Thus, DigiDisc faces a constant marginal cost of selling an additional unit.

DigiDisc's profit-maximizing price is found by first determining where the marginal revenue curve intersects with the marginal cost curve. The DigiDisc quantity at this intersection (labeled Q) is the profit-maximizing quantity. The quantity Q maximizes profits because at this level of quantity the marginal revenue from selling an additional unit just equals the marginal cost. If quantity were any lower than Q, marginal revenue would exceed marginal cost (as can be seen by the fact that the curve MR lies above the curve MC for quantity less than Q), and profits could therefore be increased by selling an additional unit. If quantity were any

---

6   Note that this means we are implicitly assuming that DigiDisc's increased demand for the inputs required to make and sell DVD players does not affect the prices of those inputs.

Figure 2. DigiDisc's Profit-Maximizing Price

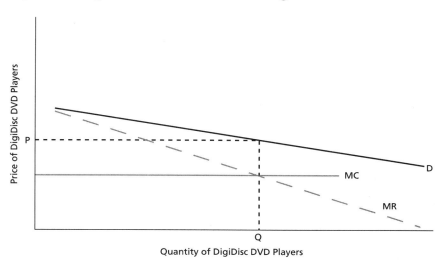

Quantity of DigiDisc DVD Players

higher than Q, the marginal revenue would be less than the marginal cost (as can be seen by the fact that the curve MR lies below the curve MC for quantity greater than Q), and therefore profits could be increased by reducing the quantity sold. DigiDisc's profit-maximizing price can be determined by reading the price off of the demand curve that corresponds to Q. This price is labeled P in Figure 2.

Now let us consider what happens in the but-for world where the InfrCorp DVD player would not have been available for purchase in the market. Without the InfrCorp product in the market, the demand curve for the DigiDisc DVD player would have been different from the demand curve with infringement (see Figure 1) in two respects. First, at any given price, the demand for the DigiDisc product would have been greater, which is represented by an outward shift in the demand curve. The reason for this is that since the InfrCorp DVD player would not be available in the but-for world, some of the consumers who purchased this product in the actual world would have instead purchased a close substitute product— the DigiDisc DVD player—in the but-for world. The amount by which the DigiDisc demand curve shifts out depends on the number of InfrCorp customers who would switch to DigiDisc at each price. The more switching, the greater would be the outward shift of the demand curve.

Figure 3. Lost Profits on Lost Sales

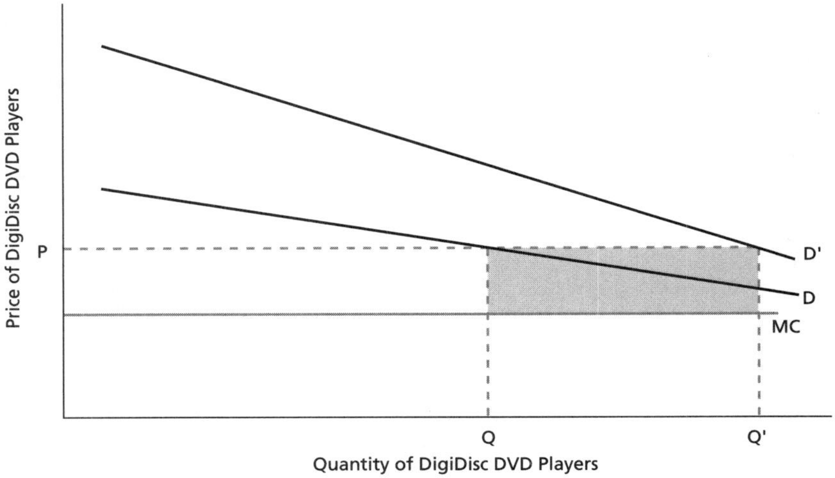

Quantity of DigiDisc DVD Players

Second, the price-sensitivity of the demand for the DigiDisc product would be reduced because in the but-for world there would no longer be a close substitute product. Consumers of the DigiDisc product would not have the InfrCorp DVD player as a substitute to which they could turn if DigiDisc increased the price of its product. This decrease in price-sensitivity would lead to a steeper overall demand curve for DigiDisc than had existed when DigiDisc competed with InfrCorp (recall that the slope of the demand curve is related to price-sensitivity). As a result of these two effects, in the but-for world the demand curve for DigiDisc would change from the curve labeled D in Figure 3 to the curve labeled D'.

Assuming DigiDisc maintained the same price and experienced the same per-unit costs as it did when competing with InfrCorp, we can measure both the quantity of lost sales and the magnitude of lost profits sustained by DigiDisc. If DigiDisc charged the same price P in the but-for world as it charged in the actual world, DigiDisc would have sold Q' units, or (Q' − Q) more units than it sold in the actual world.[7] The (Q' − Q) sales, shown in Figure 3, are often called *lost sales* because they are sales

---

7   As discussed further, one would have to check that DigiDisc had sufficient capacity to make these additional sales. "Capacity" in this context would encompass both DigiDisc's capability to manufacture (or have manufactured) the additional quantity as well as its ability to market and sell those additional units to InfrCorp's customers.

Figure 4. Lost Profits on Lost Sales and Price Erosion

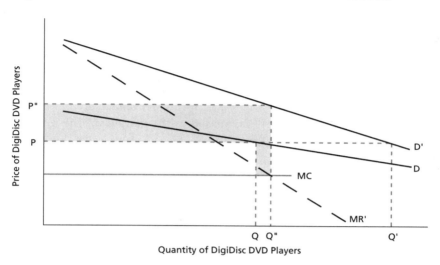

lost to the plaintiff due to the infringement by the defendant. Profits on these lost sales are represented by the shaded area in Figure 3, which is equal to the lost sales multiplied by the per unit profit margin, or (Q' − Q) x (P − MC).[8]

In Figure 3, it is assumed that DigiDisc charged the same price P in the but-for world as it charged in the actual world. However, with the reduced competition from InfrCorp—as represented by the steeper (less elastic) demand curve D'—DigiDisc would have the incentive to increase its price above P. DigiDisc would choose the price where its but-for marginal revenue curve, represented by the dotted line labeled MR' in Figure 4, intersected its marginal cost, again represented by the horizontal line labeled MC. The resulting price would be P'', which is higher than P, the price DigiDisc charged in the actual world. The difference (P'' − P) is referred to as the amount of *price erosion* caused by the infringement.

At price P'', DigiDisc would sell Q'' units, which is less than Q', the number of units DigiDisc could sell at P, the price with infringement. This is a consequence of the demand curve still exhibiting price-sensitiv-

---

[8]   This example assumes that the incremental cost required to make these sales consists solely of the marginal cost of production. As discussed further, an analysis of costs needs to be performed to determine whether any additional (traditionally fixed) costs would change with an increased level of sales.

ity in the but-for world (although less than in the actual world), so that a higher price (P'' versus P) reduces demand (to Q'' down from Q'). DigiDisc's total lost profits—taking into account both lost sales and price erosion—is represented by the lightly shaded area in Figure 4. The shaded area is equal to the increase in profit margin on existing sales plus the incremental profit on the additional sales, or (P'' − P) x Q + (P'' − MC) x (Q'' − Q). Although DigiDisc would cause its sales to decrease from Q' to Q'' by raising its price from P to P'', it would still make greater overall profits at this higher price: the increased profit margin on the retained unit sales more than makes up for the decrease in unit sales due to the higher price (put another way, the lightly shaded area in Figure 4 is larger than the shaded area in Figure 3).[9]

Construction of the But-For World

With an understanding of the economics of how and why infringement may cause a plaintiff to lose profits, we turn to the question of how one goes about measuring lost profits damages in practice. As discussed above, a lost profits damages analysis requires a reconstruction of the world as it would have existed had the infringement not occurred. This requires determining the actions that each party—the plaintiff, the defendant, other companies in the market, and customers—would have taken in this but-for world given the elimination of one of the products from the market. To perform this analysis, an economist starts with the presumption that each party would act in its best economic interest. Then, applying economic principles and case-specific facts, the economist determines for each party the likely actions that would have served to maximize its position in the but-for world.[10]

The Defendant's Actions in the But-For World

Determining the defendant's actions in the but-for world requires an assessment of the various alternatives available to it. Economic theory says that the defendant would have taken the course of action that would have

---

9 Note that DigiDisc's level of sales at P'' in the but-for world, Q'', still exceeds its actual level of sales Q.

10 In some situations, as will be pointed out, the economic analysis may also necessarily be guided by legal principles. For example, based on purely economic reasoning, damages would include the profits on the additional sales of any of the plaintiff's products that would have been made in conjunction with the lost sales of the patented product. However, as discussed below, legal principles limit a plaintiff's ability to recover its lost profits on so-called "convoyed sales."

maximized its expected profits.[11] In some cases, the defendant might have had no economically feasible alternative other than to stay out of the market entirely. In other cases, however, the defendant might have been able to offer a noninfringing (albeit potentially inferior) alternative. For example, if prior to introducing the infringing product the defendant had sold a noninfringing product based on the prior art, it might have continued selling this product in the but-for world. Alternatively, if the defendant would have been able to redesign its product in a way that was noninfringing, it might have sold this redesigned product in the but-for world.[12]

In evaluating the defendant's potential strategies in the but-for world, the economist will generally consider each alternative strategy's costs, benefits, and technical feasibility during the period of infringement.[13] Information regarding the defendant's own knowledge and assessment of these alternatives at the time may be helpful in this analysis, as may be input from technical experts. Information from the postinfringement period may be useful for determining what was known and feasible at the time, but one must be careful when using such information not to ascribe to a party more knowledge and capabilities than it actually had at the time.

Customers' Choices in the But-For World

Once the defendant's but-for strategy has been identified, the stage is set to analyze the actions customers would have taken in the but-for world. Customers who purchased the infringing product in the actual world would have had to make some other choice in the but-for world because

---

[11] The case law is consistent with this point. See, e.g., *Grain Processing,* supra note 4.

[12] This point relates to the first two of the so-called *Panduit* factors. In *Panduit Corp. v. Stahlin Bros. Fibre Works Inc.,* 575 F.2d 1152 (6th Cir. 1978), the court identified four factors that a plaintiff must establish in order to be awarded lost profits. The first two factors are (1) demand for the patented product or feature and (2) absence of "acceptable" noninfringing substitutes. If there is no customer demand for the patented feature (as opposed to the rest of the product), and it would have been technically feasible to do so, the defendant would have had the incentive to introduce a noninfringing version of the product in the but-for world by simply dropping the patented feature. By doing so, the defendant could likely have made the same level of sales in the but-for world as it actually had because, by assumption, consumers did not care about the patented feature. Similarly, if the defendant could have offered an "acceptable" noninfringing substitute (which we take to mean a nearly perfect substitute for the infringing product from the point of view of consumers), again the defendant would likely have made the same level of sales in the but-for world as it actually did because consumers would have viewed the noninfringing substitute as being virtually identical to the infringing product. In either case, there would be no lost profits for the plaintiff.

[13] As *Grain Processing* (supra note 4) indicates, a noninfringing alternative must have been "available" to the defendant during the period of infringement.

the infringing product would not have been available to them. The set of potential choices for these customers would include purchasing an alternative noninfringing product within the market in question or not making any purchase within this market at all. The questions to be answered regarding customers, then, are as follows: To which other products would these customers have turned in the but-for world? How many customers would have turned to each product? How many customers would have chosen to forego purchasing any product within the market?

As our stylized example above illustrated, the answers to these questions depend on the extent to which noninfringing products are *economic substitutes* for the infringing product from the point of view of customers. Product A is a substitute for Product B if the demand for Product A increases when the price of Product B increases. This increase in demand for Product A occurs because some of the customers who would have otherwise purchased Product B decide that Product A is now more attractive given that Product B's price has increased. Economists measure the extent to which consumers view two products as substitutes using the *cross-price elasticity of demand*. The cross-price elasticity of demand for Product A with respect to Product B's price is defined as the percentage change in the demand for Product A that would result from a 1 percent increase in Product B's price. A large cross-price elasticity between two products indicates that customers view them as close substitutes.

A product's *own-price elasticity of demand* measures the extent to which the demand for the product is sensitive to its own price. It is defined as the percentage change in demand for the product that would result from a 1 percent change in the product's price. The larger a product's own-price elasticity of demand, the more price-sensitive are the product's customers, and thus the more likely they are to switch away from the product in response to a price increase. In our stylized example, the price-sensitivity of the demand for the DigiDisc DVD player—and, accordingly, its own-price elasticity of demand—was smaller in the but-for world than in the actual world, and this was reflected in the steeper but-for demand curve.

The own-price elasticity of demand for a product is related to the cross-price elasticities of demand between that product and substitute products. A product's own-price elasticity will tend to be larger the closer are the substitutes for the product because an increase in the product's price will lead more customers to switch to close substitutes. A product's own-price elasticity of demand will also be larger when more substitute products exist. Thus, it is theoretically possible that a product may have a large own-price elasticity of demand even though it has no close substitutes because it has many relatively distant substitutes.

It is common in a patent infringement case to define a "market" consisting of the set of close substitute products.[14] Less close substitute products are typically excluded from the defined market. For this reason, the own-price effect for a product inside the market often will exceed the cross-price effects of that product on other products inside the market. This is an indication that a price increase for the product would lead some customers to switch to products outside the defined market.

We now turn to answering the question of how customers would have behaved in the but-for world. If the infringing product were not available, it is likely that some customers who purchased that product in the actual world would have switched to substitute noninfringing products. In other words, the demands for the noninfringing products would have increased. In our stylized example, the absence of the infringing InfrCorp product led to an outward shift in the demand curve for the DigiDisc DVD player (a greater demand for the DigiDisc player at every price).

A greater fraction of the infringing sales would flow to those noninfringing products that were the closest substitutes for the infringing product—those noninfringing products that had the largest cross-price elasticities of demand with the infringing product.[15] If the own-price elasticity of demand for the infringing product is sufficiently large relative to the cross-price elasticities between the infringing product and the noninfringing products being analyzed, some of the infringing sales would flow outside of the set of noninfringing products being analyzed. Thus, the key to understanding customer behavior in the but-for world is understanding the own- and cross-price elasticities of demand.

The Plaintiff in the But-For World

The Plaintiff's But-For Price

Given the but-for choices of the defendant and the but-for customer demands for the noninfringing products, the plaintiff and other remain-

---

[14] A detailed discussion of defining markets in patent infringement cases and antitrust cases is addressed in Chapter 18. Here, we merely note that the term *market* is a term of art with specific meaning in antitrust and patent infringement contexts.

[15] To an economist, the question of "causation" (i.e., Did the defendant's infringement cause the plaintiff's lost profits?) is largely resolved by establishing that the plaintiff's product is a substitute for the infringing product.

ing competitors may have chosen to change aspects of their competitive strategies. In particular, the plaintiff may have charged a different price than the one it charged in the actual world.[16] Without the competition from the infringing product, the plaintiff (and other remaining competitors) might have found it profitable to increase its price to customers.[17]

Referring to our example, the absence of the infringing InfrCorp product led to a rotation in the demand curve for the DigiDisc product, making the but-for demand curve D' steeper than the actual demand curve D. The steeper demand curve meant that the demand for the DigiDisc product in the but-for world was less price-sensitive (i.e., had a smaller own-price elasticity) than the demand for the DigiDisc player in the actual world. This would allow DigiDisc to raise its price in the but-for world to P'' above the price P that it charged in the actual world.

A company's decision regarding pricing is constrained by the price-sensitivity of its customer demand. Thus, as a general matter, if demand becomes less price-sensitive (due, for example, to the removal of a significant competitor from the market), the pricing constraint is reduced and the company generally would have the incentive to increase its price. Applying this principle to the context of a patent infringement case, the plaintiff would generally have the incentive to charge a higher price in the but-for world.[18]

However, there is an offsetting effect that must be taken into account. If the plaintiff increased its price, customer demand would decrease—again as a result of price-sensitivity. In our stylized example, the effect on quantity demanded of DigiDisc charging a higher price was represented by the

---

[16] Other aspects of the plaintiff's competitive strategy that might have changed in the but-for world include the amount of advertising and promotion of the product and the positioning of the product (i.e., the set of characteristics and features possessed by the product).

[17] An argument is sometimes made that the infringer did not "cause" the price erosion in cases where the plaintiff, not the infringer, was the first to lower its prices. However, if the only reason that the plaintiff started the price erosion was because it faced competition from the infringer, then one could reasonably conclude that the defendant did, in fact, "cause" the ensuing price reductions.
A showing that the plaintiff's price would have been higher in the but-for world satisfies the fourth *Panduit* factor, which requires that the plaintiff prove the amount of (additional) profit it would have made but for the infringement.

[18] One exception to the general principle that entry by a new product leads to lower prices might be the case of generic entry in the pharmaceutical industry. Branded drugs have sometimes increased their prices in response to generic entry. The reason is that only price-insensitive customers remain with the branded product after generic entry (all the price-sensitive customers switch to the generic). Thus, the elasticity of demand faced by the branded product actually falls in magnitude, and the branded drug firm has the incentive to increase its price.

movement from Q' to Q'' when the price of the DigiDisc DVD player increased from P to P''.[19] Although the plaintiff's customers might exhibit reduced price-sensitivity in the but-for world (which allows the plaintiff to increase its price profitably), they would still exhibit some price-sensitivity and therefore decrease their demand for the plaintiff's product somewhat.

The amount of demand adjustment depends on the relevant own-price elasticity of demand.[20] Several methods exist that may allow the elasticity of demand to be estimated in a given situation. First, if the necessary data are available, the relevant demand curve can be estimated using econometric methods. Second, the occurrence of a "natural experiment," such as an increase in price due to some exogenous factor such as a cost increase, may provide the opportunity to observe the sensitivity of demand to a price change. Third, the relevant elasticity of demand can be inferred from product gross margins and appropriate economic theory.[21] Fourth, results from a consumer survey may provide the necessary information to determine the sensitivity of demand to price. In any specific case, other methods may be available.

The Plaintiff's Capacity

To have made additional sales in the but-for world, the plaintiff would have required sufficient excess capacity or the ability to expand capacity to accommodate the increase in sales.[22] "Capacity" in this context encompasses all aspects of bringing a product to market, including manufacturing, sales, and distribution. If capacity constraints in any of these areas would have been binding in the but-for world, either the plaintiff's lost sales would be limited to its excess capacity in the bottleneck area, or the plaintiff must demonstrate that it could have profitably expanded capacity sufficiently to make the lost sales. In the latter case, the costs associated

---

[19] Note that this is a movement along the DigiDisc demand curve D', while the removal of the InfrCorp product from the market resulted in an outward shift and rotation in the DigiDisc demand curve from D to D'.

[20] If the plaintiff's product would be the only noninfringing product to increase its price in the but-for world, its demand elasticity is the appropriate one to use. If, however, the prices of all other noninfringing products would increase in line with the plaintiff, the overall market demand elasticity is the appropriate one to use. In the latter case, the demand adjustment for the plaintiff would be smaller because the substitute noninfringing products have higher prices as well, a fact that would blunt consumer switching to these products.

[21] For example, under a commonly used model of pricing in differentiated product industries, the gross margin is equal to the inverse of the absolute value of the own-price elasticity. Thus, given the gross margin, one can solve for the elasticity.

[22] The issue of sufficient capacity is the third *Panduit* factor.

with making the necessary capacity expansion must be accounted for in calculating the incremental profit on the lost sales. For example, suppose a defendant made infringing sales in a geographic area where the plaintiff did not operate. If the plaintiff seeks lost profits related to this geographic area, it would have to account for the incremental costs (and, perhaps, time) required to operate in that area. Such costs might include additions to the plaintiff's sales force, extensions to its distribution network, and so on.

The Plaintiff's Convoyed Sales

In some situations, the sales of one product are driven by the sales of another product. For example, sales at the Apple iTunes music store are driven, in part, by sales of iPods. The more iPods that Apple sells, the greater are its sales at iTunes. The iPod and iTunes example is one in which the two products work together—they are functional *complements*. In other situations, two products might have little functional relationship, but the sales of one product nevertheless lead to sales of the other product. Milk and other grocery products are an example. Milk is sometimes used by supermarkets as a "loss leader" to generate store traffic and thus sales of other grocery products. This again is an example of complementarity. In the law, the term *convoyed sales* is used to describe sales that are driven by sales of the plaintiff's patented product.[23]

When the sales of the patented product drive the sales of a second product, the loss of sales of the patented product would cause a loss in sales of the second product as well. Accordingly, infringement may cause the plaintiff to lose sales not only of the product that competes with the infringing product, but also of any complementary products the plaintiff sells. The law allows recovery of profits lost on such convoyed sales under certain conditions. Specifically, the convoyed product and the patented product must function as a "single unit."[24] The iPod-iTunes example would appear to pass this test, while the milk-other groceries example generally would not.[25] This distinction is a legal one, not an economic one.

---

23 By "patented product," we mean the product that incorporates the patented technology.

24 See *Rite-Hite Corp. v. Kelley Co.*, 56 F.3d 1538 (Fed. Cir. 1995).

25 iTunes also provides an example of a convoyed product or service for which sales continue into the future after the purchase of the "primary" product (in this case the iPod). In this situation, past infringement may cause the plaintiff to continue to lose profits on the convoyed product after trial. From an economics perspective, a damages award should include the present discounted value of future damages, as long as the future damages are not speculative. See Chapter 11 for a discussion of the appropriate discount rate to use in calculating present discounted value.

The Plaintiff's Incremental Costs

Once the plaintiff's lost sales have been determined, the plaintiff's profits on those lost sales can be calculated as the difference between the revenues on the lost sales and the *incremental costs* required to make the lost sales.[26]

Methods for Determining Lost Profits

There are a variety of approaches for determining the amount of lost profits. Which method is appropriate in a given situation depends on whether the plaintiff is claiming lost sales alone, price erosion in addition to lost sales, lost profits on convoyed sales, or some combination of these losses. The discussion below is illustrative of the most frequently used methods for determining lost profits. It is not meant to be exhaustive—other approaches may be appropriate in a given situation.

Share-Based Approaches for Determining Lost Sales

An approach to determining the plaintiff's lost sales commonly used in patent infringement cases is to assume that the plaintiff would have made a fraction of the infringing sales proportional to its share of the appropriately defined market.[27] This *market share approach* is straightforward to apply, and the necessary information on market shares is typically available.

The market share approach relies on three assumptions. The first assumption is that the defendant would have completely removed the infringing product from the market in the but-for world. The second assumption is that all of the infringing sales would have stayed within the market. This is a reasonable assumption to make if the products in the market are nearly homogenous (very close substitutes). In that case, the customers of the infringing product would readily switch to another product within the market in the but-for world because they would view the products as nearly equivalent. Alternatively, the assumption that all of the infringing sales would have stayed within the market is reasonable if the overall market elasticity of demand is nearly zero. An elasticity of demand near zero means that customers view the products in the market

---

[26] A showing of incremental profit on the lost sales satisfies the fourth *Panduit* factor. The economic principles of calculating incremental cost are addressed in Chapter 12.

[27] This principle was used by the court in *State Industries Inc. v. Mor-Flo Industries Inc.,* 883 F.2d 1573 (Fed. Cir. 1989), and subsequent cases, as discussed in Chapter 4. Under this approach, if the infringer's share of the market is x and the plaintiff's share of the market is s, the plaintiff would get a fraction of the infringing sales equal to $s/(1-x)$.

as necessities (must haves), regardless of whether they were equivalent or not, and would readily switch to a competing product if the product that they initially chose were unavailable. This condition may hold, for example, for products used in a medical procedure for which there are no substitutes outside the market. If neither of these two conditions holds, some of the infringing sales would likely go outside the market.[28] In this case, the market share approach would likely fail to provide a reliable basis for calculating the plaintiff's lost sales.

The third assumption made under the market share approach is that the market shares provide a good indication of the closeness of substitution (i.e., the cross-price elasticities) between products in the market. This assumption would likely be violated if the overall market was broken into segments, where two products within the same segment were much closer substitutes for each other than they were for the products in other segments.[29] Segmentation typically occurs based on product attributes. For example, imported beers such as Heineken are perceived to be in a different segment within the beer market than "popular price" beers such as Old Milwaukee. Consumers of Heineken are substantially more likely to switch to another "high end" beer than they are to Old Milwaukee. As a result, Heineken competes less closely with Old Milwaukee than would be indicated by its overall market share. As another example, the toothpaste market is segmented along several characteristics such as tartar control and whitening properties. Consumers of a tartar control and whitening toothpaste would likely switch in greater numbers to other tartar control and whitening toothpastes than would be reflected by these products' overall market shares because these products are closer substitutes for each other than they are for products outside the tartar control and whitening segment.

If the assumptions of the market share approach are sufficiently inconsistent with the economic reality of the marketplace at issue, a different approach must be used. One such approach is the *segment share approach*. This approach seeks to address the situation where the market is segmented and where products within the same segment compete more

---

[28] This phenomenon is sometimes referred to as "market expansion by the infringer," which is another way of saying that the infringer brought sales into the market that would otherwise not have been made by any product in the market.

[29] This issue arose in *BIC Leisure Prods. Inc. v. Windsurfing Intl. Inc.*, 1 F.3d 1214 (Fed. Cir. 1995), and *Crystal Semiconductor Corp. v. Tritech Microelectronics Intl. Inc.*, 246 F.3d 1336 (Fed. Cir. 2001). These cases are discussed in more detail in Chapter 4.

closely with each other than they do with products in other segments. The plaintiff's lost sales are based on its share of the segment of the market in which the infringing product competes, rather than on the plaintiff's share of the overall market as is done in the market share approach.[30] Note though, that if the plaintiff's product and the infringer's product are in different segments, the plaintiff is deemed to have zero lost sales.

While the segment share approach partially addresses the second assumption of the market share approach—that competition between products is completely characterized by their market shares—it makes a similar assumption that competition within the segment is completely characterized by segment shares. Again, the validity of this assumption also needs to be evaluated. In addition, similar to the first assumption of the market share approach, the segment share approach assumes that no infringing sales would leave the segment in the but-for world. This assumption requires either that the products within the segment are nearly perfect substitutes or the segment own-price elasticity of demand is nearly zero.[31]

The Before-After Approach

In some situations, data will be available on the plaintiff's sales, prices, and profits from a time period before the infringer entered the market with the infringing product as well as from the time period after the infringer entered. In that case, it may be possible to estimate the effect of infringement on the plaintiff's sales, prices, and profits by performing a comparison of the preinfringement period to the postinfringement period.[32] If, for example, the plaintiff's sales decreased by 15 percent after the infringement, it might be reasonable to conclude that this decrease was caused by the infringement and that the plaintiff would have maintained its level of sales in the but-for world. As another example, a decrease in the plaintiff's price that was observed after the entry of the infringing product might provide an estimate of the amount of price erosion the plaintiff sustained as a result of the infringement.

---

[30] This approach was used in *BIC Leisure* and *Crystal Semiconductor*.
[31] The second condition is less likely to hold in the case of a segment than in the case of a market because a segment own-price elasticity is typically higher than the corresponding market own-price elasticity. For example, the own-price elasticity for imported beers is greater in magnitude than the own-price elasticity for all beers.
[32] In a situation where the plaintiff's sales, prices, or profits are growing or declining over time, it may be appropriate to perform the before-after analysis based on trends rather than levels of sales, prices, or profits.

In performing this type of before-after analysis, one must be mindful of the possibility that some other economic factor was at least partially responsible for the observed changes in the plaintiff's sales, prices, or profits. For example, if the plaintiff's costs of producing the product decreased at approximately the same time as the entry of the infringing product, at least part of the observed price decrease might be due to the plaintiff's passing on part of the cost decrease as opposed to competition from the infringing product driving down the price.[33] If such factors may be important, econometric methods can be used to control for them and thereby isolate the effect of the infringement on the price or sales of the plaintiff.

Customer Surveys

Surveys can be used to assess the likely choices of customers in the event that the infringing product or product feature was not available to them. For example, a sample of customers of the infringing product could be asked to which alternative toothpaste product they would turn (if any) if the infringing toothpaste product was not on the shelf when they went into the store. Customer surveys can be used to determine customers' cross-price elasticities of demand between products, their willingness to pay for certain attributes of a product (including the patented feature), and the degree to which they purchase certain products together. Customer surveys can therefore be used to determine the effects of the infringement on the plaintiff's sales, prices, and profits.[34]

In performing a consumer survey, one must take care in the design of the survey questionnaire to ensure that the respondents' answers to questions regarding hypothetical purchasing situations reliably reflect what they would do in actual purchasing situations. In addition, the sample of respondents must be chosen using scientific sampling methods to ensure that the survey results can be reliably projected to the relevant population of consumers.

Merger Simulation Techniques

Merger simulation techniques were developed by economists to help assess the likely competitive effects of mergers. A simulation approach

---

[33] A basic principle of economics is that firms set their prices on the basis of marginal cost, demand conditions, and the nature of strategic interaction with competitors.

[34] The use of surveys in intellectual property cases is discussed in more detail in Chapter 8.

can also be used to evaluate the lost sales, price erosion, and lost profits sustained by a plaintiff in a patent infringement case.[35] Specifically, the but-for world can be simulated based on, among other inputs, the own- and cross-price elasticities of demand between the products. The effects of the infringement on the plaintiff's sales, prices, and profits can be determined by comparing the outcomes in the simulated but-for world to the outcomes in the actual world.

For example, consider a case where the plaintiff was claiming lost sales but no price erosion. A but-for world could be simulated by removing the infringing product from the market and asking what customers of the infringing product would have done based on the own- and cross-price elasticities of demand assuming that the prices of the remaining products would have remained at their actual levels. (This is what was done in Figure 3.) Alternatively, consider a case where a plaintiff was claiming both lost sales and price erosion. In that case, the but-for world could be simulated by removing the infringing product from the market and allowing the plaintiff and other remaining competitors to change their prices in a profit-maximizing fashion. (This is what was done in Figure 4.) Note that a properly specified simulation will take into account the quantity-reducing effects of the plaintiff charging a higher price in the but-for world.

A similar analysis can be performed to simulate the but-for world in situations where it would have been economically feasible for the infringer to offer its product after having removed the infringing feature. Specifically, the demand for the various products and the prices charged by the various suppliers can be simulated under the but-for scenario that the infringer's product would have lacked the patented feature. Damages can be calculated by comparison of the but-for world outcomes to the actual outcomes.

A simulation of the but-for world requires detailed knowledge of the structure of demand for the set of products with which the infringing product competes. Consequently, a simulation approach may have somewhat greater data requirements than other methods. For example, transactions data or customer survey data may be required to econometrically estimate the structure of demand.

---

[35] This approach is discussed in more detail in Chapter 7.

*Approaches to Determining Plaintiff's Capacity to
Make Additional Sales*

As discussed above, the plaintiff must demonstrate that it would have
had sufficient excess capacity in the but-for world to make the claimed
lost sales. An analysis of the plaintiff's manufacturing capacity might
involve determining the amount of excess manufacturing plant capacity
and comparing it to the level of potential lost sales. An analysis of the
plaintiff's selling capacity might involve checking that the sales force was
of sufficient size to call on the customers of the defendant.[36] An analysis
of the plaintiff's distribution capacity might involve seeing whether the
plaintiff sold through the same channels of distribution as the defendant.
This list is not meant to be exhaustive; other analyses may be required in
a given situation.

*Approaches to Determining the Extent of Lost Profits
on Convoyed Sales*

To determine the amount of lost convoyed sales, one can examine the
way in which the two products are marketed. As a simple example, if one
unit of the convoyed product is typically packaged with one unit of the
patented product, one could reasonably infer that the lost unit sales of
the convoyed product equals the lost unit sales of the patented product.
In other situations, it may be possible to analyze statistically the relationship between sales of the patented product and sales of the convoyed
product and use this relationship to estimate the likely amount of convoyed sales that were lost in conjunction with the lost sales of the
patented product. An assessment of causation is important as well. One
should demonstrate to a reasonable degree of certainty that sales of the
patented product drive the sales of the allegedly infringing product and
not vice versa.

Once the amount of lost convoyed sales is determined, it is necessary
to determine the incremental profit on these lost sales. This can be done in
a manner similar to that described above for the patented product.

---

[36] One may also want to analyze the extent of the overlap in the customer lists of the
plaintiff and defendant. If they are selling to essentially the same customers, in general there would be little question that the plaintiff had sufficient selling capacity to
make the defendant's sales. If, on the other hand, they are selling to different customers, one might undertake further investigation, e.g., as to whether the plaintiff's
existing sales force called on the defendant's customers.

Summary

We have outlined the economics of how and why infringement may lead to a decrease in profits for the plaintiff. The underlying economic principles provide the basis for the reconstruction of the but-for world that is necessary to calculate lost profits damages. We have discussed practical methods used by economists to determine lost profits in patent infringement cases. Below, we turn to a discussion of determining a reasonable royalty to compensate the patent owner for infringement of its patent.

Reasonable Royalty

An economist's contribution to an intellectual property case is the application of economic principles to a particular valuation problem. In intellectual property, the typical valuation problem is to determine a fair value that compensates the patent owner for the infringement (use) of its patent by an unauthorized entity. As stated at the outset of this chapter, the federal patent statute describes two approaches to determining patent damage awards: lost profits and reasonable royalties.[37] Where lost profits are damages equal to the amount of additional profit that the patent owner would have received had infringement not occurred, a reasonable royalty is computed on sales that the patent holder would not have made. In some cases, a plaintiff may seek reasonable royalty damages on all sales made by the defendant, while in others the plaintiff may seek lost profits damages on sales it can prove it would have made itself but for infringement and reasonable royalty damages on the remaining sales.

The legal requirements for obtaining lost profits are generally more rigorous than the requirements to establish damages from foregone royalty payments. As discussed above, to be awarded lost profits, the patent owner needs to prove that the infringement *caused* the claimed lost profits and prove the amount of damages. In contrast, to prove the fact of damage and obtain damages in the form of a reasonable royalty, the patent

---

[37] 35 U.S.C. § 284. See also *Lam Inc. v. Johns-Manville Corp.*, 718 F.2d 1056, 1065 (Fed. Cir. 1983). The law also allows a patent owner to obtain its "established" royalty on infringing sales. An *established* royalty has been defined as a royalty "paid by such a number of persons as to indicate a general acquiescence in its reasonableness by those who have occasion to use the invention" (where general acquiescence implies a willing licensor and licensee). See *Panduit*, 575 F.2d at 1164, n. 11, 197 U.S.P.Q. at 736i, n. 11 (6th Cir. 1978).

owner needs only to establish validity and infringement, which needs to be done in the liability phase of the case in any event. If the patent at issue is found to be valid, enforceable, and infringed, the patent owner is entitled to compensation for the infringement of its patent. Such compensation shall be "in no event less than a reasonable royalty for the use made of the invention by the infringer."[38] The reasonable royalty is the outcome of a hypothesized arm's-length negotiation between the patent owner and the infringer. The hypothetical negotiation is a reconstruction of a negotiation between a willing licensor (the plaintiff)[39] and a willing licensee (the defendant) wherein the two parties would have arrived at some royalty agreement. As a legal matter, the negotiation is hypothesized to take place on the eve of first infringement wherein the parties assume that the patent is valid and infringed.[40]

The higher bar set for showing the fact of damages from lost profits generally encourages a more scientific approach to determining damages from lost profits than from a reasonable royalty. There is, however, a clear link between the factors that make a royalty reasonable and the factors that influence lost profits. A reasonable royalty is one that imitates the royalty bargain in market-based (as opposed to court-ordered) negotiations. A market-based royalty will be influenced by the same economic factors that go into determining lost profits: namely price, costs, volume (quantity produced and sold), and the presence of alternatives. This means that the same scientific principles that are applied to determining lost profits should also be applied to royalty determination.

Methods of Royalty Determination

In addition to a market-based approach, there are a number of other methods for determining royalties that analysts use, some of which are not rooted in scientific principles and are, therefore, not what we would call "reasonable," from an economics point of view. We classify royalty determination methods into four categories according to whether they are based on market factors, comparables, industry averages, or a rule of thumb (Figure 5).

---

[38] 35 U.S.C. § 284.

[39] But see *Rite-Hite* 56 F.3d. 1538, at 1554 n. 13: "this is an inaccurate, and even absurd, characterization when, as here, the patentee does not wish to grant a license."

[40] See *Georgia-Pacific Corp. v. United States Plywood Corp.*, 318 F. Supp. 1116, 1120 (S.D.N.Y. 1970), *modified on other grounds*, 446 F.2d 295 (2d Cir.), *cert. denied*, 404 U.S. 870 (1971).

Figure 5. Methods of Royalty Determination

1.	Market-Based Method	Reasonable
2.	Comparables Method	Can Be Reasonable
3.	Industry Averages Method	Reasonable Only with Luck
4.	Rule of Thumb Method	Unreasonable

Market-Based Method

Market-based methods mimic market forces: factors that affect a licensing negotiation in the "real world" (i.e., outside of a courtroom) are considered in determining a market-based royalty in a hypothetical negotiation.

In goods markets, we think of buyers and sellers, each acting individually, coming to terms that collectively determine the price that will clear the market of the quantity proffered at that price. Patent licensing fees or royalties are the prices set in technology market transactions. Unlike many goods market transactions, technology market transactions are idiosyncratic because patents (or bundles of patents) are highly heterogeneous. The value of any one of those transactions will depend upon its profit-enhancing prospects for a given licensee, the cost to the specific licensor of granting the license, and the alternatives available to both parties. The value of the technology will also depend upon the number of times it has been sold, or licensed. In some cases, the value is diminished by the creation of additional user-licensees; in other cases, its value may be enhanced.

Market-based royalty determination methods must take explicit account of the idiosyncrasies of the particular patent being licensed, the parties to the negotiation, the alternatives to the technology at issue, and the timing of the hypothetical negotiation. If the resulting royalty would have been acceptable by rational parties in a real-world licensing negotiation, the resulting royalty is "reasonable."

Comparables Method

The second commonly used method to determine royalty damages is to compare the hypothetical license in question to a preexisting comparable license that was negotiated in the market. The value of this method (and whether it is reasonable) depends on the quality of the comparable. A poorly chosen comparable—one that bears little or no resemblance to the products, market conditions, or competitive relationship of the litigating parties—is of little value. On the other hand, if there are insufficient data to use the market-based method, a comparable chosen with care can be more informative than a poorly estimated market-based royalty. Thus, this method may yield a reasonable royalty.

Industry Averages Method

The third method used for royalty determination is to use an industry average. We label this method "reasonable only with luck." As we will explain further, there may be no reason to expect that the particular patent being litigated will be representative (in other words, equal to the average) of other patents in the industry. If we use an average or typical value for the royalty, we may incorrectly value the technology more often than we will properly value it.[41]

The distribution of patent values is highly skewed, which means that the mathematical "average" is not a reliable indicator of the value of any particular patent. Most patents are worth very little. The holy grail of inventive activity is the blockbuster patent that generates millions of dollars in profits for the patent owner. A problem with using industry averages to determine a reasonable royalty is that the industry averages will mix together the value of a one-of-a-kind blockbuster patent with the lower-value patents. The average value overestimates "typical" patents and underestimates the value of a blockbuster (Figure 6).

If the patent in question is a blockbuster patent it should be awarded a high royalty. If it is a run-of-the-mill patent, it should be awarded a much lower royalty. A blockbuster patent that has no close substitutes may be worth virtually all of the profits associated with the invention. A run-of-the-mill patent that has close substitutes may be worth only a small fraction of the profits, if it is worth anything at all. There is no justification for awarding a middle value if the patent falls into one of the two categories.

Rule of Thumb Method

Finally, the fourth method, which we are labeling unambiguously "unreasonable," is the 25 percent rule.[42] This rule can take many forms (and

---

[41] Of course, we acknowledge that one cannot let the perfect be the enemy of the good. If no other data were available, industry average royalty rates may provide the best market data to be had.

[42] For a description of this method of royalty determination see R. Goldscheider, *Technology Management Handbook* (New York: C. Boardman Co., 1984). See also R. Goldscheider, John Jarosz, and Carla Mulhern, "Use of the 25% Rule in Valuing IP," *les Nouvelles* (December 2002), for a discussion of how the authors feel the 25 percent rule has been misapplied by courts or economists.

Figure 6. What is Wrong with Using Industry Averages?

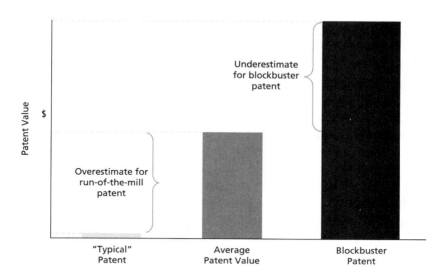

may be 33 percent or some other share), but the general category of unreasonable royalty methods is to take an arbitrary share of the operating profits associated with the allegedly infringing products and assert that that is the royalty to which the patent owner is entitled. The 25 percent rule takes no account of the importance of the patent to the profits of the product sold, the potential availability of close substitutes or equally effective noninfringing alternatives, or any of the other idiosyncrasies of the patent at issue that would have affected a real-world negotiation.[43]

For example, a royalty based on 25 percent of profits is unreasonable if the prospective licensee can obtain near identical profits by turning to the next-best alternative. A 25-percent-of-profits royalty may also be unreasonable if the patent owner earns a substantial margin on every sale and is in a position to serve the entire market if the infringer were kept out of the market.

The fundamental principle of a market-based approach to royalty determination is that the resulting royalty must consider the value of the

---

[43] See Chapter 5 for a further discussion of the potential pitfalls in using this rule-of-thumb method of determining patent value.

patent to both parties to the negotiation. Only by doing so do we ensure that the royalty is connected to the underlying value of the patented technology. The same cannot be said of rules of thumb and industry standard profit splits. The reason is simple: for an invention to be patentable it must be novel. It therefore makes little sense to assume that the value of a unique invention could be approximated by the value of some other, by definition, different, invention even if it is used or applied in the same industry.

The Market-Based Royalty Range

So how does the market determine the value of a patent? In the real world, royalties are the outcome of a negotiation between the patent owner and the licensee. The key element of a market-based negotiation is that both sides win—or expect to win at the time they sign the licensing agreement. Since the hypothetical negotiation in a patent damages context is designed to mimic a real-world bargain between a licensee and a licensor, the outcome of that negotiation (i.e., the reasonable royalty) must be one in which both sides benefit from the bargain. If it were otherwise (i.e., if either party *expected* to be worse off for having negotiated the license), the license would simply never materialize. One of the parties would have walked away from the negotiating table and not signed the licensing agreement.

The Hypothetical Negotiation

The first step in determining a reasonable royalty is to establish a bargaining range, or, the range of royalties over which both sides can benefit from having completed the transaction. The hypothetical negotiation is like any other bargaining transaction. Economics tells us that the outcome of such transactions depends on the costs and benefits to each party entering into the agreement as well as on their relative bargaining strengths. The costs and benefits dictate the range of feasible outcomes whereby both parties can benefit from the licensing agreement, while the relative bargaining power dictates which party gets more of the benefit of the agreement. Since both parties must ultimately agree on the outcome, the benefits of the hypothesized agreement must outweigh the costs for each party.

An agreement will be reached only if there exists a royalty that compensates the patent owner for the costs it incurs from licensing its patent to a competitor but still affords the licensee some of the benefits of using the patented technology. The royalty that exactly compensates the patent owner for its costs of licensing represents the *minimum* royalty that the patentee would be willing to accept. The licensor would not grant any license that leaves it with lower profits than could be earned by refusing to grant a license and being the sole practitioner of the patent or maintaining the option of granting an exclusive license to a third party. At the other end of the spectrum, the licensee will not accept any royalty that leaves it with lower profits than could be earned by designing around the patent or adopting a noninfringing alternative technology, if available.[44] The value of the benefits to the licensee from using the patented technology compared to the next-best alternative represents the *maximum* royalty that the licensee would be willing to pay. If the maximum amount exceeds the minimum that the patent owner would be willing to accept, the difference between these two amounts represents the negotiating range for the royalty associated with the license. Royalties within this range can leave both parties better off for having negotiated the license than either party would be by walking away from the bargaining table.[45]

The emphasis on the value of the invention to both sides of the transaction means that the negotiation is rooted in the economics of the product and market at issue. A royalty that reflects the value of the invention to both parties and leaves no party worse off (in expectation) for having signed the agreement is a "reasonable royalty" (Figure 7).

Willingness to Accept

The minimum of the bargaining range is the lowest royalty that makes the patent owner better off for having licensed his technology. The minimum royalty must compensate the patent owner for any costs it stands to incur by granting the license. The minimum could be quite low—at or near zero—if the two parties operate in different markets or locales or if the patent owner is seeking a reasonable royalty on sales made by the licensee that the patent owner would not have made. Alternatively, the minimum

---

[44] See *Grain Processing,* supra note 4.

[45] It may well be the case that the licensor's minimum willingness to accept exceeds the licensee's maximum willingness to pay. This can happen when the patent owner is a more efficient producer of products embodying its technology or when the patent owner stands to earn a substantial volume of ancillary profits on products sold with products embodying the patented feature that are not offered by the licensee. When no bargaining range exists, the patent owner may be better off seeking lost profits as compensation for infringement.

**Figure 7.   The Bargaining Range in a Hypothetical
Negotiation**

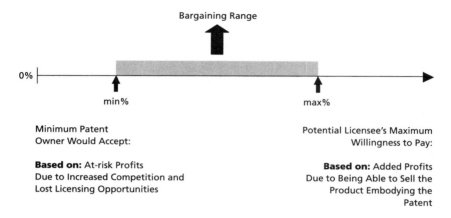

Bargaining Range

0%

min%

max%

Minimum Patent
Owner Would Accept:

Based on: At-risk Profits
Due to Increased Competition and
Lost Licensing Opportunities

Potential Licensee's Maximum
Willingness to Pay:

Based on: Added Profits
Due to Being Able to Sell the
Product Embodying the
Patent

could be relatively high—up to or greater than the patent owner's own profit margin—if every sale made by the licensee represents a lost sale of the patented product and any ancillary products.

The costs to the patent owner include, generally, the profits that the patent owner would lose on its competing products, as well as any perceived costs of facing a stronger competitor in the overall market. These at-risk profits could take the form of profits on sales lost to the licensee, reduced profits on retained sales due to price erosion caused by competition with the licensee, profits on lost sales of related products, profits associated with foregone economies of scale, profits from foregone royalties from other licensees, and profits on lost future sales of follow-on or upgrade products to customers lost to the infringer, among other things.[46] The minimum of the bargaining range could be affected by other licenses that the patent owner has signed or hopes to sign with other competitors. For example, if the patent owner has signed licenses containing "Most Favored Nation" clauses, then agreeing to a royalty lower than the rates specified in those other licenses may force the patent

---

[46] One must take care to avoid "double counting" lost profits. The determination of a reasonable royalty should only consider those costs to the licensor that are not explicitly accounted for elsewhere. If there is a lost profits calculation and the royalty under consideration is being determined for sales that the patent owner would not have made, then the factors already accounted for in the lost profits calculation should not again be considered in the royalty determination.

owner to lower the royalty offered to other licensees and lose royalty revenue from these parties.

Granting a license could deprive the patent owner of some of the benefits associated with holding the patent because it would confer a competitive advantage on the licensee. If the patent owner sells products that embody the patented technology, granting a license may adversely affect its profitability because the licensee may now be better able to compete with the patent owner. Even if the patent owner does not manufacture a product embodying its own patent, if the patent owner sells products that nonetheless compete with the prospective licensee's products, the patent owner stands to lose profits as a result of licensing a competitor.[47] The problem then is to identify and evaluate the costs to the patent owner from granting the license. The scientific approach to royalty determination requires quantifying these costs with the same rigor that one would use to quantify lost profits.

Willingness to Pay

The benefits to the licensee are those that accrue from using the patented technology; they might include lower costs, higher sales, or some combination of the two. The maximum willingness of the licensee to pay for the right to practice the technology depends on the lifetime profits from using the invention compared to the lifetime profits of the next-best alternative.[48] The lower the perceived benefits of being able to practice the patent, the lower will be the maximum royalty the licensee would be willing to pay (Figure 8).

The licensee's willingness to pay for the patent at issue is primarily driven by the profits flowing from the patent relative to the next-best alternative. Most important in making this determination are the full economic costs of avoiding the patent. The patent can be avoided by abandoning the infringing features or product lines and focusing on sales of other products, incorporating a noninfringing alternative into the accused product lines, or designing around the patent. Thus, a fundamental determinant of the value of the patent to the licensee is the availability of noninfringing alternatives.

---

47 See *Rite-Hite Corp. v. Kelley Co.*, 56 F.3d 1538 (Fed. Cir. 1995).
48 Where the lifetime may be truncated to the date the patent expires, or the economic life of the product embodying the technology, which could be shorter than the statutory life, such as in industries marked by rapid technological progress.

Figure 8. Infringer's Maximum Willingness to Pay

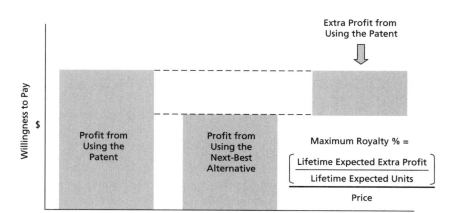

This means that a necessary step in determining a reasonable royalty is to evaluate the options available to the licensee and, if possible, to determine the cost (in both time and dollars) of designing around the patent. If, for example, it would cost the licensee $1,000 and take only a week to redesign its products without the infringing feature, *and* if the resulting noninfringing product would achieve essentially the same market acceptance as the product incorporating the infringing feature, then the most the licensee would be willing to pay is a royalty that cost him, in present value terms, no more than $1,000 over the lifetime of the patent. In comparison, if the alternative product were inferior to the infringing product (in the sense that the patented technology allowed for lower production costs or a higher selling price), then these added "costs" of switching to the alternative (the foregone benefits provided by the patented technology) would serve to increase the maximum royalty the licensee would be willing to pay.

Moreover, if there are no clear alternatives to the patented feature, and abandoning the patented technology means abandoning the product line, then the costs of avoiding the patent would be closer to the entire profits generated by sales of the products embodying the patent. In a situation such as this, the licensee would be willing to pay a significantly higher royalty because there are fewer options.

In determining the licensee's maximum willingness to pay, the analyst measures both the costs of avoiding the patent and the benefits (in terms of additional profits) of attaining a right to use the patented technology. If the proposed royalty exceeds the full economic costs of turning to an alternative technology, the licensee will be better off refusing the license. The maximum royalty, therefore, is the royalty that is precisely equal to the sum of the design around costs plus any foregone profits from switching to the next-best alternative.

The Timing of the Negotiation

One additional consideration that can affect the endpoints of the bargaining range is the timing of the hypothetical negotiation. By legal convention, the hypothetical negotiation is supposed to take place "on the eve" of first infringement.[49] This generally is taken to mean the later of the date of first infringing sale (or other "use") or the date that the patent issued. In situations where there are substantial set-up costs or where the licensee has been manufacturing and selling the infringing product prior to any patent being issued, this timing of the negotiation can lead to substantially higher royalties than would have been realized had the negotiation taken place prior to any sunk costs being incurred by the defendant.

By making investments that are (1) sunk costs and (2) specific to the patented technology, the licensee may become locked into using the patented technology. Sunk costs are costs that cannot be recovered if the licensee were later to switch away from the patented technology. Before sunk costs are incurred, the licensee would consider them in assessing the patented technology versus the next-best alternative. After the sunk costs are incurred, however, because they could not be recovered, the licensee would not consider them in its assessment. Thus, after the sunk costs are incurred, on a going-forward basis the patented technology looks more profitable relative to the next-best alternative than it did prior to incurring those sunk costs.

Sunk costs can lock a licensee into using a particular technology by making switching to alternatives impractical or excessively costly. Consider the following simple example. Suppose that after making a sunk cost investment of $15, the licensee could make a profit of $20 from the product incorporating the patented technology. The net profit for the licensee before any costs are sunk would therefore be $5. The next-best

---

49 See e.g., *Georgia-Pacific*, 318 F. Supp. 1116, 1120, or *Ajinomoto Co. Inc. v. Archer-Daniels-Midland Co.*, 1998 WL 151411 (D. Del., Mar. 13, 1998) (No. 95-218-SLR).

alternative would have to offer a net profit of at least $5 to get the licensee to switch. Now consider what happens once the investment is sunk and cannot be recovered. At that point, the licensee would recognize that if it went forward with the patented technology, its net profit (from that point forward) would be $20. Now, the next-best alternative would have to offer a net profit of at least $20 to get the licensee to switch. Thus, sinking costs can lock the licensee into the patented technology, not in a literal sense, but rather as a matter of economic rationality.

Technology-specific sunk costs might include, for example, the costs of installing manufacturing facilities or specialized equipment that could not be used or sold if the accused infringer were to avoid the patent at issue by switching to an alternative technology, or the costs of designing the product to the specifications of the patented technology. If the same facilities, equipment, or design can be used to produce the next-best alternative, then the sunk costs would not create any lock-in. On the other hand, if switching to the next-best alternative requires investing in additional facilities or equipment, then these additional costs of switching must be considered in calculating the profitability associated with switching to the next-best alternative.

Technology-specific sunk investments allow for the possibility of *hold-up* in the negotiating process. In such a situation, the patent owner can seek higher royalties than he would have been able to negotiate had the sunk investments not been made. The hold-up value is attributable only to the timing of the negotiation and does not reflect the inherent value of the patented technology to the prospective licensee. One way of avoiding the potential for hold-up to affect the royalty negotiation is to consider the "eve of first infringement" to refer to the date prior to any investments being made that lock the licensee into using the particular technology at issue, even if that date is prior to the patent actually being granted. In this case, the parties would be negotiating future royalties payable once the patent is granted (and by assumption is valid, enforceable, and infringed). While this approach can effectively eliminate the potential for hold-up, current case law may not provide for sufficient flexibility to allow the separation of hold-up value and patent value in this way.[50]

---

[50] If, however, the date of first infringing use occurs while the development costs are still in the process of being incurred, then there may be a legal justification for moving the negotiation date to a point in time that reduces (but may not eliminate) the hold-up problem.

The Final Reasonable Royalty

The difference between the patent owner's minimum willingness to accept and the infringer's maximum willingness to pay represents the *bargaining range* for the negotiation.[51] Royalty terms within this range leave both parties better off for having negotiated a license than either party would be by walking away from the bargaining table without having traded the property right at issue. Where within the range of feasible outcomes the final agreed-upon royalty is likely to fall depends upon the relative bargaining strengths of the two parties.

Bargaining Power

Bargaining power can be thought of as the ability of one negotiator to "hurt" the other party by walking away from the negotiating table. Suppose, for example, that the parties were to consider a royalty at, or very near, the minimum of the bargaining range. At this price, the licensee has the most to gain by entering into an agreement, but the patent owner has very little to lose by walking away from the bargaining table and refusing to grant a license. The patent owner would be in essentially the same position by refusing to grant a license as it would be by agreeing to license the technology at issue at this low price. Thus, the patent owner has little incentive to agree to a price at the minimum of the bargaining range.

Similarly, the licensee has little incentive to agree to a price at the maximum of the bargaining range. If the patent owner were to try to force a price at the upper end of the bargaining range, the licensee would have little to lose by walking away from the bargaining table (because such a royalty leaves it without any additional profits from licensing the technology), but the patent owner risks giving up all of the benefits of reaching an agreement at this price. For these reasons, one typically would not expect to see an agreement struck precisely at either end of the bargaining range, but rather somewhere in the middle of the range.

At the midpoint of the bargaining range, each party can hurt the other party equally by walking away from the negotiating table. The midpoint of

---

[51] As mentioned above, it may be the case that the minimum the patent owner is willing to accept exceeds the maximum that the licensee would be willing to pay. In this case, there does not exist a bargaining range as defined in this Section. If there is no positive bargaining range, then an economist might consider other factors such as what the bargaining range might look like if the licensee were an equally efficient or similarly situated competitor to the patent owner. By doing so, an economist can ensure that the patent owner is not penalized for the possibly inefficient use made of its invention by the prospective licensee.

the bargaining range allows both parties to share equally in the benefits of reaching an agreement and is therefore a useful starting place for considering other factors that affect the relative bargaining strengths of the two parties to the negotiation.

The Georgia-Pacific Factors

The United States Court of Appeals for the Federal Circuit (CAFC) encourages lower courts to consider 15 factors described in *Georgia-Pacific Corp. v. United States Plywood Corp.* (*Georgia-Pacific* factors) in determining a reasonable royalty.[52] These factors are listed in Figure 9. Many of the *Georgia-Pacific* factors are, or can be, subsumed in the scientific determination of the bargaining range described above. In particular, the final *Georgia-Pacific* factor (factor 15), states directly that a reasonable royalty is one that a willing licensor and willing licensee would have agreed upon had they been voluntarily trying to reach an agreement. This is at the heart of the method one employs to determine the bargaining range. The remaining *Georgia-Pacific* factors can either be taken into account explicitly when determining the endpoints of the bargaining range, or may be used to analyze the relative bargaining strengths of the two parties to determine whether the final agreed-upon royalty would fall above or below the midpoint of the range.

The impact of each factor on the final royalty or on the endpoints of the negotiation depends on the particular circumstances of the patent, industry, and parties at issue. Not every factor will be relevant or economically meaningful in every negotiation. Below we discuss *Georgia-Pacific* factors 1 through 13 and some of the ways that each could affect either the bargaining range or the bargaining power of the parties to the hypothetical negotiation. Our discussion is not meant to be exhaustive.

1. **Royalties received by the patent owner for the patent in suit:** If a preestablished arm's-length royalty for the patent in suit lies within the bargaining range established for the parties to the litigation, then that royalty will be a logical starting place for determining the final royalty. Other *Georgia-Pacific* factors can then be considered to determine whether the idiosyncrasies of the particular license at issue suggests a royalty above or below the estab-

---

[52] See, for example, *Dow Chemical Co. v. Mee Industries Inc.*, 341 F.3d 1370 (Fed. Cir. 2003).

Figure 9. The *Georgia-Pacific* Factors

1.	Royalties received for the patent tending to prove an established royalty
2.	Rates paid for comparable patents
3.	Nature and scope of the license
4.	Licensor's established policy and marketing program
5.	Commercial relationship between the licensor and licensee
6.	Effect on sales of other products of the licensee
7.	Duration of the patent and term of the license
8.	Established profitability of the products made under the patent
9.	Advantages of the patent over old modes or devices
10.	Benefits of the patent to users
11.	Infringer's use of the patent
12.	Customary profit split
13.	Portion of the profit credited to the patented invention
14.	The opinion of qualified experts
15.	The amount that would be agreed upon by a willing licensor and a willing licensee

---

lished royalty.[53] The patent owner may be unwilling to accept a royalty less than the preestablished royalty if doing so would trigger costly renegotiations with established licensees. Similarly, the patent owner may be unwilling to accept a royalty less than a preestablished royalty if it stands to lose royalty revenue from established licensees that compete for sales with the prospective licensee. On the other hand, if the licensee can access markets not accessible to the patent owner or established licensees, then the patent owner may be willing to grant a discount to the prospective licensee in anticipation of broadening the sales base for products embodying the patent. As mentioned above, one needs to consider the comparability of prior licensees to the prospective licensee in the hypothetical negotiation to determine how much weight to place on preestablished royalties.

2. **Royalties paid by the prospective licensee for comparable patents:** This factor explicitly asks the expert to consider industry practices or use of comparables to help determine the final

---

[53] Note that according to *Panduit,* "where an established royalty rate for the patented invention is shown to exist, the rate will usually be adopted as the best measure of reasonable and entire compensation." See *Panduit,* 575 F.2d at 1164, n. 11, 197 U.S.P.Q. at 736i, n. 11.

reasonable royalty.[54] While, as described above, industry practices in general may not yield meaningful information about the value of a particular invention, a review of the licensee's past licensing practices may provide useful information on the prospective licensee's ability to exert bargaining power over other patent owners in arm's-length negotiations.

3. **The nature and the scope of the license:** This factor can be important in determining the comparability of other royalties considered under factors 1 and 2. A nonexclusive license is typically less valuable than an exclusive license, and therefore, consideration of this *Georgia-Pacific* factor can lead to a final royalty that is lower than established or "comparable" royalties described in exclusive licenses.

4. **The licensor's established licensing policy:** A licensor with an established policy of refusing to grant licenses to a competitor may be able to receive a higher royalty than a licensor that routinely licenses its patents. This stems in part from the fact that the license under consideration could be more valuable to the prospective licensee if there are fewer manufacturers in the industry with a right to practice the patent. This factor should be considered in determining the licensee's maximum willingness to pay for the patent at issue.

5. **The commercial relationship between the licensor and licensee:** All else being equal, a patent owner would be willing to accept a lower royalty from a licensee with which it does not compete than from a licensee that is a direct competitor to the patent owner. Licensing a competitor licensee enhances the potential for the patent owner to lose sales and profits as a result of granting the license. As with factor 3, this *Georgia-Pacific* factor can be important in weighing the comparability of prior licenses. One would expect the hypothetical negotiation to yield a higher royalty than prior licenses, if prior licenses were granted to noncompeting licensees.

---

54 We mentioned earlier that the use of industry averages or rules of thumb lead to reasonable royalties "only with luck." The key point is that these royalty shortcuts should be considered only after one has established the reasonable royalty range and typically should not be the first and only consideration in determining a reasonable royalty.

6. **The effect of selling the patent in promoting sales of other products of the licensee:** The additional profits from sales of noninfringing products that the licensor and licensee stand to make by practicing the patent at issue can be explicitly considered in determining the licensee's maximum willingness to pay and the licensor's minimum willingness to accept for the patent. However, to the extent that data permitting a calculation of the expected profits from increased sales of noninfringing products are not available, consideration of this *Georgia-Pacific* factor would increase the bargaining power of the patent owner.

7. **The duration of the patent:** The longer the time frame over which a licensee will have to pay royalties for the use of the patent at issue, the greater will be the incentive for the licensee to attempt to invent around the patent. Thus, for long-lived patents, a patent owner may be willing to settle for a lower running royalty rate than it would be willing to accept on short-lived patents, in order to discourage technological leap-frogging of the invention at issue. However, in industries characterized by rapid technological progress, the life-cycle of the products at issue, as opposed to the patent at issue, may be the greater determinant of the final royalty, and the parties may agree to a higher royalty rate because they expect the economic life of the patent to be short-lived.

8. **The commercial success of products embodying the patent:** This factor should be considered in determining a prospective licensee's maximum willingness to pay for the patent. The higher the incremental sales and profits attributable to the patented technology or features, the more a licensee would be willing to pay for the right to practice the patent. However, if the maximum of the bargaining range is explicitly tied to the profits that the licensee could earn by practicing the patent, then this factor should not also play a role in determining bargaining power.

9. **The advantages of the patent over old modes or devices:** "Old modes or devices" represent potential noninfringing alternatives to the patent at issue. If the patent at issue is a minimal advance over prior art, then the patent will not command a substantial royalty, even if products embodying the patent are profitable for the licensee. As discussed above, if the licensee can earn substantially the same profits by employing an older technology, then the profits from sales are not rightly attributable to the invention at

issue. To the extent that sufficient data are available, this factor can be incorporated directly into determining the licensee's maximum willingness to pay and need not be considered separately in determining bargaining power. If data are unavailable, then one should allow the bargaining power of the patent owner to rise or fall with the advantages of the patent over old modes or devices.

10. **The nature of the patented invention and benefits to those who have used the invention:** As with factors 8 and 9, this factor affects the licensee's willingness to pay for the invention. If the invention is a cost-saving invention, the most the licensee will pay for the invention is approximately the resulting cost savings. The cost-saving characteristics of the invention should be explicitly considered in determining the upper end of the bargaining range and should not also then be considered to affect bargaining power within that range. If the invention is a demand-enhancing invention, then the increased sales and profits attributed to the invention will have been considered under factor 8.

11. **The use made of the invention by the infringer:** This factor can also be explicitly considered in establishing the bargaining range for the hypothetical negotiation. The licensee would be willing to pay more for a patent that it uses extensively and from which it derives significant profits and would be less willing to pay for a patent that it uses infrequently. If data do not allow an explicit determination of the upper end of the bargaining range, then this factor can be considered in determining how the final reasonable royalty should compare to other royalties received by the patent owner or paid by the licensee.

12. **The portion of the profit that may be customary for the use of the invention:** Factor 12 encourages the expert to consider whether there are established rules of thumb for determining patent value in the industry at issue. As noted above, industry rules of thumb are not related to the value of a particular license to a particular licensee. However, to the extent that consideration of this factor yields a royalty *within* the established bargaining range, then this factor establishes a focal point on which the parties may settle as the final royalty. In particular, the parties may be willing to be guided by industry norms if they are likely to be engaged in repeated negotiations in the future and are equally likely to be the licensor as licensee in these future negotiations.

13. **The portion of the profit that should be credited to the invention:** Econometric and other methods exist that allow an expert to establish the value that consumers place on the specific attributes of the patent as opposed to other attributes of the final product. If data do not exist to allow an explicit accounting of the portion of the total value attributed to the patented feature, then this factor may be considered in determining where within an established bargaining range the final royalty will fall. If the invention is a "blocking patent," such that the product cannot be sold at all without infringing the patent at issue, then even if the product incorporates other features, the licensee's maximum willingness to pay is based on the entire profit earned on the product.

To summarize, consideration of the *Georgia-Pacific* factors is consistent with the market-based royalty method described in this chapter as a means to establish a reasonable royalty. Data permitting, many of the *Georgia-Pacific* factors will be explicitly taken into consideration in determining the boundaries of the hypothetical negotiation. Those factors that are not readily quantifiable can be considered in weighing the bargaining power of the negotiating parties. Factors that favor the patent owner weigh in favor of a final royalty at the upper end of the bargaining range, while factors favoring the licensee weigh in favor of a final royalty in the lower end of the bargaining range. Where the final royalty will fall depends on the specific characteristics of the technology at issue and the parties to the litigation.

Departures from a Market-Based Negotiation

While the primary thesis of this chapter is that a reasonable royalty is one that is market-based, we do of course have to acknowledge that there are considerable differences between an unencumbered market-based royalty negotiation and the hypothetical negotiation envisioned by the courts. In constructing hypothetical negotiations, damages experts are required to assume that the negotiations take place on the eve of first infringement, that both sides are willing to enter into the transaction, and that the patent in suit is valid and infringed (and is acknowledged to be so by the litigating parties). These assumptions are, of course, contrary to fact when the parties have resorted to litigation.

In all likelihood, there was no negotiation on the eve of first infringement. The parties are decidedly unwilling participants in the hypothetical negotiation (if they were willing participants, there would not have been a lawsuit). And in real-world royalty negotiations, the parties may not know with certainty whether the patent is valid or infringed. This uncertainty could affect the real-world royalty negotiation in a way that would not occur in the hypothetical version of the negotiation.

Moreover, there is no guarantee that there will exist a bargaining range that would yield a reasonable royalty as we have defined it. In some cases, the foregone profits of the patent owner are greater than the profits gained by the alleged infringer. In those cases, there would be no royalty that a licensor and licensee would willingly agree on, were they not bound by law to do so. In these situations, a reward of lost profits (or the patent owner's minimum willingness to accept) rather than a reasonable royalty may be necessary to compensate the patent owner for infringement.

These differences between the hypothetical negotiation and a real-world bargaining transaction can represent a departure from the "make-whole" standard employed as the basis for determining economic damages. If the final reasonable royalty resulting from an assessment of a hypothetical negotiation is less than the lost profits of the patent owner, the patent owner is not made whole for the infringement it suffered. In addition, if the final royalty is precisely equal to the patent owner's established royalty from other arm's-length licenses, the patent owner is not made whole for the fact that the royalty payments it receives in compensation for past damages do not compensate for the time, costs, and risks involved in litigating the patent at issue—costs and risks that were presumably saved in negotiating preexisting licenses for the technology at issue. Therefore, we note that while the courts consider a reasonable royalty adequate to compensate for infringement, it may not always be the case that the reasonable royalty fully compensates the patent owner for the damages it incurred.

Conclusion

There are a variety of techniques for estimating patent damages, not all of which are scientific or reliable. The focus of this chapter has been to provide an overview of the methods of determining patent damages that are rooted in economic theory and are scientifically defensible. Estimates of damages from lost profits consider the interplay between price, cost, quantity, and competition. The same economic variables that determine lost profits also come into play in determining a reasonable royalty for an infringed patent. Both lost profits and reasonable royalty damage calculations should be built on scientific analyses of patent value. Without a rigorous analysis of factors that determine the value of a patent, the damage figure associated with infringement of that patent is no better than unfounded speculation and thus not appropriately the subject of expert opinion.

4

The Evolution of the Courts' Thinking on Damages

Phillip A. Beutel and Bryan Ray

As economists, we measure progress in the evolution of the courts' thinking on intellectual property damages by the degree to which damage determination is rooted in economic principles. While the case law on patent infringement damages has increasingly recognized the importance of economic principles, the road to economic rationality has suffered from a few wrong turns along the way.

We describe the evolution of patent damages in two broad stages. First, early patent damage calculation was essentially mechanistic and, for the most part, awarded reasonable royalty damages with little, if any, reference to market-based evidence. *Georgia-Pacific Corp. v. United States Plywood Corp. (Georgia-Pacific)* represented a significant advance in this early period in that it recognized the importance of economic factors in royalty calculation.[1] Even so, damage calculation in the early stage was, from an economic perspective, in its infancy. The second stage began with *Panduit Corp. v. Stahlin Bros. Fibre Works, Inc. (Panduit),*[2] in which the United States Court of Appeals for the Sixth Circuit provided a framework to guide the courts in measuring this loss.[3] Since *Panduit,* the courts have increasingly applied economic principles in determining damages and have relied less on formulistic approaches.

This chapter is based in part on Phillip A. Beutel and Richard T. Rapp, "Patent Damages: Updated Rules on the Road to Economic Rationality," *Patent Litigation 1996*, vol. 2, Practicing Law Institute/Patents, Copyrights, Trademarks, and Literary Property: Course Handbook Series No. G457 (November 1996).

[1] *Georgia-Pacific,* 318 F. Supp. 1116, 1120 (S.D.N.Y. 1970); modified 446 F.2d 295 (2d Cir. 1971).

[2] *Panduit,* 575 F.2d 1152, 1164 (6th Cir. 1978).

[3] We divide our discussion of the case law into pre- and post-*Panduit* periods only for expositional purposes. We recognize that others may divide this evolution differently.

Pre-*Panduit:* Early Economic Reasoning

The recovery of damages due to patent infringement is governed by 35
U.S.C. § 284, which states: "the court shall award the claimant damages
adequate to compensate for the infringement, but in no event less than a
reasonable royalty for the use made of the invention by the infringer." In
1964, the Supreme Court of the United States put this statutory language
into an economic context in *Aro Manufacturing Co. v. Convertible Top
Replacement Co. (Aro II).*[4] It followed the statute's directive by recognizing
that, as a matter of economics, compensation for a patent owner's loss
from infringement should be measured as the difference between the
patent owner's profits "had the infringer not infringed" and its actual
profits. However, the *Aro II* Court did little to establish the methods for
determining this loss.

Georgia-Pacific represented the next important advance. Here, the U.S.
District Court for the Southern District of New York concluded that a reasonable royalty sufficient to compensate a patent owner should be determined as the result of a hypothetical voluntary negotiation between the
patent owner and the licensee (infringer) at the time of first infringement.
The court also provided a list of primarily market-based evidentiary factors
to consider when calculating the royalty. These broad factors cover many of
the economic issues that may be useful for determining a reasonable royalty.
However, the court correctly recognized that it was impossible to assign
fixed weights to these various factors that would be applicable to each and
every case. In effect, the *Georgia-Pacific* court recognized that patents exist
in markets and that a reasonable royalty for any particular patent depends
on the specific opportunities and competitive conditions in the market (or
markets) in which that patent is used.

The *Georgia-Pacific* factors fall into four basic categories:

- directly and indirectly comparable royalty rates,
- factors affecting the profits of the potential licensee (infringer)
  if it gains a license,
- factors affecting the patent owner's losses resulting from awarding
  a license, and
- factors influencing the bargaining power each party brings to the
  hypothetical negotiation.

---

4   *Aro II,* 377 U.S. 476, 84 S. Ct. 1526 (1964).

Panduit: A Turning Point

With *Panduit,* the U.S. Court for the Sixth Circuit established two significant principles: (1) it ruled that the hypothesis of a voluntary negotiation between *willing* parties may be inappropriate, and (2) it provided a four-point test with which a patent owner could prove entitlement to lost profit damages.

The *Panduit* court strongly disagreed with the district court's conclusion (in the same matter) that a reasonable royalty should be based on a hypothetical negotiation between a *willing* licensor and licensee.[5] Instead, the court found that the reasonable royalty must fully account for the patent owner's *unwillingness* to license its patent.[6] Specifically, the *Panduit* approach to royalty determination focuses on the commercial relationship of the infringer and the patent owner (i.e., *Georgia-Pacific* factor 5). In particular, the court ruled that the royalty should reflect the patent owner's policy with respect to licensing a competitor and the patent owner's *expectations,* at the time of first infringement (when the hypothetical negotiation takes place), of the profits it would lose by licensing a competitor. Under this approach, therefore, the so-called "reasonable" royalty to which the infringer is assumed to agree could potentially exceed both its expected gain (and therefore the amount it would have been willing to pay in the hypothetical negotiation) and its actual realized profits from infringement.[7]

The *Panduit* court also, for the first time, provided a market-based test with which the patent owner could prove entitlement to damages based upon lost profits.[8] To receive lost profit damages, the patent owner

---

5   The *Panduit* court actually focused on certain conclusions made by a master appointed by the district court.
6   The court concluded that the assumption of a "willing" licensor would enable competitors to use infringement as a means by which to impose a compulsory license policy upon the patent owner.
7   As we discuss below, the *Panduit* court used an all-or-nothing approach to determine the plaintiff's entitlement to lost profits and in the end ruled that, in that matter, lost profits were *not* appropriate. However, that ruling was based primarily on a finding that the plaintiff could not accurately quantify the amount of profit that it would have made absent the infringement. Even so, the court found that the reasonable royalty should reflect, to the extent possible, the *patent owner's* expected lost profits if it were to grant a license. In this vein, in the absence of forecasts developed prior to the hypothetical negotiation date, it may be appropriate for a damages expert to consider the sales and profitability that existed in the market during the damage period to infer what the parties' expectations might have been at the time of the negotiation.
8   Consistent with economic theory, the court not only considered lost profits resulting from lost sales, but also considered lost profits resulting from price erosion. That is, the patent owner's sales during the infringement period may have been made at prices below the level that would have prevailed in the absence of infringement.

must demonstrate (1) a demand for the patented product,[9] (2) an absence of acceptable noninfringing substitutes, (3) the marketing and manufacturing capability to exploit the demand, and (4) the amount of profit it would have made in the absence of infringement. With this test, damage calculation becomes an all-or-nothing issue: if all four points are proven, lost profit damages may be awarded; if any one of the four points is not proven, damages are limited to a reasonable royalty—the statutory floor.

The all-or-nothing nature of the four-point *Panduit* test clearly promotes judicial efficiency, but does so at the expense of economic rationality. On the one hand, requiring a demonstration that demand for the product existed (point one) and that the claimant had the capacity to produce and sell the product (point three) prevents "workshop" inventors from falsely claiming that in the absence of infringement they would, with certainty, have become giant monopoly manufacturers. On the other hand, the *Panduit* test for the absence of noninfringing substitutes (point two) wrongly focuses attention on the extent to which technical—as opposed to economic—substitutes exist for the patented product.

The patent owner's entitlement to lost profit damages should depend upon the market power the patent confers—i.e., the ability of the patent owner, solely as a result of the patent, to profitably raise price and/or exclude competitors. In this context, the market power conferred by the patent depends on the availability of noninfringing economic substitutes for the patented invention and/or the products that embody it. All else being equal, economic substitutes are the alternatives to which consumers would turn in response to a price increase on the product that embodies the patented invention or if the (accused) product embodying the patented invention is no longer available. Thus, the presence of technical substitutes does not necessarily imply that the patent owner should not be entitled to a recovery of lost profits. As an economic matter, the extent to which the patent owner lost profits from infringement depends on consumer behavior, not on the technical similarity of products in the marketplace.

---

9   This factor, by itself, does not address the economic logic for why "demand" might play a role in determining entitlement to lost profits. In fact, demand for the product(s) that embody the patent is *not* the same as demand for the patented *feature(s)* unless, without the patent, the product(s) could not be offered for sale. If an accused infringer could turn to alternative, noninfringing technology and still offer a product that consumers would equally prefer, it could retain all of its sales, leaving none to be captured by the patent owner. Accordingly, as a matter of economics, what matters is the extent to which consumers demand (have a preference for) the *features* covered by the patented technology.

From *Panduit* to the Present

Infringement damage decisions after *Panduit* have tended to provide either a nudge toward application of economic principles or, occasionally, evidence of the economic inconsistencies inherent in the test. In *Lam Inc. v. Johns-Manville Corp. (Lam)*, the United States Court of Appeals for the Federal Circuit (CAFC) added to the *Panduit* test the *but-for* standard for determining entitlement to lost profits.[10] Here, the patent owner must prove *causation* of lost profits by infringement. The factual basis for causation is that but for the infringement, the patent owner would have made (all of) the sales that the infringer made, charged higher prices, or incurred lower expenses. The court's requirement of proof of causation implies a need to examine the but-for market and the patent owner's behavior within it.

In finding that the patent owner had adequately passed the *Panduit* test and had proven causation, the *Lam* court awarded lost profit damages arising from both lost sales and price erosion. However, among other factors, the court ignored (1) the marginal cost increases or decreases that the patent owner may have incurred in making the infringer's sales, and (2) the possibility that the patent owner may not have made *all* of the infringer's sales at the hypothetical but-for price, possibly higher than the price in the actual marketplace. First, to the extent that the patent owner's costs rise (or decline) with additional sales, lost profit damages should be accordingly reduced (or increased). Second, the court's assumption that, absent infringement, the patent owner would capture *all* of the infringer's sales at a higher but-for price is inconsistent with the law of demand. Unless demand is completely unresponsive to changes in price (or perfectly inelastic), the patent owner would be expected to capture *all* of these sales only by holding price at the infringer's level.[11] Even despite

---

[10] *Lam*, 718 F.2d 1056 (Fed. Cir. 1983). "Lost profits may be in the form of diverted sales, eroded prices, or increased expenses. The patent owner must establish a causation between his lost profits and the infringement.... In proving his damages, the patent owner's burden of proof is not an absolute one, but rather a burden of reasonable probability."

[11] This error remains prevalent in patent damage litigation. In *TWM Manufacturing Co. Inc. v. Dura Corp. and Kidde Inc.*, 789 F.2d 895 (Fed. Cir. 1986), the court allowed $100 for each sale made by the infringer, claiming that the patent owner would have made all of those sales at a higher price. In *Yarway Corp. v. EUR Control USA Inc. et al.*, 775 F.2d 268 (Fed. Cir. 1985) *(Yarway)*, the court determined lost profits based upon 100 percent of lost sales to the infringer, adjusted only for customers that were not known or inaccessible to the patent owner. In *Bio-Rad Laboratories Inc. v. Nicolet Instrument Corp.*, 739 F.2d 604 (Fed. Cir. 1984) *(Bio-Rad)*, the court ruled that merely because there existed a lack of noninfringing substitutes, all of the infringer's sales were assumed lost by the patent owner.

these problems, however, *Lam* indicates the court's willingness to accept multiple components of lost profits.

The next important advance occurred in *Bio-Rad* (see note 11).[12] This decision followed both the *Georgia-Pacific* and *Panduit* rulings in finding (1) market-based evidence is fundamental to royalty calculations, and (2) the patent owner must be compensated for unwilling licensure. Hence, the court established that industry royalty rates are not a ceiling for the royalty that may be assessed against an infringer, an important insight that should have received more attention than it has. The unquestioning use of industry-wide royalty rates as benchmarks for royalties—in both damage cases and license negotiations—is probably one of the leading sources of error in patent valuation. Established industry royalty rates may be useful as comparables only if the patents are of similar character and strength and the licensors and licensees face similar economic conditions. However, that is rarely the case. Moreover, the *Bio-Rad* court further moved toward economically sound damages by using incremental cost measures when estimating lost profits on sales made by the infringer.[13]

Lam and *Bio-Rad* represent modest adjustments to the *Panduit* methodology that moved damage calculation further toward achieving the make-whole standard. Not all post-*Panduit* decisions, however, follow this trend. *Yarway* (see note 11), for example, illustrates how the misuse of *Panduit* point two (the absence of noninfringing substitutes) may lead to damage awards entirely inconsistent with good economic sense. In ruling that the patent owner was entitled to lost profit damages, the *Yarway* court precluded the existence of the noninfringing substitutes test by defining a "mini-market" consisting only of the patent owner and the infringer—even though there were acknowledged economic substitutes in the market. This further illustrates the inherent problems with the

---

12 *Bio-Rad*, "Though established (industry) royalty rates are normally applicable...they do not necessarily establish a ceiling for the royalty that may be assessed...."
Similarly, in *Del Mar Avionics v. Quinton Instrument Co.*, 836 F. 2d 1320 (Fed. Cir. 1987) (*Del Mar Avionics*), the court ruled that the purpose of reasonable royalty damages "is not to provide a simple accounting method but to set a floor below which the courts are not authorized to go."

13 In *Paper Converting Machine Co. v. Magna-Graphics Corp.*, 745 F.2d 11 (Fed. Cir. 1984) (*Paper Converting*), the court ruled that the incremental income approach to computing lost profits is well established, recognizing that only costs incremental to making and selling some portion of the accused sales are appropriately deducted from the extra revenues earned on those sales, while costs not caused by capturing those sales, so-called fixed costs, do not enter the lost-profits calculation. Further, the incremental cost approach used in *Bio-Rad* takes into account both variable and fixed cost increases associated with the patent owner's recovery of proceeds from infringer's sales.

court's use of the *Panduit* four-point test: the extent of profit lost derives from the loss of the market power inherent in the patent, *not* from the mere absence or presence of technical substitutes. Therefore, *Yarway* provides an illustration of how the *Panduit* test can lead to economically irrational outcomes. To make the patent owner whole requires that one recognize that it may have captured only a portion of the accused sales, depending on the extent to which consumers would have turned to available *economic* alternatives in the but-for market. That is not likely to be, and should not be, an all-or-nothing market outcome.

The court made progress toward correcting the *Panduit* all-or-nothing approach to lost profit damages in *State Industries Inc. v. Mor-Flo Industries Inc. (Mor-Flo)*.[14] Rather than debate the existence of technical substitutes for the patented product, the court accepted a market-based standard—State Industries' (the patent owner) market share—as evidence of its claim to lost profits. Here, *Panduit's* noninfringing substitutes hurdle was neutralized by crediting all rivals with their market shares. State Industries' pro rata share of sales (i.e., after assuming Mor-Flo's accused sales were not in the market) was 40 percent; as such, it claimed lost profits on only 40 percent of Mor-Flo's infringing sales and took a royalty on the remaining 60 percent.

Reaffirming the principle that intellectual property infringement requires compensation regardless of whether the plaintiff would have made the sale or not, the court granted both lost profits and royalty damages covering, in total, *all* of the infringer's sales. *Mor-Flo* demonstrated the court's increased willingness to employ market-based evidence in describing the but-for environment.

Despite its advances, *Mor-Flo* inadequately recognizes that the value of a patent is not absolute. While, in some settings, it may make sense to award a patent owner only a share of the infringing sales in proportion to its overall market share, it does not follow—as in *Mor-Flo*—that this market share necessarily accurately reflects the patent owner's market power and ability to make (or likelihood of making) these sales. Neither does it follow that the patent owner is necessarily entitled to damages on *all* sales made by the infringer. Rather, the damage suffered by the patent owner depends on two related factors: (1) the number and efficacy of economic substitutes and (2) the responsiveness of demand to changes in price. *Mor-Flo* may be applauded for its attempt to recog-

---

14 *Mor-Flo*, 883 F.2d 1573 (Fed. Cir. 1989).

nize these two factors, albeit using market shares, an imperfect and arbitrary standard.[15]

The 1995 *en banc* decision in *Rite-Hite Corp. v. Kelley Co. (Rite-Hite)*[16] is a two-steps-forward-one-step-back decision marred by an internal inconsistency in the application of the make-whole standard. The *Rite-Hite* court affirmed that the patent owner is entitled to full compensation for commercial damages caused by infringement as long as the "injury was...reasonably foreseeable by an infringing competitor in the relevant market." Rite-Hite lost sales of its vehicle restraints—devices used to secure trucks to loading docks—to infringing competition. But the sales it lost in competition with the infringing device did not embody the patented invention, a releasable hook employed on another Rite-Hite vehicle restraint. The decision:

- awarded Rite-Hite lost profits on a product that was not covered by the patent at issue but that competed head-to-head with the product that had been found to infringe,
- rejected damages for a second product (so-called dock levelers) that was often sold together with the vehicle restraints, on the grounds that the convoyed product was not "functionally inseparable" from the patented product and therefore not covered under the entire market value rule,[17] and
- permitted a mixed award of lost profits on lost sales and a reasonable royalty on other infringing sales.

Six judges from the eight-judge majority concluded that, as the second point indicates, "unpatented components must function together with the patented component in some manner so as to produce a desired end prod-

---

[15] That is, how consumers would substitute other products absent the infringing product is not necessarily proportional to the market shares of even a properly defined relevant market. See Chapter 7 and 18.

[16] *Rite-Hite,* 56 F.3d 1538 (Fed. Cir. 1995).

[17] Consider a situation in which the patent covers a product typically sold in an apparatus, or package, with other features, or items. In that instance, the so-called "entire market value rule" refers to the practice of awarding lost profits to a patent owner on the sale of the entire apparatus or package, rather than apportioning sales between the patented and nonpatented elements of the package. In effect, this rule defines the patented "product" on which the patent owner may claim lost sales as including certain nonpatented elements. The extent of its application depends, among other things, on the extent to which the patented component is separable from the other elements of the package and the extent to which it drives the sale of the package as a whole. See, e.g., *Lesona Corp. v. United States,* 599 F.2d 958 (Ct. Cl. 1981).

uct or result. All the components together must be analogous to components of a single assembly or the parts of a complex machine, or they must constitute a functional unit." Thus, the majority would not extend liability to "include items that have essentially no functional relationship to the patented invention and that may have been sold with an infringing device only as a matter of convenience or business advantage." By this reasoning, they rejected Rite-Hite's demand for damages on lost sales of dock levelers that, while often sold together with the vehicle restraints that represented lost sales in the main, were also sometimes sold separately.

Here, the court moved both toward and away from economic rationality. The court first concluded that simple causation should determine what damages may be recovered. That is, a patent owner may be entitled to lost profits if infringement caused it to lose sales, even if those lost sales were of an unpatented alternate product. However, the court also concluded that the patent owner may not be entitled to lost profits on ancillary items, even if infringement *caused* it to lose those sales. The problem is obvious: If the make-whole principal is to dominate, then a patent owner that lost reasonably foreseeable and predictable sales of ancillary goods should be compensated for those losses as long as causality is proven, quite apart from issues of functional relationship.[18]

The functional (i.e., technical) relationship between products is ambiguous and immeasurable. There is no recognizable boundary line between products that are closely related functionally and those that are not. Is toner more "functionally related" to photocopiers than paper? If so, then *functionally related* may mean something like "incompatible with other brands." As a matter of economics, it is not clear why this should matter and, more important, why the case law on damages should create an incentive to reduce compatibility.

From our perspective, a sounder standard would be *complementarity*, defined in economic rather than technical terms. Complementary goods are goods that are sold together for market-determined reasons. The distinguishing characteristic of highly complementary goods is that when the price of one goes up the quantity sold of the other declines. When goods are such strong complements that they are always sold and priced together, then two products become as one—e.g., left shoes and right shoes. For the most part, however, complementary goods are priced and

---

[18] We do not address here whether the "reasonably foreseeable" aspect of this standard is, as an economic matter, necessary to fully and properly compensate the patent owner for its losses from infringement.

sold separately, but sales of one such product depend on the sales of its complement (like service on or supplies for durable equipment).

Complementarity may or may not be dependent on technological factors such as technical compatibility. For example, televisions and VCRs are probably weak complements in that the price of one brand of television going up will only mildly affect sales of the same brand of VCR, since there are so many brands of televisions that can interface with so many brands of VCRs. By contrast, where compatibility among rival brands is lower, the interdependence of demand may be greater. The quantity sold of Nikon 35 mm single lens reflex camera bodies is likely to depend importantly on the price of Nikon's lenses because of the noninterchangeability of lenses among brands. In the end, as a matter of economics, the patent owner should be eligible to receive lost profits on lost sales of complementary convoyed items so long as those lost sales were *caused* by the infringement. This principle should hold even if the convoyed items are sold with the patent owner's product "only as matter of convenience or business advantage." Regrettably, *Rite-Hite* represented a missed opportunity to set the record straight on convoyed goods.

King Instrument Corp. v. Luciano Perego et al. (King)[19] reinforces *Rite-Hite*'s affirmation of the but-for standard.[20] King was awarded damages for Tapematic's infringement of a patent for competing machines that splice and wind magnetic tape into video cassettes. Tapematic's appeal to the federal circuit against the award of lost profits by the district court was based upon its argument that lost profits can be awarded only to one who makes or sells the patented device, as King itself did not.[21] The federal circuit affirmed that "Section 284 imposes no limitation of the types of harm resulting from infringement that the statute will redress." Thus, the patent owner is permitted to earn its reward for investing in innovation by means other than practicing the patent. The court also stated: "As long as the patent owner receives a proper economic return on its investment in the acquisition of a patent, the Act does not require that return to come from the sale of patented products." That is, excluding competitors in addition to manufacturing or licensing the patented technology is a reasonable method of exploiting a patent. Consequently, *King* apparently reaffirmed *Rite-Hite*'s finding that patent owners may be eligible for lost profits on lost sales of unpatented competing items.

---

[19] *King*, 65 F.3d 941, 947, 952 (Fed. Cir. 1995).
[20] See also, e.g., *Juicy Whip Inc. v. Orange Bang Inc.*, 2004 WL 1950287 (Fed. Cir. [Cal.]).
[21] In *Rite-Hite*, the patent owner did make and sell a product embodying the patented invention, although that was not the product upon which lost sales were claimed.

Finally, there have been several relatively recent cases that most heart-eningly point in the direction of economic rationality and the avoidance of formulaic approaches. These are *BIC Leisure Products Inc. v. Windsurfing International Inc. (BIC)*, *Mahurkar*, and *Grain Processing Corp. v. American Maize-Products Co. (Grain Processing)*.[22]

In *BIC*, the district court relied on *Mor-Flo* and divided lost profits on the assumption that the patent owner, Windsurfing, would have captured a share of BIC's sales in direct proportion to Windsurfing's share of a so-called sailboard market. Judge Rader's appellate decision reveals the error in the district court's formulaic use of *Mor-Flo*: The appellate decision wisely describes evidence of a lack of actual substitution between the higher price Windsurfing sailboards and the less expensive infringing BIC products. The implication is that absent infringement, BIC's customers would not have turned to the patent owner—i.e., its products were not economic substitutes of the infringer's. Instead, BIC's customers would have purchased inexpensive boards sold by other competitors. In effect, the court found that Windsurfing and BIC did not compete in the same market, and therefore, Windsurfing could not have captured a pro rata share of the infringing sales.[23]

Relying on indicators of economic substitution represents a substantial improvement over *Yarway* and its vaguely defined "mini-markets." However, in another light, *BIC* may be interpreted as the flip side of *Yarway* and *Crystal Semiconductor Corp. v. Tritech Microelectronics Intl. Inc. et al. (Crystal)* The latter cases allowed the patent owner to claim lost profits on all infringing sales, because the court found all were within the same market as the patent owner.[24] While all three cases correctly recog-

---

[22] *BIC*, 1 F.3d 1214 (Fed. Cir. 1993); and *In re Mahurkar Double Lumen Hemodialysis Catheter Patent Litigation*, 831 F. Supp. 1354 (N.D. Ill. 1993); and *Grain Processing*, 185 F.3d 1341 (Fed. Cir. 1999).

[23] Alternatively, as an economic matter, the court may have reasoned that BIC and Windsurfing *did* compete within the same market but were sufficiently distant alternatives—i.e., certainly not the next-best alternatives to one another—that naked market shares within the broader market no longer provide a reasonable measure of the likely substitutability between the companies' products.

[24] In *Crystal*, 246 F.3d 1336 (Fed. Cir. 2001), the court perpetuated that failure of *Mor-Flo*. In *Crystal*, the court stated "to determine a patent owner's market share, the record must accurately identify the market. This requires an analysis which excludes alternatives to the patented product with disparately different prices or significantly different characteristics." In fact, as described above, this is not necessarily correct. Economic substitutes—i.e., as described above, those products among which consumers turn when relative prices change—may have "disparately different prices or significantly different characteristics." Indeed, economic substitutes cannot be defined based solely on arbitrary price points or technical features.

nize that certain products may compete more closely than others, and therefore overall market shares may get things wrong, it should be more explicitly recognized that, in the language of *Crystal,* the presence of disparate prices or different characteristics may *not,* by themselves, indicate the appropriate breaks in consumer substitution among products. Again, as a matter of economics, what matters is the degree to which consumers would actually substitute among available alternatives in the market, regardless of whether they competed only in part within certain identifiable segments.

Judge Easterbrook's decision in *Mahurkar* affirms that calculating patent infringement damages is, in the end, an exercise in economics, requiring careful economic analysis and presentation of evidence. Confronted with a failure of both parties to carry out any meaningful economic analysis of their own, Judge Easterbrook found a few fragments of evidence on which to build an estimate of price erosion damages. In the course of so doing, he explains to the reader the difference between real and nominal price increases, the elasticity of demand, and how to tease information about elasticities out of price-cost margins.

Underlying the mechanics, Judge Easterbrook affirmed the basic economic principle that fewer sales are made at higher prices. Consequently, if there is a price erosion claim, the patent owner is *not* entitled to lost profits on every but-for sale. Rather, economic evidence about the elasticity of demand is vital to explain how quantities will be affected by the higher price that the patent owner would have charged absent infringement.[25]

The CAFC further refined judicial precedent on patent infringement damages with its *Grain Processing* opinion where it recognized and put forth succinctly that a "competitor in the *but-for* marketplace is hardly likely to surrender its complete market share when faced with a patent, if it can compete in some other lawful manner."[26] This economic concept has several important implications for both lost-profit and reasonable-royalty damages.

As the *Grain Processing* court rightly understood, lost profit damages should account for the ability of the infringer to turn to readily available noninfringing alternatives.[27] To the extent that an infringer could avoid infringement by selling a noninfringing alternative product and still

---

[25] This point was further reinforced in *Crystal.*
[26] *Grain Processing,* at 1351.
[27] More generally, the court in *Grain Processing* directed that it "requires sound economic proof of the nature of the market and likely outcomes with infringement factored out the economic picture." *Grain Processing,* at 1349.

retain some (or all) of its infringing sales, any claim for lost profits by a plaintiff must be correspondingly reduced. Furthermore, the *Grain Processing* decision viewed broadly the conditions under which a noninfringing alternative should be considered available to the defendant. American Maize-Products (the defendant) argued that it could have readily switched to a noninfringing product (a different formulation of the infringing food additive) at the time of its first infringement. However, at that time the noninfringing alternative had never been made available for commercial sale. The court was aware that the noninfringing alternative was not yet a commercialized product, but based on fact testimony, the court found American Maize-Products' claims credible—i.e., (1) that it could have readily turned to the noninfringing product and (2) that consumers would not have noticed any difference between the noninfringing alternative and the infringing product.[28] Thus, in this case, the only difference between the noninfringing alternative and the infringing product was that the non-infringing alternative cost more to manufacture. Under these circumstances, the court determined that lost profit damages were not appropriate because the defendant could instead sell the non-infringing alternative and still retain all of its sales.[29]

The *Grain Processing* decision applied similar economic logic with regard to its determination of reasonable royalty damages. Here, it also relied on the ability of an infringer to turn to an available noninfringing alternative (even one that was not commercially sold) as the primary factor setting the upper bound for a reasonable royalty. That is, because the

---

[28] In contrast, the court in *Micro Chemical Inc. v. Lextron Inc.*, 318 F.3d 1119 (Fed. Cir. 2003), considered the defendant's claim that it could have turned to a noninfringing alternative, but the court ultimately rejected this claim because it concluded that the alternative was not *readily* available (i.e., it would have taken almost 1,000 hours of design work to develop). As an economic matter, if there is evidence that an accused infringer could turn to a noninfringing alternative within the damages period and in so doing retain some portion of its accused sales, then that should be taken into consideration in determining the damages to which the patent owner is entitled. Put differently, it should be *economic principles* that govern the analysis rather than an arbitrarily chosen time period that determines those alternatives that are and those that are not "available."

[29] More precisely, this outcome is based on the assumption that the defendant would have charged the same price for the product even if it had used the noninfringing alternative technology and, in so doing, would have made the same sales as it actually made in the marketplace. As a result, there would be no accused sales for the patent owner to capture. The only difference, therefore, is that infringement allowed the defendant to earn a higher margin than if it had turned to the noninfringing alternative. To the extent that the infringer may have charged *higher* prices in the but-for market—e.g., to keep its percentage profit margin unchanged—then there may be certain competitive consequences to the patent owner.

infringer could avoid infringement by turning to a noninfringing alternative and thereby avoid the need for a license to the patented technology,
the cost of turning to the noninfringing alternative "effectively capped the
reasonable royalty award."[30] As discussed above, in this case, because the
infringing product and noninfringing product were perfect substitutes for
consumers, the cost of turning to the noninfringing alternative was simply equal to the higher cost to manufacture the noninfringing alternative.

More generally, economics teaches that the cost of turning to the noninfringing alternative should be the entire economic cost incurred by the
infringer as a result of turning to that alternative (i.e., including both out-
of-pocket expenses and opportunity costs) instead of using the patented
invention. These opportunity costs may be higher costs, lost sales, and/or
lower prices caused by the act of turning to and implementing the noninfringing alternative technology.

In the end, the *Grain Processing* court affirmed a reasonable royalty
equal to all of the infringer's cost savings from using the patented invention. We note that the choice of how to allocate an infringer's gains from
infringement for purposes of determining the reasonable royalty is also a
matter of economics; however, the *Grain Processing* court was silent on its
basis for the allocation that it chose. As a general matter, the allocation
depends on such factors as the relative bargaining strengths of the two
parties and the willingness of the patent owner to grant a license.

Conclusion
Over the years, the courts have made important progress in adopting economic principles as the basis for what constitutes acceptable means of
calculating damages due to patent infringement. There have been set-
backs along the way, but, in general, judicial precedent has become
increasingly consistent with those principles.

---

[30] *Grain Processing*, at 1346.

5

A Critique of Noneconomic Methods of Reasonable Royalty Calculation

Christine Meyer and Bryan Ray

To determine a reasonable royalty for the purpose of calculating the damages due to patent infringement, the court in *Georgia-Pacific Corp. v. United States Plywood Corp. (Georgia-Pacific)* specified a framework for a hypothetical negotiation in which the licensee (infringer) and licensor (patentee) are "prudent" in that both consider the costs and benefits of licensing the patent at issue.[1] Economic theory teaches that the relevant costs and benefits to consider in constructing the hypothetical negotiation are the *incremental* costs and benefits flowing from the license. In other words, the most that a licensee would be willing to pay for a license is the additional profit that it expects to earn from using the patented invention as opposed to pursuing its next-best alternative. Similarly, a licensor would not grant the license for less than the profit that it would expect to lose by licensing. A reasonable royalty based on this framework will compensate the patent owner for the loss that it would expect to incur by licensing its patent, and possibly also award the patent owner some portion of the infringer's gain from using the patented invention.

Since *Georgia-Pacific*, the courts have continued to build upon this economic framework. For instance, the court in *Grain Processing Corp. v. American Maize-Products Co.*[2] *(Grain Processing)* recognized that a reasonable royalty should be no higher than the infringer's opportunity cost of avoiding infringement. To measure this cost, the court considered the difference between the infringer's profit from using the patented invention and the infringer's profit from pursuing its next-best noninfringing alternative. Consistent with the framework that we described above, this

---

[1]   *Georgia-Pacific Corp. v. United States Plywood Corp.*, 318 F. Supp. 1116, 1120 (S.D.N.Y. 1970).

[2]   *Grain Processing Corp. v. American Maize-Products Co.*, 185 F.3d 1341 (Fed. Cir. 1999).

approach implements the economic principle that the infringer would not be willing to pay more for a license to the patent than the *incremental* benefit of the license.[3] In *Grain Processing,* the court effectively determined that the full incremental cost of avoiding infringement stemmed from manufacturing cost savings attributable to the patented invention. By infringing, the infringer thereby avoided this cost and thus realized a benefit from infringing equal to the amount of that cost.[4]

While in *Grain Processing* the court awarded the plaintiff a reasonable royalty that was equal to the entire difference between the infringer's production cost using the patented production method and its cost if it used its next-best noninfringing alternative, other courts have ruled that a reasonable royalty should be only a fraction of the cost savings attributable to the patent. For example, in *Tights Inc. v. Kayser-Roth Corp.*[5] *(Tights)* the court determined that the reasonable royalty was 33 percent of the infringer's cost savings from using the patented product design, and, in general, the *Tights* court stated that this percentage could range between 25 percent and 50 percent, depending on the infringer's contribution to the commercialization of the product.[6]

Although in *Grain Processing* and *Tights* the courts came to different conclusions about how to allocate the cost savings attributable to the patented invention, in each of these cases there was agreement to focus on the *incremental* benefit of the patented invention to the infringer. In framing the hypothetical royalty negotiation around the *incremental* gains

---

3 See also, for example, *Ajinomoto Co. Inc. v. Archer-Daniels-Midland Co.* 155 F.3d 567, 1998 WL 322563 (Fed. Cir. 1998) *(Ajinomoto).*

4 Implicitly, this conclusion assumes that the higher-cost noninfringing alternative would only reduce the infringer's margin, and not affect its prices or sales levels. In this case, evidence was presented that showed consumers were indifferent to the differences between the product that embodied the patented invention and the noninfringing alternative. However, there may be cases where the patented invention may be preferred by consumers, thereby, all else being equal, enabling the product that embodies the patented invention to capture more sales or sell at a higher price relative to the next-best noninfringing alternative. There have also been cases where courts have resisted attempts to establish a reasonable royalty based on estimated cost savings due to the patented invention if it was determined that those cost savings were not accurately quantified or were speculative. For example, in *Mobil Oil Corporation v. Amoco Chemicals Corp.,* 915 F. Supp. 1333 (D. Del. 1995), the court found the analysis of the expected benefits of the patented invention done by the plaintiff's expert to be "unsound" for several reasons, including a disregard for certain marketplace and competitive conditions.

5 *Tights Inc. v. Kayser-Roth Corp.,* 442 F. Supp. 159 (M.D.N.C. 1977).

6 See also, for example, *Alden W. Hanson v. Alpine Valley Ski Area Inc.,* 718 F.2d 1075, 1078 (Fed. Cir. 1983). Here the court also awarded a reasonable royalty based on 33 percent of the cost savings from using the patented invention.

to the infringer, the courts in *Grain Processing* and *Tights* applied sound economic reasoning.[7]

Failing to assess a reasonable royalty based on the incremental costs and benefits of licensing may lead to royalty rates without a solid economic basis. For example, to determine a reasonable royalty some experts use so-called "rules of thumb" and other noneconomic shortcuts that avoid a careful analysis of the incremental costs and benefits of the license. In the main, these methods are divided into two types. The first type bases the calculation of the reasonable royalty on a split between the patent owner and the infringer of the total profit the infringer earned (or is expected to earn) on the product that embodies the patented invention. Methods of this type rely on rules of thumb (the most common being the 25 percent rule) to determine the split. The second type of method uses licenses that are not directly comparable to the one at issue as benchmarks from which to determine (or corroborate) a reasonable royalty. As we explain below, while each of these shortcuts may derive from a valid analytical concept, the way in which each is generally applied in practice makes them unhelpful, at best, and misleading, at worst.

Rule-of-Thumb Profit Splits

As described above, one economically grounded way to think about the calculation of a reasonable royalty is as some reasoned split between the patent owner and the infringer of the *additional* profits garnered by the infringer as the result of its use of the patented invention. However, a profit split based on a rule of thumb avoids the rigor of measuring the *incremental* benefit of a patented invention and instead reverts to an arbitrary calculation that has no basis in the specific facts of the case. Specifically, the 25 percent rule divides the *total* profits—generally, the total net pretax profits—associated with the products that embody the patented technology without considering what portion of those profits could still be earned by the infringer if it did not have access to the patent at issue.[8] Proponents of this rule maintain that an analyst with "years of

---

7   The portion of the infringer's incremental benefit from the patented invention that the patent owner should capture in a royalty is also a matter of economic analysis that examines, for example, the relative bargaining strengths of the parties to the hypothetical negotiation and the potential losses to the patent owner by licensing.

8   Robert Goldscheider, "Royalties as Measure of Damages," *les Nouvelles* (September 1996): 119. Note that although the 25 percent rule is the most commonly used rule-of-thumb profit split method, experts also employ profit splits using other ratios (e.g., 33 percent). Our discussion of the 25 percent rule applies broadly to reasonable royalties based on rule-of-thumb profit splits that use other ratios, as well.

experience" can "'tune' the ratio up or down with considerable accuracy to reflect the existence of particularly valuable rights being transferred, shifts in the risk factor, or other special legal or market circumstances."[9]

The general idea of a profit split is embodied in two of the *Georgia-Pacific* factors. The twelfth *Georgia-Pacific* factor reminds the expert to consider "[t]he portion of the profit or the selling price that may be customary in the particular business or in comparable businesses to allow for the use of the invention or analogous inventions."[10] The thirteenth *Georgia-Pacific* factor prompts the expert to bear in mind "[t]he portion of the realizable profit that should be credited to the invention as distinguished from non-patented elements, the manufacturing process, business risks, or significant features or improvements added by the infringer."[11] The 25 percent rule explicitly ignores the economic underpinnings of those two *Georgia-Pacific* factors. These factors specifically call for the expert to consider the industry and market conditions in which the patent is used and the specific invention at issue when determining the profits attributable to the patent. Accordingly, the basis for a well-reasoned, economically grounded royalty analysis must be a consideration of the incremental costs and benefits facing the two parties in the hypothetical negotiation. However, use of the 25 percent rule, which suggests that one rule can be implemented across all patents, businesses, and industries, and, furthermore that consideration of the specific profits that are attributable to the patent at issue is not necessary, is not an economically sound analysis.

Practitioners of the 25 percent rule defend its use based on the belief that actual royalties tend to be about 25 percent of the profits earned on the products that embody the patented technology.[12] For example, they cite to studies that show patent royalty rates that are on average about 25 percent of the estimated operating profit margins earned on the products that embody the patents.[13] Even if average royalty rates for some sample of licenses tend to be about 25 percent of the operating margin for the products that embody the licensed patent, this is no justification for not estimating the specific contribution of the patented invention to the infringer's profits. In fact, practitioners of the 25 percent rule acknowl-

---

[9] Id.
[10] *Georgia-Pacific.*
[11] Id.
[12] See, for example, Robert Goldscheider, John Jarosz, and Carla Mulhern, "Use of the 25 Per Cent Rule in Valuing IP," *les Nouvelles* (December 2002): 123.
[13] Id., figures 6 and 8.

edge that actual royalty rates as a percentage of operating profit margins vary substantially around the "average."[14] This variance is indicative of the case-specific and fact-intensive nature of the determination of a royalty for a patent license. Reliance on broad averages is an inappropriate shortcut that is a poor substitute for thorough research and analysis. Furthermore, any "tuning" of these broad averages is still at most a second-best approximation of an actual investigation of the specific costs and benefits of the infringer taking a license to the patent at issue.

It has been noted that "if you represent the prospective licensor then of course you apply the 25% against anticipated gross profit; if you represent the prospective licensee, you contend that the 25% applies to net profit!"[15] This statement highlights the arbitrary nature of the way the 25 percent rule has been applied and its overarching conceptual flaw: Neither gross profit nor net profit on a product alone inform us about the value of the patent, and thus about a reasonable royalty. Total gross or net profits are likely the result of many factors, only one of which is likely to be the patented technology. The profits that do inform an economic analysis of the reasonable royalty are the incremental profits attributable to the patented technology. For a patent that is essential for a particular product such that the infringer has no available alternative to the patented technology, a royalty rate substantially higher than 25 percent of either gross or net profits may be appropriate. On the other hand, for a narrow patent for which the infringer has a viable alternative that would be inexpensive for the infringer to implement and equally as profitable as the infringing product, the royalty rate may well be substantially less than 25 percent of either profit measure.

Imagining a case for how the 25 percent rule can lead to the determination of a royalty that is inconsistent with the premise of a hypothetical negotiation is not hard. Consider an example included in an article espousing the usefulness of the 25 percent rule.[16] In this example, the would-be licensee has a choice between producing a product in one of two ways: one that embodies the patent, and one that does not. The assumption in this example is that the patent would allow the licensee to reduce the costs associated with producing the product, as shown in the table below.[17] The authors conclude that a 10 percent royalty is reasonable in this case.

---

[14] Id.

[15] William Marshall Lee, "Determining Reasonable Royalty," *les Nouvelles* (September 1992): 126.

[16] Goldscheider et al., 125–126.

[17] Id., figure 2.

Table 1. 25 Percent Rule—Cost Side[18]

	No patent	Cost-reducing patent	25 percent rule
Revenues	$100	$100	
Cost of sales	$40	$30	
Gross margin	$60	$70	
Operating expenses	$30	$30	
Operating profits	$30	$40	($40 x 25%)/ $100=10%

A well-reasoned economic analysis in this example would consider the costs and benefits of licensing to each of the parties. In this hypothetical example, there is no information about the would-be licensor. However, the would-be licensee's benefits are clearly outlined. The licensee earns revenue of $100 whether or not it uses the patented invention, but by using the patented invention it is able to lower its cost of sales by $10 thus increasing its profits by $10 (or 10 percent of the total revenue). As a result, the would-be licensee should be willing to pay a royalty of no more than 10 percent of the infringing product's total revenue for a license to this patent. Instead of sharing profits, as proponents of the 25 percent rule believe is fair and customary, the licensor in this example would receive the *entire* incremental profit associated with this patent.

That outcome could make economic sense, depending on what is assumed about the relative bargaining strengths of the parties in the hypothetical negotiation. However, only modest changes in the under-lying parameters of this example make the 25 percent rule produce out-comes that contradict economic logic. Consider the case where operating expenses are only $10, the 25 percent rule would imply that a reasonable royalty of $15 (or, in this case, 15 percent of the total revenue) be paid for a license to a patent that only increased the would-be licensee's profits by $10.[19] Alternatively, consider the case in which the cost-reducing patent only decreases the cost of sales by $1 (or 1 percent of the total revenue) such that the operating profits with the patent would total $31. In that case, the 25 percent rule would imply that a reasonable royalty of $7.75 (or 7.75 percent of the total revenue) be paid for a license to a patent that only

---

[18] See Robert Goldscheider, John Jarosz, and Carla Mulhern, "Use of the 25 Per Cent Rule in Valuing IP," *les Nouvelles* 37, no. 4 (December 2002).

[19] Operating expenses of $10 would lead to operating profits of $60 if the firm used the cost-reducing patent. Following the formula used by the authors, ($60 x 25%)/$100 = 15%. Converting this to a dollar amount (15% x $100) yields $15.

reduces costs by $1.[20] Clearly, that defies both rational economic behavior and common sense.

Rule-of-thumb profit split methods have been used and considered by the courts,[21] though noticeably absent from these opinions are well-defined economic bases for doing so.[22] For example, the courts in both *Standard* and *Bose* began with a baseline royalty rate based on a profit split of the infringer's total operating profits on the infringing products. Then, based on an analysis of various *Georgia-Pacific* factors, this amount was adjusted upward by an essentially arbitrary amount. The court in *Standard* did consider an analysis that attempted to measure the incremental cost savings of the product embodying the patented invention over a possible noninfringing alternative and accorded this calculation significant weight in its *Georgia-Pacific* factor analysis, but the court ultimately concluded: "As this is but one factor which would influence the hypothetical negotiation of the royalty rate, and it is not being used as the royalty compensation base, it is unnecessary to further pinpoint an exact savings figure." The court in *Bose* similarly asserted that the patented inventions "substantially contributed to the demand for, and success of, the product," but apparently made no attempt to quantify this contribution. Thus, in each case more arbitrary methods (e.g., rule-of-thumb profit splits) prevailed over sound economic reasoning and measurement of how a license to the infringed patent would have incrementally benefited the infringer or harmed the patent owner.

---

[20] Following the formula used by the authors, ($31 x 25%)/$100 = 7.75%. Converting this to a dollar amount (7.75% x $100) yields $7.75.

[21] The 1997 opinion in *The Procter & Gamble Co. v. Paragon Trade Brands Inc.* stated: "Although the Court will consider the Rule-of-Thumb analysis in determining the royalty rate, this approach will not receive substantial weight...the court has found no case adopting this test as a matter of law" (989 F. Supp. 547 [D. Del. 1997]). See also, for example, *W.L. Gore & Associates Inc. and Gore Enterprise Holdings Inc. v. International Medical Prosthetics Research Associates Inc.*, 1990 WL 180490 (D. Ariz.); *Polaroid Corp. v. Eastman Kodak Co.*, 1990 WL 324105 (D. Mass.) (*Polaroid*); *Standard Manufacturing Co. Inc. v. United States*, 42 Fed. Cl. 748 (1999) (*Standard*); *Fonar Corp. and Dr. Raymond V. Damadian v. General Electric Co., and Drucker & Genuth, MDS, P.C., d/b/a South Shore Imaging Associates*, 107 F.3d 1543 (Fed. Cir. 1997); and *Bose Corp. v. JBL Inc.*, 112 F. Supp. 2d 138 (D. Mass. 2000) (*Bose*).

[22] In *Howard A. Fromson v. Western Lithoplate and Supply Co. and Bemis Co. Inc.*, 853 F.2d 1568 (Fed. Cir. 1988), the United States Court of Appeals for the Federal Circuit (CAFC) remanded the damages issue based on errors made by the district court. The district court contrived a reasonable royalty rate based on taking a percentage of a percentage of a standard profit rate for the infringer that it had determined. The CAFC recognized the lack of foundation for the approach used by the district court and ordered the district court to take "into account all of the particular operative facts and individual circumstances" in determining the reasonable royalty rate.

Incomparable Comparables

The royalty embodied in a real-world license reflects the outcome of an actual negotiation between a licensee and licensor. Therefore, royalties from real-world licenses reflect the economic conditions of the participants, including the competitive conditions in the market, and patent-specific costs and benefits. As a result, to the extent that a benchmark license is truly comparable to the one contemplated by the damage calculation, an actual license may be a useful benchmark to assist with the determination of a reasonable royalty for purposes of calculating patent infringement damages.[23] However, the use as benchmarks of licenses that are not comparable can lead to unreliable damages calculations.

The use of comparables in a reasonable royalty analysis derives from *Georgia-Pacific* factors 1, 2, and 12, which instruct the expert to consider "royalties received by the patentee for the licensing of the patent in suit, proving or tending to prove an established royalty"; "rates paid by the licensee for the use of other patents comparable to the patent in suit"; and "[t]he portion of the profit or of the selling price that may be customary in the particular business or in comparable businesses to allow for the use of the invention or analogous inventions," respectively.[24] These factors provide some guidelines regarding the types of licenses that are truly comparable. First, for factors 1 and 2, the licenses must involve at least one of the parties involved in the current dispute, on the same side of the negotiation as they would be in the hypothetical negotiation, whereas for factor 12, the business must be comparable. Second, the technology must either be the same as or comparable to the technology in the patents at issue. While some have correctly argued that "[evaluating] comparability of licenses involves comparisons of economic benefits rather than technology," without a full analysis of the technology embodied in the conceivably comparable licenses, the technological and economic alternatives, market opportunities and potential profits associated with the products that embody that technology and all convoyed sales, it is generally not possible to understand the economic benefits

---

23 Some have argued that because validity and infringement of the patent have not yet been determined before most license agreements are signed, the royalties for these actual licenses likely understate, all else being equal, a reasonable royalty for purposes of a damage calculation that should be based on a hypothetical negotiation in which both sides acknowledge the validity and infringement of the patent. See Stephen H. Kalos and Jonathan D. Putman, "On the Incomparability of 'Comparables': An Economic Interpretation of 'Infringer's Royalties,'" *Journal of Proprietary Rights* (April 1997).

24 *Georgia-Pacific.*

conferred to the licensee and thus whether the license in question is actually comparable.[25]

In addition, licenses are often more complex than the type of license contemplated in the hypothetical negotiation in which prospective licensor and licensee are negotiating over the royalty rate for a single patent or well-identified bundle of intellectual property and all the patents at issue are known to be valid and infringed. Real-world licenses may be unidirectional licenses or cross-licenses. They may involve up-front payments, royalties as a percentage of revenue, or payments based on reaching certain sales milestones. All of these factors make it difficult to find licenses that are truly comparable and that inform the expert conducting a reasonable royalty analysis.

Courts have recognized the idiosyncrasy of licenses and have both accepted and rejected the use of comparable transactions as being probative of a reasonable royalty for the case at issue. In general, there is case law precedent for the position that royalty rates actually negotiated for the patent at issue represent a principled basis from which to estimate reasonable royalty damages.[26] However, courts have rightly not accepted these rates at face value and have looked to extrinsic evidence to determine whether the negotiated royalty is indeed applicable to the circumstances for the hypothetical negotiation contemplated in the instant litigation. For example, in *Ajinomoto*[27] the court rejected, in favor of a cost-savings approach (see above), two different royalty rates that had been negotiated for the patent at issue. The court recognized that the party taking the license can affect the rate that a patent owner would reasonably accept—e.g., a license to a competitor may impose greater costs on the patent owner than a license to a party that is not a competitor. In the *Ajinomoto* case, the infringer was a competitor, while the negotiated rates were for licenses to parties who were not competitors of the plaintiff, and thus the court determined that the actual licenses were not comparable for purposes of determining a reasonable royalty.[28] In other cases, actual licenses have been found to be reasonable benchmarks for the

---

[25] Peter B. Frank, Vincent E. O'Brien, and Michael J. Wagner, "Patent Infringement Damages," in *Litigations Services Handbook: The Role of the Financial Expert* (2001), p. 24.19.

[26] See, for example, *Trell v. Marlee Elecs. Corp.*, 912 F.2d 1443 (Fed. Cir. 1990).

[27] *Ajinomoto.*

[28] See also, *Bio-Rad Laboratories Inc. v. Nicolet Instrument Corp.*, 739 F.2d 604 (Fed. Cir. 1984): "Though established (industry) royalty rates are normally applicable...they do not necessarily establish a ceiling for the royalty that may be assessed...."

hypothetical negotiation. For example, in The *Procter & Gamble Co. v. Paragon Trade Brands Inc.,*[29] the court compared the market conditions and competitive relationships of the parties of the actual license and the hypothetical license and found that the conditions were comparable and thus determined that the established royalty rate (which, in this case, was the result of a license that was consummated after the date of hypothetical negotiation) was indeed a reasonable royalty rate.

Courts have similarly both accepted and rejected the use of comparable licensing transactions that do not expressly involve the patent at issue for purposes of determining and evaluating reasonable royalty rates. For instance, in *Code-Alarm Inc. v. Electromotive Technologies Corp.,*[30] the court concluded that the royalty rates that were "commonly exhibited" in the industry at issue could be used to evaluate the reasonableness of the royalty rate as determined by the trial court based on other facts and testimony. However, in this matter, these industry rates ranged between 2 and 8 percent. With such a wide range of rates, this sort of benchmarking may have little value.[31] In *Utah Medical Products Inc. v. Graphic Controls Corp.,*[32] the court was much less sympathetic to the use of comparable licenses without rigorous scrutiny. The court excluded the expert's reasonable royalty testimony based on purported comparable licenses because the court found that it had not been shown that these licenses were actually "in any way comparable" to the patent at issue.[33]

These opinions reveal that the examination of other licenses, while sometimes useful, requires careful analysis. Their comparability must be evaluated against the conditions of the hypothetical license being con-

---

[29] *The Procter & Gamble Co. v. Paragon Trade Brands Inc.,* 989 F. Supp. 547 (D. Del. 1997).

[30] *Code-Alarm Inc. v. Electromotive Technologies Corp.,* 185 F.3d 877, 1998 WL 5690000 (Fed. Cir. [Mo.])

[31] The CAFC in reviewing the findings of the trial court (that relied on the opinion of a special master) stated that "the special master considered the testimony of experts that the automotive industry commonly exhibited royalty rates between zero and five percent, that royalties for highly profitable companies such as Code-Alarm ranged between two and eight percent, and that Code-Alarm's profitability, before taxes, was eight or nine percent, despite its dubious attempts to prove that it cannot satisfy the damage award. This testimony is sufficient to support the special master's recommendation and the trial court's conclusion that a reasonable royalty would be 2.5 percent applied to the entire royalty base...." As a matter of economics, this is not a sufficient basis from which to determine a reasonable royalty. It rests on broad industry averages with no confirmation that the licenses used for these averages are indeed comparable and provides no independent analysis of the incremental value of the patent to the parties in this case.

[32] *Utah Medical Products Inc. v. Graphic Controls Corp.,* 350 F.3d 1376 (Fed. Cir. 2003).

[33] See also *Polaroid.*

templated. For example, are the terms of the licenses similar? Are the relative market positions and competitive relationships of the parties similar? Are the relative benefits of the patented inventions compared to noninfringing alternatives similar? In all hypothetical negotiations, the fundamental questions facing the economist are the *incremental* value and cost of the patented invention and a license to it. When actual licenses shed light on these fundamental questions, they are a useful tool in the analysis. When actual licenses are sufficiently different from the hypothetical negotiation in economically important ways, they provide no guidance regarding the outcome of the hypothetical negotiation at issue.

Conclusion

Royalty negotiations are idiosyncratic and the resulting licenses and royalty rates are highly variable. Each party to a license negotiation evaluates its incremental costs and benefits of licensing and thereby determines the amount that it is willing to pay or accept for that license. An expert opinion is at best speculation if it fails to analyze the particular circumstances that would confront the parties to the hypothetical negotiation that is contemplated for purposes of determining a reasonable royalty in the context of litigation. In short, the determination of a reasonable royalty is fundamentally an economic analysis that involves an examination of the evidence and a quantification of each party's gains and losses due to the hypothetical license. No shortcut can substitute for a careful analysis.

6

Valuation of Nonpatent Intellectual Property: Common Themes and Notable Differences

Phillip A. Beutel

Most people immediately think of patents when they hear that a company is concerned about its intellectual property (IP) portfolio. However, the average company's IP portfolio contains far more than just patents. Other types of IP include trademarks, copyrights, trade secrets, trade dress, brands, distribution agreements, customer lists, and noncompete/nonsolicitation clauses in employment agreements.[1] Litigation has arisen involving many of these types of IP, such as allegations of theft or infringement of the IP, claims that the terms of a license were breached, claims by a tax authority or by joint venture partners that an internal transfer price was inappropriate, and antitrust claims in connection with a licensing program. Valuation of IP assets is typically required in these types of lawsuits.

Nonpatent IP assets may need to be valued in a variety of situations. As the following hypothetical examples illustrate, these include setting the proper intracompany royalty for the use of trademarks, assessing potential damages from theft of trade secrets, meeting tax requirements for the valuation of certain nonpatent intangibles, and calculating the diminution of a patent owner's brand value from its licensee's failure to properly mark certain patented products.

---

[1] While I refer in this paper to certain types of assets as IP, they are also appropriately called intangible assets.

Intracompany Trademark Licensing

U.S. Oil Inc. (USO) is a U.S.-based gasoline company that has a well-known trademark that it plans to license to a foreign affiliate. Its trademark is the logo that customers recognize when they drive by its service stations and pull up to the pump. That trademark distinguishes its service stations from those of its rivals. The royalty, or price, it obtains from the foreign affiliate (an offshore company-owned operation) will undoubtedly affect USO's overall tax burden.[2] Getting the royalty right, in a way that will both satisfy the tax authorities and make its shareholders happy, requires that USO answer two questions: (1) How would its domestic profits (both short- and long-term) be affected from granting a license; and (2) How much money does its affiliate expect the trademark to contribute to its operations? In effect, USO needs to perform a valuation analysis.

Theft of Trade Secrets

Acme Hospital Beds competes primarily with Beds-R-Us (BRU) for the patronage of local hospitals. John Smith, the former president of Acme, left the company about six months ago and has turned up as an internal advisor to BRU. The companies sell to hospitals by submitting sealed bids. Within the last month Acme has lost a couple of large accounts and is concerned that Mr. Smith's knowledge of its costs and client lists has given BRU an unfair advantage in the bidding process that will result in a substantial market share loss. Acme believes that there is a strong relationship between its recent losses and Mr. Smith's arrival at BRU. Accordingly, it needs a valuation of its allegedly stolen trade secrets so that it may decide whether to file suit to recover damages.

Accounting Rules Governing the Acquisition of Noncompete/Nonsolicitation Agreements

Big Consulting Co. recently acquired HotShot Sales LLP. In closing that transaction, it required all HotShot principals to sign employment agreements that contained noncompete/nonsolicitation clauses. Under Financial Accounting Standards Board (FASB) rules, within one year of that transaction, Big must identify the value of all intangible assets asso-

---

2   These royalties are often called transfer prices (see Chapter 22 for more on transfer pricing methods). If USO licenses the trademark to the affiliate, the royalties it receives will qualify in the U.S. as taxable income; to USO's affiliate, the royalties paid may qualify as a tax deduction. The risk of getting the royalty wrong is obvious: either USO's overall corporate tax bill will be too high or it will face the risk of tax litigation.

ciated with the transaction, including the employment agreements.[3] What principles govern the value of those clauses?

Lost Brand Value from a Licensee's Failure to Properly Mark Its Patented Products

YouKnowMe Inc. (YKM) licensed certain technology to National Sales Group (National), a larger rival that was better able to expand the market for its patented products. As part of that licensing deal, YKM also asked that all products embodying its technology be marked with language informing consumers that the technology came from YKM. As sometimes happens, YKM was unhappy with National's behavior as a licensee and filed suit for breach of contract. Among other things, YKM claimed damage to its brand value from National's failure to provide appropriate name attribution. YKM needs a valuation expert to measure this allegedly lost brand value.

A Primer on Valuation Principles

Two Concepts of Value

Regardless of the type of IP at issue, there are at least two concepts of value that are appropriate to any valuation assignment: value-in-use and fair market value (FMV). To simplify the discussion that follows, I refer only to a trademark valuation assignment involving the first hypothetical example introduced above: USO's trademark. In general, the principles governing this valuation will be applicable to other nonpatent IP analyses as well.

---

3   In part to impose a more transparent and economically meaningful accounting for acquired intangibles, in June 2001 FASB instituted Statement of Financial Accounting Standard (SFAS) Nos. 141 and 142. (See SFAS No. 141, *Business Combinations*, and SFAS No. 142, *Goodwill and Other Intangible Assets*.) SFAS No. 141 most generally addresses the financial accounting and reporting for business combinations. Among the several aspects of business combination accounting that it covers is the recognition of acquired intangible assets. SFAS No. 142 "addresses financial accounting and reporting for intangible assets acquired individually or with a group of other assets (but not those acquired in a business combination) at acquisition."

Prior to these standards, companies typically reported as goodwill the entire difference between the purchase price and the book value of identified tangible assets. Intangibles were *not* required to be separately identified; rather, they typically were capitalized as part of a company's overall acquired goodwill and amortized over some finite period. Now, SFAS Nos. 141 and 142 stipulate that companies that issue debt and/or equity to the public must report the fair value of acquired intangible assets and determine those assets' useful lives. As a result, goodwill is now calculated as the overall purchase price less the value of both tangible assets *and* identifiable intangible assets that have a finite useful life. (Goodwill is now considered to have an indefinite life, and instead of being amortized, it is tested annually for impairment. Intangibles that have a finite useful life are amortized.)

Value-in-Use

If USO's promotional spending has been successful, its trademark will signal to customers that with each purchase they will get the quality fuel and service they know and trust. These customers may even become brand loyal: Given a choice between roughly similar alternatives, they will always choose USO's service stations. How can USO cash in on this loyalty? All other things being equal, as customers develop a preference for the trademarked USO service station, USO will be able to charge higher prices or attract a higher volume of customers than if those stations did not fly USO's flag.[4] If the trademark has value, there is a price premium associated *only* with the USO mark. This premium must be disentangled from the overall price premium USO obtains from the sale of its trademarked product.[5] Specifically, it equals the extra, or incremental, revenue USO's stations can earn relative to the market price of retail fuel that is equivalent *in all other respects* but is sold by a nontrademarked or generic service station.[6] If the cost of maintaining the trademark is subtracted from this incremental revenue, we are left with the incremental profits attributable solely to the mark.

This is the first concept of value: the mark's commercial value, or value-in-use. It equals the stream of incremental profit that a single party, in this case the owner of the trademark, expects its mark to generate—i.e., incremental in the sense that all other attributes are held constant.

Fair Market Value

Fair market value refers to how much money USO's trademark would fetch if it were sold or licensed in a competitive market. Imagine there is an

---

4 The trademark may also have value if it lowers USO's costs, for example, if the presence of the mark (once it has acquired value) reduces the advertising and promotion expenses needed to maintain traffic flow through those service stations.

5 A variety of other factors could contribute to the price premium USO charges for its gasoline. These include, for example, USO's use of other intellectual property, such as patented technology in its products; USO's policy of providing additional (free) services to its customers, such as checking the oil levels and washing the windshields of customers' cars; or USO's tendency to site its gas stations in premier locations making it easier for customers to find them.
The incremental contribution of the trademark can be measured in a variety of ways, including, for example, by using so-called hedonic models, which utilize data on sales, prices, and product attributes to statistically isolate the impact of particular characteristics. Survey techniques can also be used to quantify the incremental contribution of nonpatent IP. (See Chapters 8 and 9 for a discussion on survey techniques and hedonic models.)

6 Ideally, in measuring the incremental contribution of the mark, the analyst should also consider the full economic cost associated with turning to its next-best alternative. As I explain in more detail below, that alternative provides a ceiling on the value of the mark.

active marketplace to which USO could go to buy or sell trademarks. Assume each buyer and seller in that market negotiates as an unaffiliated, arm's-length entity, is a willing partner at the bargaining table (that is, does not negotiate under duress), and has complete information about what an agreement would contribute to its own operations. The price or royalty that results from an agreement in this market is the trademark's FMV.

In the absence of an active market for IP assets, how can FMV be calculated? Economists typically assess both sides of the negotiation by asking questions such as the following: How would the agreement affect the owner/licensor? What would the buyer/licensee expect to gain from the agreement? What alternatives are available to each party? These questions determine the boundaries for the negotiation. At one side of the negotiating table, the current owner of the asset considers the incremental income that the mark generates (i.e., its value-in-use) and the portion of that income that would be lost or otherwise placed at risk if the mark is licensed or sold. On the other side of the table, the prospective buyer considers the incremental profit that it expects to gain from obtaining the mark, relative to the next-best alternative. Put differently, the buyer also measures the mark's value-in-use, but to its own operations.

To see how commercial value-in-use and FMV are related, consider both sides of the negotiation for USO's trademark. To simplify matters, assume USO sells only in the U.S. and is considering licensing the trademark for use by an unaffiliated company in another country. What effect will granting a license have on USO's profits? In this situation, granting a license will not create a competitor that can take business away from USO. This means USO does not require compensation for potential lost profits resulting from strengthening a competitor.[7] Instead, USO will merely gain licensing revenues and, perhaps, incur costs to maintain the mark's value in an additional country.[8] Given this situation, USO would likely be willing to accept a low price. That is, the commercial value to USO of the trademark in that other country is low. But this does not mean the trademark has a low FMV. Thus far, we have considered only the lower bound of the negotiation.

---

[7] Moreover, it is possible that the use of USO's trademark abroad by a third party will strengthen USO's image in its home country. Any valuation analysis should also take into account these sorts of additional effects.

[8] To the extent there are opportunity costs associated with granting a license to the affiliate (e.g., foregone licensing income from the next-best alternative licensee) this may provide a basis for the least USO would willingly accept in the negotiation.

What is the buyer/licensee willing to pay? The answer depends, in part, on what it expects the trademark to contribute to *its* bottom line— i.e., the commercial value the mark is expected to contribute if the buyer/licensee can acquire those rights from USO. The concept is the same: What price premium (and associated incremental profit) will the buyer/licensee get that it would be unable to earn without the trademark? The present value of the expected stream of profit represents the most it would be willing to pay. This is the upper bound of the negotiation.

There is one caveat: The buyer/licensee knows that it may have an alternative. Instead of obtaining the rights to USO's mark, it could develop and promote a new trademark. Assume that after spending a certain amount of promotional funds over a certain time period, that new mark is expected to generate the *same* incremental stream of profit as would USO's mark. In that case, the full economic cost of creating a trademark of identical commercial value—that is, including both out-of-pocket costs and foregone profits during the implementation period—is a ceiling on the amount the buyer/licensee would be willing to pay.

Given the boundaries of the negotiation—based on the commercial value of the asset to each side—the trademark's FMV lies between the least USO will accept and the most the buyer/licensee will pay. Where precisely in this range does it lie? The answer depends on bargaining strength and strategy, as defined by which party can hurt the other more by leaving the bargaining table.

Typical Valuation Methods

Once one determines which concept of value is appropriate for the assignment, there are several valuation approaches that are generally accepted. For each method that I describe below, it is important to remember that in every instance the IP's economic value is determined by the stream of future benefits it is expected to generate at the time of the valuation.[9]

---

9   A valuation analysis must be forward-looking because the amount any buyer is willing to pay for an asset measures that buyer's *expectations* about the likely future benefits from owning and/or using the asset. In generating expectations about the future performance of an asset, it is essential to consider both (1) the commercial status of the asset as of the valuation date and (2) its expected future status. Note that the past revenues attributable to an asset are, for the most part, irrelevant except to the extent they can be used in forming expectations about the future. Of course, for both the buyer and seller, the willingness to pay/accept reflects the benefits from having the asset relative to each party's next-best alternative.

Income Method

Any asset's commercial value is the discounted value of the expected returns attributable to that asset (i.e., "discounted cash flow," or "DCF"). Under the income method, the valuation expert explicitly models these expected returns. More precisely, a DCF analysis requires (1) that the asset's expected future returns be estimated over a reasonable forecast period (itself determined by analysis); (2) that an appropriate discount rate be determined that adequately reflects the underlying risk of those future returns;[10] and (3) that when appropriate, the asset's expected returns beyond the forecast period, known as the asset's terminal value, be estimated.

Returning to the trademark example, it is the *incremental* return that the trademark provides relative to the next-best alternative mark that determines its value. Moreover, this incremental return must be independent from the contribution of other tangible or intangible assets. For example, assume USO's fuel generates a 10 percent price premium relative to its generic equivalent, and that this premium is attributable *only* to the trademark. In this instance, the value of the USO mark equals the discounted value of the future incremental profits attributable to that premium. Using this method to calculate the commercial value at risk to the seller and expected value of the mark for a buyer, one could also determine that mark's FMV.[11]

There is a cautionary note about the income method of valuation: In the end, a DCF analysis is very sensitive to its inputs. To get it right, it is critical that the valuation expert conduct a sufficiently thorough analysis of the market(s) in which the parties expect to use the IP. Unless the financial analysis is grounded in economic reality and appropriately tested for sensitivity to reasonable changes in the underlying assumptions, the projections are unlikely to yield reliable results, regardless of the specific modeling techniques used.[12] Indeed, the assumptions that provide the

---

[10] See Chapter 11 for a discussion on selecting an appropriate discount rate.

[11] As I discuss below with respect to the replacement cost approach, the amount that a willing buyer will pay (or a seller will accept) for a trademark depends importantly on the alternatives available to it for achieving the same result. If a trademark developed in-house, for example, can yield the same incremental return at very low cost, then the trademark will likely have a relatively low *market value*.

[12] For example, economic models, econometric methods, and survey techniques can be used to measure and forecast the incremental contribution of the IP at issue. Whether the appropriate model involves simple linear or nonlinear projections, logistic (S-shaped) sales growth, discrete choice modeling, simulation models that take into consideration oligopolistic reactions of rivals to the use of this IP, or some other model, the incremental contribution will be determined by the underlying facts about the market in which the IP is expected to be used.

foundation for income projections are the most important aspect of this valuation method.

Market Transaction Method

This method is based on the concept that the FMV for an asset can be discerned from real-world marketplace transactions either involving the asset at issue or involving other, substantially similar assets. To ascertain the value of a tangible asset—a home, for example—one can examine recent market transactions for homes of comparable size, location, age, and other key characteristics. For IP, the concept is the same: Look at the prices at which comparable IP has been bought, sold, or licensed. But, as known to anyone who has ever looked at "comps" used by realtors to value a home, the quality of the analysis depends entirely on the comparability of the benchmarks.

To provide a reasonable basis for the value of nonpatent IP, candidate benchmark transactions should be carefully evaluated. More precisely, the valuation expert should assess, among other things, the extent to which the parties conducting the transactions differed from the owner and potential licensee of the IP asset at issue, included other types of IP, or took place at a different point in time from the valuation assignment at issue. In addition, the valuation expert should consider the extent to which the market in which the benchmark IP was expected to be used differed from the situation at hand. Unless all of the relevant differences between candidate benchmarks and the IP at issue are taken into consideration, this method can yield unreliable answers.

For example, suppose USO's valuation expert learns of several transfer pricing valuations performed recently by other retail gasoline companies. To the extent that those other companies had operations of a similar size, were able to charge similar price premia due to their brand recognition, had affiliates with comparable growth expectations, and so forth, then those third-party transactions may provide reasonable benchmarks for USO's valuation. However, the valuation expert should conduct a full assessment the comparability of those candidate benchmark transactions.

Cost Method

All other things being equal, a profit-maximizing firm will choose the least-cost way (including opportunity costs) to obtain an asset. As a general matter, a prospective buyer of an asset will not pay more than the lesser of (1) the expected cost to create that asset itself and (2) the expected incremental benefits of having that asset relative to the next-best alternative.

Economic reasoning indicates that a company would not make an investment in any asset, tangible or intangible, unless it expects the return on that investment to exceed the cost.[13] For example, brand equity is created by advertising and promoting one's company and its products. This spending generally has lasting effects by creating a "stock" of advertising capital. These effects, however, do not last forever. They *will* accumulate, but without additional, ongoing investment, the effects will decay.[14] All other things being equal, the company's trademark can become a storehouse for the goodwill built with customers. Therefore, for a trademark, for example, the amount spent on advertising and promotion may provide one measure (albeit an understatement) of the return that the company obtained (or expected to obtain) from that IP.[15] Thus, a complete analysis of the economic costs associated with creating (or replacing) the IP asset provides one measure of value. For USO, the valuation expert might consider the out-of-pocket design and promotion costs associated with developing a new trademark and the foregone sales and profits—e.g., from USO no longer being able to charge the same price premium for its fuel—while it invested in, and customers adjusted to, the new name.

---

[13] More precisely, companies will invest in a particular project up to the point at which for one additional dollar of spending only one additional dollar of revenue is earned.

[14] Trademarks can also lose value for reasons beyond the company's control. For example, "Ayds" was once a trademark for a diet product. The negative connotation of AIDS has destroyed that trademark.

Advertising capital, like any durable good, will depreciate unless replenished. It is this characteristic that makes possible an explicit calculation of the current value of brand equity. Certain empirical research estimates that the effect of current advertising depreciates between approximately 30 percent and 80 percent per year. This research suggests that the capitalized value of advertising is likely to be between 1-1/4 and 3 times the current advertising expenditures. See, for example, William S. Comanor and Thomas A. Wilson, *Advertising and Market Power* (Cambridge, MA: Harvard University Press, 1974); James M. Ferguson, *Advertising and Competition: Theory, Measurement and Fact* (Cambridge, MA: Ballinger Publishing Company, 1974); Richard Schmalensee, *The Economics of Advertising* (Amsterdam-London: North-Holland Publishing Company, 1972); and Elisabeth M. Landes and Andrew M. Rosenfield, "The Durability of Advertising Revisited," *The Journal of Industrial Economics* 42 (September 1994): 263-276.

[15] Brand equity can also be created or destroyed by other things. For example, staff training may improve brand equity. Alternatively, if customers have bad experiences when they visit a service station or if there is a government warning that USO gas is dangerous for automobiles, brand equity may suffer.

Hybrid Methods

In addition to the income, market, and cost approaches, valuation experts sometimes also refer to several so-called hybrid approaches. These include, the 25 percent rule-of-thumb, relief-from-royalty, and profit-split approaches, among others. For example, the relief-from-royalty method presumes that the value of a trademark can be derived from (1) the fact that a licensee will willingly pay a stream of royalties for access to the mark, and (2) that ownership of that asset "relieves" the owner of having to pay a royalty for it. If one can identify the asset in question and determine the royalties that would result from an arm's-length license for that mark, then those royalties can approximate the royalties saved and, therefore, the trademark's market value. Thus, this method requires, in effect, that the valuation expert use at least one of the other typical valuation methods to determine the proper royalty and then describe that royalty in slightly different terms. Rules of thumb are, at best, rough approximations for some of the other methods discussed here and therefore are best used as a starting point for further analysis and not as the primary basis of any valuation assignment.

Common Themes in Valuation/Damages Assessment

Regardless of the method chosen or the specific type of nonpatent IP at issue, there are several common principles that govern any valuation assignment.

Causation is Central—The value of any asset is based on its *incremental* contribution, that is, the profits that would have been lost had that asset not been employed.

Understand the Market—Whether one is measuring the value to the current owner, the FMV for a sale or licensing situation, or calculating economic damages, the assumptions providing the underpinnings of the valuation should be based on factual evidence.[16] The economic

---

[16] I recognize that in the real world data may not be available that readily permits an estimation of the incremental contribution of certain IP assets. In those circumstances, a valuation expert need not immediately throw up his or her hands and conclude that a quantitative foundation is impossible. Rather, survey methods, if appropriately prepared and carried out, may provide a useful tool. As discussed in Chapters 8 and 9, certain survey methods may be well suited to measure the incremental contribution of this type of IP. For example, to measure the value of a trademark or particular trade dress, certain surveys can isolate the role played by the IP in consumers' purchase decisions.

circumstances in which the IP is expected to be used must be taken into consideration.[17]

Consider Availability of Alternatives—To the extent an alternative asset can provide the *same* incremental contribution, the economic cost of turning to that alternative provides a ceiling for the value of the asset at issue. The analyst should take care to consider both out-of-pocket and other economic costs associated with that effort.[18]

Time Is Money—Any valuation should properly consider the fact that money earned in the future in worth less than money earned today. Accordingly, projections of income should be properly discounted to reflect the risk associated with future income streams.

General Principles Also Govern Damages Valuations—In a damages context, actual losses from the theft or infringement of that property can be based on lost profits on lost sales, price erosion, lost royalty opportunities, costs that were incurred that, absent the alleged conduct, the plaintiff would not have incurred, and so forth. In each instance, all of these general valuation principles apply.

Some Differences in Valuation Approaches Among Nonpatent IP

As a general rule, the same economic principles should govern the valuation analysis, regardless of the specific type of nonpatent IP involved. However, in certain circumstances, the valuation expert should recognize a few important differences. In particular, valuations done in the context of a damages claim may be required to meet the terms of the relevant statute. For example, unlike the patent infringement damages context, there generally is no legal or economic reason to conclude that a plaintiff in a trademark or copyright dispute should be entitled to reasonable roy-

---

[17] For example, the value of noncompete/nonsolicitation clauses in an employment agreement depends on the extent to which each of those clauses incrementally contributes to the likelihood that some business will be protected in the event the employee leaves. Evidence about prior competition from former employees, customer loyalty, the likelihood the employee would leave even in the absence of the agreement, and the probability that the company would be able to enforce its agreement in court should be considered (to the extent available) while preparing a valuation. Rules of thumb based on accounting conventions say little, if anything, about the *economic* contribution provided by these nonpatent IP assets.

[18] As noted above, surveys and econometric techniques are often useful tools for determining the acceptability of alternatives from a consumer's perspective.

alties.[19] Indeed, the phrase "reasonable royalty" itself derives from the patent statute as a floor for damages. No such floor exists for damages in those other types of infringement disputes.

However, plaintiffs in trademark and copyright infringement actions can ask for disgorgement of the defendant's unjust gains, or "unjust enrichment" damages.[20] In a trademark case, for example, the law allows the plaintiff to initially provide evidence only about the revenues the defendant gained on infringing sales.[21] The burden then shifts to the defendant to show proper deductions from those revenues.[22] Moreover, in these types of cases, a plaintiff can claim *both* the defendant's unjust enrichment *and* its own actual losses, so long as there is no double-counting. Finally, a plaintiff in a trademark or copyright dispute can also ask the court to award an amount of money needed for so-called corrective advertising—i.e., the amount of future spending needed to correct any confusion in the marketplace about the true owner of the mark or copyright. Thus, while there is no statutory floor in trademark and copyright disputes, there are other avenues for the calculation of economic damages.

Conclusion

Trademarks, brand names, and other intangible assets are not used in a vacuum; they are used in *markets*. The amount that the seller (or licensor) would accept and the buyer (or licensee) would pay depends on their market positions and on their expectations of how the markets in which they participate will evolve. The damages to the owner of an impaired IP asset depends on the marketplace within which that asset is used. The value of a noncompete/nonsolicitation agreement depends on the alternatives

---

[19] A plaintiff in a trademark or copyright dispute may claim damages in the form of lost royalties if evidence can be provided that the infringement caused it to lose licensing opportunities. In that respect, royalties lost are merely another form of "actual loss."

[20] For trademarks, see *Lanham Trademark Act,* 15 U.S.C., §1117; for copyrights, see, 17 U.S.C. §504.

[21] Id. To an economist, revenues "on infringing sales" means the revenues incrementally attributable to the use of the IP at issue, therefore holding constant all other attributes and considering the opportunity costs associated with the next-best alternatives.

[22] In practice, a plaintiff may satisfy its burden by showing only total revenues earned by the defendant. Once the burden shifts, the defendant may provide evidence to support not only the relevant incremental costs (to allow a calculation of allegedly unjustly gained profits), but also a deduction of revenues that are not incrementally attributable to the IP at issue (and that the defendant would have been able to retain even if it had not used the property at issue).

available to the former employee, the incremental business the employee was truly responsible for, and the likelihood that those clauses incrementally altered behavior. Without careful analysis of these market-based factors, cookie-cutter valuation or damages methods will give the wrong answer and may not survive a *Daubert* challenge.

III

Advanced Topics in Economic Analysis in Intellectual Property Litigation and Damages

7

Applying Merger Simulation Techniques to Estimate Lost Profits Damages in Intellectual Property Litigation

Gregory K. Leonard

Economists have a long history of building models of economic phenomena, fitting the parameters of those models to real-world data, and using the fitted models to predict the effects of potential changes in economic conditions or policy. Merger simulation was developed in this tradition by economists to predict the competitive effects of a merger between two companies that sell potentially competing products.[1] In analyzing the likely effects of a proposed merger, the Federal Trade Commission (FTC) and United States Department of Justice (DOJ) consider whether the merger is likely to lead to higher prices or lower output. The merger simulation technique has proven helpful in quantifying merger-induced price effects and focusing the regulatory review on the products most likely to create competitive concerns.

While the technique is called *merger* simulation—because it was developed primarily for use in analyzing mergers—it is useful in a much broader range of contexts. The simulation technique can be applied to

---

[1] See, e.g., R. Deneckere and C. Davidson, "Incentives to Form Coalitions With Bertrand Competition," *RAND Journal of Economics* 16 (1985): 473-486; J. Hausman, G. Leonard, and J.D. Zona, "Competitive Analysis with Differentiated Products," *Annales d'Economie et de Statistique* 34 (1994): 159-180; G. Werden and L. Froeb, "The Effects of Mergers in Differentiated Products Industries: Logit Demand and Merger Policy," *Journal of Law, Economics, & Organization* 10 (1994): 407-426; J. Hausman and G. Leonard, "Economic Analysis of Differentiated Products Mergers Using Real World Data," *George Mason Law Review* 7 (1997): 321; A. Nevo, "Mergers with Differentiated Products: The Case of Ready-to-Eat Cereal Industry," *RAND Journal of Economics* 31 (2000): 395-421.

analyze virtually any situation where a structural change in a market has
occurred or is hypothesized. For example, simulation techniques can be
used to evaluate the competitive effects of a new product introduction, to
analyze damages in antitrust cases, and to predict the effects of imposing
new taxes on industry prices.[2]

In the field of intellectual property economics, simulation techniques can be used to evaluate the damages to a patent owner resulting
from infringement of its patent. The (hypothetical) absence of the
infringing product in the but-for world represents a structural change
in the market. The effects of this structural change on the profits of the
patent owner can be evaluated using simulation techniques. It is intuitive that the extent of a patent owner's lost profits damages depends
upon how closely the infringer's product competes with the patent
owner's product. Economic principles demonstrate that, all else being
equal, the closer the competition is between the two products, the
greater will be the patent owner's lost sales and the more extensive will
be the erosion in its price. Simulation provides a method for quantita-
tively assessing these forms of lost profits damages in a unified framework that avoids some of the pitfalls of other methods of damages
calculation.[3]

Application of Simulation Techniques to Calculating
Patent Infringement Damages

A patent owner loses profits as a result of the infringement of its patent if
it loses sales to the infringer or if its price decreases as a result of competition from the infringer.[4] Lost profits damages are equal to the difference
between the patent owner's profits in the but-for world, where the patent
owner would not have faced competition from the infringing product, and

---

[2] J. Hausman and G. Leonard, "The Competitive Effects of a New Product Introduction:
    A Case Study," *Journal of Industrial Economics* 50 (2002): 237-264; G. Leonard and J.D.
    Zona, "Simulation" (NERA working paper).
[3] Simulation techniques can also be used to evaluate the "walk-away points" of parties
    involved in a licensing negotiation. Thus, simulation techniques provide useful infor-
    mation that could be used both in actual licensing negotiations and in analyses of
    reasonable royalty damages. However, this chapter focuses on the use of simulation
    models in determining lost profits damages.
[4] The patent owner may sustain other forms of lost profits damages in addition to
    those identified. For example, it may pay higher prices for an input due to competi-
    tion from the infringer in the input market or it may lose profits on lost convoyed
    sales. These other forms of lost profits damages can be addressed using simulation
    techniques as well.

the patent owner's profits in the actual world, where it competed with the infringing product.[5]

We can construct the but-for world by modeling the actual world and then simulating what would happen if we raised the price of the infringing product to its reservation level (the price at which demand for that product falls to zero). In so doing, we are able to identify where the infringing sales would have gone in the but-for world and how the infringer's rivals would have adjusted their prices.

A simulation requires modeling (1) the demand conditions faced by products in the industry, (2) the cost conditions faced by producers, and (3) the nature of strategic interaction between producers. The parameters of the model should be calibrated to the actual economic conditions in the industry.

In principle, the demand functions for the products in the industry can be econometrically estimated using transaction (price and quantity) data on the individual products at issue. While the data requirements for this type of econometric estimation are substantial, there are various sources from which this type of data can be obtained. First, the data may be collected by a third party. For example, in consumer product industries, the market research companies AC Nielsen and Information Resources, Inc. (IRI) compile and sell "retail scanner data" based on a sample of retail stores. Data from these sources have proved to be quite useful to economists interested in investigating the competitive interactions between products.[6] As another example of third-party data, in the pharmaceutical and medical device industries, IMS Health (an AC Nielsen company) compiles and sells price and quantity data based on a sample of invoices. Where the necessary data are not routinely gathered or reported by a third party, a properly designed and executed customer survey may provide the necessary information to estimate demand

---

5   One question that needs to be answered in an actual case is whether the infringer had a noninfringing alternative to which it could have turned in the but-for world. Simulation techniques can address this possibility, but for the balance of this chapter, I will assume the less complex case where the infringer had no noninfringing alternative available to it except any noninfringing products that it was already selling.

6   See, e.g., Hausman, Leonard, and Zona, supra note 1; Werden and Froeb, supra note 1; G. J. Werden et al., "The Use of the Logit Model in Applied Industrial Organization," *International Journal of the Economics of Business* 3 (1996): 83-105; J. Hausman, "Valuation of New Goods Under Perfect and Imperfect Competition," in T. Bresnahan and R. Gordan, *The Economics of New Goods* (1997): 209-248; Hausman and Leonard, supra note 1; Nevo, supra note 1; A. Nevo, "Measuring Market Power in the Ready-to-Eat Cereal Industry," *Econometrica* 69 (2001): 307-342; Hausman and Leonard, supra note 2.

functions. Alternatively, in two company markets, the sales data obtained in discovery may be sufficient to estimate demand functions.

If the data necessary for full-fledged econometric estimation are not available, company prices and shares along with some assumptions on the form of the demand functions can be used to specify the demand conditions.[7] However, when using this approach, one must be careful to consider the validity of the underlying assumptions.

Data requirements for cost conditions may be fulfilled through discovery. It may be possible to estimate marginal cost directly from the companies' internal financial data. Alternatively, it is common in merger simulations to assume that companies face constant marginal cost over the relevant range of output. This assumption will be valid in many circumstances in intellectual property cases as well. Under this assumption, the marginal cost for each product can be inferred given the product's price, the elasticities of demand, and the nature of strategic interaction between companies.[8]

Finally, economic theory provides us with guidance for modeling the nature of strategic interaction between the companies in the industry. For example, it has been common in merger simulation to assume that firms choose their prices in each period such that each firm is satisfied with its price given the prices chosen by other firms (this is known as a Nash-Bertrand equilibrium). This Nash-Bertrand assumption can be tested by comparing the price-cost margins implied by the Nash-Bertrand assumption to the actual margins from the companies' financial information. In some circumstances, other tests might be available.[9] Other possible assumptions concerning the nature of strategic interaction include joint profit maximization and a leader-follower model.[10] The ultimate model of strategic interaction chosen will depend on the specifics of the industry at issue.

---

7   See, e.g., G. J. Werden et al., supra note 6; R. Epstein and D. Rubinfeld, "Merger Simulation: A Simplified Approach with New Applications," *Antitrust Law Journal* 69 (2002): 883-919.

8   For example, if the price is $1, the elasticity of demand is -2, and the companies' strategic interaction can be modeled as static Nash-Bertrand (described below), we can infer that the company's marginal cost is $0.50.

9   See Hausman and Leonard, supra note 2.

10 Hausman, Leonard, and Zona, supra note 1.

Contrasting Simulation and Other Approaches to Calculating Lost Profits

One of the significant advantages of the simulation approach to damage analysis is that it avoids some of the unrealistic assumptions imposed by other commonly used damage models. Other approaches to determining lost sales, described in Chapter 3, include the "market share rule" outlined in the *Mor-Flo* case[11] and what can be termed the "market segment rule" described in *BIC Leisure* and *Crystal Semiconductor*.[12]

Under the market share rule, the infringer's sales are assigned to (noninfringing) products in proportion to these products' shares of the appropriately defined "market."[13] Thus, the patent owner's lost sales are assumed to be proportional to its share of the market.[14] Two issues arise with the *Mor-Flo* approach. The first is how the market should be defined for the purposes of calculating shares. As with market definition in an antitrust case, a product must be classified as either "inside" or "outside" the market. A second issue, discussed below, is that the *Mor-Flo* approach makes particular assumptions about the nature of competition between the products that are deemed to be in the market. Specifically, it assumes that market shares completely characterize the extent of competition between the products. This assumption will generally be violated when, for example, products are grouped into product segments and competition within each segment is greater than the competition between the segments. For example, minivan models compete more closely with each other than they do with sports car models. In this situation, shares of the overall car market likely give an inaccurate characterization of the nature of competition between minivans and sports cars. The use of the *Mor-Flo* approach when this assumption is violated can lead to an overstatement or understatement of lost sales damages.

---

[11] *State Industries Inc. v. Mor-Flo Industries Inc.*, 883 F.2d 1573 (Fed. Cir. 1989).

[12] *BIC Leisure Prods. Inc. v. Windsurfing Intl. Inc.*, 1 F.3d 1214 (Fed. Cir. 1995); *Crystal Semiconductor Corp. v. Tritech Microelectronics Intl. Inc. et al.*, 246 F.3d 1336 (Fed. Cir. 2001).

[13] Specifically, a product would get a fraction of the infringing sales equal to $s/(1 - w)$, where s is the product's share and w is the infringer's share.

[14] It should be pointed out that the market share rule is itself just a simulation of the but-for world, albeit under a particular set of assumptions. Specifically, the market share rule is a simulation where consumer demand is of the logit form and the market elasticity is zero. With this demand structure, and assuming the prices of the noninfringing products remain at their actual levels in the but-for world, an increase in the price of the infringing product to infinity (its reservation price in this model) will lead the infringing sales to go to the noninfringing products in proportion to their market shares in the actual world. This is exactly the market share rule.

In recognition of this issue, the courts have ruled that if the market is significantly segmented, the market share rule should be applied using the shares of the appropriate segment rather than the shares of the market as a whole. In *BIC Leisure,* for example, the infringer's products were low-end surfboards while the patent owner's products were high-end windsurfing boards (this determination was made largely on the basis of the products' price points). The court ruled that the patent owner could not use the market share rule to calculate lost sales, where the share was defined to be the share of the market consisting of all surfboards, because it was not clear that the patent owner would have captured its share of the infringing sales at its higher price point. Lost sales were instead set to zero, which is equivalent to applying a share-based rule where the share is defined to be the share of the low-end segment rather than the share of the overall surfboard market (the patent owner had a zero share of the low-end segment).

In *Crystal Semiconductor,* the infringer and the patent owner were in the same segment of a larger overall market. The court ruled that the patent owner could calculate its lost sales by applying a share-based rule where the share was defined on the basis of the segment rather than the whole market. Again, the rationale was that competition within the segment was much stronger than competition between segments.

While the approach used in *BIC Leisure* and *Crystal Semiconductor* recognizes the second issue with the *Mor-Flo* approach, namely that the nature of competition is sometimes not well characterized by overall market shares, it shares the first issue with the *Mor-Flo* approach. Specifically, a decision must be made as to which products are included in the same segment as the infringing product and which products are outside the segment. This again is an all-or-nothing approach that may not correctly reflect the actual nature of competition. For instance, in many cases some competition exists between segments. Thus, even if the infringer is in one segment and the patent owner is in another, we may expect some level of lost sales for the patent owner, even though this level may be well below what would be indicated by the patent owner's share of the overall market. The *BIC Leisure* approach would conclude that there were no lost sales based on the products being in different segments. Similarly, even if the infringer and the patent owner are in the same segment, we may expect some of the infringing sales to go outside the segment as long as there existed some competition between the segments. The *BIC Leisure* approach would overstate lost sales in this case.

Because of the all-or-nothing characteristic of the *Mor-Flo* and *BIC Leisure* approaches, the debate when using these approaches will typically center around which products should be included in the market or segment for which the shares are to be calculated. A candidate product will either be ruled in or ruled out and no intermediate determination is possible.

Simulation avoids this all-or-nothing assumption and provides the opportunity to use a more nuanced approach. Products need not be ruled entirely in or entirely out in order to assign infringing sales in the but-for world. Instead, the products are assigned more or fewer of the infringing sales based on the extent of their competition with the infringing product. However, the trade-off to introducing more nuance into the analysis is that simulation has substantially higher data and information requirements than the *Mor-Flo* or *BIC Leisure* approaches. Identifying the extent of competition—rather than just determining whether two products are in the same market or market segment—requires an understanding of the structure of consumer demand for the products. It may well be the case that the necessary data are not available to perform a simulation, while the *Mor-Flo* or *BIC Leisure* approaches would still be available. However, when feasible, simulation will generally be expected to provide a more accurate calculation of lost profits damages.

The Simulation Approach: A Hypothetical Example
The benefits of the simulation approach can be illustrated by means of a hypothetical example comparing the results of the simulation with the results of applying the *Mor-Flo* and *BIC Leisure* approaches.

Suppose the industry at issue consists of four products. Two of the products, H1 and H2, are high-end products in a premium segment. The other two products, L1 and L2, are low-end products in an economy segment. H1 is the product sold by the patent owner, while L1 is the product sold by the infringer. The two remaining products, H2 and L2, are noninfringing. For simplicity, the infringer is assumed to have had no noninfringing alternative that it could have offered in the but-for world in place of the infringing L1. Thus, in the but-for world, L1 would not have been offered for sale and the industry would have consisted of H1, H2, and L2 only. To construct the appropriate but-for world, we need to determine the prices, sales, and profits that the three remaining products would have achieved in the absence of L1.

Data Requirements

Suppose the high-end products each have a marginal cost of $100 per unit while the low-end products each have a marginal cost of $110 per unit. Given this set-up, the prices, sales, market shares, and profits of the respective products in the actual world are expressed in Table 1.[15]

Economists measure the extent of consumers' willingness to switch away from products and the extent of their willingness to substitute between products using the *own- and cross-price elasticities of demand*. The own-price elasticity of demand is a measure of the responsiveness of a product's demand to its own price (the own-price elasticity is formally defined as the percentage change in demand for the product that would result from a 1 percent increase in the product's price). The cross-price elasticity of demand is a measure of the responsiveness of demand for one product, say company A's product, with respect to the price of a second product, say B's product (the cross-price elasticity of demand for A's product with respect to the price of B's product is formally defined as the percentage change in the demand for A's product that would result from a 1 percent change in the price of B's product). The larger the cross-price elasticity of demand between two products, the closer the two products are as substitutes in the eyes of consumers.

The own- and cross-price elasticities of demand for the four products in this example are provided in Table 2. In an actual intellectual property case, these elasticities would be obtained through the methods described above. The implications of the elasticities will be discussed in more detail below. For the time being, note two aspects of the elasticities that are consistent with the existence of low-end and high-end segments. First, by looking across the cross-price elasticities in a row for a given product, one can tell which other products are the strongest competitors for that product. For example, in the row for H1, H2 has a cross-price elasticity of 0.80 and L1 has a cross-price elasticity of 0.22, indicating that H2 is a closer substitute for H1 than is L1. This pattern of cross-price elasticities is consistent with the existence of two distinct market segments. Second, the own-price elasticities for L1 and L2 are much larger than the own-price elasticities for H1 and H2. This pattern of own-price elasticities indicates that purchasers of L1 and L2 are more price-sensitive than are purchasers of H1 and H2.

---

[15] The pricing equilibrium in this industry is assumed to be of the Nash-Bertrand type both in the actual world and in the but-for world.

Table 1. Actual World Outcomes

Brand	Price per unit	Unit sales (thousands)	Share	Profit (millions)
H1	$173	214,500	33.9%	$15.67
H2	$169	207,100	32.8%	$14.30
L1	$132	105,200	16.6%	$2.36
L2	$132	105,200	16.6%	$2.36

Table 2. Own- and Cross-Price Elasticities of Demand

		With Respect to the Price of...			
		H1	H2	L1	L2
Elasticity of Demand For...	H1	−2.37	0.80	0.22	0.22
	H2	0.83	−2.45	0.24	0.24
	L1	0.77	0.77	−5.90	3.71
	L2	0.77	0.77	3.71	−5.90

Lost Sales with No Price Erosion

I start by estimating lost profits damages under the assumption of no price erosion. In other words, I assume that the prices of H1, H2, and L2 in the but-for world would have remained at their actual levels.

I first apply the market share rule of *Mor-Flo*.[16] Under this rule, the 105,200 units of L1 that were sold in the actual world would have been divided in the but-for world among the three remaining products in a manner proportional to their actual shares. For example, given that L1's share was 16.6 percent and H1's share was 33.9 percent, H1 would have received 42,761 additional units under this approach, or (105,200) x 0.339/(1-0.166). The prices, unit sales, shares, and profits of the products in the *Mor-Flo* but-for world would have been as shown in Table 3. Lost profits damages to the patent owner would be calculated to be $3.12 million using this approach (the but-for profit of $18.79 million less the actual profit of $15.67 million from Table 1).

As a comparison, under *BIC Leisure,* estimated lost sales (and hence damages) would have been zero. This is because H1 and L1 are in distinct market segments and are priced at very different price points. Thus, the *BIC Leisure* approach would not attribute any of L1's infringing sales as

---

16 Recall that the *Mor-Flo* approach is just an application of simulation with a particular set of assumptions.

Table 3. But-For World Outcomes Based on the *Mor-Flo* Market Share Rule

Brand	Price per unit	Unit sales (thousands)	Share	Profit (millions)	Damages (millions)
H1	$173	257,335	40.7%	$18.79	$3.12
H2	$169	248,457	39.3%	$17.14	
L1	—	—	—	—	
L2	$132	126,208	20.0%	$2.78	

Table 4. But-For World Outcomes Based on Simulation Methods

Brand	Price per unit	Unit sales (thousands)	Share	Profit (millions)	Damages (millions)
H1	$173	224,600	35.9%	$16.40	$0.73
H2	$169	217,400	34.7%	$15.00	
L1	—	—	—	—	
L2	$132	184,100	29.4%	$4.05	

lost sales to H1. In that case, lost profits damages would be zero. As can be seen from this example, the two commonly used legal approaches to calculating lost profits damages give widely diverging answers due to their all-or-nothing nature.

The simulation approach avoids making this type of all-or-nothing assumption and instead allows the data to dictate the extent to which sales made by the infringer would have been made by the patent owner.[17] Consumers who purchased L1 in the actual world would have the choice of switching to one of the other products (H1, H2, or L2) or not purchasing any product at all (I will refer to this latter possibility as going "outside the market"). The demand elasticities tell us how many consumers take up each of these options. The results of the simulation are listed above in Table 4. The damages estimate based on the simulation is $0.73 million as compared to the $3.12 million obtained under the *Mor-Flo* approach or the zero obtained under the *BIC Leisure* approach.

The large differences between the damages obtained under the three methods arise from the differences between the methods in terms of the

---

[17] When price erosion is assumed to have not occurred, simulation requires only the demand structure to determine the but-for sales of the patent owner.

Table 5. But-For World Comparison: Where the L1 Sales Would Have Gone

	Simulated but-for world	Mor-Flo but-for world	BIC Leisure but-for world
H1	9.6%	40.7%	0.0%
H2	9.8%	39.3%	0.0%
L2	75.0%	20.0%	100.0%
Outside the market	5.6%	0.0%	0.0%

share of L1's sales that the patent owner (H1) would have obtained in the but-for world. Table 5 summarizes where the L1 sales would have gone in the absence of L1 in the three alternative but-for worlds. Two differences between the but-for worlds are immediately obvious. First, in the simulated but-for world, H1 receives a much smaller fraction of the L1 sales than does L2, while in the *Mor-Flo* but-for world, the reverse holds. Second, in the simulated but-for world, some of the L1 sales go outside the market (i.e., some of the L1 sales do not go to any of the three remaining products), while in the *Mor-Flo* but-for world, all of the L1 sales go to one of the products inside the market.

Competition Within a Segment and Between Segments

As discussed above, the *Mor-Flo* but-for world assigns the L1 sales to the remaining products in proportion to their market shares. Thus, H1 captures the largest fraction, 41 percent of the L1 sales, while L2 captures only 20 percent. The underlying economic assumption behind the market share rule of *Mor-Flo* is that the cross-price elasticities of H1, H2, and L2 with respect to L1's price are all equal. However, Table 2 demonstrates that this assumption is violated in this example. The cross-price elasticity of L2 with respect to L1's price (3.71) is much larger than the cross-price elasticity of H1 with respect to L1's price (0.22). This pattern of cross-price elasticities indicates that the low-end products L1 and L2 compete more closely with each other than they do with the high-end products H1 and H2. Again, this is consistent with there being two distinct market segments. In this case, if L1 were absent from the market, we would expect consumers who would otherwise have purchased L1 to turn to L2 in greater numbers than L2's share would indicate. The simulated but-for world, which is explicitly based on the cross-price elasticities of demand, incorporates the fact that the competition between products within the low-end segment is greater than competition between low-end products and the products in the high-end segment. Thus, in the simulated but-for world, H1 captures only 10 percent of the L1 sales while L2 captures 75 percent.

Note that the *BIC Leisure* approach errs in the opposite direction from the *Mor-Flo* approach. Under *BIC Leisure,* if it were determined that L1 and H1 were in different market segments (as seems likely, given the facts provided here), H1 would get zero lost sales. However, as the simulated but-for world demonstrates, competition exists between products in different segments (although it is less strong than competition between products in the same segment). Thus, in contrast to the assumption of the *BIC Leisure* approach, H1 would have captured some of the L1 sales if L1 were absent from the market.

Product Differentiation

The simulated but-for world also incorporates another economic factor neglected by the *Mor-Flo* and *BIC Leisure* approaches. Because the products are differentiated in terms of the attributes they offer to consumers, and consumers differ in their tastes for these attributes, some consumers of L1 might have decided to forego purchasing a product altogether if L1 were not available.[18] Thus, some of the L1 sales might not be made by H1, H2, or L2. The extent that this outcome would occur depends on the own- and cross-price elasticities of demand. Because the simulated but-for world is explicitly based on these elasticities, it correctly determines that 6 percent of the L1 sales would have gone outside the market rather than to H1, H2, or L2. The *Mor-Flo* but-for world, in contrast, assumes that all of the L1 sales would have stayed within the market. This assumption is correct either if the overall market demand for these products is perfectly inelastic or if one or more of the products is a perfect substitute for L1. However, neither of these conditions holds in this particular example.

Price Erosion

The increased competition due to the infringer being present in the market would generally be expected to lead to lower prices for the other prod-

---

[18]   This effect is sometimes referred to as a "market expansion" effect of the infringing product.

Table 6. But-For World Outcomes Based on Simulation Methods

Brand	Price per unit	Unit sales (thousands)	Share	Profit (millions)	Damages (millions)
H1	$178	223,500	35.4%	$17.43	$1.76
H2	$174	216,400	34.2%	$16.01	
L1	—	—	—	—	
L2	$147	153,800	24.3%	$5.69	

Table 7. Extent of Price Erosion by Brand

Brand	Price increase in the but-for world
H1	2.9%
H2	3.0%
L2	11.4%

ucts in the market.[19] Thus, if L1 were absent from the market, the prices of the remaining products would be expected to be higher. The simulated but-for world is able to take price erosion into account in a straightforward manner. The own- and cross-price elasticities of demand along with the companies' costs and the nature of their strategic interaction are used to determine how much the prices of H1, H2, and L2 would have increased in the but-for world. Those results are summarized in Table 6. Relative to Table 4, which assumed no price erosion, the prices of the remaining brands are higher. The extent of price erosion by brand is described in Table 7. Because L2 was L1's closest competitor, the producer of L2 would be able to increase its price the most once L1 was no longer competing in the market. The prices of H1 and H2 would also increase, although by lesser amounts because these high-end products are less close substitutes for L1 than is L2.

The simulated but-for world also takes into account in a straightforward manner the "adjustment" to demand that would result from the higher prices in the but-for world. Specifically, at the higher but-for prices, the customer demands for H1, H2, and L2 would be lower than

---

[19] It is theoretically possible that the addition of a competitor has no price effect or even leads to a price increase for existing products. However, this latter outcome is observed only rarely in the real world. Studies of the effects of generic entry on the prices of branded pharmaceutical products are one example.

they would be at the actual prices. A price erosion analysis must take this demand adjustment into account or it will overstate damages.

Price erosion is not dealt with by the *Mor-Flo* or *BIC Leisure* approaches. Instead, price erosion is typically treated as a separate "add-on" component of damages. The amount of the patent owner's price erosion is determined in some fashion and the associated adjustment to the patent owner's demand is made. However, this analysis may fail to account for the fact that the other remaining competitors would also likely increase their prices in the but-for world. This could either give the patent owner additional room to increase its price or reduce the size of the demand adjustment that needs to be made. Again, the simulation method takes these considerations into account in a straightforward and unified manner.

Conclusion

Simulation provides a framework for calculating lost profits damages that is unified, internally consistent, and based firmly on well-established economic principles. A properly specified simulation model can avoid the all-or-nothing problem associated with the existing approaches commonly used in patent litigation, thereby incorporating the nuances of competition among differentiated products. While these benefits come at the cost of increased data requirements, which at times may preclude their use, simulation methods offer the potential for bringing increased reliability to the calculation of lost profits damages in patent litigation.

8

The Use of Surveys in Intellectual Property Disputes

Eugene P. Ericksen and Sarah M. Butler

Surveys are commonly used in intellectual property disputes. In Lanham Act trademark and trade dress cases, surveys have been used to establish the validity of a trademark and to evaluate the possibly infringing nature of a competitor's mark. In Lanham Act false advertising cases, surveys have been used to determine whether consumers are typically misled by an advertisement, especially where the advertisement makes a claim that is known to be false. More recently, in patent infringement cases, surveys have been used both by plaintiffs and defendants to estimate damages.

The advantage of using surveys in intellectual property disputes is that they are able to address directly the question of interest. However, the scientific validity and trustworthiness of the survey results depends crucially on the methodology used to implement the survey.

Conducting Surveys for Litigation

Like any other litigation survey, a survey in an intellectual property matter needs to be both scientifically valid and trustworthy. By trustworthy we mean that the data were collected in a manner that did not unfairly influence the outcome. The *Manual for Complex Litigation*[1] lists seven criteria for deciding whether or not a survey is trustworthy. They are:

1. The population was properly chosen and defined.
2. The sample chosen was representative of the population.
3. The data gathered were accurately reported.
4. The data were analyzed in accordance with accepted statistical principles.

---

[1] *Manual for Complex Litigation,* 3rd ed. (Washington, DC: U.S. Government Printing Office, 1995), 101-103.

5. The questions were clear and not leading.
6. The survey was conducted by qualified persons following proper interview procedures.
7. The process was conducted so as to assure objectivity.

We now discuss each criterion briefly, as these are the standards to which any intellectual property survey is likely to be held.

Choosing and Defining the Population to Be Sampled

In the typical trademark or patent survey, the correct population consists of current or potential users of the product in question. In most cases, respondents who have decided to cease using the product category would be ineligible for the survey. To illustrate how eligibility might be defined, if the survey concerned the trademark of a movie title, eligible respondents might be people who have seen a movie in the past six months and plan to do so in the next six months.

In order to determine whether a particular respondent is part of this population, one typically would ask the respondent a hypothetical question concerning likely future use of the product at issue. Respondents generally find it easier to answer questions about their actual behavior, meaning that they find it easier to say whether or not they have used a product recently rather than whether or not they will use it in the future. However, the question of future use is relevant because the goal is to learn whether there will be confusion or effects of infringement in the future. Asking about past behavior first usually helps to get clear answers about likely future use. For example, in a survey about a possible trademark infringement of a movie title, asking respondents about their attendance at movies over the past several months helps them to focus on the likely answer for the next few months.

A Representative Sample

Lists of respondents may be obtained from three types of sources. First, manufacturers may keep lists of people who have purchased their product and perhaps obtained a warranty. Such lists are often incomplete, and the customers obtaining warranties may not be typical of all purchasers. This can be tested for by comparing the listed customers to a small random sample of unlisted purchasers.

Second, in many cases it is a good strategy to take a sample of residential telephone numbers, to call these numbers and to screen for people in the relevant market. This strategy is particularly useful for products such as movies, where the frequency of usage is high and it is not necessary to show the actual products or pictures of the product to the consumer.

Third, in other cases samples may be obtained by approaching shoppers in malls and screening to see if they are in the relevant market. In cases where it is necessary to show the product to the respondent, this may be the optimal, and possibly the only feasible, method. While mall shoppers are clearly not random samples of the relevant market, their relevant characteristics may not be materially different from those of such a sample.

When we say that the sample is representative of the population, we mean that we can generalize from the former to the latter. This occurs statistically when the survey is based on a probability sample, i.e., each member of the population has a known, nonzero chance of selection. We are not always able to use a probability sample in surveys for intellectual property cases.

Many intellectual property surveys involve showing pictures or lists of choices to respondents. Obtaining a probability sample from the universe of consumers and interviewing them in their homes or having them come to a central location is prohibitively expensive. A more cost-effective method is to recruit respondents from available shoppers passing by an interviewing facility in a shopping mall. Groups of such recruits typically have distributions of characteristics similar to those of an actual probability sample. Because the identities and opinions of these recruits are not known to the interviewers in advance, the procedure satisfies the need for an objective method of selection. The population of mall shoppers is frequently taken to be an adequate substitute for a probability sample.[2]

Data Accuracy

The accurate reporting of data is guaranteed in a telephone survey by the use of Computer Assisted Telephone Interviewing (CATI). A CATI questionnaire is programmed into the computer in such a way that the each question appears on the screen for the interviewer to ask. The interviewer then keys in the answer, which causes the CATI program to go to the appropriate next question. With supervisors having the capability of listening to any interview, this method assures that questions will be asked and answers recorded in the proper manner.

---

[2] This is discussed by Shari Diamond in "Reference Guide on Survey Research," in *Reference Manual on Scientific Evidence,* 2d ed. (Washington, DC: U.S. Government Printing Office, 2000), especially sections I and IIIC. In particular, she cites the Federal Rule of Evidence 703 recognizing "facts or data of a type reasonably relied upon by experts in the particular field."

The second characteristic of accurate reporting is that the questions must be asked exactly as they are written in the questionnaire and the answers must be recorded exactly as they are answered. Otherwise, the answers are subject to the interpretations of the individual interviewers, and they will not be comparable.

When intellectual property surveys are conducted in shopping malls, the interviewing must often be done by survey firms who have exclusive contracts with the malls. In such cases, we have an extra need for close supervision, and this can be accomplished by a validation follow-up survey, on-site supervision, and close analysis of the questionnaires received from each mall. It is important in such cases to provide written interviewing instructions.

Appropriate Statistical Analysis

The analyst should calculate confidence intervals for important estimates and indicate whether observed differences between groups are statistically significant. The analyst should also indicate whether all responses or just a subgroup of responses are included in each calculation and should make clear the rules by which responses are excluded. In particular, the analyst needs to make clear how answers like "don't know" or "not sure" are treated.

Survey Questions

Questions should be written clearly and in a nonleading manner. In intellectual property surveys, this frequently means that key questions should be asked in an open-ended fashion, such as "What do you think the ad is about?" or "Who do you think it is who made this pizza?"

It is not always self-evident whether a question would be clear to the typical respondent, and this must be learned through pretesting the questionnaire. As stated by Sudman and Bradburn:

> Even after years of experience, no expert can write a perfect questionnaire. Between us we have more than fifty years of experience in questionnaire construction and we have never written a perfect questionnaire on the first draft.[3]

When performing the pretest, it is important that the analyst either listen to the telephone interview pretest or observe the interviewing in a

---

3   See Seymour Sudman and Norman Bradburn, *Asking Questions: A Practical Guide to Questionnaire Design* (San Francisco: Jossey-Bass, 1982), 283.

shopping mall. Nearly every pretest involves some type of unexpected glitch that needs to be fixed before the survey can proceed. If there are many such glitches, the survey should be pretested again to be sure that it is working smoothly.

A nonleading question is one that does not suggest an answer. When asking a respondent what she or he saw in an ad, what a particular logo represents, or what the story associated with a movie title might be, use of the open-ended format allows us to learn just what thoughts are in the respondent's mind. By minimizing the length of the question and not suggesting alternatives, the question writer reduces the possibility that the question is leading.[4]

Survey Procedures

The surveys should be conducted by qualified interviewers following proper procedures. Qualified interviewers are those who have been screened, trained, and monitored by a good survey research company or academic center. Good interviewers know how to ask questions properly, to listen to answers, and to record them properly. Every question should be asked as written on the questionnaire and answers should be recorded verbatim. A survey research company can apply appropriate supervision and guarantee that proper procedures are followed.

When surveys are conducted in shopping malls, it is not possible to supervise them as closely as you would a telephone survey. This is why validation is necessary. A validation survey should be conducted by a third party. In this survey, the third party would contact a representative subsample of respondents and ask them questions to determine (a) if they were actually interviewed, (b) if they were qualified, and (c) if their answers to key questions match the data they had provided on the original survey. Such a validation survey is not needed on a telephone survey where close supervision is provided by on-site monitoring. In a telephone survey, supervisors are able to listen to any particular interviewer without the knowledge of the interviewer or respondent, and thereby validate the survey as it is being conducted.

---

4   Psychological experiments suggest that the length of the answer is related to the length of the question, i.e., shorter questions will elicit shorter answers. To overcome this problem, and retain the nonleading nature of a shorter question, interviewers must be trained to probe for complete answers in a similarly nonleading manner. This can be done by probing with questions such as "Could you tell me more about that?" or "Could you explain what you mean by that?" See Sudman and Bradburn, *Asking Questions,* 50.

Objectivity

The final criterion is that the survey be conducted in a manner that would assure objectivity. This means that the survey should be "double-blind." In other words, neither the interviewer nor the respondent should know who the sponsor of the survey is or what the sponsor hopes to accomplish in the survey. This is easily accomplished by having the data collected by a subcontractor who is not responsible for data analysis.

Trademark and Trade Dress Surveys

Establishing Secondary Meaning and Confusion

Perhaps the most common use of surveys in intellectual property matters involves trademark and trade dress issues. A trademark is a name or symbol that identifies the source or manufacturer of a product. It can also be the look of the actual product, e.g., the shape of the original Volkswagen Beetle. The trade dress of a product is the packaging of that product, which also identifies the source or manufacturer of a product.

Surveys are commonly used in cases where a competitor creates a trademark or trade dress that appears to copy the original trademark or trade dress. When a competitor allegedly infringes on a trademark or trade dress, the holder of the original mark must show two things. First, that the original mark has *secondary meaning,* which is defined as a large percentage of the relevant market being able to identify the source of the trademark. Second, the holder of the original mark must show that the infringing mark creates confusion in the minds of consumers, which means that they would see the competitor's mark and think that the holder of the original mark was the source. This commonly means that consumers look at the trademark and misidentify its source, but it can also mean that consumers (incorrectly) believe that the competitor received permission from the original holder of the trademark to use it.

To demonstrate secondary meaning, the survey research firm selects a sample of consumers in the relevant market and shows the original trademark to this sample. If a large enough share of respondents correctly identify the source of the trademark without guessing (discussed further below), the mark is said to have secondary meaning. There does not appear to be a consistent legal standard for how large this percentage must be, but we have observed that benchmarks in the range of 40 to 50 percent have been used.

The standard is lower to establish confusion. To show confusion, the survey research firm would show the competitive mark to a sample of consumers and determine what share mistakenly identifies the source to be the same as that of the original mark. In general, 10 percent of the sample making this mistake without guessing is sufficient to demonstrate confusion.

Controlling for Guessing

In both secondary meaning and confusion surveys, the plaintiff must show that the apparently demonstrated secondary meaning or confusion is not due to guessing. Guessing occurs in a variety of situations, but is more likely in an industry where a small number of competitors hold large shares of the market. For example, an automobile consumer might see a Ford and not recognize it as such, but guess "Ford" because it is a well-known brand with a large market share. Such an answer would not indicate true recognition on the part of the consumer. Tests for guessing commonly involve the use of control products but may also rely on follow-up questions for the respondent.

In a secondary meaning survey, two groups of respondents will correctly identify the source, those who really know it and those who simply guess it. The most common way of estimating the percentage guessing is to show the respondents a second product from a source other than the plaintiff or defendant. The percentage of respondents who incorrectly identify this second product as being made by the plaintiff can be used to estimate the share of "guessers."

To illustrate, suppose 70 percent of a sample of automobile consumers identify a Volkswagen Beetle as being a product of Volkswagen. Of a second sample that is shown the product of a Japanese competitor, 8 percent guess "Volkswagen." We would then subtract, 70 − 8 = 62, to obtain the percent of the sample who correctly identified the Volkswagen without guessing.

In situations where it is not possible to use a control, follow-up questions can be used to identify guessing. For example, we participated in one recent case in which the goal was to establish whether the movie title *Bridge on the River Kwai* had secondary meaning. Respondents were asked if they knew of a movie title with the words *River Kwai* in it. Those respondents who gave the correct answer were asked follow-up questions to see if they could identify the story, the location, or any of the actors in the movie. Unless the respondent could correctly answer at least one of these questions, the respondent was not counted as giving the correct answer.

We followed a similar strategy for a confusion survey, except that respondents are shown the allegedly infringing defendants' product or trademark. The same issue of "guessed answers" must also be taken into account here. For example, if 20 percent of a sample mistakenly identified a competitor's automobile as a Volkswagen, by itself it would not allow us to say that confusion had occurred. We would want to show the sample a control product to identify the guessing percentage. If, as in the previous example, 8 percent guessed "Volkswagen" when they were in fact shown some other automobile, we would say that (20 − 8 =) 12 percent of consumers were confused, once an allowance had been made for guessing.

It is quite common in these surveys to use only one control, but the selection of this control may be arbitrary. It is possible that the control product could have features that could inadvertently increase or decrease the amount of guessing. The use of multiple controls can provide a better estimate of guessing.

In the trademark case involving the movie titles, the allegedly infringing mark was the movie title *Return to the River Kwai*. This movie had never been released in the United States, and the plaintiff sought to prevent the release. It was unlikely that any more than a very small percentage of a sample of moviegoers had actually heard of *Return to the River Kwai* and that even fewer had seen it. Yet, 42 percent said that they had heard of the movie and 20 percent said that they had seen it. Each of these respondents were then asked the follow-up questions about the story, location, and actors and were not counted as "confused" unless they gave answers to at least one follow-up question that would have been correct had the actual movie been *Bridge on the River Kwai*.

To obtain additional evidence on the possibility of guessing, we asked the respondents if they had ever heard of, and if so, had seen, eight additional titles. Five of the titles were actual movies, some of which were very well known and others less so. The other three were fictitious. When we asked about the fictitious titles, an average of 18 percent said that they had heard of the title, and 2 percent said that they had seen the movie. Subtracting, we estimated that (42 − 18 =) 24 percent were confused into thinking that they had heard of *Return to the River Kwai* and 18 percent (20-2 percent) were confused into thinking that they had seen it.

Surveys to Establish a Brand Name

Secondary meaning surveys may also be used to establish a brand name. This can be an issue when a manufacturer creates a new product, names it, and wishes to register the brand name for its exclusive use. There have been many instances where a prominent brand name, for example Xerox or Kleenex, has become a practical synonym for a product, in these cases, copiers and facial tissues. A manufacturer would not be able to register a word commonly used to describe a product, such as *tricycle,* but if a manufacturer invented a four-wheeled version and wished to call it a "quadricycle," the manufacturer could apply to have the word *quadricycle* registered as an exclusive brand name. The test is whether consumers associate the term with the products of one company or many companies. It is not necessary for consumers to identify the name of the one company.

The producers of an energy drink, we will call it "Lightning Juice" for purposes of this example, wished to register its name as a brand name. To test whether consumers recognized the drink's name as a brand name, we conducted a telephone survey of consumers of energy drinks in three different markets. We qualified consumers by asking, "Within the next three months, which, if any, of the following products do you expect to purchase?" We asked about five products, energy bars, herbal tea, energy drinks, yogurt, and fruit smoothies, to mask the objective of the survey. We included as respondents in the survey only those who said that they planned to purchase an energy drink.

To establish that respondents were giving focused answers rather than guessing, we employed two strategies. The first was to ask each respondent, "Have you ever heard of 'Lightning Juice'?" and only ask the key question of respondents who said "yes." The key question was, "Do you associate 'Lightning Juice' with beverages from one company, beverages from more than one company, or do you not know?"

The second strategy was to ask the same pair of questions about four additional products. Two of these, lemonade and iced tea, were clearly not brand names. The other two, Kool Aid and Gatorade, were well-known brand names. In the survey, 97 and 95 percent, respectively, identified lemonade and iced tea as products made by more than one company, while 88 percent identified Kool Aid and 92 percent identified Gatorade as products made by one company. This established that the large majority of respondents were paying attention to the questions and giving focused answers rather than guesses.

Just over half of respondents, 51 percent, told the interviewers that they had both heard of "Lightning Juice" and that it was a product made by one company. The contrast of this result with the results for the four control products allowed us to draw the conclusion that "Lightning Juice" was a brand name rather than a product name. Our report was part of a successful application to the United States Patent and Trademark Office to obtain the exclusive use of the brand name.

False Advertising Surveys

False advertising claims are filed under the Lanham Act when plaintiffs believe that a competitor has produced an advertisement that is false or misleading. The key question in false advertising surveys is to identify the impression made by the ad on the consumer. In some cases, the survey can be used to show that the misleading nature of the ad influenced actual purchasing decisions.

In a typical situation, the interviewer would show a video of the ad to a respondent and ask what the respondent thought the ad was about. This question would be open-ended, meaning that the interviewer would make a verbatim record of the respondent's answer. Use of a general question without answer categories assures that the question is not leading, and this is an important design goal for a false advertising survey.

For example, suppose a hairspray manufacturer accused a competitor of running advertisements that claimed that its brand was more effective than the plaintiff's brand. After asking initial general questions such as whether the respondent was a frequent or occasional user of hairspray, the interviewer might ask "Other than getting you to buy the product, what was the main idea of the commercial?" The quality of information given in the answers to this open-ended question can be improved with a follow-up question: "Do you have anything else to say about that?" A skillful interviewer will probe to make sure that full and complete answers are obtained.

Once the answers to the open-ended questions have been obtained, it is frequently useful to ask specific follow-up questions. After sufficient probing to assure that the first question was answered completely, a second question might be more specific, for example, "Did the commercial say that [named product] was more effective than [competing product name]?" The open-ended questions should be asked first to eliminate the possibility that respondents' answers to them could be influenced by the answers they gave to the specific questions.[5]

Allegations of misleading sales techniques create the need for a second type of false advertising survey. The allegedly false statements may exist in sales documents, or they could simply be part of the pitches given by sales representatives. These allegations appear to occur with some frequency in the pharmaceutical industry, especially with sales pitches made to doctors. It is again critical that the survey questions not be leading. To start, we might ask whether the doctor has ever been told by a sales representative that the allegedly false statement was actually true. For example, the doctor might have been told that Medicine A did not cure headaches as well as Medicine B when Medicine A was in fact equal or superior.

If the answer to this first question is "yes," the interviewer could ask follow-up questions, again in an open-ended manner, regarding the source of this information. In many cases, this strategy will be conservative, because the doctor might not remember the source, even though it did in fact come from a sales representative. Once this information has been obtained, it may be helpful to ask whether the doctor has been less likely to recommend the use of Medicine A because of what the doctor has been told.

In one case, a brand of baby food (Brand A) was incorrectly described in marketing materials sent to doctors as having less food value than a competitor's brand (Brand B). In this case, there was a target list of the physicians who had received the marketing materials. The survey sample included two groups, one of physicians from the target list and a control group that had not been targeted. In the survey, the physicians on the target list were more likely, by 37 to 22 percent, to have a negative opinion of Brand A. They were also more likely, by 40 to 18 percent, to say that they had been told negative things about Brand A. Of the physicians who had heard negative comments, 70 percent had heard them from a sales representative, though the physicians could not always remember the employer

---

5   There is a substantial research literature indicating the influence of the survey context on respondents' answers. This is especially true for subjects that respondents have not thought about very much or that have low salience for other reasons. In such situations, respondents look to previous questions, the specific wording of the question at hand, and any signals that they might receive from the interviewers for guidance in how to provide an appropriate answer. Seymour Sudman, Norman Bradburn, and Norbert Schwarz, *Thinking About Answers* (San Francisco: Jossey-Bass, 1996), especially chapters 4 and 5; and Jean Converse and Stanley Presser, *Survey Questions: Handcrafting the Standardized Questionnaire* (Newbury Park, CA: Sage, 1986) are two good references on the subject.

of the sales representative. Another 11 percent had read the negative comments in a sales brochure. The negative comments did appear to have an impact on the recommendations made by the doctors: 21 percent of the target list sample, compared to 12 percent of the control sample, said that they had heard negative comments that made them less likely to recommend Brand A. These results provided moderately strong evidence indicating the negative impact of the advertising campaign.

Survey Strategies in Patent Infringement Cases

Many technological devices, such as computers, medical equipment, and automobiles, incorporate multiple patents, and infringement claims may only involve one of several hundred patents taken out on the device. For example, an infringement claim could involve just one part of the software that a computer uses to browse the Internet.

Quantifying damages in such a case is a daunting task, but a survey can play an important role. Computers provide a useful example, for they are complex machines with hundreds of features, many of which are covered by patents. The litigation could involve just one of these many features and patents. Determining the effect that the patented feature had on consumer demand for the overall product is an important goal. A survey can help to attain this goal.

In the computer example, we start by obtaining a sample of survey respondents. For the survey design discussed below, a random sample of the population is probably not feasible, but respondents may be recruited in shopping malls. For surveys where we need to have respondents look at pictures or other advertising materials, or engage in an activity like web searches on the computer, it is not possible to conduct a telephone survey. It is very expensive, prohibitively so in the eyes of most clients, to conduct personal interviews in the homes of a random sample of consumers or to recruit a random sample of consumers and bring them to a central location.

As a result, intellectual property surveys are frequently taken in shopping malls, with shoppers who happen to be passing by the interviewing facility. These respondents are recruited by the interviewers who then determine whether or not they are qualified. Because the use of these surveys is so widespread, and the use of surveys based on probability samples so expensive, such shopping mall surveys will not typically be rejected by courts for the use of a nonprobability sample. There is some statistical justification for this, as the bias due to the use of a nonprobability sample is generally thought to be less when comparing two groups than when trying to estimate average characteristics for one population.[6] To minimize the biases due to the use of a nonprobability sample, it is critical that the assignment to groups be random and out of the control of either the interviewer or the respondent.

It is important that the survey respondents be diverse and include many different types of computer users. Once recruited, the respondents would be randomly assigned to a treatment or control group as described below. The random assignment, with sufficient sample size, assures that the treatment and control groups are comparable on all features except the ones being tested. Ideally, the random assignment would be "double-blind" such that neither the interviewer nor the respondent would know whether she or he was in the treatment or control group. Sample sizes of 400, with 200 in each group, will be sufficient in most applications.[7]

Once potential respondents have been found to qualify as users of the relevant product, they may be randomly assigned and asked to use the computer, perhaps to browse the Internet for 15 or 20 minutes. Other possible activities might include playing a game, sending and receiving emails, or typing a document. The infringing feature would be turned on while the treatment group was using the computer. The control group would use the computer for the same activity, but with the infringing feature turned off.

Afterward, respondents in both groups would be interviewed. They would be asked questions to find out about their enjoyment and satisfaction with the computer and the software that they used. It is a good idea to ask several questions relating to the respondents' satisfaction with and evaluation of the software. Specific questions can be asked about different features of the software, and general assessments may also be obtained. This use of multiple indicators reduces the opportunity for between-group differences to appear by random chance. The essential test is whether the satisfaction with the computer differs between the treatment

---

6   See Leslie Kish, *Survey Sampling* (New York: Wiley, 1965), section 13.2A.
7   The question of necessary sample sizes can be difficult. For a comparison of percentages, where the percentages for each group are in the range of 20 to 80 percent, a 10 percentage point difference will be statistically significant at the 5 percent level. This provides reasonable assurance that had all available members of the relevant consumer population been interviewed, the direction of the difference observed in the population would be the same as in the actually observed sample. To reduce the size of the difference necessary to achieve statistical significance, substantially larger sample sizes may be needed. For example, if a 5 percentage point difference is to be statistically significant, sample sizes of 800 in each group are needed.

and control groups. If they are different, then the use of random assignment eliminates the possibility that some other, confounding variable might have caused the difference.

As part of the interview, questions should be asked to ascertain respondents' demographic characteristics and patterns of computer usage. Answers to these questions may be checked against existing data sources to determine whether the survey respondents were typical of computer users in general. It is essential that the respondents not only have typical characteristics on average but also that they reflect the variation in computer usage. You would like to have "home experts" as well as naïve users and respondents who are familiar with different types of applications.

The design just discussed is appropriate for a situation where the allegedly infringing feature is used every time a consumer uses a computer or a particular software package. There are other features of computers or software packages that consumers can choose whether or not to use. It is likely that the typical computer owner actually uses only a small percentage of the available features of her or his software package. For a situation such as this, we might take a survey about the uses to which consumers put their computers.

In one recent case, a plaintiff company alleged that a computer operating system had infringed upon a patent for a device used to record speech. This patent was part the basic operating software, but it was used only in features that were not commonly used by consumers. In our survey, we first asked if the respondent was aware that certain features were on their computer. A large percentage of respondents, between 60 and 80 percent, were aware of commonly used word processing, spreadsheet, and Internet browsing packages that were not part of the lawsuit. When the same question was asked about the less commonly used features at issue in the lawsuit, only 10 to 30 percent of respondents were aware that their computers had these features. Fewer than 15 percent had actually used these features.

These percentages are so low that they could have been due to guessing. To control for guessing, we suggest two strategies. The first is to ask about a fictitious feature, whose name sounded like it could have been part of the operating system. Some respondents will say "yes," either because they have misheard the name of the feature, or they do not want to appear to be a naïve user. In our survey, 9 percent said that they had actually used the fictitious feature, and we used this as an estimate of guessing.

The second type of control was to ask how they used the feature in question. In some instances, respondents reported uses that were technologically impossible, further indicating that the percentages were inflated. For example, the respondents indicated that they used a meeting feature as a fax machine, which cannot be done.

In this particular survey, the contested features were not commonly used, and the survey results were therefore relevant to damage calculations. Because it was not necessary for the respondents actually to use the computer as part of the survey, we used a randomly selected telephone sample. This assured the representativeness of the sample. Follow-up comparisons of respondent averages and variation with public databases on computer users verified this assumption.

Conclusion

Many of the surveys used in intellectual property disputes concern the "state of mind" of the respondent, and hence it is perhaps most critical that key questions be asked in an open-ended, nonleading fashion. Surveys used in litigation need to be taken carefully. There should be appropriate supervision and distancing between data collection and the stated goals and objectives of the analysis. The seven rules stated in the *Manual for Complex Litigation* provide good guidance, and they are consistent with scientific standards. One version of these standards may be found at the website of the American Association for Public Opinion Research.

There are many different applications of the survey method in all three of the areas of intellectual property—trademark infringement, false advertising, and patent infringement—that we have addressed in this paper. While there is no boiler-plate method of taking these surveys, trademark and trade dress surveys commonly use a format of showing the products in question to a sample of respondents and using control groups to account for guessing.

For patent infringement surveys, there are as yet no commonly used formats. The use of surveys has a shorter history, and lawyers and experts continue to search for the best ways to use survey evidence. There is still a great deal of room for creativity in the design and implementation of surveys relevant to patent infringement cases.

9

Hedonic Characteristics in the Valuation of Intellectual Property

Joseph P. Cook

Questions about the value of a patented feature can arise in a variety of circumstances. In litigation, an analysis of the but-for world might require information on how consumer demand for the infringer's product would have changed without the patented feature. Similarly, in a licensing negotiation (whether an actual negotiation or a hypothetical negotiation in a reasonable royalty analysis), an important issue is the contribution the patented feature makes to the profits of the potential licensee. More broadly, valuing the product characteristic that a piece of intellectual property provides allows us a means of valuing the intellectual property itself, as its value is generally derived from the value it can impart to the products that embody it.

Economists have developed several econometric methods for measuring the value of a product characteristic. These approaches view individual products as a bundle of product characteristics. For example, an automobile model might be defined by its engine size, fuel efficiency, cargo space, and color. A home might be defined by its square footage, age, location, number of bathrooms, and number of bedrooms.

Consumers base their purchasing decisions on product characteristics. Products with more desirable product characteristics generate higher consumer demand and, potentially, higher prices. Econometric methods, applied to data from market outcomes, can be used to measure the size of any price premium or discount associated with a particular product characteristic or the amount by which a given product characteristic affects consumer demand for the product.

Econometric Approaches to Product
Characteristic Valuation

Regression analysis, generally speaking, encompasses statistical techniques used to measure relationships between variables. The dependent variable is modeled as a function of a number of independent variables. In performing the analysis, one estimates some measure of the responsiveness of the dependent variable to changes in each of the independent variables, holding all of the others constant.

An advantage of the use of econometric methods of product characteristic valuation is that they can extract from complex data, which has been generated by the interaction of multiple market factors, the same information one might see more readily if one could view a single market relationship in isolation. For example, suppose the only difference between two products is that one of them includes the patented feature at issue. Under certain conditions, a simple comparison of the transactions prices of the two products could be used to calculate the price premium associated with the patented feature. As it only rarely occurs that the difference between two products is reduced to only one feature (in addition to price), in general, a more sophisticated approach is required. Regression analysis may be able to provide an estimate of the price premium by allowing a comparison of a number of different products with varying characteristics.

One potential complication that this approach cannot resolve completely arises when a single patent does not provide sufficient rights to include the product characteristic of interest. If a group of patents makes a joint contribution to the characteristic, one may be left with a value for the group of patents rather than a value for each constituent patent. However, the estimated value of the group of patents may be better than could otherwise be obtained by any other means.

Generally, one can divide the regression models of interest into two principal types: hedonic price regressions and econometric models of discrete consumer choice. In the former, product characteristics are included as explanatory variables for price. In the latter, product characteristics are included as explanatory variables for the consumer's choice of product.[1]

---

[1] For more detailed discussions of these issues, see Kenneth E. Train, *Discrete Choice Methods with Simulation* (Cambridge, MA: Cambridge University Press, 2003); Sherwin Rosen, "Hedonic Prices and Implicit Markets: Product Differentiation in Pure Competition," *Journal of Political Economy* 82 (1974): 34-55; and Zvi Griliches, "Hedonic Price Indexes of Automobiles: An Econometric Analysis of Quality Change," in Zvi Griliches, ed., *Price Indexes and Quality Change* (Cambridge, MA: Cambridge University Press, 1971).

Hedonic Price Regressions

A hedonic regression is a means of estimating the contribution of each of a product's constituent features to its price. That is, a hedonic regression allows us to measure the premium (or discount) associated with each of the product's characteristics.[2] Some characteristics are binary, indicating the inclusion (or exclusion) of some feature, such as curtain airbags in an automobile or particular write capabilities for a disk drive. Other characteristics are continuous, such as the hard disk capacity or processing speed of a computer, the fuel efficiency of an automobile, or the square feet of living space in a home.

A linear regression takes the following form:

$$Y_i = \alpha + \beta_1 X_{i1} + \beta_2 X_{i2} + \ldots + \beta_m X_{im} + \varepsilon_i,$$

where Y is the dependent variable whose value depends on the values of a number of independent X variables. The βs are the coefficients that indicate the amount by which the dependent variable changes when the corresponding X variable changes, holding everything else constant. The observations in the data are indexed by i, and there are m independent variables, in addition to the constant term, α.

In a hedonic regression, the dependent variable is the price of the complete product and the estimated coefficients are estimates of the implicit prices (or contributions) of the product characteristics.[3] Returning to the case of automobiles, one might find that by including a curtain airbag in a model of automobile, the manufacturer is able to raise the average price by a certain amount or percentage.[4] Or one might find that the price

---

[2] In this way, the use of hedonic price regression is akin to income approaches focused on price premiums, as one may consider the estimated coefficients as estimates of the average increase in the transactions price attributable to the presence of the associated characteristic. In an income approach based on price premiums, one is typically focusing on transparent premiums, where one can readily see the contribution of a feature by simply comparing two models that only differ in their inclusion or exclusion of the patented feature. However, frequently the variations in product features are not so conveniently distributed and more than one feature is changing across models. Such is the case, for example, in the case of automobiles that frequently differentiate versions of the same make with packages of features. See, e.g., Gordon V. Smith and Russell L. Parr, *Valuation of Intellectual Property and Intangible Assets*, 3d ed. (New York: John Wiley & Sons, 2000), 217.

[3] More formally, we might represent our starting point as $p(z) = p(z_1, z_2, \ldots, z_m)$, where p is price and z is a vector of m product characteristics. This might then lead to an estimation based on the following specification, $p_i = \alpha + \Sigma_j \beta_j z_{ij} + \varepsilon_i$, where i indexes over n transactions, j indexes over the m product characteristics, β_j is the implicit price of the jth characteristic, the ε_i are unobserved random factors, and $m < n$.

[4] Assume for this purpose that the curtain airbag is not available as a separate option but only as part of a package of options.

increases by $x for each additional mile per gallon the automobile offers. For example, if the estimated coefficient for the inclusion of a curtain airbag were 500, one would have estimated that the implicit price of the curtain airbag, or its contribution to the overall price of the automobile, was $500.

Note, however, that because the parameters in a hedonic regression are the result of the interaction of supply and demand, it may not always be an easy matter to uncover the underlying supply and demand functions. The type of hedonic regression described above is called a reduced form model. Instead of directly estimating demand or supply elasticities or the willingness to pay of consumers, a reduced form model measures the average price premium associated with the product characteristic as revealed by the data, i.e., the incremental revenue associated with the characteristic.

One can then use this price premium in conjunction with measures of the incremental costs of providing the characteristic in the product to determine its incremental profitability. When engaged in licensing negotiations or calculating economic damages associated with patent infringement, one can subtract the costs of implementing the patented technology (and any other costs of providing the feature) from the price premium to estimate the incremental profit of the feature and of the intellectual property necessary to offer it.

Applications of Hedonic Price Regressions

Applications of hedonic price regressions comprise a broad and extensive literature. Hedonic regressions are often used as a first step toward calculating a quality-adjusted price index. The U.S. Department of Labor, Bureau of Labor Statistics uses hedonic models in the Consumer Price Index (CPI) to control for concomitant changes in product quality and price for a number of electronic products.[5] Such adjustments are particularly important in areas where technology is rapidly improving. New products improve on old features and add new ones. If one wanted to

---

5   See, e.g., U.S. Department of Labor, Bureau of Labor Statistics, "Using a Hedonic Model to Adjust Prices of Personal Computers in the Consumer Price Index for Changes in Quality," 16 October 2001, www.bls.gov/cpi/cpihedpc.htm; and U.S. Department of Labor, Bureau of Labor Statistics, "Using a Hedonic Model to Adjust Television Prices in the Consumer Price Index for Changes in Quality," 16 June 2003, www.bls.gov/cpi/cpiheo1.htm. See also Nicole Shelper, "Developing a Hedonic Regression Model for Camcorders in the U.S. CPI," 16 October 2001, www.bls.gov/cpi/cpicamco.htm.

know whether personal computers were becoming more or less expensive over time, one would need to control for the fact that processing speeds and memory have greatly improved since their introduction in the early 1980s. Failing to do so would result in a considerable understatement in the decline in computer prices.

Hedonic price regressions have often been used to estimate price premia for characteristics associated with computers, automobiles, housing, and agricultural products (including wine, horses, wheat, rice, and cotton).[6] In addition, they have been used in the study of such diverse products as pharmaceuticals, crude oil, kitchen garbage bags, group health insurance, newspapers, breakfast cereals, child care, sculptures, common carrier services, and coal rail prices.[7]

To illustrate the basic principles of this approach, consider the following example of a regression of the price of an electronic device on a num-

---

[6] See, e.g., Kenneth R. Bowman and Don E. Ethridge, "Characteristic Supplies and Demands in a Hedonic Framework: U.S. Market for Cotton Fiber Attributes," *American Journal of Agricultural Economics* 74, no. 4 (November 1992): 991-1002; B. Wade Brorsen, Warren R. Grant, and M. Edward Rister, "A Hedonic Price Model for Rough Rice Bid-Acceptance Markets," *American Journal of Agricultural Economics* 66, no. 2 (May 1984): 156-163; Robert Cervero and Michael Duncan, "Neighbourhood Composition and Residential Land Prices: Does Exclusion Raise or Lower Values?" *Urban Studies* 41, no. 2 (special issue, February 2004): 299-315; Pierre Combris, Sebastien Lecocq, and Michael Visser, "Estimation of a Hedonic Price Equation for Burgundy Wine," *Applied Economics* 32, no. 8 (June 2000): 961-967; Juan A. Espinosa and Barry K. Goodwin, "Hedonic Price Estimation for Kansas Wheat Characteristics," *Western Journal of Agricultural Economics* 16, no. 1 (July 1991): 72-85; Griliches, "Hedonic Price Indexes of Automobiles"; J. Shannon Neibergs, "A Hedonic Price Analysis of Thoroughbred Broodmare Characteristics," *Agribusiness* 17, no. 2 (Spring 2001): 299-314; and Phil Simmons and Phillip Hansen, "The Effect of Buyer Concentration on Prices in the Australian Wool Market," *Agribusiness* 13, no. 4 (July-August 1997): 423-430.

[7] See, e.g., Jeff Anstine, "Consumers' Willingness to Pay for Recycled Content in Plastic Garbage Bags: A Hedonic Price Approach: Erratum," *Applied Economics Letters* 7, no. 5 (May 2000): 347; Ernst R. Berndt, Robert S. Pindyck, and Pierre Azoulay, "Consumption Externalities and Diffusion in Pharmaceutical Markets: Antiulcer Drugs," *Journal of Industrial Economics* 51, no. 2 (June 2003): 243-270; Frederick C. Dunbar and Joyce S. Mehring, "Coal Rail Prices during Deregulation: A Hedonic Price Analysis," *Logistics and Transportation Review* 26, no. 1 (March 1990): 17-34; Alison P. Hagy, "The Demand for Child Care Quality: An Hedonic Price Theory Approach," *Journal of Human Resources* 33, no. 3 (Summer 1998): 683-710; Gail A. Jensen and Michael A. Morrisey, "Group Health Insurance: A Hedonic Price Approach," *Review of Economics and Statistics* 72, no. 1 (February 1990): 38-44; Marilena Locatelli-Biey and Roberto Zanola, "The Sculpture Market: An Adjacent Year Regression Index," *Journal of Cultural Economics* 26, no. 1 (February 2002): 65-78; Linda R. Stanley and John Tschirhart, "Hedonic Prices for a Nondurable Good: The Case of Breakfast Cereals," *Review of Economics and Statistics* 73, no. 3 (August 1991): 537-541; R. S. Thompson, "Product Differentiation in the Newspaper Industry: An Hedonic Price Approach," *Applied Economics* 20, no. 3 (March 1988): 367-376; and Z. Wang, "Hedonic Prices for Crude Oil," *Applied Economics Letters* 10, no. 13 (October 2003): 857-861.

ber of product attributes. Each firm in the market offers more than one model, but all the models sold by Firm A include a product feature that allows them to be voice-activated. No other firm offers voice activation as none have devised a means of providing voice activation that would not infringe Firm A's patent.

Given the complex array of characteristics across products, including brand and the life-cycle stage of the product, it is not possible to calculate the premium associated with voice activation by direct comparison of two products' prices. So a regression model that includes all of the important product characteristics needs to be specified, which, for this purpose, is assumed to be linear:

$$p_i = \alpha + \beta_1 V_i + \Sigma_{j \neq 1} \beta_j z_{ij} + \varepsilon_i,$$

where i indexes over n transactions, j indexes over the m product characteristics, p is the complete product price and dependent variable, V is a variable that indicates the presence of the voice activation characteristic, β_j is the regression coefficient representing the implicit price of the jth characteristic, the ε_i are unobserved random factors, and $m < n$. When voice activation is present in a product i, the value of V_i is equal to one and β_1 is included in the product price p_i. When the voice activation feature is not present and does not contribute to the complete product price, the value of V_i is zero and β_1 is not added into the complete product price.

Using transactional sales data for the prices of each model of product and engineering data and product descriptions to construct the product characteristic variables, the regression coefficients can be econometrically estimated. The variation in the complex array of product characteristics across models provides the variation required to measure the contributions of the product characteristics to the product price. One does need to ensure though that there are more transactions than there are product characteristics whose contributions we are trying to measures (i.e., n must be greater than m in the example above).

Suppose we ran the regression described above on 500 observations of (hypothetical) sales transactions for the electronic device and obtained the following results:

$$p = 1.25 + 0.50\ V + ...,$$

The regression results show that the coefficient on the dummy variable for the presence of voice activation, controlling for all other factors influencing price, is statistically significant and equal to 0.50. This would imply that the implicit price of the voice activation feature is $0.50.[8] If we put ourselves in the place of a prospective licensee that has estimated the incremental costs of voice activation at $0.10, we would approach the negotiation with a maximum willingness to pay of $0.40 per unit in royalties.

Discrete Choice Models

Discrete choice models can be viewed as coming at the issue of the valuation of intellectual property at a somewhat different angle. Unlike hedonic price regressions, where the dependent variable (price) is the result of the interaction of both supply and demand, discrete choice models focus on the demand side—consumer demand for products and their attributes.[9] Discrete choice models can be used to measure consumers' willingness to pay for product attributes. The dependent variable in a discrete choice model is the consumer's choice regarding purchase from among a number of alternative products. The coefficients in a discrete choice model are measures of the influence of the product characteristics on the probability that the consumer will choose to purchase a given product.

Using the econometric estimates from the model, one can calculate the difference in demand for the product in question with and without the characteristic in question. This yields a measure of the consumer demand for the product characteristic of interest. From the demand, one can determine how much consumers are willing to pay for the product characteristic.

An important difference in working with an estimate of the willingness to pay rather than the price premium is that the factors of supply have to be separately accounted for in the analysis. In other words, the results of the model show only the willingness of consumers to pay, and not what the marginal consumer is paying in equilibrium. If one were

---

[8] If, instead, one assumes that the correct specification were log-linear (i.e., the dependent variable were the logarithm of price instead of price), a regression coefficient of 0.50 would imply that the inclusion of voice activation leads to an increase in the base price, using the average value of the other explanatory variables, of 50 percent. The estimated coefficient of 0.50 is an approximation and is more precisely interpreted as a change of $e^\beta - 1$, or 64, percent.

[9] Again, we might represent our starting point with a basic relationship, different from the one above, i.e., $P(z) = P(z_1, z_2,..., z_m)$, where P is the probability of choice and z is a vector of m product characteristics. However, because we are now attempting to explain a probability rather than a price, and probabilities are bounded by zero and one, we would employ a discrete choice model, e.g., logit. For more details, see Train, *Discrete Choice Methods with Simulation*.

willing to assume that the supply of the product characteristic is perfectly inelastic, then one might be able to interpret the willingness to pay as the implicit price for the product.

The data required for a discrete choice model can be obtained from information on the actual purchasing decisions of consumers. The data can also be obtained from choice experiments presented to consumers as part of a properly designed survey. In some cases, survey data and transactional data, along with engineering and other descriptive data, might be combined in a process of data enrichment.

In a consumer choice survey, the respondents are presented with a number of alternatives, each with a price and a description of the product (or service) characteristics. The alternatives could include a "no buy" option. The respondent is then asked to indicate which of the alternatives is preferred. Using a variety of price and product characteristics provides the variation needed to identify the marginal utility of each attribute. Consumer willingness to pay can be determined from these results.

As with the hedonic price regression, a product's characteristics should be considered in the broadest sense as those characteristics likely to influence the price or choice of consumers. A study of housing value may, therefore, include characteristics relating to the structure and the lot, as well as to the location of the house and the associated schools and community amenities. Similarly, a study of wine or cigars may include not only characteristics about the vintages or tobaccos used, but also how these products have been rated by perceived authorities.

Application of Discrete Choice Models: Market Growth in Medical Devices

Discrete choice models have been used in a variety of market contexts. Models based on actual transactions data are necessarily restricted to evaluation of products already on the market. Models based on choice experiment data can be used to forecast the demand for products not yet on the market, such as soon-to-be-introduced automobile models.[10]

For purposes of illustration, consider the following example. Suppose that a firm called Medical Instruments (MI) has a fundamental, or pioneer, patent for a particular kind of medical device useful in

---

[10] For examples, see the references in Jordan J. Louviere, David A. Hensher, and Joffre D. Swait, *Stated Choice Methods: Analysis and Application* (Cambridge, MA: Cambridge University Press, 2004).

the treatment of cardiovascular disease.[11] It is estimated that the number of Americans with cardiovascular disease is approximately 64 million. This particular device is flexible enough to navigate a substantial portion of the human circulatory system to reach and treat diseased areas. During the first year on the market, MI sales increase rapidly and quickly reach into the millions.

About one year after the release of the MI device, a research laboratory, Young & Efficacious Research (YER), develops a similar device, but one that has greater flexibility. The YER product increased flexibility by one unit measured in terms of the angle to which the device would bend under pressure typical of that experienced with ordinary use. The new technology, enabling the increased flexibility, is granted a patent by the United States Patent and Trademark Office. However, while innovative, the new device appears, to MI, to be infringing its earlier patent.

Assuming that MI is correct, the likely outcomes are either that (1) YER will take a license from MI, or (2) MI will receive a favorable judgment against YER including damages for patent infringement and an injunction barring further unlicensed sales. However, YER's participation in the market presents an interesting problem. Some of YER's sales are competitive with MI and could have been made "based on" MI technology alone. Other of YER's sales can be said to be "based on" YER technology, as, although based on the combined technologies, they are not possible without the YER improvement.

The proportion of sales that fall into these two classes can have important implications for the negotiation and litigation. The former set of sales represents lost sales to MI, and thereby both provide the basis for estimating lost profit damages and set a lower bound on the royalties that MI would willingly accept in a licensing agreement. The latter set of sales represents profit opportunities that YER and MI can only realize cooperatively and would somehow divide between themselves. The total profits to YER on both types of sales represent YER's maximum total royalties that YER would willingly pay. MI's expected damages are likely smaller and its bargaining position weaker, all else equal, the greater the proportion of YER's sales that come from market expansion. Therefore, in the course of license negotiations, either before or after a lawsuit has been

---

[11] *Merck & Co. Inc. v. Teva Pharmaceuticals USA Inc.*, United States Court of Appeals for the Federal Circuit 04-1005 (decided 28 January 2005), contains what might be a similar situation where the issues related to validity and commercial success. There the apparent cause of the growth in the market was a patented dosage regime.

filed, or in the course of preparing damage calculations, both parties must address the source of YER's sales and ask, "Are those sales based on MI technology or YER technology?"

A more flexible device can be easier to use and may, therefore, be more widely adopted by physicians or surgeons. Such a device may become less the domain of specialists who see large numbers of patients with a given medical condition. Of course, a more flexible device may also be delivered to a greater proportion of the circulatory system.

The probability that a doctor will choose the YER device for a given patient might be expressed as follows:

$$Pr(YER) = \frac{e^{\beta_1 * t + \beta_2 * F_{YER} + \sum_{i\ 2}^{n} \beta_1 * X_{1,\ YER}}}{e^{\beta_1 * t + \beta_2 * F_{YER} + \sum_{i\ 2}^{n} \beta_1 * X_{1,\ YER}} + e^{\beta_1 * t + \beta_2 * F_{MI} + \sum_{i\ 2}^{n} \beta_1 * X_{1,\ MI}} + e^{\alpha + \beta_1 * t}},$$

where F is the measure of flexibility of each firm's product (MI or YER) and α is a constant that is representative of the "no buy" alternative.[12] The model is also a function of time, which might be thought of as controlling for the general level of experience and familiarity with the device that might also contribute to market expansion.

The results of our estimation indicate, as we might expect, that the probability of choosing a device increases as the flexibility of the device increases, all else being equal. In addition, the results provide the means to estimate the fraction of YER's sales that was derived from competition with MI and the fraction that was derived by market expansion as a result of the increased flexibility. One can calculate the marginal effect on the probability of choosing YER by taking the derivative of the probability formula with respect to flexibility and evaluating the result using the estimated coefficients; however, for the purposes of this illustration, it might be more helpful to consider the following approach of alternative forecasts. Each forecast is of the probability of choosing YER's product, which is then multiplied by the market size of 64 million, the number of Americans with cardiovascular disease, to estimate sales. In the first forecast, the values used for the independent variables are the actual data we observed. In the second, the same values are used except that the value of flexibility is limited to that of the MI product. The difference in these forecasts is then the estimate of the sales derived by market expansion.

---

12 The probabilities of the other alternatives can be expressed similarly.

The probability of choosing the YER product is derived from two sources: a reduction in the probability of the MI product being selected and a reduction in the probability of a "no buy" decision. The probability drawn from MI represents competition and the probability drawn from the "no buy" decision represents market expansion, controlling for other factors including those that could contribute to market expansion apart from the increase in flexibility. Moreover, one has a measure of the incremental contribution made by YER's enhancement of the product that is probative in licensing contexts, including those of the hypothetical license negotiations in *Georgia-Pacific*.[13]

Conclusion

Hedonic regression and discrete choice modeling offer powerful tools for valuing patented features of products in and out of a litigation context. These techniques can provide keen insights into questions of the value of intellectual property and the damages from an alleged infringement of intellectual property. Moreover, with the increasing prevalence of electronic records of transactions, the potential for using these tools and types of analyses is also expanding to cover a broad range of industries.

---

[13] *Georgia-Pacific Corp. v. United States Plywood Corp.*, 318 F. Supp. 1116, 166 U.S.P.Q. (BNA) 235 (S.D.N.Y. 1970).

10

The Use of Event Studies in Intellectual Property Litigation

John H. Johnson and Vinita M. Juneja

An event study is an econometric technique used to measure the impact of a particular event or news item on a company's stock price. Economists use event studies to quantify the effect on a company's value from a particular occurrence, such as a negative earnings announcement, a mass lay-off, or the passage of new legislation. In intellectual property litigation, event study methodology can be used to measure damages to firms that have been harmed by false patent infringement allegations. If an accuser's patent is truly invalid, then the liability phase of the litigation should provide an opportunity to demonstrate that the case should be dismissed. In certain cases, however, the defendant company may have been harmed by the mere allegation of infringement, and dismissal of the case alone will not compensate the defendant for that harm.[1] Event studies have also been used to measure lost profits in breach-of-contract cases, cases regarding failure to comply with licensing agreements, and cases involving the theft of trade secrets.

Event studies can be valuable in litigation for many reasons, including their reliance on testable hypotheses, their known measures of significance and error rates, and the existence of objective standards for their application and use.[2] Of course, event studies that are poorly constructed,

---

[1] Note that this is a different type of counterclaim than the attempted monopolization of a market, where the plaintiff's direct actions in the marketplace (versus the mere allegations themselves) are said to cause harm. The type of claim discussed here is more akin to a libel claim, and the ensuing damage is a financial damage that arises from a loss of reputation.

[2] David Tabak and Frederick Dunbar, "Materiality and Magnitude: Event Studies in the Courtroom," in *Litigation Services Handbook: The Role of the Financial Expert,* 3d ed., Roman L. Weil, Michael J. Wagner, and Peter B. Frank (New York: John Wiley & Sons, 2001), 19.1-19.22.

applied in an inappropriate setting, or otherwise do not meet *Daubert* standards may still be rejected by a court. Thus, parties in intellectual property litigation need to be familiar with the event study technique and its benefits and shortcomings.

A Hypothetical Example: The Case of GenPlus Corporation

The concept of an event study and its potential benefits or shortcomings can best be illustrated by means of a hypothetical example. Suppose "GenPlus" is a privately held biotechnology company with talented scientists on the cutting edge of genetic research. GenPlus's research appears extremely promising, but the company needs to raise $60 million in equity funding to cover the expense of the research and development required to bring additional products to market. It files a registration statement with the Security Exchange Commission (SEC) on 1 January 2004, and its investment bankers advise the company to offer three million shares at a price of $20 per share.[3] GenPlus begins the process of meeting with potential investors and stock analysts to try to drum up interest and gauge investor sentiment. A date for the initial public offering (IPO) is set for March.

On 31 January 2004, MegaBloc, GenPlus's archrival, puts out a press release summarizing an analyst report strongly touting the value of MegaBloc's forthcoming patent infringement claim against GenPlus. The press release fails to mention that MegaBloc's former CEO, a biotech analyst, authored the analyst report. GenPlus believes that the technologies listed in the press release are actually only marginally related to and not infringed by their own products. MegaBloc's press release is the first real publicity that the patent infringement claim has received, and GenPlus believes that MegaBloc intentionally timed the release to interfere with the pending IPO. Trial on MegaBloc's infringement claim is set for August 2004.

On 31 March 2004, GenPlus conducts its IPO of 3 million shares but is able to achieve only $10 a share, raising $30 million in the process, well below the expected $60 million. Figure 1 shows the expected IPO target and anticipated range from January 2004 to the time of the offering and GenPlus's actual stock price from March 2004 through December 2004.

In August 2004, the court dismisses MegaBloc's patent infringement claim. GenPlus decides to file a counterclaim against MegaBloc alleging that GenPlus has been materially harmed by MegaBloc's false patent

---

3   The target range for the IPO is between $18 and $22 per share.

Figure 1. GenPlus IPO Price is Less than Expected

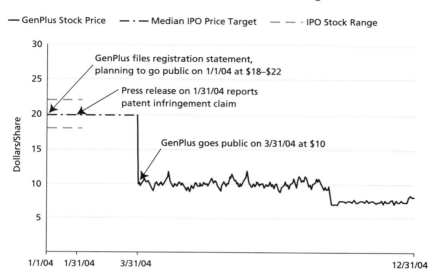

infringement allegations and that GenPlus would have raised much more money from its IPO absent the press release.[4] MegaBloc, in response, argues that March was a terrible month for biotech stocks and the GenPlus IPO was poorly timed.

If MegaBloc's actions indeed reduced the value of GenPlus's IPO, we expect to see a reduction in GenPlus's stock price from what it would have been absent the negative press release. To estimate the but-for price of GenPlus stock, we must take into account other factors that influenced the entire stock market, similar companies, and GenPlus itself to isolate the decline in GenPlus's stock due to the press release from any potential decline due to other factors. An event study can be used in this context to assess both the materiality of MegaBloc's actions and the damages to which GenPlus would be entitled if any injury occurred.

The Event Study Methodology

The goal of the event study is twofold: to determine whether or not the event of interest had a "material" (important) effect on the stock price,

---

4　To be explicit, any recovery for losses due to an initial public offering would be made by the private owners of the company. In our stylized example, we are assuming these private owners are reinvesting their earnings from the IPO into the company.

and, if such an effect existed, to determine its magnitude.[5] An event is considered to be material if it "in reasonable and objective contemplation might affect the value" of a security.[6] In most circumstances, a material event is expected to cause a statistically significant change in stock price. The usefulness of the event study methodology is that it provides a mechanism by which we can both test whether a given event had a material effect on stock price and determine the size of the effect.

An event study can be implemented in three steps: (1) define the event window, (2) model the normal returns, i.e., the daily stock price returns in a counterfactual world where no adverse event occurred, and (3) calculate the excess returns and damages for the event, i.e., the difference between the modeled normal returns and the actual returns over a given time period.[7]

Defining the Event Window

Formally, the *event window* is the time period economists analyze in an event study; it includes the event of interest and continues through the period in which the stock market would be expected to react to the event. In our hypothetical example, there is a well-defined event of interest— the issuing of the negative analyst report sponsored by MegaBloc's former CEO and the subsequent GenPlus IPO. The more concretely the event can be tied to a specific date, the more straightforward it is to isolate the true effect of the event and control for the effects other factors. The most frequently used event windows are: (1) the day of the event (if the event occurred during trading hours), (2) the day following the event, and (3) several days around or after the event. The circumstances of each individual case dictate the appropriate event window.

In our hypothetical example, the only sensible choice for the event window is the period from the day when GenPlus filed registration with SEC to the day of the IPO. It is therefore reasonable to look for effects on the stock price after the release of the MegaBloc report. However, it is not hard to imagine that if we defined our event window too broadly (e.g., three years subsequent to the MegaBloc report), it would seem much less

---

5   Tabak and Dunbar provide a description of materiality and magnitude in event studies. See Tabak and Dunbar, "Materiality and Magnitude."
6   See *TSC Industries Inc. v. Northway Inc.*, 426 U.S. 438 (1976).
7   The event study technique is frequently used in economics and finance. See, for example, A. Craig MacKinlay, "Event Studies in Economics and Finance," *Journal of Economic Literature* 35 (March 1997): 13-39. The calculation of daily excess returns is usually cumulated to derive a cumulative excess return over several days.

credible that observed movements in the stock price were causally related to the report touting the patent infringement suit.[8]

Modeling Stock Price Returns

Having defined an event window, we turn to the question of developing a statistical model that can predict what GenPlus's stock price would have been absent the negative press release from MegaBloc. For this purpose, we need to choose what is called the *estimation window,* which is the time period used to model the behavior of GenPlus's stock price. During this time period, we estimate the effects of the important factors that influence GenPlus's stock price unrelated to the press release. It is important to account for other events that caused changes in investors' valuations of the stock, possibly including any events that affect the market as a whole (such as macroeconomic policy shifts) or GenPlus's industry as a whole (such as a shift in the laws affecting genetic research), as well as any company-specific news (such as a change in GenPlus's estimated long-term earnings).

Traditionally, economists choose a period prior to the event at issue as the estimation window. In our example, we face the confounding fact that we have no pre-event data because GenPlus had no stock price history before the IPO. In situations with insufficient data prior to the first event or if there are multiple events, economists must find some other benchmark period from which to determine the relationship between stock price and other economic variables. For our example, we can use a period after the IPO. We then need to determine whether the press release at issue caused a permanent change in the stock's relationship with the market and industry.[9] This concern can be addressed by com-

---

[8] Our hypothetical example is slightly different than the standard event study in which the event of interest would directly tie in to the negative act alleged and the company would already be trading publicly prior to the event date. If we were studying the effects of a negative event on a stock price, we would choose the event window to be the period directly around the event. For example, suppose one wanted to know the impact of a preliminary injunction barring a company from using the patented technology of one of its competitors; in that circumstance, the event window likely would be centered around the date of the injunction. Patent infringement claims can also be brought by a competitor after the falsely accused infringer was already publicly traded and was in the process of a secondary offering of equity. The situation is more straightforward in that the event study can be done by looking at the impact of the allegedly false statement on the existing trading price of the falsely accused infringer's stock.

[9] One example of such a permanent change would be if the effect of the press release on the IPO price permanently caused a change in the beta of the stock price, that is the relationship between the GenPlus stock returns and the general stock market returns.

paring the model estimated over the chosen time period with models estimated over other time periods for GenPlus or with models of other similar companies over the same time period. If the parameters using a period after the event are similar to parameters estimated over other time periods or for other companies, it would appear that the press release did not cause a permanent change in the stock's relationships. In choosing a period that encompasses the event, a similar concern is that company-specific events may influence the estimation of the market model. To solve this problem, the dates of and around company-specific news events can be excluded from the event study.

In our example, we use the period from 1 August 2004 through 31 December 2004 as our estimation window.[10] The advantage of this estimation window is that it is not too far removed from the events at issue but far enough that the uncertainty created by the MegaBloc claim has been resolved. Figure 2 shows GenPlus's stock price movements between 1 August 2004 and 31 December 2004.

When we have determined the appropriate estimation window, we need to model GenPlus's stock price returns during this period. Several models can be used to predict stock price returns, and the most common ones are the *constant mean return model,* the *stock market index model,* and the *market model* (also known as the *multivariate regression model*). The constant mean return model simply assumes that the average daily return on the stock price would have been constant over time absent the MegaBloc press release. In our GenPlus event study, we would take the average stock return over the estimation window as the indicator of the stock price in the but-for world. The advantage of the constant mean return model is its simplicity, but this approach does not attempt to model the effects of any factor on the stock price during the estimation window and thus does not allow us to fully use all of the information available to us.

A more sophisticated approach, the stock market index model, looks at the relationship between a stock and a market index to predict how that stock would have performed in the but-for world. In our example, we would look at GenPlus's relationship with the market (as proxied by using

---

10 As a practical matter, we can test various estimation windows as a robustness check on our results. The trade-off the economist must make is between longer windows that may capture more information and shorter windows in which the parameters of the models are less likely to change. Estimation windows are typically three months to a year in duration, but again, the circumstances of a specific case will dictate the appropriate choice.

Figure 2. GenPlus Stock Price Moves with S&P 500 and Biotech Index

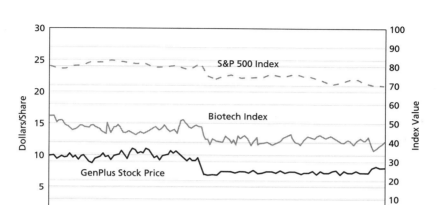

an index such as Dow Jones Industrial Average or the Standard and Poor's 500) during our estimation window. Figure 2 illustrates the statistical relationship between GenPlus's stock price ($P_{GENPLUS}$) and the S&P 500 (P_{SP500}). The statistical model underlying this relationship specifies the daily percentage change in GenPlus's stock price as a linear function of the percentage change in the market index:

Percent Change in   = $\alpha + \beta$ x Percent Change + ε
Price of GenPlus   in S&P 500

where α (alpha) is a constant that reflects the underlying trend in GenPlus's stock price and β (beta) measures how GenPlus's stock moves on average when the market moves.[11] So if the market index increases by 10 percent, and on average that is accompanied by the stock price of GenPlus increasing by 10 percent, the value of the beta is 1. If when the market goes up by 10 percent we typically observe that GenPlus stock goes up by 20 percent, the beta is 2. Of course, GenPlus will not be per-

---

[11] Common specifications for stock price returns are either the percentage change in the stock price or the difference between the natural log of stock price at time t and the natural log of stock price at time *t-1*; both specifications would also typically adjust for dividends, if any were paid.

fectly predicted by the movements in the market index, and the unexplained variation in GenPlus's stock prices is ε (epsilon), or the error term.

Although the stock market index model provides an improvement over the simple constant mean return model, we have additional information available to incorporate into our model of GenPlus's stock price that requires more sophistical statistical analysis. Economists call this more refined version of the stock market model the *multivariate regression model*. It incorporates not just the effects of movements in the overall stock market but the effects of other explanatory factors as well. For example, broad trends in the biotech industry could provide an important context for understanding GenPlus's stock price performance (not to mention MegaBloc's main defense that March was a bad month for biotech stocks). We can control for such trends by including an index of biotech companies.[12] This modification to the model helps us answer the question of how GenPlus performs relative to other similar biotech companies. Thus, our refined market model controls for both stock market movements and biotech industry trends:

$$\begin{array}{l}\text{Percent Change in} \\ \text{Price of GenPlus}\end{array} = \alpha + \beta \times \begin{array}{l}\text{Percent Change} \\ \text{in S\&P 500}\end{array} + \gamma \times \begin{array}{l}\text{Percent Change} \\ \text{in Industry Index}\end{array} + \varepsilon$$

The gamma (γ) is the historical relationship between GenPlus and other biotech companies. Although for our hypothetical example we will use this model, the approach is extremely flexible in accommodating additional control variables. We can control for a variety of factors that may be relevant and statistically test their importance. We can also control for other events that may have had a one-time effect on a stock price (for example, the approval of a new drug by the FDA) through the inclusion of additional time-specific indicator variables.

Estimating the Model

To estimate the parameters of our model, we must first collect the necessary data. Figure 2 shows GenPlus's stock prices, the S&P 500 stock index, and a biotech industry index in the estimation window.

We run a regression using the data in our estimation window, 1 August 2004 through 31 December 2004. The results of this regression can be used to predict what prices would have been at the time of the IPO

---

[12] The index should, of course, exclude GenPlus.

Figure 3. GenPlus Stock Price Has No Time Trend

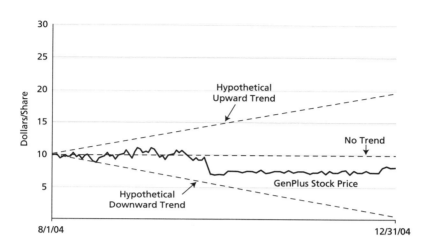

had MegaBloc not issued its press release. When we run this regression model, we get the following equation:

Percent Change in   = 1.0 x Percent Change   + 0.5 x Percent Change + ε
Price of GenPlus   in S&P 500   in Industry Index

That is, GenPlus's stock price tends to move by the same amount as over-all market movements, but only by half as much as movements in the biotech industry. To explain this model, it is helpful to look at graphs of GenPlus's stock price compared to each explanatory factor in the model. In Figure 3, we note that from August through December of 2004, GenPlus has no price trend—throughout the estimation window, the price of GenPlus's stock is fairly stable, both visibly as graphed and statistically as estimated in the equation. This trend is captured in our regression equation by the alpha term, which equals zero.[13] Figure 2 shows GenPlus's historic relationship with the S&P 500. Our regression results confirm what we observe in the graph: GenPlus's stock historically moves very closely with the market. In our regression equation, the estimated coefficient on the S&P 500 index variable (beta) is not statistically significantly different

---

[13] Figure 3 also illustrates the hypothetical situation in which GenPlus's stock price would have a positive price trend or a negative price trend.

from 1. Figure 2 also depicts the relationship between GenPlus's stock price and the biotechnology index of other biotech drug-discovery company stocks.

As the graph displays, biotech stocks and GenPlus's stock generally moved together. Our regression estimate implies that when the biotech index went up by about 10 percent, GenPlus's stock price typically went up by 5 percent.[14] Note though, that while we have discussed each factor in the model separately, the regression model estimates the relationships simultaneously. Therefore each of the coefficients (α, β, and γ) must be interpreted as the effect of a given variable holding constant the other variables.

Calculating Excess Returns and Damages

Having determined a baseline relationship for GenPlus's stock price, we now look at data around the event window on the performance of the S&P 500 and the biotech indexes. We use these data and our regression equation to predict for each date in the event window what the anticipated price of GenPlus's stock should have been absent MegaBloc's issuing the press release. Since GenPlus was not publicly traded, we use the projected $20 IPO price as the company's initial stock price on 1 January 2004, which is the date on which GenPlus's investment bankers advised them to make the offering at $20. The refined market model coefficients are used to estimate what the ensuing series of prices would have been for GenPlus absent any company-specific events.

As shown in Figure 4, in early March 2004, the market was flat, so the overall market did not contribute significantly to the reduction in the stock price of GenPlus. Looking more specifically at the biotechnology industry, MegaBloc asserted that GenPlus's IPO was badly timed because of the poor performance of biotech stocks in general in that quarter. In fact, looking at the contemporaneous data in Figure 5, we observe that our hypothetical index of biotech stocks dipped by 25 percent over this time period.

Does that mean that we can attribute $5 of the drop from $20 to $10 to trends in biotechnology and not due to MegaBloc? Figure 6, which shows the relationship between GenPlus's stock price and the biotechnol-

---

[14] Given the unique nature of the biotech research conducted by GenPlus and the greater firm-specific volatility in the biotech industry more broadly, it is not unusual to expect that GenPlus's stock moves more closely with the market than with the biotech industry.

Figure 4. Stock Market Movements Do Not Explain GenPlus's Change in IPO Price

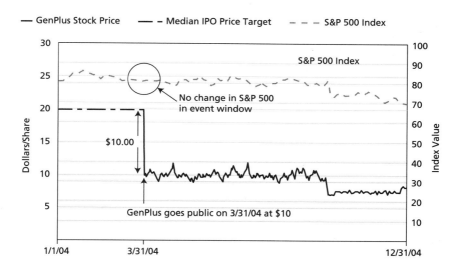

Figure 5. Biotech Stocks Fell by 25% from 1/1/04 to 3/31/04

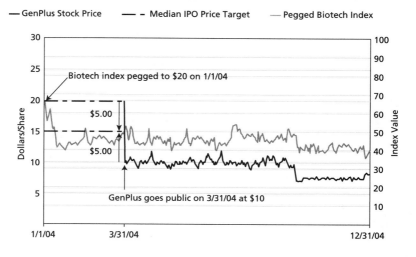

Figure 6. Industry Movements Explain Only $2.50 of the Decline in Stock Price

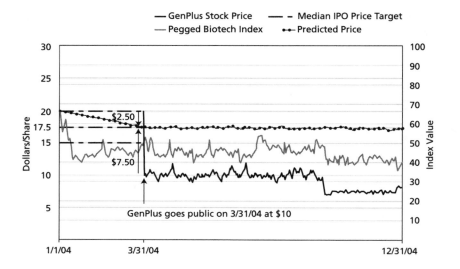

ogy industry index, and our regression result demonstrates that GenPlus's stock only moves by half as much as the industry. Thus, the 25 percent drop in biotech stocks generally would imply a drop of about 0.5 x 25 percent, or 12.5 percent, in the GenPlus stock.

By taking into account overall movements in the market and movements in other biotech stocks, we can account for $2.50 of the $10 drop in the GenPlus offering price. Put another way, we would have predicted an offering price of $17.50 given these other factors. The remaining $7.50 of the decline from $20 to $10 is known as the (negative) excess return.

No statistical model can perfectly predict stock prices, which is what the error term (epsilon) reflects. The error term reveals the variation in GenPlus's stock price that is unexplained by our model. The model not only provides a single-point estimate of $17.50, but also a range (or confidence interval) that allows us to estimate the probability that the difference between the observed price and the model's prediction is due to random variation or, alternatively, to a systematic phenomenon. We thus can construct a confidence interval, which predicts the range within which prices are likely to fall, given the company's own trend, the market, and the industry stock index movements.

Figure 7. GenPlus's Change in IPO Price Indicates the Megablock Claim is Material

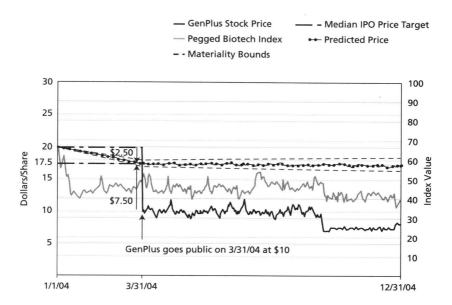

Economists traditionally use a 95 percent level of confidence in forming confidence intervals. If we used market models to form confidence intervals for 100 different days of GenPlus's stock price, and there were no systematic phenomena affecting the price on those days, we would expect the confidence intervals for 95 of the 100 days would contain the price actually observed. Therefore, if for a given day, the observed price falls outside of the 95 percent confidence interval, it is such an unusual event that we conclude that news on that day relating to GenPlus likely caused investors to reevaluate the stock. In other words, the news had a statistically significant or material effect.[15] As illustrated in Figure 7, the confidence interval in our example starts out with a band of $0.50 per share on 31 March 2004, meaning that we are 95 percent confident that the GenPlus price would lie between $17.00 and $18.00 on that day absent the press release. Given that the IPO price of $10 is far outside the confidence inter-

---

[15] A simple method for implementing this event study methodology is to run a single regression that includes both the estimation window and the event window, with indicator variables for each day in the event window. The coefficients on the event window indicator variables will provide the estimate of the event's effect, and the standard error on the coefficients can be used to derive the confidence interval.

val, we conclude with high confidence that the press release had a material negative effect on GenPlus's stock price.

To calculate damages, we must derive the excess return due to the event after excluding the effect of other factors. Using our statistical model, we estimate that $7.50 of the $10 decline in GenPlus's IPO offering price was due to the MegaBloc press release as opposed to other factors. Multiplying $7.50 by the 3 million shares offered equals $22.5 million in damages. Given the confidence interval range of plus or minus $0.50 per share, we are confident that damages are between $21 million and $24 million.

For robustness checks, we ensure that no other negative news about the company came out during the period, and we look at the performance of other contemporaneous IPO offerings.[16] Some biotech IPOs announced in January did go public at less than their initially announced price, but many went at higher-than-announced prices. On average, in our hypothetical world, biotech IPOs announced in January 2004 went public at prices 10 percent lower than originally anticipated. This fact is consistent with our estimate using our statistical model that $7.50 per share of the decline in GenPlus's IPO was due only to the MegaBloc press release.

Possible Misuse of Event Studies

Care must be taken when using event studies. To illustrate some potential difficulties that can arise if event studies are applied improperly, we describe a recent case in which a plaintiff claimed that the defendant did not fulfill its obligations in a licensing agreement. The plaintiff's economist calculated lost profits damages based on an event study of the price impact to its stock during the year following poor earnings announcements for the plaintiff. In doing so, the entire effect of the negative earnings announcement was attributed to the alleged failure by the defendants to meet their obligations in the licensing deal. In this context, the event study results were potentially misleading for several reasons.

First, the plaintiff's poor earnings were due to many reasons, including factors specific to their production techniques. For example, the company's factories had been shut down for violations of various health and safety standards. The defendant had no involvement with these violations. Any methodology to calculate lost profits would need to account

---

[16] Robustness checks include any additional modifications to the basic model or additional information that can be used to show that the results are consistent with known facts and invariant to small changes in the model.

for the effects of these production shutdowns in order to separate them from the effects of the breach of the licensing deal.

Second, the defendant's breach of the licensing agreement was known to the stock market prior to the plaintiff's poor earnings announcement. As a result, any market response to the breach of the licensing agreement likely occurred prior to the earning announcement and the plaintiff's stock price likely already reflected that information.

Third, many other events that affected the plaintiff's stock valuation occurred during the year following its poor earnings announcement. These events were unrelated to the defendant's alleged breach of the licensing agreement. For example, the plaintiff sustained a fire at one of its plants. Not only were these subsequent events unrelated to the defendant's alleged harmful actions, but they were also not market- or industry-related. As a result, the simple market model presented in this circumstance could not control for these other events and their impact was therefore (incorrectly) attributed to the defendant's actions, leading to an overstatement of lost profits.

In other situations, event studies conducted with care can be used to measure lost profits by examining a company's loss in equity value at the time that certain news was released. In performing the event study, however, one must control for the impact of unrelated events on the stock price. One should limit the study's event window so that the impact is not tainted by other events and remove the impact of unrelated events that do occur during the window. Typically, one should begin an event window at the point when the news of interest first is revealed to the market.

Conclusion

The event study methodology provides a powerful set of scientific tools for the estimation of damages when a company's value may have been affected by a negative event or events. There is a range of harmful acts—such as false infringement claims, preliminary injunctions, and misrepresentations of technology—for which this methodology may provide insight. Our example is meant to introduce how the basic event study methodology might be used in the context of intellectual property where tangible measures of damages may be difficult to derive using other methodologies. We also note that the event study technique can be misused and that care must be taken in its application. Done poorly, event studies can be highly misleading. Done with care, they can be used as a credible, scientific approach to damage estimation in intellectual property litigation.

11

Interest and Discount Rates in Intellectual Property Damages

Jesse David and Christine Meyer

Both the calculation of damages and the actual payment of compensation to harmed parties almost always occur long after the wrongful acts that caused the damage. In addition, while the wrongful acts may have occurred in the distant past, harm from those acts may extend well beyond the date of trial. As a result, methods to account for the time value of money and the risk associated with future cash flows are critical to making injured parties whole. Interest rates and discount rates must therefore be used to bring damages forward or backward from the time they occur to the time of compensation. Damages that are expected to occur subsequent to compensation must be reduced to account for the time value of money and risk. Damages that occur prior to compensation must be increased to reflect the plaintiff's lost opportunity cost. In either case, the analysis that underlies the choice of the proper interest or discount rate centers on making the plaintiff whole. In other words, the proper interest rate is one that makes the plaintiff indifferent about receiving the damage amount when the harm actually occurred or receiving the compensation at the time it was actually paid. The general concept of an interest or discount rate is well understood by economists and courts. However, in practice, the choice of a rate can have a large impact on the magnitude of damages and is often subject to debate.

Adjusting Past Damages: Prejudgment Interest Rate
In any situation where there is a lag between the loss incurred by the plaintiff and compensation received from the defendant, prejudgment

The authors would like to thank Mark P. Berkman for his early contributions to the sections in this chapter pertaining to prejudgment interest.

interest serves as an integral part of damages. Interest is necessary to make the plaintiff whole—that is, to compensate the plaintiff for the foregone opportunity to earn a return on the funds lost due to the defendant's actions from the time of the event to the end of trial.

Although prejudgment interest is a relevant consideration in many business disputes and can represent a substantial component of damages, limited attention has been paid to what the appropriate interest rate should be. Moreover, there is disagreement among the few jurists and economists who have addressed the question at any length. For example, in some recent decisions, courts have called for a rate based on the defendant's cost of borrowing.[1] In contrast, economists Franklin Fisher and R. Craig Romaine, in a widely cited article, assert that a risk-free rate is correct.[2] Even if the defendant's borrowing cost approaches the prime rate— the rate offered to low-risk borrowers—the difference from the risk-free rate, generally defined as the Treasury-bill rate, can lead to a notable difference in the calculated damages. The average duration of a patent infringement case from filing to judgment is about 2.5 years. Over this length of time, interest on $1 million in damages at the current prime rate would yield $143,000 compared to $67,000 at the current (3-month) Treasury-bill rate. In cases resolved long after the initial wrongdoing, the choice of prejudgment interest rate can make a substantial difference even if the initial loss was small. One of the authors was involved in a dispute where the loss, valued at about $20,000 annually, began over 200 years prior to trial.[3] In this admittedly extreme case, relatively small differences in the prejudgment interest rates proposed by the parties were magnified into a difference of over $1 billion in the overall damage claim.

Outside of a few notable cases, the courts generally have not limited prejudgment interest to either the risk-free rate or the defendant's cost of debt. Some states have defined statutory fixed rates for cases tried in local jurisdictions.[4] Rates based on the plaintiff's or defendant's cost of

---

1   See, for example, *Cement Division, Natl. Gypsum Co., et al. v. City of Milwaukee*, 97-1349 (7th Cir. 1998); or *First National Bank v. Standard Bank*, 93-7234 (7th Cir. 1999).
2   Franklin M. Fisher and R. Craig Romaine, "Janis Joplin's Yearbook and the Theory of Damages," in *Industrial Organization, Economics, and the Law: Collected Papers of Franklin M. Fisher*, ed. John Monz (Cambridge, MA: MIT Press, 1991).
3   See *Cayuga Indian Nation of New York v. Pataki*, 165 F.Supp. 2d 266, 366 (N.D.N.Y. 2001).
4   See American Re Corp., "Post Judgment Interest, Prejudgment Interest, Punitive Damages: United States and Canada, 2001" (booklet), for a review of statutory rates imposed by states.

capital or cost of debt also have been used. The only general consensus regards the application of compound rather than simple interest.[5]

In light of this history, is there a theoretically sound method for determining the rate of prejudgment interest that should apply? The answer to this question depends on what one considers the purpose of prejudgment interest—that is, for which costs and risks borne by the plaintiff should prejudgment interest serve as compensation? It appears that most differences between practitioners stem from fundamental disagreements on this issue.

The Purpose of Prejudgment Interest

Economists and other practitioners who have written on the subject generally agree that the purpose of prejudgment interest is to compensate the plaintiff for its lost "opportunity cost." The theoretically sound method to account for this lost opportunity would be to award the plaintiff a lottery with the same expected return and distribution of outcomes as the assumed but-for investment. We are not aware that such an approach has ever been proposed in a commercial dispute. As an alternative, one must identify a single interest rate that serves as a proxy for the lost opportunity. The disagreement arises when one attempts to identify exactly what opportunity was lost. There have been two general approaches to this issue—each raising a number of fundamental questions.

The first approach considers the plaintiff's but-for use of the funds— that is, what it would have done if it actually had use of the money. The benefits of such use represent one potential measure of prejudgment interest. Important questions related to this approach include the following: Should one account for the return the plaintiff would have earned on a *particular* use of the money or, alternatively, on its *average* opportunity? In addition, how should one account for the risks associated with those lost opportunities, and which risks should be considered? Finally, how should one account for the possibility of mitigation?

An alternative method considers the plaintiff's "actual" losses. If one views the plaintiff-defendant relationship to be one of a lender and borrower, the loss is simply the interest that the defendant would have paid to the plaintiff had the relationship been made explicit as of the date of the initial bad act. Regarding this second approach, a number of other questions become important. Should prejudgment interest, for example,

---

[5] Id. A few states, however, have imposed simple interest for civil cases decided in state courts.

reflect the plaintiff's risk associated with the litigation outcome or the risk that the defendant may go bankrupt before trial concludes? Furthermore, should the analysis consider that the case in question is a one-time event, or should it treat the battle between plaintiffs and defendants as a repeated game and attempt to make the plaintiff whole, in some sense, on average?

Finally, in either case, an overarching question arises related to the purpose of prejudgment interest itself. Should prejudgment interest be designed exclusively with the objective of making the plaintiff whole, or should it attempt to eliminate the possibility that the defendant could benefit from its actions?

Potential Choices for the Prejudgment Interest Rate

Defendant's Debt Rate

The argument for the use of the defendant's debt rate stems from a view that a damages claim may be considered equivalent to a forced loan from the plaintiff to the defendant.[6] Under such circumstances, the plaintiff should be compensated for the defendant's risk of default. Since the defendant's debt rate reflects the market's assessment of this risk, it is the appropriate rate for this "loan" and should be the basis for prejudgment interest.

This approach, however, suffers from a number of limitations. First, even under the assumption that the forced-loan framework is valid, it is unlikely that an award of interest at the defendant's debt rate will make the plaintiff whole. There is no reason to believe that the plaintiff would have made such a loan or a loan of equivalent risk voluntarily.

A more fundamental problem arises when one considers the risk of default in the context of the broader set of risks associated with litigation. As pointed out by Fisher and Romaine, the plaintiff bears a number of other types of litigation risk, including the risk that it might lose its case, perhaps on appeal, even if the defendant did, in actuality, cause the loss.[7] The plaintiff also bears the risk that, due to its own financial constraints, it may be forced to settle a strong claim at less than fully com-

---

6   See for example, James M. Patell, Roman L. Weil, and Mark A. Wolfson, "Accumulating Damages in Litigation: The Roles of Uncertainty and Interest Rates," *The Journal of Legal Studies* 11, no. 2 (1982): 341-364; and Susan Escher and Kurt Kruger, "The Cost of Carry and Pre-Judgment Interest" *Litigation Economics Review* 6, no. 1.

7   Fisher and Romaine, "Janis Joplin's Yearbook."

pensating terms or drop the case and discontinue prosecution entirely. Damages experts usually operate under the assumptions that (1) the defendant, if truly at fault, will be found liable with certainty, (2) the court's decision will be correct and final, and (3) any judgment will be collected in full. They consequently do not account for such risks in their assessment of the appropriate compensation for the loss. We agree with Fisher and Romaine that there appears to be no reason to choose the risk of default as the only litigation risk that *should* be accounted for in an assessment of a make-whole award.

Plaintiff's Internal Rate of Return

Most practitioners take the approach that prejudgment interest should compensate the plaintiff for the foregone use of the lost funds (the but-for approach). The plaintiff's internal rate of return (IRR), measured as of the time of the harm caused by the defendant, reflects the company's realized return on its internal investments and might be viewed as an appropriate basis for determining the but-for income stream lost as a result of the defendant's actions. On careful reflection, however, one must recognize that this rate reflects the *average* return on all of the plaintiff's internal investments, including the most profitable opportunities, which, presumably, would have been undertaken regardless of whether the defendant had caused the harm that it did. The funds lost as a result of the defendant's actions only affect the plaintiff's *marginal* opportunities (unless, of course, the loss represented a substantial portion of the plaintiff's capital base). Furthermore, presumably the plaintiff had the opportunity to mitigate its loss by turning to the capital markets. Consequently, prejudgment interest levied at the plaintiff's IRR may overcompensate it for its lost use of the funds.[8]

Plaintiff's Debt Rate

When considering the possibility of mitigation, the plaintiff's debt rate is a natural first proposition as a measure of its opportunity cost.[9] This approach reflects the assumption that the plaintiff could have mitigated

---

[8] An additional problem with using the plaintiff's IRR for a calculation of prejudgment interest is that while this rate reflects the actual return on the company's investments historically, it may not represent an accurate estimate of the return on future investments.

[9] Courts have frequently adopted this approach, with the caveat that the plaintiff bears the burden of proving that it incurred borrowing costs that exceed the risk-free rate. See, for example, *Laitram Corp. v. NEC Corp.*, 115 F.3d 947, 955 (Fed. Cir. 1997).

its loss through the lowest-cost means available—by borrowing the same amount at its market rate for debt. Thus, by compensating it for the cost of borrowing, the plaintiff is arguably made whole. However, while a company's average cost of debt financing is usually lower than its average cost of equity financing, the marginal impact of increasing each type of financing on the company's overall capital costs must be equal, otherwise the company would alter its mix of debt and equity. Lenders determine their required return by assessing, among other things, the amount of equity capital invested in the firm. Consequently, a firm will not be able to increase its debt at its marginal borrowing rate without simultaneously increasing its collateral (equity), particularly if the amount required is large relative to existing levels of borrowing. In summary, the plaintiff's debt rate in isolation will generally not represent an appropriate measure of the opportunity cost borne by the plaintiff.

Plaintiff's Weighted Average Cost of Capital

A more appropriate assumption might be that the plaintiff could have mitigated by raising additional mixed (debt and equity) financing. Alternatively, the plaintiff could have used the lost funds to pay down debt or repurchase shares. Many damages experts employ this line of reasoning to justify use of the plaintiff's weighted average cost of capital (WACC), which represents the firm's average financing cost across both types of capital.[10]

However, as pointed out by Fisher and Romaine, the plaintiff wasn't just deprived of a return on the lost investment opportunity, it was also relieved of the risk associated with that investment.[11] The funds likely would have been invested in a project that would have generated a return other than the plaintiff's WACC, possibly even incurring a loss. The alternatives of paying down debt or repurchasing shares both involve risk, as well.[12] By providing the same return as the firm's average investment opportunity while imposing none of the risk,[13] an award of prejudgment interest at the plaintiff's WACC therefore would overcompensate the plaintiff.

---

[10] See, for example, R. F. Lanzillotti and A. K. Esquibel, "Measuring Damage in Commercial Litigation: Present Value of Lost Opportunities," *Journal of Accounting, Auditing and Finance,* Winter/Spring 1990:125-144.

[11] Fisher and Romaine, "Janis Joplin's Yearbook."

[12] Both these alternatives involve the company reappropriating risk that had been held by its providers of capital. The risk to the firm undertaking these actions is the same as the overall level of risk associated with the firm's marginal investment opportunity.

[13] Again, this analysis does not consider the risks associated with litigation discussed above, which, in any case, are entirely unrelated to the risks that cause the firm's WACC to exceed the risk-free rate.

Risk-Free Rate

Fisher and Romaine propose a resolution to this problem.[14] Under the assumption that damages are awarded without risk (i.e., that the defendant's solvency is irrelevant and that the courts' decisions are always correct and final), interest on the original loss should reflect only the time value of money and inflation. The securities markets price an asset that has these characteristics, the risk-free asset, which is generally considered to be represented by the U.S. Treasury bill (also known as a T-bill). In our opinion, the risk-free rate, generally represented by the T-bill rate, will be the appropriate basis for prejudgment interest in many circumstances. In our experience, use of this rate for determining prejudgment interest is common among damages experts and the courts.[15]

One criticism of the risk-free rate relates back to the view that a damages award is equivalent to the repayment of a forced loan from the plaintiff to the defendant. Requiring the defendant to pay prejudgment interest at a rate lower than its borrowing cost would allow it to benefit from its actions to the extent that it had use of the funds during the intervening period. However, the courts have ruled consistently that the objective of prejudgment interest is to make the plaintiff whole—whether the defendant is unjustly enriched is not an issue.[16] Moreover, applicable statutes often contain provisions that allow the courts to eliminate any such benefits through additional damages. In patent infringement cases, for example, the court may use its discretion to award treble damages or attorneys' fees in addition to the make-whole amount.[17]

Certainty-Equivalent WACC

Under certain circumstances, however, the risk-free rate approach may not fully compensate a plaintiff for its foregone opportunities. Awarding prejudgment interest at the T-bill rate implies that plaintiff's marginal investment opportunities are the same as those of the overall securities market and that the T-bill rate provides an equivalent risk-adjusted return to these marginal opportunities. This may not be the case, however. Consider posing the following question to a plaintiff:

---

[14] Fisher and Romaine, "Janis Joplin's Yearbook."
[15] See, for example, *Datascope Corp. v. SMEC Inc.*, 879 F.2d 820, 829 (Fed. Cir. 1989).
[16] See, for example, *Transco Prods. Inc. v. Performance Contracting Inc.*, 131 F.Supp. 976, 981-982 (N.D. Ill. 2001).
[17] 35 U.S.C. § 284 and § 285.

What guaranteed return do you require in order to be indifferent to lending out the last dollar from your capital budget, rather than investing that dollar in your least profitable enterprise?

In situations where, at the margin, the plaintiff is voluntarily returning profits to its providers of capital, through a dividend or early debt retirement, for example, the likely response will be, in fact, "the T-bill rate." But in cases where the firm is capital constrained to some extent, the likely response will be a rate that is higher than the T-bill rate. For example, firms that are small, new, or in financial distress may have difficulty raising additional capital. For such firms, the loss of marginal funds may have a risk-adjusted cost that is greater than the risk-free rate. This issue becomes particularly important if the amount of funds at issue (i.e., the magnitude of the damages award) is large relative to the plaintiff's overall capital base.

In such cases, we consider the alternative that prejudgment interest be awarded at the *certainty-equivalent* WACC, which we define as the truthful response to the question posed above. This interest rate accounts for the possibility that the plaintiff could have earned a return on those marginal funds that would exceed the T-bill rate on a risk-adjusted basis and does not compensate the plaintiff for risks avoided in the time frame between the initial loss and the payment of the damages award, yet does account for the possibility that the plaintiff could have earned a return on those marginal funds that would exceed the T-bill rate on a risk-adjusted basis.

The remaining issue, therefore, is to identify a method that a damages expert could use to determine the *certainty-equivalent* WACC. While we have not considered at length the requirements for such a method, we have identified a few guideposts. As a starting point, one should recognize that this rate must be bounded by the T-bill rate at the low end and the firm's standard WACC at the high end.[18] Evidence of the plaintiff's availability of capital should also be examined. Events such as dividends, share repurchases, and early debt retirements would tend to indicate that the firm could not have profitably employed additional capital.[19]

---

[18] This upper bound reflects the assumption that the plaintiff could have obtained additional funds at its existing WACC. If any increased demand for capital would have resulted in a higher WACC, then it is this higher rate that should pertain.

[19] We note that these types of transactions, such as dividend issuance, may serve other corporate purposes, and therefore do not necessarily provide a reliable indicator that the firm has excess cash on hand. See, for example, Said Elfakhani, "The Expected Favourableness of Dividend Signals, the Direction of Dividend Change and the Signalling Role of Dividend Announcements," Applied Financial Economics 8, no. 3 (June 1998): 221-230.

Significant amounts of cash on hand not dedicated to some future use would also tend to support this finding. The size of the damages award should also be considered. A large award (relative to the plaintiff's capital base) would tend to support a rate closer to the upper bound—a small award would tend to support a rate closer to the lower bound. In general, we expect that the methods used to calculate the *certainty-equivalent WACC* will be case-specific and will depend significantly on the availability of the relevant data. In practice, an expert may make a judgment that, based on the information at hand, either the risk-free rate or the standard WACC—perhaps with some adjustment—is the appropriate rate under the circumstances.

We point out, however, that claims by a plaintiff that the defendant's actions caused it to miss opportunities with above-market risk-adjusted returns should be viewed, at least initially, with some skepticism. Presumably, whatever data that the expert views to resolve this issue would also have been available for the plaintiff to show to a prospective lender or equity investor, prompting the question of why the firm wasn't able to convince the capital markets of the value of this opportunity at the time of the loss. Nonetheless, there may be circumstances under which information asymmetries or other circumstances could result in such an outcome. Awarding prejudgment interest at a rate higher than the risk-free rate may be justified in these cases.

Adjusting Future Damages: Discount Rate

Expected future lost profits can enter into the damages analysis for many types of litigation including patent infringement, misappropriation of trade secrets, and breach of contract. In a case involving the misappropriation of trade secrets, for example, the plaintiff may argue that the misappropriation had an impact on his business in two ways. First, the misappropriation may have allowed a competitor to enter the market sooner or more effectively than he otherwise would have and, therefore, affected the plaintiff's profits in the past. Second, the plaintiff may argue that the impact of the theft is likely to persist and have a deleterious effect on future profits even if the defendant is enjoined from using the trade secret in the future. It would not, however, be proper to account for the damages associated with the expected lost future profits by simply adding up the lost profits that the company has forecast.[20] In addition to

---

[20] In *Jones & Laughlin Steel Corp. v. Pfeifer*, 462 U.S. 523 (1983), the Supreme Court of the United States does recognize the need to discount future losses.

showing that the projections are reasonable, the expert must apply a discount rate to the future lost profits projections to account for two factors: the uncertainty inherent in projections and the fact that any damages would be awarded in advance of the actual occurrence of the loss. In short, a dollar that one might get a year in the future is worth less than a dollar that one is sure to get today.

The Purpose of Discounting Expected Future Lost Profits

In any calculation of expected future lost profits, it is crucial to remember that what the plaintiff lost by virtue of the defendant's misdeeds was not a certain stream of revenue and profits. Rather, the plaintiff lost the opportunity to try to make a stream of future profits, profits that he may or may not have actually received. Although the plaintiff has to show that he would have received the profits with reasonable certainty, whether or not he would have received those profits in the absence of the alleged theft of trade secrets will never be known. There are many reasons why he may not have actually received those profits. The actual level of profits made by the plaintiff will be affected by (1) factors that affect everyone in the economy (e.g., a recession), (2) factors that affect everyone in a particular industry (e.g., introduction of a new competing technology), and (3) factors that affect only the plaintiff (e.g., the success of a certain marketing campaign).

Because of these sources of uncertainty, the future expected cash flows necessarily involve risk. For a given expected return, risk-averse firms would prefer a cash flow with less, rather than more, risk. In other words, risk-averse firms would prefer a certain amount to a gamble with the same expected value.[21] Therefore, it is necessary to adjust downward the future expected risky cash flows to make the plaintiff indifferent between those expected cash flows and a specified amount of compensation (which is received with certainty).[22]

The appropriate discount rate must not only reflect the risk inherent in predicting future cash flows, but also the fact that money received today is more valuable than the same amount of money received in the future. The time value of money is a well-understood principle of economics.[23] Because the plaintiff could invest the compensation he receives from a

---

[21] Richard Brealey and Stewart Myers, *Principles of Corporate Finance* (Boston, MA: McGraw-Hill/Irwin, 2003), 15-16.

[22] Id., 221.

[23] See, for example, William Baumol and Alan Blinder, *Economics: Principles and Policy* (Fort Worth, TX: Dryden Press, 1994), 386-387; Paul Samuelson and William Nordhaus, *Economics* (New York: McGraw-Hill, 1995), 248-249.

damages award in a risk-free instrument and receive interest payments in the future, it is again necessary to adjust downward the future expected cash flows to make the plaintiff indifferent between those expected cash flows in the future and the compensation he will receive today.

In order to fairly reimburse the plaintiff for his expected future losses, he should receive a lump sum such that he is indifferent between taking that certain lump sum today and having the opportunity to attempt to earn the expected profits at a time in the future. The correct discount rate is the rate that equates those two amounts, taking into account both the time value of money and the riskiness of the expected future cash flows.

Quantifying the rate that equates lump sums today with uncertain payoffs in the future is at the heart of pricing in capital and equity markets. A bond, for example, is priced so that the marginal investor is just indifferent between the lump sum today—the price that he pays for the bond—and the stream of future, uncertain payments. In the case of a bond, the payments are uncertain largely because the issuer of the bond may default on making the promised payments. The interest rate on the bond serves the same purpose in the financial markets as discount rates do in valuing future expected profits: the bond's interest rate accounts for the time value of money and the riskiness of the investment. Riskier investments have higher interest rates. Thus, for example, junk bonds have higher interest rates than AAA corporate bonds. Therefore, one way of thinking about finding the right discount rate is finding an investor who is essentially facing the same risks as the plaintiff for the profit stream in question.[24]

Potential Choices for the Discount Rate

Statutory Rate

Court opinions have mentioned discount rates ranging from 6 to 25 percent.[25] Discount rates applied to speculative ventures in early stages of development can be as high as 50 to 80 percent.[26] This dispersion has led to a suggestion for a rate set by statute.[27] However, economics principles

---

[24] Brealey and Myers, *Principles of Corporate Finance*, 523.

[25] For example, see *Binghamton Masonic Temple Inc. v. City of Binghamton*, 158 Misc.2d 916; and *Lleco Holdings Inc. v. Otto Candies Inc.*, Civ.A.No.93-1840, 1994, 867 F.Supp. 444.

[26] Russell Parr, "Early-Stage Technology Valuation (New)," in *Intellectual Property Infringement Damages: A Litigation Support Handbook, 2003 Cumulative Supplement*, 2d ed. (Hoboken, NJ: J. Wiley & Sons, 2003), 75-76.

[27] Christopher Bowers, "Courts, Contracts, and the Appropriate Discount Rate: A Quick Fix for the Legal Lottery," *University of Chicago Law Review*, Summer 1996.

demonstrate that the discount rate should vary according to the economic conditions present in each case. Thus, the use of the same statutory rate for every case would necessarily lead to damage awards that failed to reflect a proper valuation of what was lost as a result of the alleged bad act. Instead of a prespecified statutory rate, the appropriate discount rate should be calculated based on a few straightforward and sound principles, as outlined above. While not eliminating all uncertainty about possible damages awards, a well-reasoned discount rate grounded in the facts of the case will ensure that lost profits damages, as closely as possible, fairly compensate the party that was injured by the misconduct.

Federal Reserve's Discount Rate

The Federal Reserve's discount rate is the rate that the U.S. Central Bank charges to member banks, usually large financial institutions, for loans through the so-called "discount window." These loans are either overnight loans, loans to alleviate short-term liquidity crises, or loans to banks with recurring seasonal liquidity issues.[28] This rate is typically one of the lowest costs of borrowing because of the strict collateral requirements and the short-term nature of the loans. This rate neither matches the typical time span over which expected future profits are earned nor reflects the types of risks inherent in business profits. Therefore, the Federal Reserve's discount rate is not useful as a measure of the appropriate discount rate to apply to expected future lost profits, although it has in fact been endorsed by courts.[29]

T-Bill Rate and Other Conservative Investment Instruments

The interest rate on short-term T-bills or other similar conservative investment instruments is another suggested measure of discounting for expected future lost profits.[30] However, like the Federal Reserve's discount rate, this rate will rarely be applicable to any actual damages scenario. As described in the previous section, the T-bill rate is often referred to by economists as the "risk-free rate," reflecting the extremely low probability of default involved with an investment in U.S. government treasury securities. Furthermore, T-bills are typically short-maturity instruments, with durations of less than one year. Therefore, T-bills

---

28 Federal Reserve Board discount window, at www.frbdiscountwindow.org/.
29 See, for example, *Frey v. Smith & Sons*, 751 F.Supp. 1052, 1057 (N.D.N.Y. 1990).
30 *Northern Helix Co. v. The United States*, No. 454-70, 1980, 634 F.2d 557; *Binghamton Masonic Temple Inc. v. City of Binghamton*, 158 Misc.2d 916.

do not account for the time value of money associated with longer-term expected profit streams. While longer-term treasury securities may more appropriately account for the time value of money, they still do not reflect the types of risk inherent in any particular firm's business prospects and, as such, are not appropriate for discounting expected future lost profits.

Plaintiff's Weighted Average Cost of Capital

If the lost profit stream is similar in risk to the plaintiff's firm overall, then it may be economically appropriate to use the WACC for the plaintiff, and courts have endorsed this discount rate.[31] For example, this situation might happen if the profits that were lost were on products that are essentially the same as the products that the firm produces and the lost customers were similar to the customers that the plaintiff actually sold to. The WACC is simply a measure of the average amount that a firm pays for capital that it already raised. As mentioned previously, it considers how much a firm has raised in debt (i.e., bonds or loans) versus in equity (i.e., the stock market) and the cost of raising capital in each of those markets. The calculations are standard and well known by economists, and the data are readily available through sources like Bloomberg and Ibbotson.[32]

Cost of Capital for Similar Investments

There are several instances, however, in which the WACC of the firm is not the appropriate discount rate to use in valuing expected future profits. For example, since the WACC is the average cost of capital that a firm raised in the past, it may not be the appropriate measure of the cost of capital for the additional investments the firm enters into at the current time. If the firm's financial position has changed since its past investments were financed or if additional investments have different risk profiles than past projects, the WACC may not measure accurately the cost of capital that the firm would incur for the expected profit stream in question.[33]

---

[31] In *Cede & Co. v. Techicolor Inc.*, Civ. A. No. 7129, 1990 WL 161084 (Del. Ch.), the court endorsed the use of different costs of capital for different lines of business. See also *Jeffrey Gilbert v. MPM Enterprises Inc.*, C.A. No. 14416, 709 A.2d 663, 1997 WL 633298 (Del. Ch.).

[32] Ibbotson Associates, *Stocks, Bonds, Bills and Inflation: Valuation Edition: 2003 Yearbook.*

[33] This proposition is essentially the same as the statements in Brealey and Myers that "each project should be evaluated at its own opportunity cost of capital" and that "the company cost of capital is fine as a discount rate for average-risk projects"; Brealey and Myers, *Principles of Corporate Finance*, 244. See also I. page 222.

In addition, if the lost profit stream is on products that are very different from those the plaintiff actually sold in the past, then it may be appropriate to find investments that more closely resemble the types of risk faced by the plaintiff. One approach is to find firms in the market that have businesses that are similar to the source of the lost profit stream. For example, in a recent damages analysis conducted by one of the authors, the forecasted lost profit stream would come from a risky venture involving satellites owned by a communications firm. In such a case, the WACC of other large communications conglomerates did not provide an accurate measure of the discount rate that should be applied to this venture. The large communications conglomerates had diversified product portfolios and well-established product lines and customer bases, as compared with the risky satellite venture that had yet to earn a profit. Instead, capital costs of firms that specialize in similar (or similarly risky) projects in the satellite industry were more representative of the types of risks facing the venture at issue, and as such, the average WACC among these specialized firms was the appropriate discount rate measure.

The United States Court of Appeals for the Federal Circuit (CAFC) acknowledged the importance of considering risk in a case involving Energy Capital Corporation in 2002.[34] The plaintiff, Energy Capital, argued that the correct discount rate was a risk-free rate of return, specifically, the interest rate on Treasury securities. The argument put forward by Energy Capital was that "once [the court] determined that its profits were reasonably certain, no further consideration of risk was appropriate, because risk already had been considered in determining whether there would have been profits."[35] The CAFC disagreed. "The fact that the trial court has determined that profits were reasonably certain does not mean that risk should play no role in valuing the stream of anticipated profits."[36] The CAFC specifically noted that the purpose of the discount rate in this case was two-fold: to account for the time value of money and to account for risk. The discount rate that the CAFC endorsed was an interest rate on real estate investment trusts—an investment with risks similar to those faced by the plaintiff—plus a 2 percent risk factor. In this case, the court correctly considered risk in choosing a discount rate and, as such, properly awarded the plaintiffs an amount consistent with a "make whole" standard.

---

[34] *Energy Capital Corp. v. United States*, 14 August 2002.
[35] Id.
[36] Id.

Conclusion

The discount rate as applied to expected future lost profits and the pre-judgment interest rate both serve to adjust cash flows to reflect the fact that the cash flows are received at a different time from when they were or would be accrued. The theory that underlies the choice of both rates is the same. The rate must correctly account for the time value of money and for risk such that the plaintiff is indifferent between accepting two sums: (1) the lump sum at the time the damage award is received, and (2) the amount of the damage at the time it was or would have been realized.

While the underlying theory is the same for both past and future damages, the application of that theory leads to different results in the two cases. In choosing a discount rate to apply to expected future lost profits, it is necessary to account for the fact that the expected profit stream would have embodied some risk that the lump-sum payment does not have. Therefore, the discount rate should reflect the return that outside investors would demand for the risky profit stream in question. In choosing a prejudgment interest rate, however, there are a number of approaches to the issue of risk which depend on one's viewpoint regarding the purpose of prejudgment interest. Under a reasonable set of assumptions, which we have outlined here, unless the plaintiff can prove that the act for which it is seeking damages caused it to lose an above-market (on a risk-adjusted basis) investment opportunity, then the risk-free rate is the appropriate rate to bring past damages forward to the date of actual compensation.

12

Avoiding Misidentified Incremental Costs

Alyssa Lutz and Paola Maria Valenti

Incremental cost analysis plays a key role in intellectual property damages calculations. Incremental costs are necessary to determine a plaintiff's lost profits in patent infringement cases and a defendant's ill-gotten gains in trademark infringement cases, and they are often an important factor to be considered in reasonable royalty calculations.[1] Incremental revenues, while not necessarily simple to determine, are usually straight-forward. Incremental costs, however, often are not. The appellate opinion in *Panduit Corp. v. Stahlin Bros. Fibre Works Inc.,* which has become the reference for lost profits damages in patent infringement cases, described the cost analysis as the Achilles' heel of the plaintiff's claim.[2] Indeed, cost measurement is an exercise in subtleties, and when it is poorly performed, it can result in an over- or understatement of damages.

Implementing an Incremental Cost Analysis
The "make whole" standard requires that damages be awarded such that the plaintiff is restored to the same financial position it would have held *but for* the alleged bad act. That is, the plaintiff should be fully compensated for the losses *caused* by the bad act but not compensated for any losses resulting from unrelated factors. The basic framework for lost profit damages is to determine the plaintiff's additional profits in a but-for scenario in which the defendant would not have violated the plaintiff's intellectual property rights. Because the but-for scenario should include the impact of factors that would have occurred regard-

---

[1] In this chapter, incremental cost analysis issues are discussed primarily in the context of patent infringement and lost profits damages, but the topics discussed are applicable in other damages analysis settings as well.
[2] *Panduit Corp. v. Stahlin Bros. Fibre Works Inc.,* 575 F.2d 1152.

less of the bad act and remove the impact of those factors that occurred only because of the bad act, causation is an intrinsic requirement for the crafting of an appropriate but-for scenario. Once the but-for revenues are identified, the question for an economist is, In the absence of the alleged infringement, what additional costs would the plaintiff have incurred?

There are two main approaches to estimating incremental costs. The first approach is to analyze financial documents and, with the aid of other information gathered from the company, identify the costs that would have changed had the plaintiff made the sales lost to the defendant. The second approach is to conduct a statistical analysis of the company's historical costs to quantify the relationship between sales and costs and thus estimate how costs would have changed had the plaintiff made the incremental sales.

Identifying Incremental Costs on the Basis of Financial Documents

A careful analysis of a firm's financial documents is an appropriate method by which to identify incremental costs, but only if the analysis is conducted with a clear understanding of the information that is and is not reflected in these documents.[3] For example, companies sometimes list categories of costs as "variable" and "fixed" or "direct" and "indirect."[4] These categories are a useful starting point but often are not sufficient to properly define the incremental costs that are relevant to a damages analysis. Costs that are labeled "variable" in a financial statement may not be variable at all in the case at issue, and costs that are usually considered fixed may, in fact, increase as the plaintiff's sales increased in the but-for world.

---

3 Relevant financial documents are not limited to standard financial statements such as those typically found in a firm's annual report. Instead, these may include a much broader set of documents such as pro forma statements, operating reports, sales databases, and other sources of information that quantify the firm's operations.

4 Variable costs as reported in financial statements are typically the sum of direct costs and variable overhead costs. Depending on the type of business at issue, direct costs include product costs such as direct material and direct labor costs. Variable overhead may include indirect product costs such as manufacturing overhead (e.g., supervisors' salaries, utilities, property taxes, insurance on the factory, and depreciation on manufacturing plant and equipment). Administrative costs are typically excluded from variable costs (e.g., executive salaries, accounting and data processing costs, and the costs of various support activities, such as legal services, employee training, and corporate planning). See Clyde P. Stickney, Roman L. Weil, and Sidney Davidson, *Financial Accounting: An Introduction to Concepts, Methods, and Uses*, 6th ed. (1991), 87-88, 139, 824.

The point is *not* that companies are ignorant of their own cost structures. Rather, these cost labels are used in the business world in a variety of ways for a variety of purposes. Unless the underlying method-ology is understood and, if necessary, the cost information is adjusted, financial documents can give a distorted impression of the relevant incremental costs. This should not be surprising since few financial statements are created for the purpose of evaluating the profitability of a specific product or manufacturing process. Thus, standard financial statements should be reviewed with care and the fundamental nature of the costs analyzed in the context of the company at issue. In order to understand the nature of the costs associated with the business, an economist may need to perform additional analyses, including review of discovery related to the firm's cost structure and discussions with business personnel.

Identifying Incremental Costs Using Regression Analysis

The relationship between incremental sales and incremental costs can also be examined by conducting a statistical analysis of the company's historical costs and sales. The idea is to use historical data to quantify the amount by which costs changed in response to changes in sales volumes and use the results to predict what additional costs the plaintiff would have incurred had it made the claimed amount of lost sales.

In economics, the cost function represents the minimum cost of pro-ducing a given output level (sales volume), conditional on the technology available to the firm and the prices of the various inputs to production. By econometrically estimating the cost function—i.e., the relationship between cost and sales volume—it is possible to determine the impact of changes in sales volumes on costs. More precisely, consider the cost func-tion specification

$$TC = \tilde{\alpha} + \beta Q = \sum_i \gamma_i w_i + \varepsilon ,$$

where TC is total cost, Q is sales volume, w_i is the price of input i, and ε is an error term that captures the effects of unobserved variables on costs.[5] The coefficient on Q, β, indicates how total costs vary as sales volume

---

5   The linear functional form presented here is only one example of the possible func-tional forms that may be used. In particular, cost functions are often estimated by using a translog functional form, which is a good approximation of the cost function associated with any production function.

changes. If the input prices w_i are essentially constant over the relevant time period, one can estimate the simpler cost function

$$TC = \alpha + \beta Q + \varepsilon,$$

which separates the fixed and variable components of total costs (α and βQ, respectively). If data on unit sales are not available and output prices are stable, one may use revenues as the explanatory variable and estimate the equation

$$TC = \alpha + \beta REV + \varepsilon.$$

In this case, the coefficient β represents the variable cost as a proportion of revenues and can be used to estimate the incremental costs associated with a certain increment in dollar sales. If data on sales volumes are not available and prices change over the relevant time period, one may deflate the revenues by using, for example, an industry price index to yield a quantity index. In this case, the coefficient β on the quantity index has the same interpretation of the coefficient on output in the traditional regression, (i.e., it indicates how total costs vary as sales volume changes).

Before conducting a regression analysis of this type, it is important to understand the underlying reporting mechanisms that generate the cost data, especially in a multiproduct company. Unless these mechanisms are understood and properly adjusted for in the regression modeling, relying on the data as reported may result in cost categorizations based on how costs are recorded rather than how they are actually incurred. For instance, data processing costs may be allocated to products A and B depending on their relative revenues. If the sales of A increase, financial statements may record an increase in the costs of A that may not be driven by an actual increase in the company's data processing costs. Thus, some costs may appear variable when in fact they are not.

Potential Pitfalls

A rigorous incremental cost analysis is very much a fact-specific analysis that depends on the claim at issue and the specific circumstances of the plaintiff, defendant, and their competitors. The nature of a company's cost structure may differ across products, over time, and with the level of production. Understanding which costs vary with the additional sales regardless of the label they have for accounting purposes is crucial for a sound economic analysis of incremental costs.

Choice of But-For Scenario

There are often multiple causes for changes in a firm's cost structure over time. Changes in the firm's input costs, production methods, competitive environment, or other factors affecting the firm's cost structure that took place during the damage period but are unrelated to the infringement should be included when determining the firm's but-for cost structure. In this way, the only difference between the actual situation during the damage period and the but-for scenario is the absence of the defendant's alleged bad act.

A firm's preinfringement cost history is sometimes used as a benchmark on which to base the but-for scenario. However, because *other* factors may also differ between the period preceding the alleged violation (before period) and the damage period, it is an obvious but often overlooked fact that the before period may not be a good benchmark for the but-for scenario. For instance, if fuel costs increased substantially during the period of infringement relative to the preinfringement period, it would be inappropriate to include lower preinfringement fuel cost levels in the firm's but-for scenario. This is equivalent to assuming the plaintiff would have continued to have access to less expensive fuel in the but-for scenario.[6]

Relying strictly on the plaintiff's historical data and prior cost structure as a benchmark for its but-for costs is appropriate only if (a) the plaintiff's but-for sales are comparable to its preinjury levels and (b) other elements in the plaintiff's environment have remained essentially static. If these conditions do not hold, then differences between the before benchmark and the plaintiff's actual costs will be attributed to the incremental but-for sales despite the fact that some of these changes may have been caused by other unrelated factors.

Consequently, a simple before-and-after comparison of costs can lead to misidentified incremental costs if the plaintiff would have made its production decisions and earned its profits in the face of changing market conditions. The appropriate and relevant comparison is to compare the plaintiff's actual costs against the costs that would have been incurred in the face of realistic but-for circumstances. Thus, regardless of the approach followed to estimate incremental costs, it is necessary to craft a robust and well-supported but-for scenario to which one can compare the actual setting.

---

[6] Note that in the face of higher fuel costs, the plaintiff could also have chosen a lower production level in the but-for scenario than in the before period. Thus, changes in costs could affect but-for revenues as well.

Consideration of Capacity Constraints

The extent to which fixed costs might have increased in the but-for scenario depends on the extent to which the company was operating at full capacity in the actual world and the ratio of the incremental sales to the company's actual sales. The same increment in sales may require different incremental costs in companies of different sizes. Likewise, the same company may incur different sets of costs depending on the size of the increment in sales.

Consider, for example, a very large firm taking on the sales from a small infringer. The large firm may be able to make the additional sales with virtually no additional fixed costs if it has excess capacity, a preexisting distribution mechanism, and a large sales force. However, a small firm trying to make those same sales may have to install new production lines, outsource production, expand its distribution capabilities, and hire new sales representatives. Even if the increase in sales is the same in both cases, the costs that are incremental to absorbing those sales will vary dramatically because of the different starting sizes of the firms.

Similarly, the extent to which fixed costs may be incremental depends on the size of the sales increment. If the sales lost to the defendant are sufficiently small compared to the plaintiff's production, the plaintiff could have accommodated the incremental sales in the existing production process without increasing capacity or hiring new people. Therefore, there would be virtually no impact from changes in fixed costs on the incremental costs. In contrast, if the infringer's sales of accused products are so large that the plaintiff would have had to dramatically increase its size, a good portion of the incremental costs necessary to expand the plaintiff's production would include increased "fixed" costs.

Nonlinear Costs

The plaintiff's production function may be characterized by economies of scale over a certain range of output. For instance, as purchases of inputs in bulk allow it to take advantage of volume discounts or inputs are used more efficiently, total costs increase at a decreasing rate. At some point, however, the company may experience diseconomies of scale. For example, increasing production to serve distant markets may increase transportation costs and reduce the productivity of workers, and therefore total costs may increase at an increasing rate. Similarly, the plaintiff's production function may be characterized by economies of scope or efficiencies gained from learning. Any of these characteristics may cause costs to increase in ways that are not directly proportional to sales volume increases. Thus, the resulting cost functions may be nonlinear, with costs increasing slower or faster than volume or even increasing in steps with flat ranges followed by increases at critical volume levels.

If historical costs do not accurately reflect the nature of costs at higher production levels or in the context of a different product mix, a simplistic analysis of a firm's financial documents may lead to misleading estimates of incremental costs. Similarly, if the true underlying cost function is, in fact, nonlinear, a regression analysis that uses a linear cost function may result in an under- or overestimation of incremental costs. In addition, a regression analysis based on a cost function that expresses total costs as a function of input prices and output may provide a biased estimate of incremental costs if other cost drivers such as scope and cumulative experience affect total costs. These types of nonlinearities can be taken into account in either method of estimating incremental costs. A careful analysis of financial statements can be adjusted by investigating how particular costs change with different volume levels and product mixes. A regression analysis, on the other hand, can be adjusted by specifying an appropriate nonlinear cost function with these characteristics in mind.

Incremental Costs in a Multiproduct Setting

Which costs should be classified as incremental also depends on the relationship of the product at issue with the other products produced by the company. For example, suppose that to make the lost sales the company would be introducing a new product into an existing product line. In that case, the company may not need to hire any new sales people or make sales calls on any additional potential customers. Then, the selling costs that would normally be included in an accounting measure of variable costs would not qualify as an incremental cost for a damages analysis. Conversely, suppose that to make the lost sales the company would be introducing a new product line. In that case, the company may have to install specific machinery and hire additional support or supervisory staff (e.g., a product marketing manager). The associated costs would be incremental, even though these types of expenses may be reported as "overhead" in the firm's financial statements.

Moreover, because financial statements often do not separately report sales of different products, there may be little information on what product mix the company produces and how the product mix would have changed should the plaintiff have made the sales lost to the defendant. If the additional sales entail a production process with a cost structure substantially different from the costs characterizing the plaintiff's actual production, an analysis of the company's actual cost structure may lead to incorrect estimates of the incremental cost associated with the lost sales.

Coping with Cost Allocation Rules

Even when financial statements do list sales and costs separately for individual product lines, the costs as reported are often the result of accounting allocation rules that bring a whole new set of complications to the analysis.[7] The difficulty is that costs that have been allocated across multiple products often reveal more about the mechanism by which costs are recorded than the underlying nature of those costs. Costs are often allocated to particular business units or products on the basis of sales volume or some other "driver" of an activity. For example, a manufacturing plant supervisor's salary may be allocated to various products on the basis of units produced of each type. Thus, if output of product A is expanded and the volume of product B is held steady, more of the supervisor's salary may be shifted to product A, despite the fact that this cost does not vary at all with the output of either product A or B. Rather, this salary is essentially a common cost that is fixed with respect to the plant's overall production.[8] Allocations of this sort may make sense for financial reporting purposes (e.g., by requiring each product to bear its "fair share" of the supervisor's salary), but reveal little about how the firm's plant supervisor costs would change in response to changes in the level of production.

Accounting allocation rules are typically relied upon to apportion common costs and also to derive an estimate of variable costs when an input is too cumbersome or costly to track directly. For instance, monitoring exactly how much of an input is consumed to produce each unit may be quite expensive, so many firms estimate the per-unit costs by allocating the input's overall costs on the basis of a cost driver (e.g., the

---

7   The distortions resulting from efforts to allocate joint and common costs have long been well-known to economists. See, for example, William J. Baumol, Michael F. Koehn, and Robert D. Willig, "How Arbitrary Is 'Arbitrary'?—or, Toward the Deserved Demise of Full Cost Allocation," *Public Utilities Fortnightly* 120, no. 5 (September 3, 1987): 16-20; and William J. Baumol, "Predation and the Average Variable Cost Test," *Journal of Law and Economics* 39, no. 1 (April 1996): 49-72, particularly at page 59.

8   This, of course, assumes that the supervisor's bonus and future raises are not related to the factory's production volume. If they are linked, then this portion of the supervisor's compensation might be relevant.

number of units produced). If spending for a particular input increases evenly with increases in the volume of units produced (holding constant the price per unit of the input), the allocated cost measure for that input may be an appropriate proxy for the input's incremental cost. For example, it may not be possible for a lumber company to know exactly how much fuel is used to cut each particular board size. However, an allocation of total fuel consumed based on the number of units produced and weighted by the size and complexity of the lumber being cut may be a good proxy for the fuel necessary to produce each unit.

While an allocated cost measure may be an appropriate proxy for incremental cost in some cases, this simplification can also cause fixed costs (such as the supervisor's salary) to appear to vary or can give "lumpy" costs (costs that increase in steps rather than continuously) the appearance of increasing smoothly over ranges in which they are actually flat. For example, the costs an airline reports for each of its flights may include an allocated portion of the salary and benefits for baggage handlers and gate staff. Airlines typically require minimum staffing levels to handle each flight as it arrives and departs from an airport. If there are long gaps between flights, this staff may have downtime, allowing additional flights to be scheduled without requiring additional airport staffing. The airline's accounting system will likely use a simplifying assumption to allocate these staffing costs across all flights, even though a new flight would actually incur no additional costs. In other words, the financial statements may include these staffing costs as variable costs even though the addition of a new flight to the schedule did not cause any incremental airport staffing costs because the airline would have incurred these costs even if the new flight had not been added. The distortions inherent in accounting allocation rules are likely to be greater as the production at issue narrows relative to the overall activities of the firm. This is because a more narrowly defined product is likely to be produced with shared staff and equipment that is also used to produce other products.

Conclusion

Incremental cost measurement is quite straightforward and logical in concept, but implementation can be a more complicated process. Identification and measurement of the relevant incremental costs in a damages analysis often goes well beyond the pages of a financial statement. It involves informed practical choices that are based on a clearly defined but-for scenario, an understanding of how incremental sales would have changed the plaintiff's cost structure, and the market conditions in which the plaintiff would have produced these units. Financial documents and data can form the basis of this analysis, but an understanding of the data and underlying accounting methods is necessary to complete an accurate incremental cost analysis.

13

Commercial Success: Economic Principles Applied to Patent Litigation

Jesse David and Marion B. Stewart

A party accused of infringing a patent may contend that the asserted patent is invalid because of obviousness. That contention may be rebutted by a showing that the patented invention is a commercial success—one of several *secondary considerations* that courts look to for identifying the differences between the patented invention and the prior art. These secondary considerations—known as *objective indicia* of nonobviousness—also include such factors as copying, long-felt but unsolved need, failure of others, and licensing.[1]

Determining whether an invention has, or has not, been a commercial success is primarily an economic exercise, and economists increasingly assist courts in evaluating this issue. Case law indicates that courts have traditionally looked for characteristics such as increasing revenues, gain in share in an appropriately defined market, and public acclaim in an attempt to determine whether a product has been a commercial success. Courts have also considered whether the patent holder has established a *nexus* between the claimed invention and the product's commercial success—that is, whether the commercial success, if evident, is due to the patented feature as opposed to some other characteristic of the product or a mode of selling employed by the manufacturer.

---

[1]   *In re Denis Rouffet, Yannick Tanguy, and Frederic Berthault,* 149 F.3d 1350, 47 USPQ2d 1453 (Fed. Cir. 1998). It is our understanding that courts may consider all of these indicia in an assessment of a patent's validity. For the purposes of our discussion, we consider only those factors that should weigh in a determination of commercial success, not whether or the extent to which those factors could support a finding of validity or invalidity.

From an economic perspective, commercial success could in principle be defined by a single criterion: Does the patented invention earn a positive net return (risk-adjusted) on invested capital after accounting for all relevant costs associated with developing and commercializing the patent as well as any alternatives available to the patent holder? Patents exist to protect the human and financial investment used to develop new products, services, or processes. This investment, however, is only beneficial, from a social perspective, if consumers are willing to purchase an embodiment of the invention at such a price as to fully compensate the inventor for all costs incurred in bringing the product to market.[2] Put simply, patents are not needed to protect inventors from making poor investment decisions.

The courts' use of the previously mentioned factors is not necessarily in conflict with this definition, and many—perhaps most—previous decisions made by courts are likely to have been consistent with it. Given the limitations on available data, it is entirely reasonable that an analysis of commercial success should consider and place significant weight on the traditional measures such as market share or revenue growth. However, under certain circumstances, rapid sales growth and gains in market share will not *necessarily* reflect a profitable underlying invention. Moreover, calculating the proper measure of profitability can be a complicated task and should be considered in an appropriate context—for example, relative to an appropriate benchmark or alternative. Consequently, it is our opinion that courts should look more deeply into the economic characteristics of the product before arriving at a determination of the commercial success of the patent.

A Summary of the Case Law

In *Graham v. John Deere Co.,* the seminal case identifying commercial success as a relevant secondary consideration in a determination of patent validity, the Supreme Court of the United States cited an article in the *University of Pennsylvania Law Review* that focused on the consumer perspective for evaluating the commercial success of a patent. The article stated that "[t]he operative facts...are the actions of buyers rather than those of producers."[3] Case law since Graham has generally followed this

---

2   One could imagine that, for reasons of public policy, a patented invention related to health care could be sold at an artificially low price, or even given away, but such a strategy would not reduce the true value of the invention.

3   *Graham v. John Deere Co.,* 383 U.S. 1 (1966); and Richard L. Robbins, "Subtests of 'Nonobviousness,'" *University of Pennsylvania Law Review* 112 (1963-1964): 1175.

position. For example, in *Demaco Corp. v. Fl. Von Langsdorff Licensing Ltd.*, the court stated the following:

> The rationale for giving weight to the so-called "secondary consid-erations" is that they provide objective evidence of how the patented device is viewed in the marketplace, by those directly interested in the product.[4]

Based on this approach, courts appear to have turned to a few standard measures of consumers' demand for the patented product, such as total unit sales or revenues. Although not universally, the courts have generally recognized that this information must be placed in a "meaningful context" and consequently have noted that the sales must represent a significant and/or growing share of that product in some "market." This also follows the *University of Pennsylvania Law Review* article, which stated that "[t]he basic measure of commercial success should be the proportion of the total market for the product that the patentee has obtained."[5] Subsequent deci-sions have reinforced the standard that sales figures must at least be con-sidered in light of the size of the overall market, although the method for identifying the appropriate market has not generally been specified.[6]

However, achieving a significant volume of sales or even a large mar-ket share does not necessarily indicate that the inventor should view a patent as a success. For example, sales may be driven by characteristics other than the patented invention, such as other patented features, non-patented characteristics, and brand name. For some products, market share may also be affected by advertising. (The basic formulas for Coke and Pepsi haven't changed in decades, yet market shares appear to be affected by changing marketing strategies on the part of the two compa-nies.) As an extreme example, increasing sales and market share of a product could also be generated by simply lowering price, a tactic some-times employed by companies seeking to create customer awareness early

---

4   *Demaco Corp. v. Fl. Von Langsdorff Licensing Ltd.*, 851 F.2d 1387, 7 USPQ2d 1222 (Fed. Cir. 1988).
5   *University of Pennsylvania Law Review*, 1175.
6   For example, see *Ecolochem Inc. v. Southern California Edison Co.*, 227 F.3d 1361 (Fed. Cir. 2000); *Cable Electric Products Inc. v. Genmork Inc.*, 770 F.2d 1015, 226 USPQ 881 (Fed. Cir. 1985); and *Hybritech Inc. v. Monoclonal Antibodies Inc.*, 802 F.2d 1367, 231 USPQ 81 (Fed. Cir. 1986). An exception where a decision considered sales explicitly outside the context of the size of the overall market is *Neupak Inc. v. Ideal Manufacturing and Sales Corp.*, 41 Fed. Appx. 435; 2002 U.S. App. LEXIS 13843 (Fed. Cir. 2002). In *J.T. Eaton and Co. v. Atlantic Paste and Glue Co.*, 106 F.3d 1563, 41 USPQ2d 1641 (Fed. Cir. 1997), the court similarly found that a large number of units sold *did* represent evidence of com-mercial success, without any showing of a share in a well-defined market.

in the product life cycle. The *Manual of Patent Examining Procedure*, published by the United States Patent and Trademark Office, identifies this nexus between the success of the product and the patent itself as a key component of a nonobviousness claim:

> An applicant who is asserting commercial success to support its contention of nonobviousness bears the burden of proof of establishing a nexus between the claimed invention and evidence of commercial success.[7]

Courts have recognized some of these possibilities and have generally required a showing that any commercial success be directly linked to demand for the patented feature rather than any other factors.

Consequently, for any data on sales or market share to be relevant, one must be able to demonstrate that whatever demand for the product exists, it is due, at least in part, to the patent, not some other features or actions by the seller.[8] A simple thought experiment can shed light on the concept of a nexus. Suppose the patented invention were made unavailable and removed from the product. Could the seller attain the same level of commercial success? Or, from an economic perspective, what is the difference in net profits that would accrue to the patent holder if the patented invention were removed from the product?

Despite the courts' tendency to view commercial success from only the consumers' perspective, a few decisions have recognized profitability as a factor that might be considered along with other objective economic evidence. For example, in *Cable Electric Products Inc. v. Genmork Inc.*, the court stated:

> Without further economic evidence, for example, it would be improper to infer that the reported sales represent a substantial share of any definable market or whether the profitability per unit is anything out of the ordinary in the industry involved.[9]

Discussions of profitability or other "supply-side" considerations have been included in assessments of commercial success in only a few other

---

7   United States Patent and Trademark Office, *Manual of Patent Examining Procedure*, February 2003 revision, § 716.03. See also *Demaco*, 851 F..2d 1387.

8   Although the courts have consistently recognized that the issue of a nexus is critical in a determination of commercial success, in many cases they have found that the existence of a significant advertising budget does not in itself rebut the presumption that the commercial success of the product at issue must be due to the patented invention. For example, see *Merck and Co. v. Danbury Pharmacal Inc.*, 694 F.Supp. 1, 21 (D. Del. 1988); and *Hybritech*, 802 F.2d 1367.

9   *Cable*, 770 F.2d 1015.

cases.[10] As these cases properly point out, ultimately an inventor's success should be judged by the returns to his investment *relative* to that inventor's next-best alternatives.

Economic Criteria

In the first edition of his ground-breaking book, *Economic Analysis of Law,* the distinguished jurist Richard Posner discussed the *normative* (i.e., prescriptive) and *positive* (i.e., descriptive) roles of economics in the law:

> Economics turns out to be a powerful tool of normative analysis of law and legal institutions—a source of criticism and reform...The normative role of economic analysis in the law is fairly obvious. The positive role—that of explaining the rules and outcomes in the legal system as they are—is less obvious, but not less important. As we shall see, many areas of the law, especially the great common law fields of property, torts, and contracts, bear the stamp of economic reasoning. Few legal opinions, to be sure, contain explicit references to economic concepts and few judges have a substantial background in economics. But the true grounds of decision are often concealed rather than illuminated by the characteristic rhetoric of judicial opinions.[11]

As described above, we suggest that there is a straightforward normative role for economics in determining commercial success: A patented invention should be considered a commercial success if it can be shown to have earned, or can reasonably be expected to earn, a positive net return on invested capital after accounting for all relevant costs associated with development and commercialization as well as any alternatives available to the patent holder and the amount of risk borne by the patent holder. Although courts would do well, in our view, to adopt more explicit economic reasoning along these lines in their analysis of commercial success issues, our reading of the relevant cases suggests that a substantial amount of economic analysis has already found its way into judicial opinions regarding commercial success.

Under certain circumstances, it appears that economic analysis could provide a definitive answer to the question "Has a patented invention been a commercial success?" For example, suppose that:

---

[10] For example, see *Miles Laboratories Inc. v. Shandon Inc.*, 1992 WL 503432 (W. D. Pa.); and *In re Ben Huang*, 100 F.3d 135, 40 USPQ2d 1685 (Fed. Cir. 1996).

[11] Richard A. Posner, *Economic Analysis of Law* (Boston, MA: Little, Brown and Co., 1972), 6.

1. a start-up company, founded solely to exploit a single patented invention, incurred costs (in present value terms) of $1 million to develop a single saleable product;
2. over its entire life cycle—now completed—sales of that product generated net profits of $2 million (again, in present value terms); and
3. there is no doubt that the product characteristics and/or other factors that led consumers to purchase the product were all due to the invention.

The first assumption allows us to say with certainty that it cost precisely $1 million to develop a product embodying the patented invention, since we assume away any difficulties that would be caused by the need to associate "common costs" in, say, a central research-and-development (R&D) facility with the development of a particular invention. The second assumption eliminates the difficulty of evaluating the potential profits still to be earned by a product currently on the market. The third assumption assures that the nexus between patented invention and sales success has been established. Assuming that an appropriate interest rate has been used to "discount" (or appreciate) the investment and the resultant profits, a $2 million return on a $1 million investment would surely count as a commercially successful venture from the perspective of the producer. Since (by assumption) the patented invention is what made that return possible, then the patented invention should be deemed a commercial success.

In our experience, however, the issues that need to be addressed are always more complicated than the stylized example above, so it is hardly a surprise that—as far as we know—no reported case has reached a decision regarding the commercial success of a patented invention simply by comparing the cost of developing and selling the patented product with profits earned on that product. Our own research has made clear that even large, technology-oriented companies have difficulty associating early-stage R&D costs with what ultimately became a commercially viable product, inevitably leading to some uncertainty regarding the total cost of bringing a patented invention to market.[12] In addition, determining profitability for a single product sold by a multiproduct company can be further complicated if the growth in that product's sales comes at least partly at the expense of profits

---

[12] Even if detailed product-specific R&D cost data were not available, however, one might be able to make a reasonable evaluation of commercial success by comparing a product's profits to the average cost of developing and commercializing broadly similar products.

elsewhere in the company or, alternatively, if sales of the patented product generate additional profits for the company by drawing consumers to other products. Another complication arises from the fact that most patent disputes involve products currently or not yet on the market, not products whose life cycles have ended, adding further uncertainty regarding the profits that will ultimately be generated.[13] And finally, while there are certainly instances in which there is no doubt that the patented invention has created the performance characteristics that were responsible for the product's success, our studies have also revealed contrary examples in which it was clear that a patent played little, if any, role in generating product sales. Given the data imperfections that frequently make a "direct" measure of commercial success impractical,[14] it is therefore not surprising that courts have tended to focus on "indirect" evidence, such as growth in market share. As Judge Posner suggested, however, many of the courts' decisions on commercial success nevertheless "bear the stamp of economic reasoning."

For example, economic reasoning makes clear that pharmaceutical companies would not invest in research on a particular class of drugs, such as antibiotics, unless they believed that on an expected-value basis that research would be profitable. If companies' expectations are rational, then a bundle of "average" marketed antibiotics will generate enough profits over their life cycles to yield an acceptable return on the companies' R&D investments. A drug that clearly does much better than average is very likely, therefore, to be a commercial success.[15]

How would we know that a drug is much better than average? A large (i.e., much above-average) market share would be a likely indicator, and rapid growth in market share—particularly if the product is not too far into its life cycle—would also likely be relevant, since the expected present value of a product's profit stream will be greater the sooner those

---

[13] Sometimes, however, as with a blockbuster prescription drug that has performance features clearly due to the patent at issue, the sales and profits generated during the first few years of the product's life will be sufficiently large to leave little doubt about the patent's commercial success even if uncertainties remain regarding the precise magnitude of early-stage R&D costs.

[14] A further complication relates to the possibility that infringement by a competitor may affect the profitability of a patent holder's product, and therefore its apparent commercial success. In order for an analysis of profitability to be of use in assessing commercial success, one should account for the actions of the infringer. Moreover, assessing only the infringer's profitability, rather than the patent holder's, may not provide an appropriate measure of commercial success. Such a problem could arise if, for example, the infringer had a different cost structure or sold to a different group of customers than the patent holder.

[15] Note, however, that the inverse is not necessarily true. For example, in a highly profitable industry, a "below-average" product may still be a commercial success.

profits are earned.[16] The courts' reliance on market-share data and growth in market share, as described in the previous section, appears to be sensible in light of the likely imperfections in the data that would have shed a more direct light on the issue of a product's commercial success.

Despite the fact that, for the most part, courts' general approach to determining commercial success has been consistent with these economic concepts, it appears that some decisions would have benefited from more, or at least more explicit, economic analysis. For example, in the *Neupak Inc. v. Ideal Manufacturing and Sales Corp.* case, the court of appeals found the following:

> Because the record shows that between 1995 and 2000 Neupak's patented mobile filling carts enjoyed a significant increase in sales and constituted an increasing share of Neupak's business, the district court did not clearly err in concluding that Neupak demonstrated a nexus between commercial success and the '233 patent.[17]

In this case, not only did the courts (both the district and appeals) apparently fail to put Neupak's sales into any "meaningful context," there appears to be a possibility that the product embodying the patented invention became successful at the expense of other Neupak products. It is likely that a relatively simple analysis of the company's financial records could provide a definitive answer to that question.

In another case, *In re Ben Huang,* the United States Court of Appeals upheld a finding by the Board of Patent Appeals and Interferences that the pending claims made by Huang for a patent covering a particular kind of tennis racket grip were obvious, in part through a finding that Huang had not presented sufficient evidence of commercial success.[18] In this case, the patent holder had cited several factors that he claimed were indicators of commercial success, including 1) sales of over 1 million units for use on both new and resold rackets and 2) the fact that since Huang began selling the claimed grip, sales of his company's prior grips had decreased by about 50 percent. In this case, a relatively basic review of the economics of the claimed product by the patent holder would likely have provided a sounder basis for his claim. For example, from a review of the product and patent descriptions, it appears that development costs were likely quite low—the

---

16 The discounted net present value (NPV) of a product that generates $10 per year in profits over the next three years will be greater than the NPV of a product that generates $5 next year, $10 the second year, and $15 the third year, even though both products will generate $30 in (undiscounted) profits.

17 *Neupak,* 41 Fed. Appx. 435.

18 *Huang,* 100 F.3d 135.

patent claimed a change in the ratio of the thickness of the various materials used in the grip. If this were the case, then net profitability could have been reliably estimated for both the patented version of the product and the older version that it replaced. Assuming that Huang's sales of the new grip were not a result of discounting relative to the preexisting product and that manufacturing costs for the two products were similar, then a determination of commercial success could be made based on an evaluation of the increased revenues generated by the patented product relative to an appropriate benchmark (such as Huang's revenues prior to introduction of the new product or to revenues of competitors in the industry).

Two Case Studies
We were asked to evaluate and testify on commercial success issues in two recent cases. These cases provide an illustration of how traditional measures may be insufficient to prove commercial success, as well as an illustration of how, if properly applied, economic analysis can provide the complete picture.

In the first case, we were asked to carry out research and testify on behalf of an accused infringer who was challenging the validity of a patent allegedly covering a particular type of packaged snack product. Despite rapid growth in sales of the product embodying the patented invention (approximately $30 million in revenues during the first year rising to about $110 million by the fourth year) and attainment of a substantial share of any reasonably defined market, we identified several key facts that nonetheless indicated that the patent may not have been a commercial success.

Our first concern was that, although revenues were increasing rapidly, the trend in profits was not so promising. As shown in Figure 1, the company experienced a cumulative net operating loss of approximately $10 million to $15 million during the first five years of the product's life cycle. Moreover, the trend through the last two years was downward—offering no indication that profits would be forthcoming in the near future. Furthermore, our analysis found that sales of the product were coming, in part, from customers that were switching from other snack products manufactured by the same company. We estimated that an additional $13 million in profits had been lost due to "cannibalization" of other product lines. These data indicated to us that although the product apparently had been deemed a success in the marketplace by consumers, it did not appear to be a commercial success from the perspective of the patent holder.

**Figure 1. Snack Product Patent Holder Profitability,
Annual and Cumulative**

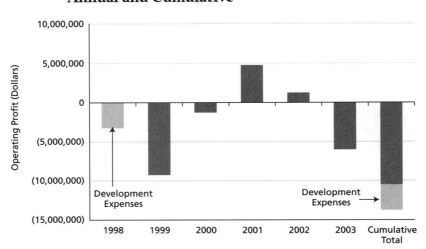

A second major concern related to the issue of the putative nexus between the revenues earned by the company and the patented invention. In this case, a competitor had entered the market one year after the patent holder with a product—acknowledged to be noninfringing and apparently not protected by any other patent or critical trade secret—that provided virtually the same benefits to the consumer as the disputed product, including such characteristics as ease of preparation, portion control, and shape of the package (important for product placement on the store shelf). Moreover, as shown in Figure 2, this product experienced a path of revenue growth almost identical to the product at issue. The patent holder claimed that the product embodying the patented invention was *one way* to achieve the benefits cited by customers. However, despite the dramatic growth in revenues, in our opinion the performance of this alternative product demonstrated that *causation* had not been established. Based on information we reviewed, it appeared that rapid growth in revenues and market share for products of this type were not dependent on the patented invention. Finally, we pointed out that the patent holder had a very well-known brand name and had used innovative techniques to introduce and market the product at issue. These factors further weakened the link between the patented invention and any success (at least in terms of gross revenues) that the product had in the marketplace.

Figure 2. Snack Product Annual Revenues Based on Number of Years Since Product Introduction

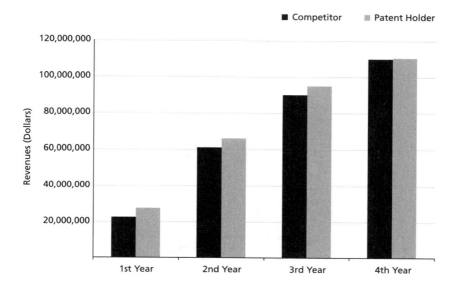

The facts were very different in the second patent dispute in which we testified for the patent holder regarding the commercial success of an anti-infective drug. First, there did not appear to be much dispute about the nexus between the patented invention and the product's efficacy, since—as one might expect with pharmaceutical products—the patent disclosed the drug itself and its methods of use. Second, although the accused infringer contended that the product's success was due to advertising and promotion, that argument was weakened by (1) physicians' testimony and other evidence that while promotional activities may well lead physicians to try a new product, repeated prescribing for patients is likely only if the product performs well; and (2) our analysis, which showed that the product at issue had the second-lowest ratio of promotional spending to sales of all major anti-infective products introduced in the past decade.

Traditional metrics, such as growth in market share, also pointed to the product's commercial success, as did a direct comparison of profits and R&D expenditures. Figure 3, for example, shows that after just four years on the market, the product ranked fourth among all oral tablet antibiotics, a market that included well over 200 products.

Figure 3. Revenues for Best-Selling Competing Brands in the Oral Tablet Antibiotic Market

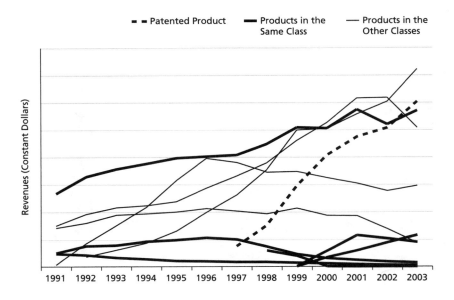

Although competition among antibiotics spans several classes of drugs, each class has a unique mechanism of action and therefore represents a distinct market segment that should be examined as part of an evaluation of the commercial success of a patented invention. As Figure 3 also shows, sales of the patented product grew faster than any other competing antibiotic. Figure 4 shows that within drugs of the same class, the market leader began losing share as soon as the patented product was introduced. The product's rapid acceptance as the treatment of choice for dangerous infections such as hospital-acquired pneumonia demonstrated both the product's commercial success and the importance of its performance characteristics (since no amount of advertising or promotion would be likely to influence the use of a product in life-threatening situations). The huge sales of the product were even more impressive in light of the long odds against success in the pharmaceutical industry[19] and a history of failed attempts to develop safe and effective anti-infective drugs, leaving no doubt in our minds that the product and the patented invention were commercial successes.

Figure 4. Shares of Revenue for a Class of Antibiotic Drugs

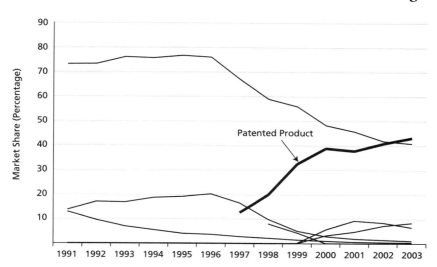

Conclusions

Based on our understanding of the purpose of patent protection and our interpretation of precedents, it is our opinion that commercial success should be evaluated on the basis of the economic contribution of a patented invention to an inventor's financial well-being. Thus, from the perspective of economics, a key indicator of commercial success ought to be the profits generated by the patented invention, relative to an appropriate benchmark or alternative. When available, financial data on these factors should be considered in an evaluation of commercial success. Courts' historic use of factors such as revenue growth and large market share is likely to be consistent with this standard in most cases, if applied correctly.

---

[19] Recent studies estimate that only one out of every 5,000 potential drug compounds synthesized during applied research ends up being marketed. See Alfonso Gambardella, *Science and Innovation: The U.S. Pharmaceutical Industry During the 1980s* (Cambridge University Press, 1995), 20; and Pharmaceutical Research and Manufacturers of America, *Pharmaceutical Industry Profile 2003*, 2–6. Only 3 of every 10 approved drugs have sales revenue that exceed the average after-tax development costs of a new drug product. See Pharmaceutical Research and Manufacturers of America, "The Lengthy and Costly Challenge of Drug Development," in "Leading the Way in the Search for Cures," (brochure), available at www.phrma.org/publications/publications/brochure/leading/index2.cfm, accessed 6 July 2004.

14

Preliminary Injunction Motions and the Economics of Irreparable Harm in Pharmaceutical Patent Infringement Cases

Jason Zeitler

When the United States Patent and Trademark Office issues a patent, it is granting to the patent holder the right to exclude others from making, using, or selling the patented invention for a fixed term. This right to exclude, the very essence of the concept of property, would be of limited value, of course, if adequate remedies at law for infringement were not available to patent holders. In the U.S., remedies for patent infringement include monetary and injunctive relief. The former remedy compensates patent holders for past infringement—in accordance with the make-whole standard[1]—while the latter enjoins infringers, either preliminarily or permanently, from future infringement.[2] Although district courts typically grant permanent injunctions in patent cases as a matter of course once infringement has been established, they must apply a four-factor standard prescribed by federal circuit law when considering motions for preliminary injunctions. The four factors include (1) whether the plaintiff will have an adequate remedy at law or will be irreparably harmed if a preliminary injunction does not issue, (2) whether the threatened injury to the plaintiff outweighs the threatened harm the injunction may inflict upon the defendant, (3) whether the plaintiff has at least a reasonable

---

[1] See 35 U.S.C. § 284, which states, "...the Court shall award the claimant damages adequate to compensate for the infringement, but in no event less than a reasonable royalty for the use of the invention by the infringer."

[2] The U.S. patent statute authorizes injunctive relief in patent cases: "The several courts having jurisdiction of cases under this title may grant injunctions in accordance with the principles of equity to prevent the violation of any right secured by patent, on such terms as the court deems reasonable." See 35 U.S.C. § 283.

likelihood of success on the merits, and (4) whether the granting of a pre-liminary injunction will disserve the public interest.[3] As a matter of law, a plaintiff may obtain a preliminary injunction for patent infringement if the balance of these four factors favors granting the injunction.

Of the three factors amenable to economic analysis—irreparable harm, balance of hardships, and public interest—irreparable harm is perhaps the most elusive.[4] What does it mean exactly for a harm to be irreparable? In the words of the United States Court of Appeals for the Federal Circuit (CAFC):

> In matters involving patent rights, irreparable harm has been pre-sumed when a clear showing has been made of patent validity and infringement.... This presumption derives in part from the finite term of the patent grant, for patent expiration is not suspended during litigation, and the passage of time can work irremediable harm. The opportunity to practice an invention during the notoriously lengthy course of patent litigation may itself tempt infringers.... The nature of the patent grant thus weighs against holding that monetary damages will always suffice to make the patentee whole, for the principal value of a patent is its statutory right to exclude.[5]

From an economic perspective, few forms of harm would appear to strictly meet the CAFC's definition of "irremediable," given the ability of

---

3   See, for example, *Roper Corp. v. Litton Systems Inc.*, 757 F.2d 1266, 1269 (Fed. Cir. 1985), hereafter cited as *Roper*; *Hybritech Inc. v. Abbott Laboratories*, 849 F.2d 1446, 1451 (Fed. Cir. 1988), hereafter cited as *Hybritech*; *Bio-Technology General Corp. v. Genentech Inc.*, 80 F.3d 1553, 1558 (Fed. Cir. 1996), cert. denied, 519 U.S. 911 (1996), hereafter cited as *Bio-Technology General*; and *Amazon.com Inc. v. Barnesandnoble.com Inc.*, 239 F.3d 1343, 1350 (Fed. Cir. 2001), hereafter cited as *Amazon.com*. A presump-tion of irreparable harm follows in a patent suit if the plaintiff has made a clear showing that the patent at issue is valid and infringed, thereby satisfying the third factor for preliminary injunctive relief—that is, that there exists a reasonable likeli-hood of success on the merits. See, for example, *Smith International Inc. v. Hughes Tool Co.*, 718 F.2d 1573, 1581 (Fed. Cir. 1983), cert. denied, 464 U.S. 496, 104 S.Ct. 493, 78 L.Ed.2d 687 (1983); *Novo Nordisk of North America Inc. v. Genentech Inc.*, 77 F.3d 1364, 1371 (Fed. Cir. 1996); *Purdue Pharma L.P. v. Boehringer Ingelheim GMBH*, 237 F.3d 1359, 1363-1365 (Fed. Cir. 2001); and *Amazon.com*, at 1350. Federal circuit law also provides an alleged infringer the opportunity to rebut any presumption of irreparable harm. See, for example, *Roper*, at 1272; *Illinois Tool Works Inc. v. Grip-Pak Inc.*, 906 F.2d 679, 681-682 (Fed. Cir. 1990), hereafter cited as *Illinois Tool Works*; *Reebok Intl., Ltd. v. J. Baker Inc.*, 32 F.3d 1552, 1556 (Fed. Cir. 1994), hereafter cited as *Reebok*; and *Polymer Technologies Inc. v. P. Bridwell*, 103 F.3d 970, 974-977 (Fed. Cir. 1996).

4   For an economic perspective on the balance-of-hardships and public-interest factors, see Ramsey Shehadeh and Marion Stewart, "An Economic Approach to the 'Balance of Hardships' and 'Public Interest' Tests for Preliminary Injunction Motions in Patent Infringement Cases," July 2000, available at www.nera.com/eLibrary.asp.

5   See *H.H. Robertson Co. v. United Steel Deck Inc.*, 820 F.2d 384, 390 (Fed. Cir. 1987).

patent holders to seek monetary damages through litigation. Economic principles provide damages experts with the tools necessary to quantify nearly every imaginable form of harm. Nevertheless, at least some forms of harm exist that appear to defy quantification or that cannot be remedied monetarily.[6] Lost future profits due to lost research and development (R&D) opportunities, for example, would probably be impossible to quantify with precision, and simply as a legal matter, any harm attributable to lost R&D opportunities would likely be regarded as irreparable,[7] since U.S. patent law stipulates that while damages calculations need not be unerringly precise, they cannot be speculative.[8] Even assuming there

---

[6] As the CAFC states, "[t]he patent statute provides injunctive relief to preserve the legal interests of the parties against future infringement which may have market effects never fully compensable in money. 'If monetary relief were the sole relief afforded by the patent statute then injunctions would be unnecessary and infringers could become compulsory licensees for as long as the litigation lasts.'" See *Hybritech,* at 1457. Moreover, the CAFC appears not to look favorably on "applications of the concept that *no* patentee could ever be irreparably harmed when an alleged infringer is capable of responding in damages." See *Illinois Tool Works,* at 683; italics in original.

[7] See, for example, *Bio-Technology General,* at 1566; and *Pharmacia & Upjohn Co. v. Ranbaxy Pharmaceuticals Inc.,* 85 Fed. Appx. 205, 2003 WL 23016042 (Fed. Cir.), 214-215, hereafter cited as Pharmacia. Other forms of irreparable harm have been cited in the case law. For example, in the well-known *Hybritech* case, which involved a biotechnology patent relating to diagnostic test kits, the United States District Court for the Central District of California found, among other things, the following factors to be reasons for granting a preliminary injunction: (1) the plaintiff would likely lose opportunities to establish a market position and to create business relationships; (2) by the time the litigation finished, the value of the patent could be diminished and the patented technology leapfrogged; (3) the potential injury was unpredictable; and (4) in the absence of an injunction, other potential infringers would be encouraged to infringe. See *Hybritech,* at 1456. In *Reebok,* the CAFC indicated that damage to a patent holder's reputation or goodwill could be irreparable: "Harm to reputation resulting from confusion between an inferior accused product and a patentee's superior product is a type of harm that is often not fully compensable by money because the damages caused are speculative and difficult to measure." See *Reebok,* at 1558. Similar logic was applied in the *Bio-Technology General* case, in which the district court determined that Genentech Inc.'s goodwill would be irreparably harmed in the absence of an injunction. See *Bio-Technology General,* at 1566. There may even be circumstances in which alleged infringers could not afford to pay damages if their accused sales were made throughout the duration of litigation. See, for example, *Illinois Tool Works,* at 682-683.

[8] The fact that permanent injunctions are matters of course when case dispositions favor the plaintiff means that damages are usually presumed to end at the date of trial. As a result, courts rarely award future damages, not because such damages never exist but because attempts at quantification too often enter the realm of speculation. For the courts' views on speculative damages claims, see, for example, *Lam Inc. v. Johns-Manville Corp.,* 718 F.2d 1056, 1065 (Fed. Cir. 1983); *Bio-Rad Laboratories Inc. v. Nicolet Instrument Corp.,* 739 F.2d 604, 616 (Fed. Cir. 1984), cert. denied, 469 U.S. 1038, 105 S.Ct. 516, 83 L.Ed.2d 405 (1984); *Standard Havens Products Inc. v. Gencor Industries Inc.,* 953 F.2d 1360, 1374-1376 (Fed. Cir. 1991), cert. denied, 113 S.Ct. 60 (1992); and *Minnesota Mining and Manufacturing Co. v. Johnson & Johnson Orthopaedics Inc.,* 976 F.2d 1559, 1579 (Fed. Cir. 1992).

were an economic model sophisticated enough to predict future payoffs from R&D projects, the inputs used in that model, as well as its outputs, might well be regarded as speculative by some courts.[9]

In the R&D-intensive pharmaceutical industry, a patent holder's ability to seek preliminary injunctive relief is particularly important, largely because of provisions contained in the 1984 Drug Price Competition and Patent Term Restoration Act (commonly known as the Hatch-Waxman Act) that limit pharmaceutical patent protection rights. Under the act, patent holders have the right to prevent competitors only from selling, not from making or using, a product protected by an unexpired patent. In essence, the act allows generic drug manufacturers to challenge patents covering innovative drugs and, therefore, to enter the market before patent expiration. Generic drug manufacturers may file patent challenges as early as three or four years after the Food and Drug Administration (FDA) approves a new innovative drug. As of 2003, patent challenges occurred in approximately 6 percent of generic drug applications for FDA approval.[10]

This chapter provides an overview of the economics of pharmaceutical R&D and considers the possible manifestations of irreparable harm that can result from pharmaceutical patent challenges and consequent early entry of generic drugs. The primary conclusion is that when R&D expenditures are funded from current earnings, generic entry has the greatest potential to lead to irreparable harm to the patent holder in the form of lost future profits. Losses in current earnings caused by the presence of a generic drug would diminish the patent holder's ability to innovate and, thus, would diminish expected future profits. Because predicting future lost profits from innovations that were never actually developed is inherently speculative, any such lost earnings potential is unlikely to be compensated for in monetary damages awards.

---

9   For example, one model input might be the probability that a particular drug under preclinical evaluation later becomes a marketed product and also recovers its R&D costs. An *ex ante* estimate of that probability would likely be highly speculative, especially if it were based solely on historical industry averages. The distribution of profit outcomes on marketed drugs is decidedly skewed. This means that the profit outcome for the average drug is unlikely to be indicative of the profit outcome for a specific drug.

10 See Pharmaceutical Research and Manufacturers of America, *Pharmaceutical Industry Profile 2003*, 60–62, available at www.phrma.org/publications/publications/profile02/index.cfm. Generic drug manufacturers may challenge an unexpired innovator patent through a "paragraph IV" certification—submitted to the FDA in conjunction with an abbreviated new drug application, or ANDA—stating that the patent is either invalid and/or would not be infringed by the sale of a generic drug. Patent holders are entitled to sue within 45 days of receiving notice of a challenge, in which case a 30-month stay is placed on the FDA's final approval of the generic drug application.

The Economics of Pharmaceutical R&D

The pharmaceutical R&D process is lengthy, expensive, and extremely risky. Pharmaceutical firms invest substantial capital, both human and financial, to discover and develop new or improved innovative drugs. According to Pharmaceutical Research and Manufacturers of America (PhRMA), annual pharmaceutical R&D spending in the U.S. has nearly doubled every five years since 1970. In 2002, R&D spending reached approximately $26.4 billion, or the equivalent of about 18.2 percent of pharmaceutical revenues.[11] As a result of this spending, the U.S. pharmaceutical industry is able to produce 30 to 50 new drug discoveries annually.[12]

Experimental drugs take an average of 10 to 15 years to commercialize.[13] The R&D process for these drugs entails five distinct development and approval steps: discovery/preclinical testing, Phase I clinical trials, Phase II clinical trials, Phase III clinical trials, and FDA approval. On average, clinical trials alone are expected to last about seven years.[14] After FDA approval, a drug may also be required to undergo additional, "Phase IV," trials in order to evaluate long-term effects. Because innovative drug patent applications are usually submitted at the beginning of the clinical development process, effective patent lives for pharmaceuticals are often no more than 11 to 12 years, even after accounting for patent term restoration periods granted under the Hatch-Waxman Act.[15]

Pharmaceutical R&D is costly in part because of the large number of drug candidates that fail to become marketed products. Only about 0.1 percent of compounds evaluated in preclinical testing actually reach the clinical trial stage, and only about 0.02 percent of compounds eventually receive FDA approval for marketing in the U.S.[16] It is estimated that out-of-pocket costs to develop the average new drug, including allocations for the cost of failed projects, exceed $400 million. Capitalizing out-of-pocket costs to the point of FDA approval increases the estimated cost per approved new drug to roughly $800 million. If the costs for Phase IV

---

[11] See PhRMA, "Leading the Way: Facts about the U.S. Pharmaceutical Industry" (brochure), available at www.phrma.org/publications/publications/brochure/leading/lead9.cfm; and PhRMA, *Pharmaceutical Industry Profile 2003*, 10.

[12] See PhRMA, "Leading the Way: America's Pharmaceutical Industry" (brochure), available at www.phrma.org/publications/ publications/brochure/leading/lead2.cfm.

[13] See John T. Kelly, "The Drug Development and Approval Process," in *New Medicines in Development for Heart Disease and Stroke*, 2003 (PhRMA), 19.

[14] Id.

[15] See PhRMA, *Pharmaceutical Industry Profile 2003*, 61.

[16] See Kelly, supra note 13.

R&D are included, the total capitalized cost per approved new drug approaches $900 million.[17]

Few marketed drugs ever recover their development costs, further compounding the risk of pharmaceutical R&D. Approximately 70 percent of commercialized drugs fail to produce revenues equal to or greater than their R&D costs.[18] Not surprisingly, this has caused the pharmaceutical industry as a whole to focus its R&D efforts on the search for "blockbuster" drugs, which tend to be drugs that have garnered a first-mover or other early entry advantage in a new therapeutic class.[19] A consequence is that an individual pharmaceutical firm's long-term economic viability may be determined by the profitability of only a small fraction of its overall drug portfolio.

Industry insiders have apparently long held the view that pharmaceutical firms generally finance their R&D from internal cash flows. This view was empirically examined in a 2001 *Health Affairs* article by Professor F. M. Scherer, who found that pharmaceutical firms' R&D expenditures are indeed significantly affected by changes in gross margins. He states the following in the introduction to his article:

> Profitability and investments in R&D can, in principle, be linked in three different ways. First, successful R&D leads, with long and variable lags, to new products, which depending upon their reception in the market, can add greatly to company profits....
>
> Second, the profits earned by a company serve as a source of funds to support R&D investments, and some managers are known to set R&D budgets using rules of thumb emphasizing an indicator of current cash flow or sales....Third, managers' expectations of future profit opportunities, which are tempered, inter alia, by contemporary market conditions, can exert a demand-pull influence on R&D investments.[20]

---

17 See Joseph A. DiMasi, Ronald W. Hansen, and Henry G. Grabowski, "The Price of Innovation: New Estimates of Drug Development Costs," *Journal of Health Economics,* 22 (2003): 151-185.

18 See PhRMA, *Pharmaceutical Industry Profile 2003,* 3-4. See also Henry Grabowski, "Patents and New Product Development in the Pharmaceutical and Biotechnology Industries," (working paper, Duke University, July 2002), 13-15.

19 See Grabowski, "Patents and New Product Development," 13-15, 17. As Professor Grabowski points out, life cycles of branded products within a given therapeutic class often follow a dynamic competitive pattern that involves breakthrough as well as incremental advances in drug formulations.

20 See F. M. Scherer, "The Link Between Gross Profitability and Pharmaceutical R&D Spending," *Health Affairs,* 20, no. 5 (2001): 216-220.

As is discussed below, the link between current earnings and pharmaceutical R&D spending has obvious implications for economic analyses of irreparable harm in the context of pharmaceutical patent
infringement cases.

Irreparable Harm Due to Reduced Pharmaceutical R&D in ANDA Cases

Branded-drug firms respond to generic entry in a number of fairly predictable ways. First, despite facing significant price competition, branded-
drug firms sometimes respond to generic entry by raising prices. The
economic rationale for higher brand prices is that the demand side of a
particular drug market consists of segments with differing sensitivities to
price. The more price-sensitive buyers shift away from the branded drug
to generics, while the more price-insensitive buyers continue to purchase
the branded drug, the result of which is a less elastic demand function for
the branded drug. For their part, branded-drug firms choose to maximize
profits, raising price and supplying only to the more price-insensitive
market segments.[21] The net financial effect of generic entry for the
branded-drug firms is higher per-unit profit margins but substantially
lower sales and overall profits.

Second, branded-drug firms reduce or eliminate their marketing and
detailing activities, which may include laying off or redeploying dedicated
sales staff. This response to generic entry makes intuitive sense, as it
would be economically irrational for branded-drug firms to send sales
representatives into the field and to distribute samples or marketing
materials for the purpose of increasing brand awareness when prescrip-
tions would more likely be filled with a less expensive generic.

Third, branded-drug firms reduce or cancel spending on clinical trials
or other R&D, either because the presence of a generic diminishes the
incentive to innovate within a given class of drug or because the

---

[21] See, for example, Richard G. Frank and David S. Salkever, "Generic Entry and the
Pricing of Pharmaceuticals," *Journal of Economics & Management Strategy* 6, no. 1
(Spring 1997): 75-90. Price responses to generic entry for anti-infective drugs may be
more consistent with traditional market models. Research conducted by Steven
Wiggins and Robert Maness shows that in the anti-infectives market, brand prices
decline sharply with initial entry of a generic. See Steven N. Wiggins and Robert
Maness, "Price Competition in Pharmaceuticals: The Case of Anti-Infectives,"
Economic Inquiry 42, no. 2 (April 2004): 247-263. There may also be instances in
which generic entry causes branded-drug firms to lower rather than raise prices in
non-anti-infectives drug markets. Regardless of whether the branded-drug firm
raises or lowers price in response to generic entry, the overall effect is to reduce gross
profits earned from sales of the branded drug.

decreased profits caused by generic competition limit the resources available to innovate. Although branded-drug firms may not cancel existing clinical trials, perhaps for patient-health and public-relations reasons, they may cancel planned clinical trials. They may also cancel existing or planned nonclinical trials or studies that might otherwise have led to the discovery of new indications for compounds, to product improvements, or to advancements in public education programs.

Of the three types of responses to generic entry, it is the third type that has the greatest potential to lead to irreparable harm. If infringement were found, lost sales and concomitant lost profits on the branded drug would, in principle at least, be fully compensable by money. The infringer's sales would be permanently enjoined, and the branded-drug firm's right to exclude would be restored. Reduced or eliminated marketing and detailing could possibly result in irreparable harm to the branded-drug firm's reputation—in the sense, for example, that relationships with physicians, who provide patients with samples and who rely on medical information regarding available treatments provided by sales representatives, may be tarnished. But depending on the expected length of the litigation, the branded-drug firm may decide not to reduce its marketing and detailing, since the costs of severance packages, sales staff redeployments, and subsequent rehiring and training of new sales staff might outweigh any short-term savings in selling and marketing expenses.[22]

However, the branded-drug firm *would* likely suffer irreparable harm if the presence of an infringing generic product caused a decrease in R&D expenditures. In theory, any lost opportunities to conduct R&D, and in turn any lost future profits on new or improved products that might have resulted from that R&D, could at least partially be regained once damages were awarded at trial: the branded-drug firm could simply earmark for R&D the portion of the damages award that it would otherwise have spent on R&D *but for* the infringement. That notwithstanding, the damages award would not be expected to precisely compensate the branded-drug firm for its losses. Because of their time-sensitive nature, most R&D opportunities available at the commencement of litigation likely would not be available months or years later by the time of trial. At a minimum, the delay in R&D spending would lead to losses equal to the time value of money on future profits generated by any new or improved drugs. At

---

[22] Irrespective of the branded-drug firm's exact response, a proper damages calculation would reflect any differences between actual and but-for selling and marketing expenses.

worst, the branded-drug firm could lose a first-mover or other early entry advantage if competing drugs reached the market sooner as a consequence of the delayed R&D. The extent of the harm would depend in part on the financial position of the branded-drug firm. For example, in relative terms, a large, well-established pharmaceutical firm would likely suffer less harm than a start-up with a modest drug portfolio, since the latter would necessarily be more heavily reliant on its near-term R&D opportunities to remain financially viable. But regardless of where along the spectrum of possible outcomes the harm would ultimately lie, because future profits resulting from the branded-drug firm's R&D spending could never be known with certainty ex ante, any harm caused by a delay in R&D would likely be impossible to quantify and would therefore be irreparable.

The Courts' Rulings on Claims of Irreparable Harm Due to Lost R&D Opportunities

CAFC and district court rulings have been mixed with regard to motions for preliminary injunctions that involve claims of irreparable harm due to lost R&D opportunities.[23] Perhaps the most prominent rulings were made in the mid-1990s case of *Eli Lilly and Co. v. American Cyanamid Co.*[24] In *Eli Lilly,* American Cyanamid and three other defendants were accused of infringing an Eli Lilly patent relating to the compound cefaclor, a member of the cephalosporin class of anti-infectives. At the time, two of the defendants had recently received FDA approval to market generic versions of cefaclor in the U.S., while a third defendant's ANDA was pending approval. All three companies had imported supplies of cefaclor from the fourth defendant, an Italian manufacturer. In its complaint, Eli Lilly requested a preliminary injunction to enjoin the defendants from importing or selling their cefaclor products. Eli Lilly argued, among other things, that competition from generic versions of cefaclor would result in

---

[23] Overall, from October 1982 through December 1993, district courts granted motions for preliminary injunctions in patent infringement cases approximately 61 percent of the time. Of those, about 23 percent were reversed on appeal, indicating an effective success rate for preliminary injunctions of about 47 percent [(1 - 0.23) x 0.61]. See M. A. Cunningham, "Preliminary Injunctive Relief in Patent Litigation," *IDEA: The Journal of Law and Technology,* 1995:230-232. Success rates appear not to have changed substantively since 1993. According to University of Houston Law Center statistics, which exclude unpublished court decisions, the effective success rate (i.e., after accounting for appellate-court decisions) for preliminary injunctions during the January 2000-June 2004 period was about 40 percent. See www.patstats.org/editors_page.html.

[24] See *Eli Lilly and Co. v. American Cyanamid Co.,* 82 F.3d 1568 (Fed. Cir. 1996), hereafter cited as *Eli Lilly.*

irreparable harm to its R&D programs. The United States District Court for the Southern District of Indiana denied Eli Lilly's request, finding that there was not a reasonable likelihood of success on the merits and that Eli Lilly would not suffer irreparable harm in the absence of a preliminary injunction.[25]

On appeal, the CAFC affirmed the district court's decision. With regard to Eli Lilly's contention of irreparable harm due to lost R&D opportunities, the CAFC stated:

> [Eli] Lilly contends that the loss of profits on sales of cefaclor because of competition from the appellees will result in irreparable injury to [Eli] Lilly's overall pharmaceutical research efforts. As the district court pointed out, however, that claim of injury is not materially different from any claim of injury by a business that is deprived of funds that it could usefully reinvest. If a claim of lost opportunity to conduct research were sufficient to compel a finding of irreparable harm, it is hard to imagine any manufacturer with a research and development program that could not make the same claim and thus be equally entitled to preliminary injunctive relief. Such a rule would convert the "extraordinary" relief of a preliminary injunction into a standard remedy, available whenever the plaintiff has shown a likelihood of success on the merits. For that reason, adopting the principle that Lilly proposes would "disserve the patent system."[26]

The CAFC's position here is unfortunate, as it seems to miss the point of Eli Lilly's contention.[27]

There is a clear distinction, which the CAFC fails to draw in *Eli Lilly,* between what might be termed "ordinary" business investments and those associated with pharmaceutical R&D. Ordinary business investments would include capital equipment purchases as well as any other outlays where expected returns can be valued using capital budgeting techniques, such as discounted cash flow analyses. These investments differ from investments in pharmaceutical R&D in two meaningful ways: (1) their returns are likely to be normally distributed and are therefore reasonably

---

[25] Id., at 1569-1571 and 1578.

[26] Id., at 1578.

[27] Equally unfortunate is the fact that district courts have since cited to *Eli Lilly* as justification for rejecting pharmaceutical patent holders' contentions of irreparable harm due to lost R&D opportunities. See, for example, *Minnesota Mining and Manufacturing Co. v. Alphapharm Pty. Ltd.,* 2002 WL 1299996 (D. Minn.), at 5.

predictable, and (2) companies undertaking them are not dependent on internal cash flows for funding but instead may turn to the financial markets. Consequently, in motions for preliminary injunctions, not just "any manufacturer with a research and development program" could legitimately claim irreparable harm due to lost investment opportunities, since any company that could turn to the financial markets to fund its investments would not have opportunities to lose in the first place. While it is true that pharmaceutical firms seem likely to suffer irreparable harm if R&D opportunities are lost, the courts' application of a "rule" based on that fact would appear to be no more of a "standard remedy" than is the presumption of irreparable harm that follows in a patent suit whenever a plaintiff has shown a strong likelihood of success on the merits.[28]

Despite the CAFC's commentary in *Eli Lilly,* district courts have been willing to entertain the possibility that pharmaceutical patent holders could be irreparably harmed as a result of lost R&D opportunities. In the recent *Pharmacia* case, for instance, which involved the challenge of a patent that covered a cefpodoxime proxetil anti-infective drug sold by Pharmacia & Upjohn Co. (Pharmacia), the United States District Court for the District of New Jersey granted a preliminary injunction, based in part on a finding of irreparable harm due to the "loss of current research opportunities resulting from loss of funding."[29] The district court cited additional economic factors in support of its conclusion that irreparable harm was likely, including loss of the remaining relatively short life of the patent, irretrievable price and market erosion for the patented product, the speculative nature of damage assessments, and the difficulty of pursuing collection of any damages in international courts. For its part, the CAFC did not consider the district court's finding of irreparable harm to be erroneous.[30] Notably, all of the economic evidence of irreparable harm cited by the district court was

---

[28] The CAFC's stance on the irreparability of lost pharmaceutical R&D seems to be rooted more in a dislike of extremes than in economics: "Past applications of the concept that *no* patentee could *ever* be irreparably harmed when an alleged infringer is capable of responding in damages frequently disserved patentees and the patent system. ... That disservice would not be cured by a rash of patentee motions for preliminary injunctions filed without full basis in equity. Application of the concept that *every* patentee is *always* irreparably harmed by an alleged infringer's pretrial sales would equally disserve the patent system. Like all generalities, neither concept is universally applicable and, knowing that the court will do so, patentees should consider, weigh, and balance all of the equitable circumstances, in light of the established jurisprudence, before moving for a preliminary injunction." See *Illinois Tool Works,* at 683; italics in original.

[29] See *Pharmacia,* at 207-208 and 214-215. See also *Pharmacia & Upjohn Co. v. Ranbaxy Pharmaceuticals Inc.,* 274 F.Supp.2d 597, 614 (D. NJ).

[30] See *Pharmacia,* at 215.

secondary to the presumption of irreparable harm that proceeded from Pharmacia's clear showing of patent validity and infringement. One implication is that district courts may more readily accept evidence of irreparable harm due to lost pharmaceutical R&D opportunities when the plaintiff also makes a strong showing of a likelihood of success on the merits.

Conclusion

Uncertainties pervade pharmaceutical R&D and commercialization processes. Only about 0.006 percent of compounds evaluated in preclinical testing eventually become marketed products that generate revenues equal to or greater than their R&D costs. Recent empirical research seems to corroborate conventional wisdom that innovative pharmaceutical firms generally finance their R&D spending with internal cash flows. In an ANDA case involving a patent challenge—or in any pharmaceutical patent infringement case, for that matter—irreparable harm in the form of lost future profits would likely occur if infringement were to lead to a loss in R&D opportunities. The courts have rendered seemingly divergent opinions on the issue. In the recent *Pharmacia* case, however, the United States District Court for the District of New Jersey accepted the plaintiff's contention that irreparable harm would result from lost pharmaceutical R&D opportunities, and on appeal the CAFC affirmed the district court's finding of irreparable harm.

This chapter has focused on irreparable harm due to lost pharmaceutical R&D opportunities, but other forms of irreparable harm may occur in pharmaceutical patent infringement cases, including lost future profits caused by permanent price erosion or by losses in non-R&D business opportunities that derive from internally generated funds.[31] Also, while the conclusions drawn in this chapter are specific to the pharmaceutical industry, they could in principle equally apply to other R&D-intensive industries (e.g., the biotechnology, computer, and semiconductor industries), particularly to the extent that companies in those industries finance their R&D with internal cash flows instead of with venture capital or other external sources of funds. Ultimately, the possibility of irreparable harm, regardless of what form it might take and in what industry it might occur, is an empirical matter to be determined by the unique facts of each patent infringement case.

---

[31] As is evident from the *Pharmacia* case, for example, infringing pretrial sales of a generic anti-infective product could potentially lead to irreversible price erosion for the branded drug.

IV

The Intersection of Antitrust and Intellectual Property

15

Standard Setting and Market Power

Richard T. Rapp and Lauren J. Stiroh

Patents, Standards, and Value

Most patents do not create market power, despite the implications of terms such as *patent monopoly*. This is because most patents protect technologies that, while novel and useful, have close substitutes. However technically original an invention may be, its value is no greater than the price people are willing to pay for the advantage the invention confers over the next-best alternative. An invention that is merely different from, but not an improvement over, existing alternatives will not be worth much, no matter how new and exciting the inventors claim their technology is.

In certain industries and in a very specific set of technical and economic circumstances, the combination of standard setting and patents can create market power where none might otherwise exist. It bears emphasizing, however, that just as one should not infer market power from the existence of a patent, neither should one assume that standard setting in the presence of patenting creates market power.

Standard setting has the potential to create market power (i.e., increase the value of a technology) when a technology with close substitutes wins a formal standard-setting competition and the fact of having been named a standard separates the standardized technology from its formerly equivalent substitutes. Standard setting creates market power by making otherwise close substitutes inferior, and thereby increasing the royalty rate (price) a technology can command. By contrast, when the invention would dominate the alternatives in a technology market on its

---

An earlier version of this chapter was first presented as part of the joint hearings of the United States Department of Justice and the Federal Trade Commission, "Competition and Intellectual Property Law and Policy in the Knowledge-Based-Economy," Washington, DC, 18 April 2002.

own inherent merits, ratification of the market outcome by formal standard setting is an afterthought; it changes nothing.

One of the goals of a standard-setting organization (SSO) is to choose a technology as the standard that will yield the best performance at the lowest possible cost. The technology that offers the best technical performance is not necessarily the first choice if the cost of that technology exceeds its performance advantage. A predicament facing the SSO in trying to choose the technology with the best price-performance trade-off is that the price of the chosen technology can change after the standard is determined if the technology owner attempts to extract the value added by the standardization process in royalty fees for the standard technology. If the SSO were not aware that the technology it was including in the standard was proprietary, it would not be aware of the likely *ex post* cost of the standard.

To ensure that it has the most information possible about the potential for the technologies it is considering being subject to royalties, many SSOs request that their members disclose any relevant patents that they have to the SSO during the standard-setting process. In addition, the SSO also typically requires that a member whose proprietary technology *is* included in the standard will license that technology to other members of the SSO either free of charge or on "fair, reasonable, or non-discriminatory terms."

The Impact of Disclosure Rules

SSOs rely upon disclosure rules to accomplish important objectives. Disclosure rules enable the SSO to obtain information about whether technologies under consideration for inclusion in the standard are proprietary and subject to licensing. They thereby reduce the potential for a technology to be included in a standard without the knowledge that there may be a technology owner with intellectual property that reads on the standard who may try to extract opportunistic royalties for the use of the technology.

In the absence of knowledge about proprietary intellectual property rights in the technologies under consideration, manufacturers may find themselves the victims of opportunism after the standard has been set. That is, the patent owner may charge a royalty that reflects a premium arising from the cost of revising the standard to save the cost of royalty. A patent owner may charge such a premium when the patent emerges after manufacturers have made sunk investment in the patented feature of the standard without having predetermined the license fee.[1] Avoiding the technology (and the required license) entails undertaking additional investment costs if the old (potentially infringing) investments cannot be modified to evade the patent. The manufacturers are in a weak negotiating position compared to the patent owner because the patent owner can credibly seek high licensing fees backed up with the threat of lawsuit if the manufacturers' product infringes upon the patent. The manufacturers could redesign their product around the patent, but this could require a major redesign effort and cause a significant disruption to production. The manufacturers could still be potentially liable for any products sold after the patent issued and before the redesigned products were available. Furthermore, the new product could be incompatible with other products or different versions of the product, which would further increase redesigning costs for manufacturers.

In order for a technology owner to profit from opportunism of this sort and for such opportunism to be a concern to the SSO, three important conditions must be met. First, the proprietary technology must be essential to the standard or else it could simply be omitted. An attempt by the patent owner to charge opportunistic royalties would result in manufacturers leaving that particular technology out of the final product. Second, there must be costs associated with changing either the standard or the manufacturing process that are greater than the royalty demanded. Finally, there must be alternatives to the chosen patented technology that could plausibly have been adopted had disclosure taken place. If there were no economic alternative, the patent owner would have been able to extract the full value of preventing manufacturers from making on-standard products by means of the exclusionary power of the patent alone. Thus, if there were no economic alternatives, the SSO could not benefit from the proprietary nature of the technology at issue having been disclosed.

Because of the potential for opportunism in standard setting, SSOs employ a variety of disclosure rules and enforce them with varying degrees of strictness. An example of one such rule is that issued patents essential to the standard be disclosed by standard-setting participants

---

[1]   Sunk investments are those that cannot be recovered if the manufacturer decides to adopt a different production process or manufacture his products according to an out-of-standard technology.

who are active proponents of the adoption of their technology.[2] A more rigorous rule is a requirement that all participants disclose issued patents, essential or otherwise, and whether or not the technology owner is an active proponent of its own technology. More rigorous still is a rule requiring disclosure of both issued patents and patent applications.

Disclosure rules vary because along with the potential benefits of disclosure, described above, there are costs of compliance. Compliance costs fall into two categories: transaction costs and the risk of diminishing the property right. These costs are borne directly by the organization members and indirectly by the SSO if compliance costs cause some technology owners to opt out of the SSO, making the SSO less effective. The more rigorous the disclosure rule, the higher the cost of complying. It is costly for the SSO representative of a member firm to first learn the patent portfolio of his firm, particularly if that firm is a large, research-based organization, and then to ascertain whether any patents read on the standard. The need to do this for as-yet-unpatented projects increases the cost.[3]

Rules that require the disclosure of unprotected intellectual property such as patent applications pose obvious risks for the IP owners. U.S. patent applications are kept secret for 18 months so that premature disclosure does not lead to unprotected use of the invention. Disclosure of unpublished or even published applications in standard-setting bodies opens the applicant up to the risk of interferences in the patent application procedure. These interferences will be costly to the applicant and may be brought by a competitor whose goals are to increase its rivals' costs or steer the standard-setting committee toward a less desirable technology.

In addition, a disclosure requirement covering patent applications reduces the value of a patent later obtained because it affords others— typically, competitors in the technology market—a head start toward evasion or design-around efforts that will diminish the value of the patented

---

2   Since patents are public documents, a rule requiring disclosure of patents merely saves the SSO patent-searching costs. If the disclosure rule is accompanied by a requirement that a standard-setting participant's patents be licensed on "reasonable and non-discriminatory" (RAND) terms, as is often the case, the SSO's objective is to nullify, not merely discover, the potential for opportunistic licensing.

3   Without a requirement that a firm's representative be knowledgeable about the firm's actual and potential intellectual property, any disclosure rule can be evaded by sending a deliberately ignorant representative. Because full compliance by an ignorant representative does not yield any of the benefits of disclosure to the SSO, we assume that member firms feel some obligation to send a knowledgeable representative.

technology. Application owners will weigh the benefits of joining a standard-setting organization against the cost of revealing potentially valuable intellectual property before it is protected by a patent.

The costs of disclosure fall not only upon members but upon the standard-setting organizations themselves: As cost and risk rise for individual member firms, the attractiveness of opting out of participation in standard setting increases. This is dangerous for the SSO and for economic efficiency in industries for which formal standard setting is an efficiency-enhancing activity.

In addition, mandating disclosure of patent applications has the potential for facilitating coordination among various factions of standard-setting members to the detriment of other members. Buyers of technology have an incentive to depress prices while sellers of technology have an incentive to raise prices. Technology buyers may work against technology sellers by attempting to design around prematurely disclosed patentable claims to depress royalties and to deter the entry of technological mavericks. This would create a disincentive for nonmanufacturing firms (i.e., firms specializing in R&D) to participate in standard-setting organizations. Alternatively, some members of the SSO may try to get the standard to move in a particular direction to create a weaker competitor to its own proprietary technology. That is, a committee member with a proprietary competing technology may object to any features of the standard that may become patentable by other members of the committee if those features add performance benefits to the standard, thus making it a more formidable competitor to the member's own out-of-standard proprietary technology.

It is unlikely that there is a single "one size fits all" optimal disclosure rule for standard-setting bodies. There is bound to be variation by industry or technology in the value sacrificed by an inventor as a result of premature disclosure, just as there are inter-industry differences in the value that patent protection affords.[4] To the extent that the benefits and costs described above cannot be measured in a given industry, the optimal rule for that industry may be, in fact, unknowable.

Because of differences across industries in the reward afforded by patent protection and in the incentives of standard-setting members, no rule would be optimal for all situations. Because of this heterogeneity across industries, the policy choice that leaves the disclosure rule and the

---

4   See, for example, Mark Schankerman, "How Valuable Is Patent Protection? Estimates by Technology Field," *RAND Journal of Economics*, 29, no. 1 (Spring 1998): 94.

rigor of enforcement up to standard-setting organizations themselves may be best. Standard-setting bodies may be the best suited (1) to understand their industry, (2) to determine how susceptible they are to capture or holdup by one of their members,[5] and (3), absent capture, to optimize the trade-off between the benefits and costs of disclosure that these rules entail. This conclusion does not rule out antitrust enforcement against firms which abuse standard setting to monopolize technology markets. It does, however, imply an approach to antitrust enforcement that is tailored to the specific characteristics of the industry and the technology.

Reasonable and Non-Discriminatory Royalty Rates in Standard Setting

Having learned through disclosure what elements of the standardized technology may be proprietary and subject to royalties, the standard-setting body is still left with the problem of trying to forecast what royalty or licensing fees the technology owner is likely to charge after the standard is determined. The typical SSO patent policy mandating that a royalty be "fair, reasonable, and non-discriminatory" gives little guidance for royalty determination because "reasonable" can mean different things to a technology owner and a technology buyer.

The economist's approach is to consider as reasonable a royalty that reflects the inherent benefits of the technology over the next-best alternative. A reasonable royalty for a standardized technology should not be less than the expected royalty the technology owner would have been able to command had the standard-setting body never been formed and technology owners competed in the market to become a *de facto* standard. This gives a target for a reasonable royalty for a *de jure* (formal) standard: The technology owner should be able to earn at least the expected royalty he could have earned in an open and competitive market.

A useful way of thinking about the reasonableness issue is to imagine the outcome of a royalty negotiation as a sharing of the gains from achieving a bargain between a patent owner and potential licensees. Whether any particular split of the value created by the standard is "fair" is not up to an economist to decide. Economics, though, can provide useful insights into the incentive properties of any solution and rule out

---

5   Capture and holdup refer to the ability of a patent owner to exclude manufacturers from manufacturing according to the defined standard unless those manufacturers agree to the patent owner's royalty demands.

solutions that yield incentives that are undesirable from the point of view of economic efficiency.

It is desirable to encourage firms to design technology with an eye on achieving compatibility in industries where technology users benefit from compatibility. It is also desirable to encourage technology-intensive firms to offer their technologies to standard-setting bodies for consideration in industries where standards matter, or when the technology of one firm represents such a significant improvement over alternative modes that it is socially desirable to have that technology become the standard. If the firm with the superior technology were not assured of receiving appropriate compensation for its invention, it might opt not to participate in the standard-setting process. If inventors of great advances opt out of standard-setting bodies, we are left with the potential of either the chosen standard being an inferior alternative or the chosen standard being irrelevant and the act of determining the standard an inefficient use of resources. The implication is that, built into the definition of reasonableness, there ought to be an incentive for bringing technology to a standard-setting body. Put another way, the reasonable and non-discriminatory standard should not be set so as to deprive patent owners of the incentive to propose their technology as a standard.

Note, however, that incentives are already in place to design for standardization. Since market forces can determine the winner in a standards war, and becoming the standard can create market power, firms wishing to see their technology become the standard will invent with the objective of winning in the market. They will have incentives to submit their inventions for consideration to formal standard-setting agencies in hope of saving the cost of a standards war, but only as long as doing so does not deprive them of the fruits of winning. If all gains were taken away, firms would rather go to war in the market than submit to the profit-destroying restrictions of a standard-setting body.

The gains from formal standard setting can be defined as the difference between the royalty that the technology owner can charge after being selected formally as the standard and the royalty that the technology owner could charge if no formal standard were set.[6] To award the patent owner all the gains from formal standardization creates a strong incentive

---

[6] And, by implication, the ability to charge was set by the cost of employing the next-best alternative. A technology with a close substitute will gain value from formal standard setting as the substitute will be ruled out-of-standard. A technology with no close substitute will gain little or no value from formal standard setting because it would have been the de facto standard.

for firms to invent with the goal of becoming a formal standard and for bringing inventions, especially those which are not major advances, into the formal standard-setting process. However, because all of the gains of standardization will be absorbed by the patent owner, users of the standardized technology will be no better off than if a standard had not been chosen (the value to them of having a standard will equal the cost of purchasing the standardized technology).

Alternatively, if the patent owner were not awarded any of the gains of standard setting, it may choose to try to win a standards war in the market, which would allow it to capture all of the gains from becoming a de facto standard. The patent owner will weigh the probability of winning a standards war in the market and earning higher royalties against the probability of being chosen as a de jure standard and earning royalties reflecting only the prestandardized value of his technology. The expected value of a technology reflects the probability of winning the standards war, the costs of waging the war, and the price the technology could command if it became a de facto standard. The probability of winning a standards war depends on the extent of the price-performance advantage of the patented technology at issue. Technology owners whose patents represent significant advances in improving performance or manufacturing efficiency will have a greater incentive to let the market choose the standard than technology owners whose patents represent minimal advances.

Dividing the gains from standardization between the patent owner and the standard users can ensure that innovators have an incentive to join SSOs and that technology users maintain some benefit from having a standard. Note though, that the minimum royalty that will induce an innovator of a significant technological advance to join a standard-setting organization will be different than the minimum royalty that will induce the owner of a technology with many economically equivalent alternatives to join. The inventor of a significant technological achievement will likely require a greater share of the benefits of standardization to be willing to forego the chance of becoming a de facto standard and having freer rein to set his royalty.

As to the "free of unfair discrimination" condition that standard-setting bodies strive to impose, one possible interpretation relates to the economist's definition of price discrimination. Price discrimination refers to the act of charging two or more customers—licensees in this case—different prices where the differences are not explained by differences in the economic costs of dealing with them. Economic costs include not only direct costs but also, for example, opportunity costs and the risks imposed on the licensor by the licensee and other economic costs. If this interpretation is appropriate, its implication is that to agree to license on terms free of unfair discrimination entails an agreement to charge licensees the same royalty rate, except where the economic costs of licensing customers differ. In those instances, the prices (royalties) should differ with differences in licensing costs.

Limiting the ability of a licensor to charge different royalties to different licensees may reduce the use of technology.[7] Allowing a patent owner to charge different licensees different royalties induces more licensing than imposing a single-rate rule would. Indeed, this is economically efficient and can enhance social welfare because a licensor can establish low prices for price-sensitive licensees and higher prices for less price-sensitive licensees. The result is that output (i.e., licenses sold and, conceivably, goods or services sold with licensed technology) increases. If a patent owner were forced to set one royalty rate schedule for all licensees, then the chosen royalty rate may be too high for some manufacturers, and they would opt out of the technology market. Since these manufacturers would be willing to license the technology at a lower royalty rate and the patent owner would be willing to charge them a lower price if he could do so without sacrificing the higher royalty he gets from other licensees, the one-price rule can create what economists refer to as dead-weight loss—a loss in social welfare as a result of market imperfection. To avoid these social welfare losses, economic price discrimination can be beneficial.

However, a standard-setting body may legitimately be concerned that a participant in the standard-setting process may attempt to raise its rivals' costs or otherwise discriminate against its rivals for the purposes of reducing competition. Thus, a rule against "unfair" discrimination that requires that the same royalty be offered to "similarly situated" licensees enables the technology owner to expand output to the benefit of welfare without the risk that it could use price discrimination to hinder its rivals in competition in the product market. It permits both pricing where the cost differences of licensing different parties fully explain price differences and price discrimination where it cannot harm competition.

---

7   For example, a requirement for no price discrimination might rule out the use of lump-sum payments, either alone or in combination with running royalties. Lump-sum payments that are not calibrated to different levels of sales are likely to imply price discrimination because, with lump-sum payments, high-volume licensees will pay lower per-unit licensing fees than low-volume licensees.

Conclusion

We tend to think about patents and standards as conveying market power because that is the interesting case. Reality is more varied, not only because few inventions are blockbusters, but also because patents matter more in certain industries than others. The same applies to standards. Realism requires looking beyond the convenient abstractions to the specific characteristics of individual technology markets.

Disclosure rules have benefits and costs whose balance will vary with the nature of technology markets, including the extent of their dependence on compatibility and standardization and the characteristics of innovative and imitative activity within them. In standard-setting policy determination, preserving the incentive to participate in standard-setting activities must be part of the solution. Because the link between economic efficiency and standard-setting participation is likely to vary by industry, so must the rules.

The reasonableness of a royalty may be assessed in terms of the division of the gains from licensing between licensor and licensees. While there is no single right answer that would apply to all situations, we may be able to rule out as unreasonable those royalties that leave the patent owner worse than he would have been had he not joined the SSO and those royalties that absorb all of the gains from standardization. The threshold for what is reasonable will depend on the nature of the invention that is chosen as the standard.

16

Essential Issues in the Competitive Analysis of Patent Pools

Lawrence Wu and Thomas R. McCarthy

In the U.S., the pooling of patents by multiple patent owners has been instrumental in many markets in clearing the way for new product development and innovation. Indeed, as noted in *Antitrust Guidelines for the Licensing of Intellectual Property,* issued by the United States Department of Justice (DOJ) and Federal Trade Commission (FTC), patent pools and cross-licensing arrangements

> may provide procompetitive benefits by integrating complementary technologies, reducing transaction costs, clearing blocking positions, and avoiding costly infringement litigation. By promoting the dissemination of technology, cross-licensing and pooling arrangements are often procompetitive.[1]

These concepts are reiterated in the business review letters that have been issued on matters involving joint licensing arrangements and in testimony submitted to the DOJ and FTC Joint Hearings on Competition and Intellectual Property Law and Policy in the Knowledge-Based Economy.[2]

---

[1]   See DOJ and FTC, *Antitrust Guidelines for the Licensing of Intellectual Property,* section 5.5, 6 April 1995 at http://www.usdoj.gov/atr/public/guidelines/ipguide.htm.

[2]   See, for example, a business review letter to Garrard R. Beeney, Esq., from Joel I. Klein regarding the DVD-ROM and DVD-Video joint licensing arrangements, 16 December 1998; a business review letter to Carey R. Ramos, Esq., from Joel I. Klein regarding the DVD-ROM and DVD-Video joint licensing arrangements, 10 June 1999; and a business review letter to Ky P. Ewing, Esq., from Charles A. James regarding the 3G Patent Platform, 12 November 2002. The DOJ's analysis of these patent pools was conducted at the request of the parties as part of the DOJ's business review procedure. In addition, numerous individuals submitted testimony on the subject of patent pools at the DOJ and FTC hearings, and their presentations and papers can be found on the FTC's website, at www.ftc.gov.

By bringing together related patent rights held by different patent owners in a single package license, patent pools permit one-stop shopping for prospective licensees. Rather than have licensees identify all of the relevant owners of patents that may be needed to practice a given technology or industry standard and then undertake potentially time-consuming, costly, and uncertain individual negotiations with each of those licensors, patent pools allow a prospective licensee to obtain all of the patent rights they desire at one time from a single administrator. This reduces transaction costs, the possibility of inadvertent patent infringement, uncertainty regarding the technology needed to meet industry standards, and the amount of time associated with becoming licensed. As a result, products and competitors can come into the market more quickly to the benefit of consumers.

Patent pools further promote efficiency by clearing the potential blocking positions of individual patent owners whose patents are needed to make use of patents owned by others. These necessary and inter-dependent patents are often called *essential* patents. Without one-stop shopping for all of the essential patents from a single administrator, any single owner of an essential patent could simply refuse to license its technology, thus rendering economically worthless the other patentees' technologies for the licensees' purposes. Alternatively, the last-to-license patent holder of an essential patent could demand a disproportionately high royalty in exchange for agreeing to license its patent. By eliminating this hold up problem, patent pools enhance efficiency. In addition, by reducing transaction costs, reducing litigation risk, and facilitating access to technology, patent pools enable the rapid introduction of new products and the dissemination of nascent technologies.

Notwithstanding these benefits, patent pools have been the source of much controversy in the area of antitrust and intellectual property law and economics.[3] At the heart of the debate is the following tension: While it is clear that the benefits of a patent pool stem from the creation of a single license to all of the patents needed to create a product, it is this single license that gives the pool the right to be the sole licensor of the patents needed to practice a standard and perhaps the power to exclude potentially competing technologies.

---

[3]   For a historical overview of the legal and economic issues that have arisen in the regulation of patent pools in the U.S., see Steven C. Carlson, "Patent Pools and the Antitrust Dilemma," *Yale Journal on Regulation,* 16 (1999): p 359-399. See also Richard J. Gilbert, "Antitrust for Patent Pools: A Century of Policy Evolution," manuscript, 3 October 2002.

The Economics of Procompetitive Patent Pools

Benefits from the Pooling of Essential Patents

Patent pools tend to be unambiguously procompetitive when the patents covered by the joint licenses are both essential and complementary in that they reflect the interdependent and essential technologies needed to make a product that is of consistent quality or functionality across licensees.[4] By combining these patents, a patent pool can facilitate the manufacturing of a new product category that did not exist before. This is related to standard setting in that pools often help to ensure the creation of and adherence to technological standards that benefit consumers and manufacturers. In addition, patent pools can lead to lower royalty rates compared to the rates that would be obtained if the licensee had to negotiate separately with each patentee. As described below, this is the result of two principal forces: the elimination or reduction of the potential for hold up and the incentive for the owner of a group of complementary patents to set royalty rates at a lower level.[5]

A patent pool that combines complementary patents also avoids the possibility that the pool will prevent the development of a competing technology or eliminate possible competition among the developers of competing technologies that could be sold to the same licensees as an alternative way to produce the product or its close substitute. This is

---

4   A patent could be complementary but not essential to making the product at issue. For example, a patent pool needed to make a recordable DVD (DVD-R) may not include a patent that allows the manufacturer to make the DVD-R in various colors. Such a patent would be complementary to the technology in the patent pool but may not be essential to producing a universally compatible, fully functioning DVD-R. Its inclusion in the patent pool may or may not raise competitive concerns, depending in part on whether there are alternative and competing technologies for adding color to DVD-Rs, how acceptable the alternatives might be as a substitute, when they were developed compared to when the pool was formed, and whether there are benefits to licensees for buying a complementary but nonessential patent as part of the pool (e.g., one-stop shopping). Still, inclusion of a patent in the pool that is nonessential or one that may have substitutes now or in the future may require a deeper analysis into whether the pool generates net benefits overall. In this respect, analyses of the competitive effects of patent pools have elements common to economic analyses of tying, product bundling, and package discounts. The general lesson of recent business review letters by the DOJ is that including nonessential or substitute patents in the pool will require a more extended analysis of the competitive effects of the pool.

5   The incentive to lower royalty rates for a complementary group of patents is similar to the incentive of a manufacturer of a group of complementary products to set the price of each of its products at a lower level. For example, in the product or service market setting, the seller of complementary products recognizes that a reduction in the price of one product encourages the customer to buy its complementary products, which makes such pricing a more profitable strategy. This effect on customer demand is an externality that would not be considered by a single-product seller.

analogous to the competitive concerns that are often raised in the context of mergers involving sellers of competing products.[6] For example, suppose three firms have technologies that are substitutable in that they are alternative methods of making the same or similar products. If all three technologies were included in a patent pool, then licensees wishing to use any of the alternative technologies would have to obtain a license from the pool. In other words, the three developers of the technology would no longer have to compete for licensees. Absent the pool, licensees would be able to choose from among the three technologies. The competitive concern is that a patent pool may preclude competition among the patent holders of competing technologies that could well have led to lower royalty rates on licenses for each of the competing technologies. For this reason, a key issue in assessing the competitive implications of a pool is to understand whether the pooled patents are substitutes or complements.[7]

Categorizing patents as substitutes or complements is similar to the analysis that is used to identify patents that are *essential* to making a particular product that embodies the patented technologies. If essentiality is properly defined, a pool would not, by definition, include competing patents or substitutable technologies.[8] Put differently, if the members of the pool have competing patents, then by definition, not all of those patents can be essential patents.

Benefits to Licensees

Pools that contain only essential patents (i.e., patents that are, by definition, complementary) tend to be unambiguously procompetitive because

---

6   In the context of a merger involving sellers of competing products, the chief competitive concern is that the transaction will eliminate competition between the merging parties, thereby leading to higher prices in the marketplace.

7   See Josh Lerner and Jean Tirole, "Efficient Patent Pools," NBER working paper 9175, September 2002, for a theoretical analysis of how and why the substitutability or complementarity of the patents in a pool are central in determining whether the pool is welfare enhancing or not.

8   The distinction between complementary and substitute patents is not always clear in practice. Because patents normally contain many separate claims that describe the invention, a specific patent might include claims that are complementary and some that are substitutes for the claims found in another patent in the pool. If the complementary claim in the patent is also essential, it is efficient to include it in a pool because the new technology cannot be practiced without the patent. In many cases, it may be difficult to assess the complementarity or substitutability among patents as the specific contribution of a patent may not be known fully until later as the downstream product markets develop and as the technologies at issue are adopted and accepted by consumers. For this reason, decisions regarding the inclusion or exclusion of patents in a pool often are made with incomplete information and uncertainty about the future.

they help to eliminate the possibility of hold up, resolve problems when there are blocking patents, and reduce transaction costs for licensees.[9] By transaction costs, we mean the additional administrative and other costs (including time) associated with the need to negotiate separate licenses with the relevant patent holders. Moreover, in cases where licensees may not be certain about the patents that must be licensed, the cost of negotiating separate licenses includes the risk that the licensee does not obtain a license for all of the patents needed to produce a noninfringing product. In other words, pools often help to ensure licensees that they have access to all of the technologies needed to produce a particular downstream product.

Benefits to Consumers

By bringing together complementary technologies, a patent pool can facilitate the process by which new products are brought to market. Moreover, patent pools may help manufacturers by establishing standard technical specifications and making available the intellectual property needed to manufacture the products that meet those specifications. In this way, the pool may have created, or at least stimulated, an innovative and vigorously competitive industry, which benefits consumers.

To assess the conventional measures of consumer welfare, an economic analysis would begin by focusing on evidence that prices have fallen over time, product quality has increased, or new products have been introduced based on the pool's technology. Lower prices and the greater availability of new and valuable products to consumers are typically associated with increases in consumer welfare. In markets with such evidence, there is typically little controversy regarding the procompetitive effects of the pool.[10] Another indicator of possible harm to competition is whether innovation has been stopped or significantly retarded. It is important to focus on these measures of consumer welfare—prices,

---

9   For examples and a general discussion of the benefits of patent pools for licensees, see Carl Shapiro, "Navigating the Patent Thicket: Cross Licenses, Patent Pools, and Standard Setting," in *Innovation Policy and the Economy,* ed. Adam Jaffe, Joshua Lerner, and Scott Stern, (Cambridge, MA: MIT Press, 2001), vol. 1.

10 It could be argued that absent the pool, prices would have fallen even further, output would have been even higher, and the rate of innovative activity even greater. However, this is often very speculative since proof of such assertions must demonstrate that alternative technologies would have been developed, but for the pool, and that the products embodying the alternative technology would have come onto the market in a timely and sufficient manner to force royalty rates and final product prices for the patent pool products to be lower. Again, the likelihood of these problems occurring depends heavily on the essential and complementary nature of the patents in the pool at issue.

quality, and innovation—because they help to distinguish activities that harm competition from activities that harm competitors.[11]

Evidence of increasing production and innovative activity clearly demonstrates the procompetitive benefit of a patent pool. Lower prices are helpful, as well, although the analysis of prices is more complex. For example, suppose the products that are based on the pool's technology become widely accepted by customers. The widespread adoption of such a technology could well lead to higher, not lower, prices because of significant quality improvements contained in the products covered by the pool. Thus, analyses of price trends must account for changes in product quality and the other supply and demand factors that are important determinants of market prices.

The Determination of Royalty Rates in a Patent Pool Context

The process by which royalty rates are determined in the context of a patent pool is similar to the process by which a royalty rate is determined for any individual patent. The key market factors that affect the relative bargaining positions of the pool and potential licensees include (1) the alternative technologies that are available to licensees to produce a competing downstream product or if there is an existing standard, a comparable product that meets the standard, and (2) the demand for the downstream product that incorporates the pool's technology relative to substitute products that do not rely on the pool's technology.

Both factors are important. If there are alternative technologies available to licensees, then the presence of this next-best substitute would limit licensees' willingness to pay for the pool's technology; if consumers can purchase comparable alternatives, then the value of the patented technology or process—as embodied in the downstream product—may be relatively limited. That is, should the price of the new patented product rise, consumers may be willing and able to switch to alternative

---

[11] Harm to a *competitor* means that an individual firm has lost some economic advantage that it otherwise would have achieved but for the actions taken by another firm. Taken alone, this type of injury is not the concern of the antitrust laws largely because it can occur even if competition has not been harmed; indeed, it can often occur as a result of competition being *enhanced*. For example, to compete for new business, a firm may introduce a new service or find a way to lower its costs, thereby lowering price. As a result, the firm may be successful in winning more business and in taking market share away from a competitor. This may harm a competitor, but there is no harm to the competitive process. In fact, we would say that this is just the process of competition at work.

products, which might include the same product without the patented feature or products that are based on different technologies yet serve the same purpose or function. Thus, a license to a patent pool is only as valuable as the enhanced profit the new products will generate for the manufacturer.

However, patent pools raise unique questions. First, does a patent pool *necessarily* lead to increased market power because the pooled patents are, by definition, *essential* to licensees if they are to manufacture the product(s) that incorporate the patents at issue? Second, does the joint licensing of multiple patents always lead to royalties that are higher than those which would have been obtained under separate licensing with the owners of each of the individual patents? The answer to both questions is "no," and the underlying logic hinges on the nature of the benefits that patent pools can bring to consumers and licensees.

Do Patent Pools Necessarily Create Additional Market Power?

The administrator of a patent pool may appear to have substantial bargaining power as it would be setting royalty rates and licensing agreements for a group of patents, each of which is essential to making or using a particular technology. However, while it is the case that the administrator is pricing a license for a group of patents, the pooling of essential patents does not necessarily give a pool's administrator more bargaining leverage or market power compared to the patent holder of just one of the essential patents.

The reasoning is that even if each of the patents in the pool is essential, the only power that the pool would have is, at most, the same power that would be held by the owner of any of the essential patents, which is the legitimate power to hold up or refuse to license its patents or attempt to do so by bringing an infringement action and seeking an injunction. In other words, if there are monopoly profits to be had, those returns could potentially be extracted by the owner of one of the essential patents just as it could potentially be extracted by the administrator of the entire set of patents. Thus, the pooling of essential patents does not make it more likely or plausible that a patent pool would have more market power or negotiating leverage than that held by an owner of one of the essential patents in the pool.

In addition, even if a pool comprises a set of essential patents needed to produce a particular downstream product, the pool will not have much market power or leverage over licensees if licensees can turn to other technologies that, in their view, present a superior quality-to-price proposition. For example, depending on the nature of production and the ease with which production lines can be reconfigured to produce alternative products, many licensees may have options when deciding whether to accept a given royalty rate or choosing which technology to adopt.

Another factor that can favor licensees in the calculus of setting royalty rates is their ability to produce a wide range of products so that a licensee may be able to change its productive capacity in favor of other products (i.e., decide not to produce the product covered by the pool at all if the royalty rate being asked for is considered to be too high).[12] This supply response and the degree to which sunk costs can be minimized are other factors that should be considered when evaluating the competitive forces that affect the royalty rates that are and were set for the patent pool's technology.

Does Joint Licensing of Multiple Patents Always Lead to Royalties that are Higher than Those that Would Have Been Obtained Under Separate Licensing?

By definition, patent pools have the authority to negotiate royalties on behalf of the owners of multiple essential patents. While it may appear that such joint licensing gives the patent pool a great deal of control and leverage, the outcome is likely to be lower, not higher, royalties.

There are a number of reasons why the royalty rate charged by a patent pool may be *below* that which would have been charged absent the pool due to the complementarity of the pooled patents. Absent the pool, the patent holder of each essential patent would want to charge the most that the market will bear for that patent alone. Pooling changes the process by which royalty rates are determined because the licensing decision is in the hands of the pool's administrator, who has a different interest in mind—the profits associated with licensing the *entire set* of patents in the pool. If the patents in the pool are essential and complementary, the patent pool's incentive is to charge a lower price for the package, not a higher price. This is because a reduction in the royalty rate of one of the essential patents increases the likelihood that a licensee will also want to license other essential patents. A patent holder that only owns one, not multiple, patents

---

[12] Whether the ability to turn to alternative technologies gives a licensee significant bargaining leverage will depend on other market factors. For example, the presence of a standard and the magnitude and nature of the sunk cost investments that may have been made in specific production technologies prior to the licensing negotiations may limit licensees' bargaining position vis-à-vis the patentee.

would not consider this effect. In other words, while monopoly-level royalties on a per-patent basis would benefit each patent holder individually, such a pricing strategy would reduce the overall demand for all of the patents collectively, which is not in the best interest of the pool. Indeed, if each patent holder charged a monopoly-level royalty, then the total royalties demanded may be so high that licensees may be discouraged from entering the market at all. By putting the negotiation of an entire complementary set of essential patents in the hands of a single administrator, patent pools can facilitate technology development and adoption by eliminating per-patent pricing by individual patent holders and removing the ability of any individual patent holder to hold up a potential licensee by demanding higher or even monopoly-level royalty rates. As noted earlier, holders of complementary patents (as opposed to holders of a single patent or competing or substitute patents) have an incentive to charge lower royalty rates.

The benefits of pooling are often reflected in a comparison of the royalty rates set by the pool against the royalty rates that might have been paid had licensees purchased or negotiated licenses individually with each of the members of the patent pool. The theoretical basis for such a calculation is sound in that the difference in royalty rates captures the cost savings to the licensee from a joint license with the pool. However, in practice, the computations are complex and the data requirements fairly high. For instance, it could well be the case that there are no licensees who have sought to license separate contracts with the pool members. In fact, if the pool were efficient, this outcome would be expected. Thus, absent data on individual licensing, the royalty rates that would be paid under separate licensing must be estimated or modeled.[13]

Depending on the industry, this can be complex, as royalty rates can be influenced by a number of factors, such as cross-licensing discounts and rates that vary depending on the volume produced in a particular time period (e.g., sales or production over a three-month period) or the cumulative volume produced over a longer time span (e.g., one year). Also, the royalty rate often needs to be adjusted to account for geographic territories. For instance, even though there is a pool, some or all of the pooled technology may not have to be licensed in particular countries.

---

[13] Such an analysis can be complex, particularly if it incorporates the element of time. For example, in the but-for world, each individual patent pool holder will want to be the last party to negotiate a license with a licensee. This is because the party in the last-to-license position may have an opportunity to hold up the licensee and extract a higher royalty. Depending on the technology and downstream market at issue, this could delay the licensing process and therefore the adoption and diffusion of the underlying technology.

This analysis also requires a clear specification of what would have happened to the process of invention and distribution of the patented product *but for* any alleged anticompetitive design of the patent pool. Moreover, an analysis of royalty rates also must account for differences in bargaining position between the pool and each licensee. The timing and dates of the negotiation will also matter because the information that was known in the market at that point in time is critical to interpreting the evidence on royalty rates. For example, was the royalty rate determined at a time when the pool had market power? In the case of patent pools, this is not always clear because at the time the pool was formed, there may have been a number of competing technologies whose future prospects were unknown, or even likely to be better than that of the pool. This is particularly true for products that rely on their invention catching on and creating the network effects of widespread adoption. For example, inventors of five-channel audio technology (e.g., the Super Audio CD [SACD] or Audio DVD) rely on equipment manufacturers to produce the compatible players and content/software producers (i.e., music studios) to provide the five-channel recordings if the technology is to catch on. Thus, the history of innovation and a careful accounting of the information that was known about competing technologies at the time licenses were negotiated are important elements of the analysis. When the success of the product is uncertain, the patent pool may not have much market power. In fact, in such circumstances, the licenses may be priced at relatively low levels to encourage early adoption to trigger the network effects needed for the product to succeed.

Potential Anticompetitive Effects of Patent Pools

Patent pools that contain only essential patents tend to be unambiguously procompetitive, yielding benefits to both consumers and licensees. These patent pools do not necessarily create market power that stems from the formation of the pool itself. Moreover, by eliminating problems associated with multiple monopoly markups, patent pools often lead to lower, not higher, royalty rates. However, notwithstanding these procompetitive benefits, there are certain licensing practices that could raise competitive concerns. These include tying, grantback provisions, and discriminatory licensing.

Tying

Patent pools that contain only essential patents are typically procompetitive, but when a pool also includes nonessential patents, the possibility of anticompetitive tying arises. The issue is whether the nonessential patents are tied to the essential patents in a way that reduces consumer welfare. Tying of this nature is a common complaint because a license for a pool typically involves a license for all of the pool's patents at a single price. If some other inventor's patent were foreclosed from being used by licensees who receive the allegedly nonessential technology as part of the joint license, it is possible that an anticompetitive effect may be the result.[14] Alternatively, the pool may be charging supracompetitive royalties by forcing licensees to license unwanted patents (i.e., nonessential patents).

To assess such possibilities, it is important to understand the nature of the alleged tie. Specifically, for there to be tying, there must be some coercion imposed upon licensees. In the case of patent pools, the tying is usually related to the fact that patent pools often license multiple patents under a single license. Such joint licensing could then give rise to claims that licensees can only obtain access to the essential patents if they also agree to license other patents (e.g., nonessential patents), which they otherwise would not have licensed under competitive conditions. Joint licensing also can give rise to claims that licensees would have preferred to license the patents separately with each of the owners of the essential patents.

Moreover, because patent pools are organized in many different ways, the analysis must consider the alternatives available to licensees. For instance, in many patent pools, potential licensees are given the option to sign licenses with the individual patent holders. Alternatively, some pools offer a menu of choices for licensees, who can choose to license all of the patents or some subset of patents (e.g., essential patents only). When such options are available—particularly if they have been chosen by licensees—there is no coercion, and the licensing of a pool's patents cannot plausibly be called tying.

However, if tying is plausible and foreclosure the source of the alleged anticompetitive effect, the analysis proceeds by identifying the allegedly tied nonessential technologies, the downstream products that incorporate them, any other technologies that are alternatives to the non-essential technologies, and alternative downstream products that compete with the downstream products that incorporate the nonessential technologies. For there to be harm to competition (as opposed to harm to competitors), the nonessential patents that are supposedly foreclosed would have to be

---

[14] It is, however, also possible that a tie of this type is procompetitive despite the fact that a competitor is foreclosed.

patents that are (1) substitutes to the patents in the pool, (2) superior to those patents, and (3) not being licensed because of the creation of the pool, despite being clearly superior. Given the near zero marginal cost of licensing, the likelihood that a valuable nonessential technology would not be licensed is low.

Whether the alleged tie is likely to harm competition also requires an analysis of whether the allegedly foreclosed inventor can sell its technology in other uses that are not affected by the pool. Such an approach is therefore similar to analyses that are typically conducted when assessing anticompetitive foreclosure generally. Without a clear definition of the alternative technologies and their possible uses, one cannot estimate the degree of foreclosure that might have resulted from the alleged tying.

Allegations of tying involving patent pools are also often accompanied by claims that had the pool excluded the allegedly nonessential patents, royalty rates would be lower. However, while possible in theory, this is not often the case in practice. This is because a patent pool typically sets the royalty to reflect the value of being able to manufacture the downstream products that incorporate the patented technology. Thus, whether the pool has one essential patent or multiple essential patents, the royalty rate is unlikely to be different, even with the inclusion of a non-essential patent. Why? Because the royalty rate measures the value of access to a technology that allows a manufacturer to make a product. As a result, the royalty rate is based on the value of the downstream product and not on the number of patents needed to make that product. In other words, the value of the pool is based on the value of the downstream product and not necessarily on a *per-patent* valuation of the pool's intellectual property portfolio.[15]

From an economic perspective, a reduction in the royalty rate therefore would not be expected upon the expiration of a single patent in the

---

15 Whether and by how much a pool that includes a nonessential patent can obtain a higher royalty rate is an empirical issue, one that will depend on the incremental value to consumers of the downstream product incorporating the nonessential patent compared to the downstream product that does not incorporate the nonessential patent. If a patent is truly nonessential, it is more likely to have a relatively low value because (1) it has substitute technologies to compete with or (2) its nonessentiality means that its share of the pool royalty rate might reduce the royalty shares to the essential patent holders (i.e., the single monopoly power issue). Thus, its presence in the pool and its effect on the reasonable royalty is likely to be minimal in terms of competitive effects. If, on the other hand, it is a valuable and somewhat unique nonessential patent, its inclusion in the pool may be warranted, based on buyer preferences for one-stop shopping. Put differently, if the vast majority of buyers would license a given nonessential patent anyway—even if it is not part of the pool—it is hard to conclude that a significant anticompetitive foreclosure of a less-well-accepted substitute patent has occurred.

portfolio. This is true for any essential patent so long as there are essential patents that remain unexpired in the pool and for any nonessential patent that does not contribute incrementally to consumers' valuation of the downstream product. Further, there is no reason why one would expect there to be a correlation between the royalty rate and the composition of the patents in the pool. As noted earlier, a patent pool is not valued simply by the composition of the patent portfolio, but more by its providing the ability to manufacture the ultimate product and the revenue and profit stream associated with the sale of that product. In other words, having even just one essential patent is enough for the patent holder to capture the value of the ability to manufacture the product. Accordingly, the royalty rate is generally independent of the number of patents, so long as one of those patents remains essential.

Grantback Provisions

Under a grantback clause, a licensee that develops an innovative new technology that is or becomes essential to the pool's technology would be required to license that patent through the pool. Grantback provisions are common clauses found in joint licensing arrangements because they often have procompetitive benefits. As noted in the *Antitrust Guidelines for the Licensing of Intellectual Property,* grantback provisions "provide a means for the licensee and the licensor to share risks and reward for making possible further innovation based on or informed by the licensed technology, and both promote innovation in the first place and promote the subsequent licensing of the results of the innovation." [16]

Grantback clauses are often included in patent pool licenses because they facilitate the entry of other essential patents into the portfolio of patents that are covered by the joint license, thereby lowering licensees' costs of assembling the patent rights that are essential to complying with a standard and limiting the potential for a licensee to "exact a supracompetitive toll" from other licensees. [17] In other words, a grantback provision serves to remove the possibility of new blocking patents on new innovations so that all of the licensees can continue to compete on an equal basis and so a new inventor cannot hold up the other licensees by refus-

---

[16] See U.S. DOJ and FTC, *Antitrust Guidelines for the Licensing of Intellectual Property,* section 5.6.

[17] See, for example, a business review letter to Garrard R. Beeney, Esq., from Joel I. Klein regarding the DVD-ROM and DVD-Video joint licensing arrangements, 16 December 1998.

ing to license its essential patents to all other licensees (and licensors) on reasonable and nondiscriminatory terms.

Grantback clauses that are likely to encourage innovation tend to have provisions that cover essential patents only. They also tend to be royalty-bearing, thereby giving licensees an incentive to innovate and to add the patents into the pool. If innovations are made stemming from access to the patents in the joint licenses, the owners of the joint licenses should be rewarded through protective grantbacks. Some of these procompetitive features of grantback provisions were the subjects of the DOJ business review letters that approved joint licensing programs.[18]

Despite these benefits, grantback provisions can be the source of competitive harm under the theory that licensees may reduce their research and development activities if they knew ahead of time that anything they develop will be added to the patent pool. In other words, by giving the rights of that intellectual property to the pool, the returns to research and development are potentially lower, particularly if patent pools eliminate or reduce the potential for the inventor to hold up licensees for greater royalty rates. These claims are difficult to assess, but one important area of analysis is to understand the historical rate of innovation in the industry. If there is no evidence that innovation has declined after the formation of the pool, then it is unlikely that a grantback provision has diminished innovation.

More importantly, perhaps, innovation through entirely different technological approaches for accomplishing the same functions (e.g., USB drives as a substitute for CD-R based data storage) is not affected by the pool and its grantback provisions. In fact, grantbacks arguably stimulate such new technologies. Similarly, it is important to remember that an analysis of the competitive effects must involve some analysis of the market for the downstream products that embody the pooled technology. For a grantback provision to retard innovation, it must be shown that there has been a reduction in innovation in the development of substitute downstream products, assuming such products exist.

Discriminatory Licensing

Discriminatory licensing refers to differences in royalty rates charged to similarly situated licensees. Charging lower royalty rates to certain cross-licensees is sometimes alleged to be a form of price discrimination and a

---

[18] See, for example, business review letters, supra note 2.

source of "unfair" competitive advantage to the licensees who receive lower royalty rates. Unlike analyses of tying and grantback clauses, most questions about discriminatory licensing focus on how the terms of a pool's licensing agreements can affect competition among licensees. As a general matter, concerns about the competitive implications of discriminatory licensing tend to arise in circumstances where the members of the pool also manufacture the licensed product. In this case, licensees may be concerned that they are at a disadvantage by paying higher royalty rates.

In an analysis of discriminatory licensing, a key aspect of the analysis is to determine the extent to which the licensees at issue are similarly situated. For example, some may be cross-licensees who own valuable intellectual property. In return for access to this intellectual property, these licensees could well receive lower royalty rates. This is not only legitimate, but also procompetitive. Lower royalty rates is another way of rewarding the inventor for developing valuable intellectual property. In addition, lower royalty rates often translate into lower marginal costs and therefore lower prices to wholesalers, retailers, and consumers.

There are other differences among licensees that may legitimately lead to differences in royalty rates across licensees. These would include the volume of downstream product produced, the geographic areas into which they sell their products, and the end uses to which their products are put.

If there has been discriminatory licensing, we can assess the competitive effects by examining the downstream marketplace. If cross-licensees' royalty savings are passed on to wholesalers, retailers, and consumers in the form of lower prices for the downstream product, then such savings by the cross-licensees could not be the source of any harm to competition.

Discriminatory royalty rates can be procompetitive for many reasons. It is a strategy that is often used by sellers attempting to enter a new market or to reach new customers because it is an important way by which discounts are given to customers. It is also a practice that is widely used to respond to or meet the demands of the marketplace, particularly when there are differences across geographic regions or types of licensees.

In addition, there are benefits that are commonly associated with price discrimination more generally. For example, a manufacturer may charge different prices to its wholesalers and retailers because it is less expensive to distribute goods to certain types of customers (e.g., it may be less costly for a manufacturer to ship an entire truckload of product to a customer than half a truckload). Price discrimination is also viewed favorably when the price may be lowered to customers to provide valuable services in return (e.g., the provision of retail inventory space). Finally, where there are large fixed or sunk costs of production (or product development and, thus, economies of scale), price discrimination can expand sales to those who might not be able to buy at the higher marginal cost that would be associated with the single price that a profit-maximizing firm would choose. It is for these reasons that price discrimination is viewed favorably by economists in most situations.

Although discriminatory royalties have their virtues, there are often reasons why pool administrators may charge one low price to all licensees, particularly in circumstances where the commercial success of the pooled technology depends on consumer acceptance of the downstream products. This is particularly true in network industries, where it is counterproductive to keep prices high and to reduce output. In these markets, the pool has a strong incentive to get consumers and manufacturers interested in the product and underlying technology by keeping royalty rates (and therefore downstream product prices) as low as possible to fuel the growth of the network effects needed to make the products a commercial success. Such a strategy could involve licensing many manufacturers on a *nondiscriminatory* basis in an effort to encourage manufacturers to compete by achieving production efficiencies rather than by trying to get the lowest royalty rate in negotiations. The result is that pools often have a strong incentive to license as many manufacturers as possible on an equal basis.

Conclusion

Patent pools are often procompetitive because they bring complex new technologies to market sooner and at lower cost. By putting the licensing decisions in the hands of an administrator whose interest is to license all of the essential patents that are needed by licensees to make a particular downstream product, patent pools eliminate the potential for hold up and problems associated with blocking positions that can arise when licenses must be obtained from multiple patent holders. In this way, patent pools generally yield benefits to both licensees and consumers. However, there are certain licensing terms and arrangements that can raise competitive concerns. Among these are tying, grantback provisions, and discriminatory licensing. Analyses of these issues tend to be highly fact-specific, requiring an understanding of the underlying patents and technology. This would include an assessment of the alternative technologies that are available to licensees, as well as an evaluation of the downstream product markets that embody the pool's patents. The ability of consumers to switch among products, their preferences regarding product features and characteristics, and the degree of competition in these downstream markets may seem far removed from the technology-based analysis of patents generally, but they are critical to competitive analyses of patent pools and an assessment of their net benefits and competitive effects

17

Antitrust Implications of Pharmaceutical Patent Litigation Settlements

Gregory K. Leonard and Rika Onishi Mortimer

In recent years, antitrust concerns have arisen concerning patent litigation settlement agreements between branded drug manufacturers and generic drug manufacturers. The Federal Trade Commission (FTC), in particular, has challenged several such agreements in court.[1] The FTC has alleged that the settlements in question prevented or delayed the introduction of generic drugs, thus harming consumers by denying them access to lower prices. Of particular concern to the FTC was the inclusion in the settlement agreements of so-called *reverse payments* by the patent owners to the defendants.

The question raised by these cases is, under what conditions is the settlement of patent infringement litigation anticompetitive? A patent litigation settlement represents a negotiated compromise between the patent owner and the potential entrant. For a settlement to be mutually acceptable, it must make both parties better off than they would be if they pursued the litigation. Consumers, however, are not party to the negotiation and thus their interests are not represented. As a consequence, the settling parties—in seeking to reach a compromise based on their own respective best interests—may have incentives to reach an agreement that makes consumers worse off. How does one tell whether a settlement will maintain consumer welfare at a level no lower than would be expected from litigation?

---

[1] See Federal Trade Commission, "Generic Drug Entry Prior to Patent Expiration: An FTC Study," July 2002, for more details.

Settlement of Patent Litigation in the Pharmaceutical Industry

Before proceeding with an economic analysis of patent litigation settlements, we address the question of why the issue of reverse payments has arisen in the context of the pharmaceutical industry rather than other industries.[2]

The Implications of the Hatch-Waxman Act

Patent disputes between branded and generic drug manufacturers are different from patent disputes in other industries due to the 1984 Drug Price Competition and Patent Term Restoration Act (also known as the Hatch-Waxman Act).[3] The Hatch-Waxman Act was passed with the intention of promoting the introduction of generic drugs without damaging the incentives of branded drug manufacturers to innovate. Hatch-Waxman provides for an abbreviated approval procedure for generics, which is designed to help control rising prescription drug expenditures. Generic drugs, which must demonstrate *bioequivalence* to their branded counterparts, are typically substantially discounted.

Pursuant to the act, a generic firm that files an abbreviated new drug application (ANDA) with the Food and Drug Administration (FDA) before the expiration of one or more patents relating to its branded counterpart is required to certify that the patents at issue are either invalid or not infringed by the generic version (Paragraph IV Certification) and to notify the owner of the patents regarding its intent to enter. If the patent owner files a patent infringement lawsuit within 45 days of receipt of notification of a Paragraph IV Certification, FDA approval of the ANDA is automatically stayed for 30 months unless the patents expire or are found invalid or not infringed by the court. As a result, patent lawsuits have been typically filed before the generic firm actually begins marketing its product.

Moreover, the Hatch-Waxman Act grants the first filer of an ANDA the right to exclusively market its generic version of a branded drug for 180 days before the FDA approves any other generic manufacturer's ANDA relating to the same branded drug. Under Hatch-Waxman, the

---

2   See D. Crane, "Exit Payments in Settlement of Patent Infringement Lawsuits: Antitrust Rules and Economic Implications," *Florida Law Review* 54, no. 4 (September 2002): 747-797, which points out that reverse payments may in fact exist in other industries, but are obscured by offsetting forward payments made by the defendant to the plaintiff (e.g., as compensation for damages due to past infringement). In other words, the net of the reverse and forward payments still results in a forward payment.
3   FTC, "Generic Drug Entry."

180-day exclusivity period does not initiate until the first generic entrant commercially markets its product or a court determines the patents are either invalid or not infringed. As a result, if the first ANDA filer settles the patent dispute before the court enters judgment regarding patent validity and then decides not to market its generic drug, the 180-day exclusivity period would not begin and no other generic could enter. The 180-day exclusivity provision in the Hatch-Waxman Act, therefore, has created an opportunity for settling parties in the pharmaceutical industry to delay generic entry for a significant period of time. In other words, the settlement has an externality on other potential entrants. This feature of Hatch-Waxman has provided the parties with a much greater incentive to settle and delay generic entry than would exist in a typical patent infringement lawsuit.

The Medicare Prescription Drug, Improvement, and Modernization Act of 2003 made changes to the 30-month stay and 180-day exclusivity provisions of the Hatch-Waxman Act, altering incentives of litigating parties regarding patent settlements.[4] The new rule allows only one 30-month stay per product whether or not a brand-name manufacturer lists any new patents during the lawsuit. In the past, brand-name manufacturers were able to receive successive 30-months stays by listing additional patents after an ANDA was filed. Some brand-name manufacturers have been alleged to have listed patents that did not meet the FDA requirements in order to delay generic entry.[5] Moreover, the 2003 Act added new categories of events that would cause the first ANDA filer to forfeit its 180-day exclusivity: for example, an agreement with another applicant, the listed drug application holder, or a patent owner that is found anticompetitive, failure to market within 75 days of approval or within 30 months after submitting the ANDA, and expiration of all relevant patents.[6] These changes to the 180-day exclusivity and 30-month stay provisions reduce the potential for using them to delay generic entry through patent lawsuits and settlements.

---

4   The Medicare Prescription Drug, Improvement, and Modernization Act of 2003, title XI, sec. 1101–1118, 8 December 2003.
5   See FTC, "Generic Drug Entry," for further discussion of this issue.
6   Other forfeiting events are failure to market within 75 days after any court decision, withdrawals of an ANDA, amendment of Paragraph IV Certifications, and failure to obtain tentative approval within 30 months. The 2003 Act also stipulates that the 180-day exclusivity will be triggered only by the commercial marketing of the generic drug and not by a favorable court decision. In addition, under the 2003 act, multiple firms can qualify for the 180-day exclusivity if more than one applicant submits an ANDA for the same product on their first day of eligibility.

FTC v. Bristol-Myers Squibb Corp.

The *FTC v. Bristol-Myers* case provides an illustration of the potential antitrust concern that arises with a settlement agreement where a reverse payment is involved.[7] Bristol-Myers marketed a brand-name antianxiety drug called BuSpar. Schein was the first to file a Paragraph IV ANDA with the FDA to market a generic version of BuSpar. Bristol-Myers sued Schein for patent infringement, and they fully settled their litigation in December 1994. As part of the settlement, Bristol-Myers agreed to pay Schein $72.5 million, and in return, Schein agreed not to market any generic versions of BuSpar until six years later, in November 2000, when Bristol-Myers' patent would expire.

From the FTC's perspective, the settlement was designed to delay generic entry, with the payment from Bristol-Myers to Shein reflecting a split of the monopoly rent that Bristol-Myers was able to generate in the absence of generic entry. Note that, from the perspective of consumers, continuing the litigation could not have led to a worse outcome. Even if Bristol-Myers had won the infringement case, the worst that could have happened was that generic entry would be delayed until patent expiration. But, this is exactly the outcome under the settlement agreement.

The FTC and the defendants settled the case with a consent decree, prohibiting agreements involving either defendant in which 1) the generic rival agrees not to enter the market with a noninfringing generic product or not to relinquish its 180-day exclusivity rights, and 2) the branded drug firm pays the potential generic competitor in exchange for its agreement not to market its generic product.

FTC v. Schering-Plough Corp.

The *FTC v. Schering-Plough* case illustrates the complexities that can arise in an alleged reverse payment case.[8] Schering-Plough marketed a branded potassium chloride supplement called K-DUR 20. Upsher and ESI filed ANDAs to produce and sell generic versions of K-DUR 20. Schering-Plough filed patent infringement suits against both companies and then

---

7   FTC complaint, *In the Matter of Bristol-Myers Squibb Co.*, docket no. C-4076, available at www.ftc.gov/os/2003/04/bristolmyerssquibbcmp.pdf.

8   *Schering-Plough Corp. v. FTC*, docket. no. 04-10688, 2005 U.S. App. Lexis 3811, 8 March 2005, 5-6. FTC complaint, *In the Matter of Schering-Plough Corp., Upsher-Smith Laboratories, and American Home Products Corp.*, docket no. 9297, available at www.ftc.gov/os/2001/04/schringpart3cmp.pdf.

entered into settlement agreements with both companies. In those agreements, Upsher and ESI agreed not to produce any generic versions of K-DUR 20 until a certain date, in both cases prior to the expiration of the K-DUR 20 patent. As part of the settlement agreement with Upsher, Schering paid Upsher $60 million and other royalty fees and obtained licenses to market five of Upsher's products, including an exclusive license to market Upsher's Niacor outside North America. Similarly, as part of the settlement agreement with ESI, Schering paid ESI $30 million for the settlement and was granted licenses to enalapril and buspirone.

The FTC alleged that Schering and the defendants had agreed to delay generic entry in order to allow Schering to maintain monopoly profits, and in return for their participation, the defendants were to receive reverse payments from Schering. However, the case was complicated by two factors that distinguished it from earlier cases such as *FTC v. Bristol-Myers*. First, while the settlement did involve setting a date of generic entry, that date was well before the date of patent expiration. Thus, the parties were able to argue that as a result of the settlement, generic entry was certain to occur prior to when it would have occurred if litigation had continued and Schering had won.

The second distinguishing factor was that it was unclear whether there was even a reverse payment at all. Schering argued that the alleged reverse payments were instead forward payments of royalties for the licenses granted by the defendants to Schering. The FTC responded by arguing that the payments were in amounts well above the market value of the licenses given to Schering. The United States Court of Appeals for the Eleventh Circuit ruled in favor of Schering in March 2005. At the time of writing, the FTC has asked the Eleventh Circuit to rehear the case *en banc*.

An Economic Model of Patent Litigation Settlement

In litigation between patent holders and alleged infringers, the central issue that the parties seek to resolve is, when will the defendant be able to sell its allegedly infringing product? If the patent owner wins the lawsuit, the defendant is prohibited from selling its product until patent expiration (unless the patent owner subsequently agrees to license the defendant).[9] If the defendant wins, it can begin selling its product immediately (or, if it was already selling its product, it can continue to do so).

---

[9]   To simplify the discussion, we will assume that the defendant has no economically feasible design-around alternatives.

To gain an understanding of the antitrust issues, it is useful to build an economic model of patent litigation settlement.[10]

We will assume that the parties have available to them two instruments with which they can design a settlement of the litigation.[11] First, they can specify a date at which the defendant can enter the market. Second, they can specify a payment from one party to another. To lend some concreteness to the model, we will assume that the patent will expire in one year. A settlement would thus involve the choice of a date of defendant entry, which we will refer to as D, and a payment from the patent owner to the defendant, which we will refer to as P. D will lie between 0 (enter immediately) and 1 (enter at the time of patent expiration).[12] We allow P to be either positive or negative. When P is a positive number, it represents a *reverse payment* from the patent owner to the defendant. When P is a negative number, it represents a *forward payment* from the defendant to the patent owner.

If the defendant were not to enter until patent expiration ($D = 1$), the parties and consumers are assumed to have the following payoffs for the year:

Patent Owner	H
Defendant	0
Consumers	$\underline{CS}$

This represents the "monopoly" outcome where the patent owner is the only seller of the drug for the year until patent expiration. We use H to represent the patent owner's payoffs (profits) in this situation because the patent owner will make a relatively "high" level of profits. The defendant would receive a payoff (profit) of 0 for the year because it does not enter

---

[10] The model we discuss below is similar to models developed by others and described in C. Shapiro, "Antitrust Limits to Patent Settlements," *RAND Journal of Economics* 34 (2003); R. Willig and J. Bigelow, "Antitrust Policy Toward Agreements That Settle Patent Litigation," *The Antitrust Bulletin,* Fall 2004; and J. Bulow, "The Gaming of Pharmaceutical Patents," in *Innovation Policy and the Economy,* ed. A. Jaffe et al., vol. 4 (Cambridge, MA: MIT Press, 2004). Other papers that discuss patent settlements with reverse payments include Crane, "Exit Payments"; M. Schildkraut, "Patent-Splitting Settlements and the Reverse Payment Fallacy," *Antitrust Law Journal* 71:1033-1068; and T. Cotter, "Antitrust Implications of Patent Settlements Involving Reverse Payments: Defending a Rebuttable Presumption of Illegality in Light of Some Recent Scholarship," *Antitrust Law Journal* 71:1069-1097.

[11] To further simplify the discussion, we will assume for the time being that the patent owner owns only one patent and the defendant owns no patents. Thus, there are no cross-licensing possibilities.

[12] We assume that the litigation would occur instantaneously. Making this aspect of the model more realistic would not have any significant effect on the overall conclusions.

and thus has no product to sell. The payoff to consumers is measured using consumer surplus, which is the difference between the value consumers derive from use of the drug and the price they have to pay for it. The *consumer surplus* associated with the monopoly outcome is relatively low (because of the higher price under monopoly), and thus we use the $\underline{CS}$ notation to represent consumer surplus in the $D = 1$ case.

Alternatively, if the defendant were to enter immediately ($D = 0$), the payoffs for the year would be:

Patent Owner	L
Defendant	E
Consumers	$\overline{CS}$

The $D = 0$ case implies a duopoly for the year. Because the patent owner's profits would be lower under duopoly than monopoly, we use L to represent the patent owner's relatively low level of profits in the case of $D = 0$ (and we therefore assume $L < H$). The defendant, being able to participate in the market for the year, would make a profit of E. Consumers gain from entry because price would be lower under duopoly than monopoly. Accordingly, we use $\overline{CS}$ to denote consumer surplus in the $D = 0$ case and note that $\overline{CS} > \underline{CS}$.

If the defendant were to enter at some intermediary time D between 0 and 1, the payoffs would be an average of the $D = 0$ payoffs and the $D = 1$ payoffs:

Patent Owner	$DH + (1 - D) L$
Defendant	$(1 - D) E$
Consumers	$D \underline{CS} + (1 - D) \overline{CS}$

A crucial consideration for the parties when exploring settlement is their respective assessments regarding the probability that the patent owner will win the lawsuit. Initially, we will assume that the parties agree on this probability, which we will refer to as θ. We will also initially assume that the parties have no litigation costs and are risk neutral (which is to say that they care only about their expected payoffs, not the variance of their payoffs). We will explore the implications of relaxing these assumptions later in the chapter.

In entering a negotiation, the parties must first determine their *walk-away* points—the value they would get from not settling and continuing the litigation to conclusion. To be mutually acceptable to both parties, a settlement must make them better off than their respective walk-away points. If the case were litigated, the patent owner would get H if he were to win, which will happen with probability θ, and L if he were to lose, which will happen with probability $1 - \theta$. Thus, the patent owner's walk-away point is

$\theta H + (1 - \theta) L$. The defendant, however, gets 0 if she loses and E if she wins. Thus, the defendant's walk-away point is $(1 - \theta) E$.

We will define a settlement as a pair (D,P) that specifies the date of entry D (between now [0] and patent expiration [1]) and the payment P from the patent owner to the defendant. Under a settlement (D,P), the patent owner would get a payoff equal to $DH + (1 - D) L - P$. This equation reflects the fact that for a percentage of the year equal to D the patent owner would be alone in the market and would get H, while for the rest of the year $(1 - D)$, the patent owner would be in competition with the defendant and thus would only make L. In addition, the patent owner makes payment P to the defendant. Similarly, the entrant would make $(1 - D) E + P$ under the (D,P) settlement because it would be in the market for a fraction of the year (from D to 1), and it would receive the payment P.

The (D,P) settlement would be acceptable to the patent owner if its resulting payoff exceeded its walk-away point, or if

(1) $DH + (1 - D) L - P \geq \theta H + (1 - \theta) L$.

Similarly, the settlement would be acceptable to the defendant if

(2) $(1 - D) E + P \geq (1 - \theta) E$.

One settlement that is acceptable to both parties (i.e., satisfies both of these criteria) is the settlement $(\theta,0)$ that specifies that the entrant enters at a date $D = \theta$ and no payments are exchanged between the parties. Note that the negotiated date of entry in this case is equal to the patent owner's probability of winning the case. In the extreme where the patent owner is sure to win ($\theta = 1$), the negotiated date of entry is $D = 1$. In that case, the "settlement" calls for the defendant to remain out of the market until patent expiration.

Having determined that the $(\theta,0)$ settlement is acceptable to both parties, one might ask how such a settlement affects consumers. It turns out that expected consumer surplus under the $(\theta,0)$ settlement is exactly the same as it would be under continued litigation. Under the settlement, consumers get $\underline{CS}$ for the period of length D until entry occurs and then $\overline{CS}$ for the remaining period of length $(1 - D)$. But, since $D = \theta$ under the settlement, consumer surplus is

(3) $\theta \, \underline{CS} + (1 - \theta) \, \overline{CS}$,

which is precisely the expected consumer surplus under continued litigation. Thus, consumers retain the same expected surplus under the $(\theta,0)$ settlement as they had under continued litigation.

While the $(\theta,0)$ settlement is acceptable to both the litigating parties, one might ask whether there is a *better* settlement as far as the parties are concerned. We will consider two polar cases. In the first case, we assume that the profits that the defendant stands to make upon entry, E, are larger than the losses the entry will cause the patent owner, $H - L$. In that case, one possible settlement is to set D to 0 (immediate entry for the defendant) and to have the defendant make a forward payment $-P^*$ (recall that a forward payment is a negative number in our framework) to the patent owner to compensate the patent owner for its losses. For this settlement to be acceptable to both parties requires that P^* fall within the range defined by

(4) $\theta E \geq P^* \geq \theta(H - L)$.

This $(0,-P^*)$ settlement (if feasible) makes the parties better off than the $(\theta,0)$ settlement. This follows from the fact that the $(0,-P^*)$ settlement makes both parties better off than continued litigation, and continued litigation makes both parties as well off as the $(\theta,0)$ settlement. Consumers are also better off under the $(0,-P^*)$ settlement than the $(\theta,0)$ settlement because they receive consumer surplus of $\overline{CS}$ for the whole period prior to patent expiration instead of the average consumer surplus $\theta \underline{CS} + (1 - \theta)\overline{CS}$.[13]

The case just described, where the defendant's payoff after entry, E, exceeds the patent owner's loss due to entry, $H - L$, might be called the "typical" case in patent litigation. In this typical case, the defendant upon its entry would stand to gain more than the patent owner would stand to lose because the defendant would expand the market or take a significant fraction of its sales from rivals other than the patent owner. The fact that the entrant typically stands to gain more than the patent owner stands to lose is why most patent litigation settlements allow the defendant to enter (or continue selling its product) in return for a royalty payment from the defendant to the patent owner.

Patent litigation between branded pharmaceutical manufacturers and generic manufacturers is "atypical" for several reasons. For now, we will focus on one particularly important difference. It is more likely in drug patent litigation that the benefits to the entrant, E, are less than the losses to the branded manufacturer, $H - L$. There are two reasons why

---

[13] The evaluation of consumer welfare effects becomes more complicated if the settlement calls for the defendant to pay a running royalty based on its sales instead of a lump sum payment to the plaintiff. The reason is that this "tax" on the defendant will distort its pricing decisions after entry and thus affect consumer surplus.

this occurs. First, generic entry typically leads to substantial sales losses for the branded product. Second, the pre-entry profit margin on the branded product usually far exceeds the (post-entry) profit margin on the generic. As an example, consider a branded drug with sales of 100 units at a profit margin of $10 prior to generic entry. The branded drug profits pre-entry are therefore $1,000. After entry, the generic firm captures 75 percent of the market, leaving the branded product with only 25 units. Thus, the branded manufacturer—even if it maintains its profit margin— loses $750 in profits. Suppose the generic's profit margin is $5. Its gain from entry is therefore $375, well below the branded drug's losses.

In this case—where the gain to the entrant is less than the loss to the patent owner (i.e., where $E < H - L$)—a $(0,-P^*)$ settlement is not feasible as demonstrated by condition (4) above. A $(\theta,0)$ settlement is still feasible, but again we might ask whether there is a better settlement available as far as the parties are concerned. Such a settlement would involve a date of entry D after θ with a reverse payment P^{**}. The reason why this makes both parties better off is that with a later date of entry the patent owner continues to make the high level of profits H and, because $H - L$ is larger than E, the patent owner profitably can use the reverse payment to compensate the defendant for staying out of the market. In fact, in this particular version of the model, the best settlement from the point of view of the parties is a $(1,P^{**})$ settlement, where the reverse payment falls in the range defined by

(5) $(1 - \theta)(H - L) \geq P^{**} \geq (1 - \theta)E$.

Note that the size of the reverse payment is inversely related to θ. For small values of θ, the patent owner must make a large reverse payment in order to keep the defendant out.

While this settlement makes the parties better off than a $(\theta,0)$ settlement, what about consumers? Consumers receive less expected consumer surplus because they get $\underline{CS}$ for the entire period instead of $\theta\,\underline{CS} + (1 - \theta)$ $\overline{CS}$, which is necessarily greater than $\underline{CS}$ as long as $\theta < 1$. Thus, the agreement that is best for the parties makes consumers worse off than continued litigation.

The conclusion from this model is that reverse payments arise only as compensation to the defendant for delaying its entry to the detriment of consumers. Moreover, prohibiting reverse payments would not prevent settlements in this model since the $(\theta,0)$ settlement is always feasible and the parties are at least as well off under such a settlement as they would be under continued litigation.

A model of the sort just described supports the suggestion that patent litigation settlements containing reverse payments should be considered per se illegal. However, adding several features to the model reverses this conclusion and demonstrates that reverse payments may not be indicative of a consumer-welfare-reducing settlement. Thus, a rule of reason analysis would, in general, be required.

Litigation Costs, Risk Aversion, and Differing Assessments of θ

The model described so far does not take litigation costs into account. The existence of litigation costs make the parties more willing to settle because settlement would allow them to avoid incurring the litigation costs. The existence of litigation costs does not alter the feasibility of a settlement where $D = \theta$, which would maintain expected consumer surplus at the level that would be achieved under litigation. Such a settlement may, however, involve a payment (either forward or reverse) depending on the parties' relative litigation costs.

To see this, note that the patent owner's payoff from a (θ, P) settlement would be $\theta H + (1 - \theta) L - P$, while the payoff from litigation would be $\theta H + (1 - \theta) L - C_P$ where C_P represents the patent owner's litigation costs.[14] Thus, the patent owner would be willing to pay an amount up to C_P in a settlement with $D = \theta$ to avoid the litigation. Similarly the defendant would be willing to pay an amount up to its litigation costs C_D. Assuming the parties split their combined litigation cost savings upon settling, a reverse payment would be called for if $C_P > C_D$, and a forward payment would be called for otherwise (a payment of o would correspond to the case of equal litigation costs).[15] This result establishes that the existence of a reverse payment does not imply that the settlement is necessarily anticompetitive. However, the size of the reverse payment in this case would be limited to one-half of the difference in litigation costs between the two parties. This typically would be expected to be a small figure.

Risk aversion on the part of the parties has a similar effect as litigation costs. If the parties are risk-averse and are presented a choice between a settlement that provides a certain outcome that is equal to the expected outcome under the risky litigation, they would prefer the certain

---

14 A more complex model might allow the patent owner's probability of winning the litigation, θ, to be a function of the parties' litigation costs.
15 An even split of the litigation cost savings from settlement is consistent with the Nash bargaining solution.

outcome.[16] Thus, a risk-averse party would be willing to accept less in a (certain) settlement than it would expect to receive if it continued with the (uncertain) litigation. This differential is called a risk premium. It can be thought of as another form of litigation cost, and its effect on the analysis of settlements is similar. Specifically, risk aversion does not render a (θ,P) settlement infeasible. The payment P may not be nonzero and may represent a forward or a reverse payment.

A further complication is raised if the parties do not agree on the value of θ. This complication would appear to be important since in the real world disagreement regarding litigation outcome probabilities is a likely cause for the failure of parties to settle. Suppose that there is a "true" value of θ, but that this value is unknown to the parties. Instead, each party receives an unbiased "signal" regarding the value of θ. Specifically, the patent owner believes its probability of prevailing is θ_P, while the defendant believes that the patent owner's probability of prevailing is θ_D.[17] In general, the two parties will have different assessments of θ.

Consider a potential $(D,0)$ settlement (a settlement with some date of entry D and no payment). The plaintiff would find such a settlement acceptable if its payoff from the settlement exceeded its expected payoff from litigation:

(6) $DH + (1 - D)L \geq \theta_P H + (1 - \theta_P)L$.

(For ease of exposition, we go back to assuming that litigation costs are 0.) Rearranging the terms yields

(7) $D \geq \theta_P$.

For the defendant, this settlement would be acceptable if

(8) $(1 - D)E \geq (1 - \theta_D)E$

or, after rearranging,

(9) $D \leq \theta_D$.

---

[16] The claim that the parties are risk-averse is called into question by basic financial economics. The risks faced in litigation are largely unsystematic risks; that is, they are not correlated with market risks. In that case, investors could diversify away the litigation risks.

[17] By *unbiased signal*, we mean that on average the patent owner's assessment of θ is equal to the true θ, or, mathematically, $E(\theta_P | \theta) = \theta$. A similar equation holds for the defendant's assessment.

From inequalities (7) and (9), it can be seen that both sides will be satisfied by a $(D,0)$ settlement only if the patent owner believes θ is no larger than the defendant does (that is, if $\theta_P \leq \theta_D$). In the other case—where the patent owner believes θ is higher than the defendant does (that is, if $\theta_P > \theta_D$)—a $(D,0)$ settlement is not feasible because it cannot satisfy both parties.

A feasible settlement in this case requires a reverse payment. We now attempt to identify the feasible settlement that has the lowest value of D (the earliest date of entry). This settlement would be the one that consumers would most prefer out of the set of all feasible settlements. This settlement can be found by solving for the values of (D,P) that make both parties just as well off under the settlement as they would be under litigation.

From the perspective of the patent owner, this means that the settlement (D^{***},P^{***}) must satisfy

$$(10) \quad D^{***} H + (1 - D^{***}) L - P^{***} = \theta_P H + (1 - \theta_p) L ,$$

and from the perspective of the defendant, (D^{***},P^{***}) must satisfy

$$(11) \quad (1 - D^{***}) E + P^{***} = (1 - \theta_D) E .$$

Equations (10) and (11) represent a system of two equations in two unknowns that can be solved for (D^{***},P^{***}). The solution for D^{***} is

$$(12) \quad D^{***} = \frac{\theta_P (H - L) - \theta_D E}{H - L - E} .$$

Given that we are analyzing the case where $\theta_P > \theta_D$ and $E < H - L$, equation (12) implies that

$$(13) \quad D^{***} = \frac{\theta_P (H - L) - \theta_D E}{H - L - E} > \frac{\theta_P (H - L) - \theta_P E}{H - L - E} = \theta_P > \theta_D .$$

In other words, the earliest date of entry among feasible settlements exceeds both the patent owner's and the defendant's values of θ. Note that plugging (13) into (11) demonstrates that $P^{***} > 0$, which implies that a reverse payment is necessary in this case to achieve settlement.

How do consumers fare under this (D^{***},P^{***}) settlement as compared to continued litigation? In principle, the answer to that question depends on the true value of θ. However, if the true value of θ is unknown to the parties, it makes little sense to evaluate the effect of the settlement on consumer surplus assuming the true value of θ were known to the antitrust analyst. After all, the antitrust analyst (or a finder of fact in an antitrust litigation) would likely not have any better idea about θ than the parties. Instead, the settlement should be assessed given the best estimate of θ available to the antitrust analyst or finder of fact. If the signals the parties have received about θ are independent and identically distributed, the best estimate of θ would be the mean of the parties' signals, or $\hat{\theta} = 0.5 \, (\theta_P + \theta_D)$.[18] Using this estimate, consumers would obtain expected consumer surplus under litigation of $\hat{\theta} \, \underline{CS} + (1 - \hat{\theta}) \, \overline{CS}$. This exceeds the expected consumer surplus under the settlement because $\hat{\theta} < \theta_P < D^{***}$ (the first inequality follows from the fact that a mean of two unequal numbers is necessarily smaller than the larger of the two numbers). Thus, in this case with these assumptions, a settlement with a reverse payment makes consumers worse off than they would be if the parties proceeded to litigation.

We conclude that, with potential disagreements concerning the probability that the plaintiff will win the lawsuit, a settlement may not be feasible without reverse payments.[19] However, in such situations, the resulting settlement likely makes consumers worse off than under litigation.[20] This is because, to satisfy both parties, the settlement must push the date of entry beyond the patent owner's estimate of θ and have the patent owner pay the entrant for delaying entry.

We conclude the discussion of economic models by noting that a settlement that is consumer welfare reducing may nevertheless be social welfare enhancing. Social welfare is the sum of producers' profits and consumer surplus. For example, consider the case of litigation costs with the parties having the same assessment of θ. A settlement that calls for $D > \theta$ and a small reverse payment would make consumers slightly worse off. However, the firms' profits may be increased sufficiently (e.g., by

---

[18] A better estimate of θ may be possible if the probability distribution of the signals were known. The estimate described in the text assumes only that the two signals are independent, identically distributed, and have mean equal to θ.

[19] Willig and Bigelow also examine the cases where the plaintiff has better knowledge as to future demand for the product than the defendant and where future entry by a noninfringing product would affect the defendant and plaintiff differently. The asymmetry that arises in these cases may again lead to the situation where a reverse payment is needed to achieve settlement.

[20] Willig and Bigelow find that settlements in this situation may make consumers better off. This is possible in their type of model when consumer surplus is evaluated using the true θ and the true θ exceeds both parties' evaluation of it—in other words, when both parties were quite wrong about θ. However, as discussed in the text, it makes sense to evaluate a settlement using information known to the antitrust analyst since the true value of θ is unknown.

avoiding litigation costs) to offset the consumer harm, yielding an improvement in social welfare.

Conclusion

Economic models that incorporate litigation costs and risk aversion demonstrate that a reverse payment may arise in procompetitive litigation settlements. Thus a per se rule against reverse payments is not appropriate. However, such reverse payments would be expected to be small in most cases. Thus, a large reverse payment is a likely indication that the associated settlement represents an anticompetitive outcome.

The Hatch-Waxman Act made drug patent litigation somewhat different than other patent litigation in that litigation takes place prior to generic entry and the patent owner can delay all generic entry by settling and obtaining the defendant's agreement to delay its entry while retaining its 180-day exclusivity.[21] Perhaps it is not surprising that the reverse payment "problem" has arisen in the area of drug patent litigation.

The early cases brought by the FTC, such as *FTC v. Bristol-Myers,* appear to have involved the type of reverse payments that reasonably raise antitrust concerns. In that case, the reverse payment was large and seemed designed to obtain the generic entrant's agreement to delay its entry. Later cases, such as the Schering case, have been more complicated. The very existence of a reverse payment was at issue given the transfer of valuable intellectual property rights from Upsher and ESI to Schering. Moreover, the agreement called for a date of entry well before the date of patent expiration. Accordingly, there were economic arguments as to why the settlements may not have been anticompetitive. This demonstrates the need for conducting a careful economic analysis before drawing conclusions regarding the competitive effects of a given settlement agreement.

---

[21] As discussed above, the 2003 Medicare reform bill may have changed the landscape in this regard.

18

A Comparison of Market Tests for Evaluating Patent Damages Claims and Antitrust Counterclaims

Joseph P. Cook, Susan C.S. Lee, and Ramsey Shehadeh

In making a claim for lost profits in a patent infringement case, the patent owner must identify the set of substitutes to which customers would turn in the absence of the allegedly infringing product. This set of products (which potentially includes the patent owner's product) would capture the allegedly infringing sales in the but-for world. All else equal, the patent owner's lost profits damages will be larger the fewer are the number of noninfringing substitutes.

The defendant in the patent infringement case may bring an antitrust counterclaim in which it is typically alleged that the patent owner acquired its patent through fraud on the patent office and that the litigation is a sham designed to monopolize a relevant market. In making such a counterclaim, the defendant will typically be required to define a relevant antitrust market (i.e., to identify the set of products whose presence in the market constrains the pricing of the patent owner).

Some may argue that there is a natural tension between the lost profits claim and the antitrust counterclaim. Specifically, the tension faced by the patent owner is typified by the following conundrum: How can the patent owner claim large lost profits damages on the one hand (which seemingly implies that there are few noninfringing substitutes) while arguing for a "broad" relevant market on the other (which seemingly implies that there are many substitutes)? Similarly, the tension faced by the alleged infringer can be described as follows: How can the alleged infringer claim minimal lost profits damages on the one hand (which seemingly implies that there are many noninfringing substitutes) while arguing for a "narrow" relevant market on the other (which seemingly implies that there are few substitutes)?

While both the lost profits analysis and the relevant market analysis require identifying a set of products that are competitively important, the two analyses are different in several important ways. Several observers have noted sources of tension between the claims and pointed out differences of market definition processes that may lead to different markets being defined for each claim.[1] Here we follow the nature of the apparent tension between the claims and demonstrate that a genuine tension may not actually exist under certain market conditions.[2]

Differences Between the Identification of Substitutes in the Lost Profits and Antitrust Analyses

At issue in the lost profits damages analysis is the market impact of the alleged infringement. Infringement can cause sales to be diverted to the alleged infringer and prices in the market to fall. The patent owner is one potential source of the infringer's sales, but other firms may also lose sales to the alleged infringer, and new customers may be attracted to the market. The set of substitute products considered in the lost sales analysis would include all the products affected by the alleged infringement, either through the redistribution of unit sales or by price erosion.[3] Thus, the focus in the lost profits analysis is on substitutes for the *alleged infringer's product*. Moreover, the substitute products are identified as those to which customers would turn if the alleged infringer's product were removed from the market or if its price increased to such a level that no one would want to purchase it.

---

1 See, e.g., Sumanth Addanki, "The Antitrust Counterclaim and Patent Damages: The Economic Relationship," Calculating Damages in Intellectual Property Litigation: Papers for Practitioners, NERA, March 1995; David S. Evans, "Market Definition in Antitrust and Patent-Infringement Litigation," Practising Law Institute, Patents, Copyrights, Trademarks, and Literary Property Course Handbook Series, PLI order no. G4-3942, June 1995; Alyssa A. Lutz and Lauren J. Stiroh, "The Relevant Market in IP and Antitrust Litigation," *IP Litigator* May/June 2003:26-31; and Marion B. Stewart, "Calculating Economic Damages in Intellectual Property Disputes: The Role of Market Definition," *Trial of a Patent Case*, SK022 ALI-ABA 125 (The American Law Institute 2004).

2 In some circumstances, a false tension may arise as a result of peculiarities in the market such as markets in which multiple branded pharmaceuticals compete with each other as well as with their own generic counterparts. In markets such as these, price changes should be interpreted carefully to avoid mistaking reductions in the average price of one particular chemical as dispositive of market power for the branded version of that chemical.

3 This was recognized by the court in *Crystal Semiconductor Corp. v. Tritech Microelectronics Intl. Inc.*, 246 F.3d 1336 (Fed. Cir. 2001).

The antitrust counterclaim typically involves allegations of monopolization or attempted monopolization.[4] The relevant market for the evaluation of such claims is defined as the smallest set of products (starting with the patent owner's product) such that a hypothetical monopolist controlling all of them could profitably raise price on the patent owner's product by a small, but significant amount for a nontransitory period of time ("the SSNIP test").[5] Thus, the focus in the antitrust relevant market analysis is the substitutes for the *patent owner's product* and the price increase contemplated is a small, but significant one (5 percent is often used as a benchmark).

There are, then, two fundamental differences between the respective sets of products considered in the lost profits and antitrust analyses. First, the focus of the analysis differs in that in the lost profit analysis, the focus is on the alleged infringer's product, and in the relevant market analysis, that focus shifts to the patent owner's product. The set of substitutes in the lost profits analysis consists of the substitutes for the alleged infringer's product, while the set of substitutes in the relevant market analysis consists of the set of substitutes for the patent owner's product.

Second, in the antitrust relevant market analysis, we are not concerned with the full array of substitute products (i.e., all those products that are substitutes for the patent owner's product). Instead, we are focused only on the smallest set of substitute products such that a hypothetical monopolist would be able profitably to raise price on the patent owner's product by a small amount. Thus, relevant market definition limits its focus to *close* substitutes for the patent holder's product. In the lost profits analysis, the set of substitutes would generally include *all* of the substitutes for the infringer's product.

The two sets of substitutes may overlap (or even be identical if there is no differentiation between the patented and allegedly infringing

---

4   The legal elements of an attempted monopolization claim, as recited in *Full Draw Productions v. Easton Sports Inc.*, are (1) market definition (including relevant product and geographic markets), (2) a dangerous probability of success in monopolizing the relevant market, (3) the specific intent to monopolize, and (4) conduct in furtherance of such an attempt. The alleged infringer may argue that the alleged infringement suit is a sham and that the patent owner knows his patent to be invalid and is only bringing the suit to foreclose competition. *Full Draw Productions. v. Easton Sports Inc.*, 182 F.3d 745, 756 (10th Cir. 1999).
5   The SSNIP test is described in the *1992 U.S. Department of Justice and Federal Trade Commission Horizontal Merger Guidelines* ("small but significant and nontransitory increase in price").

products), but there is no reason to assume that they are identical in every case, and they often will not be identical. On the one hand, we have all the products against which the alleged infringer won sales. In cases where the alleged infringer expanded the market, we also have a group of sales that would only have been made by the infringer. On the other hand, we have the relevant antitrust market analysis, which involves a small price change, while the analysis of the infringement claim requires that we price the alleged infringer out of the market.

What Is the Basis for the Tension?

There is an intuitive appeal to the thought process that a "narrow market" necessarily implies that (1) the bulk of the alleged infringer's sales, if removed from the market, would be captured by the patent owner, and (2) the patent owner possesses substantial market power for a finding of antitrust liability. Equally attractive is the complementary argument which states that a "broad market" necessarily implies that (1) few of the alleged infringer's sales would have been made by the patent owner were the alleged infringer to be removed from the market and, (2) the patent owner does not possess substantial market power.

Reasoning such as this may lead one to conclude that the results of a relevant market analysis will predict perfectly the outcome of the lost profits analysis (and vice versa). Relying on that conclusion, one may believe that if one establishes that the bulk of the effect of the infringement is on the patent owner, then it must be the case that the patent owner would generate substantial market power through the exclusion of the alleged infringer. Or, similarly, establishing a narrow relevant market is sufficient to show that the bulk of the effect of the alleged infringer's entry is on the patent owner. In addition, this reasoning may help to explain the general concerns regarding a tension between the two types of claims.

Practical concerns about the appearance of a tension may remain an issue for litigators; however, as we have argued above, it is not necessarily the case that the set of substitutes for the lost profits analysis is the same as the set of substitutes included in the relevant market. Differences in the focus of the analysis and the degree of substitution it contemplates can lead to different groups of products being included in the analysis. Therefore, the outcome of the antitrust analysis will not necessarily be a perfect predictor of the outcome of the lost profits analysis (and vice versa), and under the right set of market circumstances, there may not be a genuine tension.

Under What Conditions Might the Tension Not Exist?
To better discriminate between cases where there is a genuine tension and those in which the tension may be more one of appearance, consider the following example. Assume that the effect of the allegedly infringing entry on existing firms in the market is quite large. However, while the alleged infringer drew some sales from the patent owner's product, its closest substitutes are other products on the market. This could occur if, for example, the patent provided an easy means of entry into the market rather than a source of differentiation among the competing products. In such a case, the proportion of the entry effects accounted for by sales lost by the patent owner might be relatively small. Nevertheless, even that relatively small amount of sales may represent sufficiently close competition to indicate that the alleged infringer and patent owner comprise a relevant market for antitrust purposes.

In Figure 1, the closest competitor to the alleged infringer (I) is the patent owner (P), and the primary competitive constraint on the patent owner is the alleged infringer. If that constraint were lifted by the removal of the alleged infringer from the market, it could provide the basis for the exercise of substantial market power by the patent owner. However, the closest competitor to the alleged infringer is a third competitor (C). It is this third competitor that will likely capture the bulk of the alleged infringer's sales in its absence, implying that the lost profits damages of the patent owner would be relatively small. The asymmetry in the closeness of substitutes underlies the difference in the results of the lost profits analysis and the antitrust analysis.

**Figure 1. An Illustration of Spatial Competition Between
Three Firms**

It may be the case that if the patent owner would have captured all the alleged infringer's sales, then the two products are likely such close substitutes that the wrongful exclusion of the alleged infringer from the market would create an antitrust problem.[6] The extreme example of such cases would be one in which the alleged infringer introduces a market clone to the patent owner's product. However, the logic is not quite so appealing the other way around. And, this asymmetry may help to explain the persistent use of antitrust counterclaims in patent infringement cases.

Let us consider a simple linear model of differentiated competition similar to the one shown in Figure 1.[7] Table 1 presents two alternative cases. In each case, the patent owner is part of a duopoly market into which the alleged infringer enters. In one case, the alleged infringer enters with a product similar to the patent owner's product. In the other, the alleged infringer enters with a product similar to the product of the other (noninfringing) competitor in the market. For both of these cases, we compare the pricing equilibria of the model for the duopoly conditions before entry and the triopoly conditions brought about by the entry of the alleged infringer.

The relative magnitude of the lost profits claim can be measured with the ratio of the change in the patent owner's profits as a result of the allegedly infringing entry to the change in the profits of all firms in the market prior to entry, including those of the patent owner.[8] By using profits, we include the effects of lost sales and price erosion. If the full impact of the allegedly infringing entry falls on the patent owner (so that the ratio is equal to one), lost profits damages could not be higher given the market conditions and nature of the infringement.

In Case 1, where the alleged infringer enters with a product similar to the patent owner's product, the results are consistent with the existence

---

6 A counterexample might exist here as well, at least in some sense, if we suppose that the market is sufficiently competitive that margins are so small that entry cannot produce a large enough price effect to reach the area of, say, 5 percent—even where the alleged infringer is the patent owner's market clone and nearly all the effects of entry are felt by the patent owner. In a small market, the patent may not be sufficiently valuable to merit a lawsuit to exclude the alleged infringer, making the case less interesting. However, in a large market, small changes in the price can accrue over large sales volumes to become large total changes in revenue and profit.

7 This model is based on the well-known Hotelling model of spatial competition where firms are differentiated based on linear transportation costs. See H. Hotelling, "Stability in Competition," Economic Journal 39 (1929): 41-57.

8 This can be written as $\Delta\pi_p / \Sigma_i \Delta\pi_i$, where $\Delta\pi_p$ is the change in the patent owner's profits associated with the infringement, and $\Sigma_i \Delta\pi_i$ is the cumulative change in profits from all firms affected by the alleged infringement, including the patent owner. A similar measure can be constructed based on quantities; however, as such a measure would not capture any price erosion, the quantity-based measure does not account for the full effects of the allegedly infringing entry.

Table 1. Market Effects of Entry by an Alleged Infringer that Represents the Patent Owner's Closest Competition

Firm		Location on Unit Interval	Price	Quantity	Profits
Case 1: The alleged infringer enters close to the patent owner					
Duopoly	Other Competitor	0.000	1.00	0.500	0.5000
	Patent Owner	1.000	1.00	0.500	0.5000
Triopoly	Other Competitor	0.000	0.58	0.290	0.1687
	Patent Owner	1.000	0.17	0.043	0.0037
	Alleged Infringer	0.995	0.09	0.667	0.1111
Market Effects of Entry on Existing Competitors	*Relative to Market Effect*				
	Other Competitor			31.44%	40.03%
	Patent Owner			68.56%	59.97%
	Relative to Duopoly Value				
	Other Competitor		−41.92%		
	Patent Owner		−83.33%		
Case 2: The alleged infringer enters close to the other competitor					
Duopoly	Other Competitor	0.000	1.00	0.500	0.5000
	Patent Owner	1.000	1.00	0.500	0.5000
Triopoly	Other Competitor	0.000	0.09	0.043	0.0037
	Patent Owner	1.000	0.58	0.290	0.1687
	Alleged Infringer	0.005	0.17	0.667	0.1111
Market Effects of Entry on Existing Competitors	*Relative to Market Effect*				
	Other Competitor			68.56%	59.97%
	Patent Owner			31.44%	40.03%
	Relative to Duopoly Value				
	Other Competitor		−71.67%		
	Patent Owner		−67.67%		

of a tension. The antitrust outcome predicts the lost profits outcome. If we first compare the prices between duopoly and triopoly, we see that the price changes are large. The patent owner's price falls with entry by over 80 percent and the third competitor's price falls by more than 40 percent. Returning to a duopoly and using the lower triopoly prices as a base would engender price increases of even greater magnitude. Such large price changes, far more than 5 percent, provide the needed support for the antitrust counterclaim. Moreover, the effect of the entry on the patent owner relative to the total effect indicates that the majority of the market effect, roughly 60 percent, is on the patent owner. So, here the results of the two analyses are consistent with a genuine tension. The patent owner's large lost profits claim is coincident with the potential for the exercise of substantial market power if the alleged infringer were to be excluded.

Similarly, in Case 2, where the alleged infringer offers a product similar to the other competitor in the market, the changes in equilibrium price based on the entry (or exit) of the alleged infringer are still substantially greater than 5 percent and supportive of the antitrust counterclaim. Each existing firm's price falls by more than 60 percent with the allegedly infringing entry. So, in this case, as in the previous one, the patent owner's equilibrium price change with the exclusion of the alleged infringer is consistent with the exercise of substantial market power. However, in contrast to the previous case, the bulk of the effect of the entry does not fall on the patent owner. Instead, it is the other competitor in the market that bears the bulk of the effect. The shares of the effect of entry are reversed, with the smaller share of 40 percent for the patent owner. Thus, in this case, the tension fails to exist, as least from the point of view of the alleged infringer, and the results of the antitrust analysis do not have predictive power with respect to the lost profits analysis as they did in the previous case.[9]

Conclusion

We have shown that there are counterexamples to the suggestion that there is necessarily a tension between lost profits claims and antitrust claims. In particular, an alleged infringer may be able consistently to argue that on the one hand, lost profits damages are relatively small and, on the other, the relevant antitrust market is narrow, and its exclusion will prompt an exercise of substantial market power. Thus, there is the potential for asymmetry in the existence of tension such that the likelihood of a genuine tension for the patent owner is more likely than for the alleged infringer. As the alleged infringer is the one to initiate the antitrust counterclaim, this asymmetry may provide at least part of the explanation for why we see so many such counterclaims, even though the tension has been widely discussed.

---

9 As the number of firms grows large, one would expect that the equilibrium price changes brought about by the alleged infringer's entry would decrease. So, as the number of firms in a market grows, the potential for substantial price effects is likely reduced, thereby making it more difficult to reach a benchmark price change such as 5 percent.

V

Intellectual Property Rights Protection in Japan and China

19

When East Meets West
Converging Trends in the Economics of Intellectual Property Damages Calculation

Christian Dippon and Noriko Kakihara

Japan is one of the world's richest countries in regard to intellectual property (IP) holdings. The United States Patent and Trademark Office (USPTO) lists five Japanese companies in its 2004 top ten organizations receiving the most U.S. patents—Matshushita Electric Industrial Co. Ltd., Canon Kabushiki Kaisha, Hitachi Ltd., Toshiba Corp., and Sony Corp.[1] Yet, despite its wealth of IP, until 1998, Japanese intellectual property law offered little protection to patent owners' rights. Intellectual property owners had little to gain by bringing a lawsuit against infringers: it typically took years to litigate a case, plaintiffs rarely received any damages, and those damages that were awarded tended to be small and were often insufficient to cover litigation costs. Consequently, many international companies brought suit in U.S. district courts or before the United States International Trade Commission (ITC) against alleged Japanese infringers.[2]

After decades of strong economic growth since World War II, Japan's economy faltered in 1990 and has been in and out of recession ever since. Convinced that propatent policies and other legislation that encouraged research and development and technology transfer were key to the United States' recovery from its recession in the early 1990s, Japan's government organized the Commission on Intellectual Property Rights in the Twenty-

---

[1] See United States Patent and Trademark Office, "USPTO Releases Annual List of Top 10 Organizations Receiving Most U.S. Patents," at www.uspto.gov/main/homepagenews/bak11jan2005.htm, accessed 1 March 2005.
[2] For instance, in 1998, Fuji Photo File Co. Ltd. brought suit before the ITC against 28 alleged infringers, some of which were Japanese firms. See U.S. ITC Investigation #337-TA-406.

First Century. The Commission was charged with improving intellectual property rights (IPR) protection, particularly for patents. Japan also was pressured by the World Trade Organization (WTO), which it joined in 1995, to harmonize its measures of IPR protection with the international community under the Agreement on Trade-Related Aspects of Intellectual Property Rights (TRIPS).[3] As illustrated in Figure 1, these forces led to widespread revisions of Japanese IPR law from 1998 to the present.

A pivotal part of Japan's IPR reform was the revision of the methods by which economic damages in Japanese patent infringement disputes were to be quantified. Prior to 1998, patent damages in Japan were predominantly based on rules of thumb, accounting standards, or other noneconomic methods of apportioning value. With the IPR reforms, these methods were largely replaced by economic principles. The revisions to the code of law and the methods of calculating harm dramatically increased a patent owner's chances of recovering damages in case of infringement.

Principles of IP Litigation in Japan

Prior to Reform

Prior to the IPR reform of 1998, Japan's patent law provided only very general guidelines as to how damages should be calculated. Japanese law merely stated that "the profits earned by the infringer are presumed to be the damages suffered by the patentee."[4] As an alternative, the law allowed the patent owners to recover "the amount which is normally received for the working of a patented invention."[5]

In the abstract, preform Japanese damage models were not substantially different from their U.S. counterparts. That is, Japanese law allowed patent owners to collect a measure of either lost profits or lost royalties. However, as detailed below, the application of these concepts differed substantially from the way they were applied in the U.S. Moreover, there existed little case law that guided parties in the interpretation of these

---

3   The objective of the WTO's TRIPS agreements is to "narrow the gaps in the way these rights are protected around the world, and to bring them under common international rules." World Trade Organization, "Understanding the WTO: Agreements, Intellectual Property: Protection and Enforcement," at ww.wto.org/english/thewto_e/whatis_e/tif_e/agrm7_e.htm, accessed 29 March 2005.
4   Japanese Patent Law, Article 102, translation from Japanese Patent Attorney Association, International Activities Committee, "Revisions of the Japanese Patent Law, Recent Revisions to the Japanese Patent Law," January 2000, at www.jpaa.or.jp/english/data/jan2000.htm, accessed 4 April 2005.
5   Id.

Figure 1. Revisions of Japanese IPR Law, 1998–2004

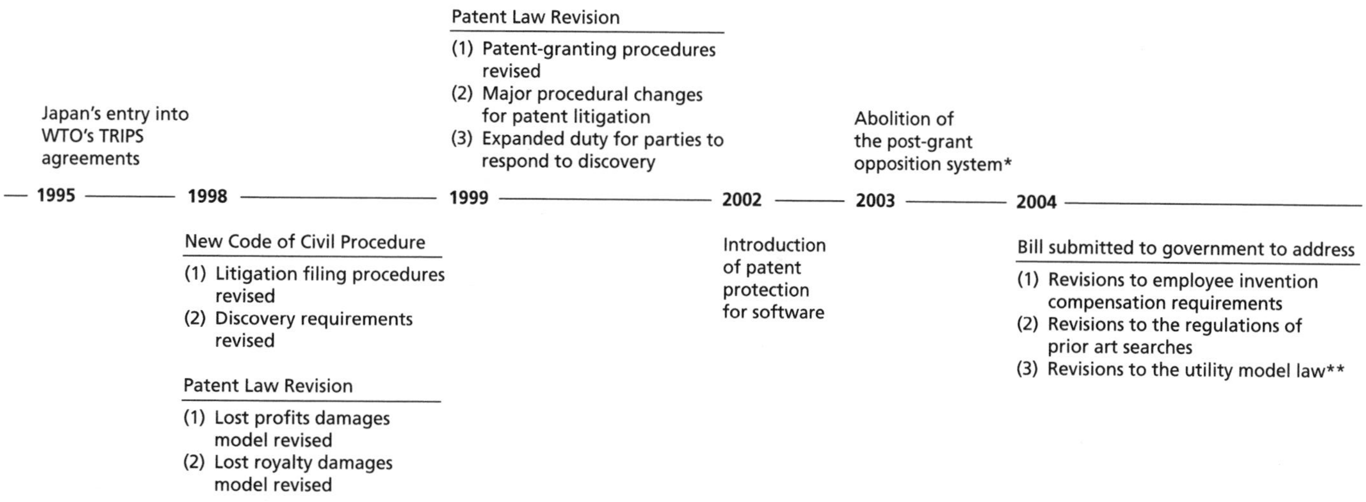

1995	1998	1999	2002	2003	2004

1995

Japan's entry into WTO's TRIPS agreements

1998

New Code of Civil Procedure
(1) Litigation filing procedures revised
(2) Discovery requirements revised

Patent Law Revision
(1) Lost profits damages model revised
(2) Lost royalty damages model revised

1999

Patent Law Revision
(1) Patent-granting procedures revised
(2) Major procedural changes for patent litigation
(3) Expanded duty for parties to respond to discovery

2002

Introduction of patent protection for software

2003

Abolition of the post-grant opposition system*

2004

Bill submitted to government to address
(1) Revisions to employee invention compensation requirements
(2) Revisions to the regulations of prior art searches
(3) Revisions to the utility model law**

* Post-grant opposition allowed any person to file an opposition against the registration of a granted patent within a certain time period.

** The utility model law is designed to promote the protection and utilization of a "device" in order to encourage technical ideas. The term device refers to a technical idea by which a law of nature is utilized.

broad guidelines: few precedents were set to provide a common framework to analyze damages. The concepts of "lost profits" and "reasonable royalty" as ultimately applied by prereform Japanese courts resulted in low damages awards in Japan, particularly when compared to those in the U.S. In fact, Japan's average damages award in a patent infringement case was less than 1 percent of the U.S. average. After accounting for litigation costs, plaintiffs frequently lost money on net when suing infringers in Japanese courts. Consequently, it was often economically worthwhile to infringe a patent in Japan. Not surprisingly, Japanese and non-Japanese companies chose to litigate their patent suits in U.S. courts. The venue of many of these lawsuits was the ITC, which not only guaranteed U.S.-style recognition of economic damages principles, but also assured a relatively fast resolution of the matter.

Lost Profits

Prior to the 1998 reform, Japanese patent law loosely permitted the recovery of lost profits. It assumed that the damages suffered by the patent owner were equal to the difference between the *infringer's* actual profit and the *infringer's* but-for profit.[6] This method is not consistent with the make-whole standard of lost profits damages applied in the U.S. Rather, the Japanese damages model was tied only to the enrichment of the infringer and not to any actual harm realized by the plaintiff. The economic harm to the plaintiff caused by an infringement may be substantially greater than the infringer's enrichment due to the infringement. For instance, a firm with a relatively high cost structure might make relatively low profits from selling an infringing product. Its competitive presence could, however, cause considerable harm to a patent owner in terms of lost sales and price erosion. Under the prereform "lost profits" model, the plaintiff would not be fully compensated for its loss, as the defendant did not derive much profit from infringement. Conversely, the method could theoretically also cause a windfall to the patent owner if the patent owner makes little use of its own patent.

As in the U.S., plaintiffs claiming lost profits were also required to show a causal relationship between the infringement and the damages.

---

[6] Japanese Patent Law, Law No. 51 of 1998, article 102, para. 1, cited by Toshiko Takenaka, HD, 2 Wash UJL & Pol'y 309, "Patent Infringement Damages in Japan and the United States: Will Increased Patent Infringement Damage Awards Revive the Japanese Economy?" at law.wustl.edu/journal/2/p309takenaka.pdf, accessed 4 April 2005.

Because in many Japanese cases, such a relationship was difficult to prove, plaintiffs often sought compensation in the form of lost royalties.

Lost Royalties

Before the reform, lost royalties were determined based on the revenue that was "normally" received from licensing the patent. The term *normally* was the cause of much dispute. Parties and courts interpreted the term differently, particularly in cases where a patent had previously never been licensed. Even if there were existing licensing agreements, parties disagreed on which agreement was representative of the royalty rate that the patent owner would have "normally" received. The term *normally* also did not require the parties to base their opinions on any economic principles, such as the ones required in the hypothetical negotiation framework. Consequently, royalty rates were often based on unsupported company or expert opinions. Japanese courts generally took "normally" to mean published standard royalty rates for the industry.[7] If such rates were not available, courts defaulted to royalty rates for licensing government-owned patents, which often were very low.[8] Thus, as interpreted by the courts, the term *normally* limited the patent owner to receive no more, and frequently significantly less, than a standard industry-wide royalty rate.[9] This, in turn, led to low damages awards, even for valuable patents, and thus was largely ineffective in deterring future infringement.

Post Reform

Recognizing the shortcomings of Japanese IPR protection, the Japanese government implemented a number of changes to its Code of Civil Procedures and the patent law beginning in 1998 and continuing to the present. As illustrated in Figure 1, on 1 January 1998, basic changes to the way a court examines IP infringement cases in Japan were made to the Code of Civil Procedures. Revisions have also been made to the patent law

---

7   See Toshiko Takenaka, University of Washington, School of Law, Center for Advanced Study and Research on Intellectual Property Newsletter, Summer 1999, vol. 6, no. 1, "Recent Legislative Updates in Japan" at http://www.law.washington.edu/casrip/newsletter/Vol6/newsv6i1jp2.html, accessed 20 June 2005.

8   Id.

9   Industry-wide royalty rates are only coincidentally indicative of the value of a license to a particular technology. First, the average is likely to be based on agreements that involve licenses to disparate technologies, forms, amounts of intellectual property, and terms. Second, there is usually no presumption of validity and infringement in real-world licensing negotiations.

during the last few years. Many of these changes were intended to improve the overall efficiency of how IP cases move through the Japanese legal system. However, there were also a number of specific changes made that impact how economic damages due to infringement are to be calculated. These changes brought Japanese IPR protection closer to the standards employed in the U.S.

Lost Profits

As part of the IPR reform, several amendments were made to the Japanese patent statute, Article 102. Under these amendments, the patent owner, for the first time, has the option to receive compensation based on lost profits, using the following formula:

$$\text{Lost Profits} = \frac{\text{Number of}}{\text{Infringed Sales}} \times \frac{\text{Patent Owner's}}{\text{Profit Margin Per Unit}}$$

The profit here is the per-unit profit that could have been earned by the patent owner, and is calculated by subtracting variable production costs from the sales price. Since this calculation of the profit margin excludes fixed costs, it can potentially yield very high profit margins and thus very high damages. As a counterbalancing measure, the courts frequently arbitrarily reduce the profit margins used in the calculation. It appears to be at the courts' discretion as to what constitutes a high profit margin and how much such a margin would be reduced.

The new Japanese lost profits model differs from U.S. standards as it determines damages based on the licensor's profit margin over variable cost rather than the *incremental* profit margin. The incremental profit margin is defined as the profit left after the deduction of those additional costs, both fixed and variable, necessary to make and sell the additional units at issue, expressed as a per-unit percentage of the price of the product. For instance, if the plaintiff could have made and sold the additional units without any capital investments, the incremental profit margin potentially could be quite high. However, if the plaintiff would have incurred significant new capital costs in meeting the additional demand or would have had to subcontract the additional demand at a high price, the incremental profit margin would be net of these capital costs and would therefore be correspondingly lower. In contrast, Japan's lost profits model is based on the profit margin over variable cost. It only incorporates variable production costs and does not include any fixed costs, even if these would need to increase in order to meet additional demand.

Japanese courts have frequently deviated from the formula above by incorporating a factor that supposedly accounts for the contribution of the patent to the sales of the products. For example, this *contribution factor* could be low if the product incorporates a large number of other patents or nonpatented features, or it could be high if the sales of the final product are primarily attributable to the patent at issue. The challenge with using a contribution factor is that it can be difficult to accurately determine the appropriate value. If the parties (either the plaintiff or the defendant) fail to provide adequate support for their proposed value for the contribution factor, the damages claim, or rebuttal thereto, is jeopardized.

Under the amendments of Article 102, to recover lost profits damages, the patent owner only has to prove the number of infringing sales, his profit margin, and his ability to have made the sales. In contrast to the requirements in the U.S., the plaintiff is no longer required to demonstrate a cause-and-effect relationship between the patent owner's sales and the number of infringed sales. This revision has the potential of significantly decreasing a plaintiff's burden of proof.

Lost Royalties

If the court awards lost profits, the patent owner is considered fully compensated and typically is not entitled to any additional damages on the same sales. However, the patent owner is always entitled to the amount of money equivalent to the royalty income he could have received from the infringing party under Article 102(3). Thus, similar to the U.S. system, lost royalties serve as a statutory floor for damages. As discussed above, the methodology for calculating royalty damages in Japan is significantly different than that used in the U.S. The IPR reform has only slightly modified the method by which lost royalties are calculated. Rather than determining damages based on the amount which is *normally* received from the working of the patented invention, the revised approach removed the word *normally,* due to the broad interpretation that parties assigned to it. The fundamental concept of determining damages based on lost royalty income remains unchanged, however. Of note is the fact that, notwithstanding the revisions to its patent law, Japan has not mandated a hypothetical negotiation framework like that used in the U.S. for reasonable royalty calculations. The reasonably expected royalty approach, however, does not necessarily preclude the use of the hypothetical negotiation framework.

Based on the authors' consulting experience in Japan, we find that Japanese parties generally welcome the idea of determining the reasonably expected royalties based on a hypothetical negotiation. However, the first full application of this concept in a Japanese court has not yet occurred.

Discovery

Prior to the 1998 reform, there was no explicit discovery process in Japan, as there was in the U.S., and document production was largely voluntary. Because the burden of proof for damages (as well as liability) was with the patent owner, the patent holder faced a significant hurdle in its effort to convincingly prove economic damages. Instead of relying on the defendant's actual financial information to assess the lost profits, the plaintiff was often forced to rely on publicly available information or rules of thumb. The new Japanese Code of Civil Procedures has expanded both parties' obligation to respond to discovery requests and produce the information necessary to establish liability and economic damages in patent infringement cases. Parties are still allowed to retain certain information from the court and opposing parties, including trade secrets and proprietary information.

Prejudgment Interest

Plaintiffs in Japan, as in the U.S., are entitled to prejudgment interest for any lost time value of money. In the U.S., prejudgment interest is calculated for each infringing sale, from the time of sale to the trial date.[10] In Japan, however, prejudgment interest starts with the filing date of the lawsuit and ends with the trial date. Besides resulting in lower prejudgment interest awards, starting the calculation with the filing date encourages the plaintiff to quickly file a patent lawsuit, rather than play a game of wait and see.

Treble and Punitive Damages

As a matter of law in the U.S., the plaintiff, after a showing of willful infringement, is entitled to treble damages as a form of punitive damages. No such damages are awarded in Japan. Treble damages were considered during the IPR reforms of 1998, however, because of a Japanese Supreme Court decision in July 1997, the enforceability of treble damages was denied. The absence of such damages in Japan is one reason why IP damages awards in Japan are generally lower than in the U.S.

---

[10] This assumes that the lawsuit is filed within the statute of limitations.

Converging Statistics

Due in part to the sweeping IPR reforms, the attitudes of Japanese businesses toward the protection of IPR have changed dramatically. In order to protect their patents, Japanese firms are now more aggressively defending their rights and more frequently resolving IP disputes in a court of law. This departure from the traditional standards (wherein lawsuits are considered distasteful) also seems to stem from changes in the business environment. For example, intensifying competition from low-cost manufacturers located in South Korea, Taiwan, and China has provided Japanese firms with strong incentives to rigorously defend their patent portfolios. Statistics that describe IP litigation in Japan (e.g., the frequency and duration of cases) show converging trends with the norms observed in the U.S. Specifically, the number of IP related lawsuits in Japan has increased, nearly doubling in the last ten years. Similarly, the average pendency time for concluded cases decreased from over 25 months in 1998 to approximately 15 months in 2003, demonstrating the improved efficiency of Japanese courts. Finally, as IPR protection increased, so did the penalty for violating it. Patent damages awards increased from an average of ¥46 million (approximately $400,000) between 1990 and 1994 to ¥111 million (approximately $1 million) between 1998 and 2000, an increase of over 140 percent.[11]

Number of Lawsuits

The change in attitudes toward litigation and protecting a firm's IP portfolios, in particular, becomes apparent when reviewing the number of cases filed in a court of law. As shown in Figure 2, the number of cases filed in eight Japanese district courts increased steadily since the early 1990s, from 311 new cases in 1991 to more than 600 new cases a year during most years after the 1998 reform.[12] An important part of the IPR reform was restructuring the court system to make it more efficient, thus decreasing the time it took from hearing a case to issuing a ruling. Prior to the IPR reform, the courts' caseloads were increasing yearly, as more new cases were filed than were resolved. This increase in cases filed added

---

[11] Japan Patent Office, "Report Presented by the Intellectual Property Committee of the Industrial Structure Council," December 2001, p. 7, at www.jpo.go.jp/shiryou_e/toushin_e/shingikai_e/pdf/bukai_report_e.pdf, accessed 4 April 2005.

[12] It is unclear how much of the increase in the number of cases can be directly attributed to the IPR reform rather than to other factors, such as the recession or the anticipation of the IPR reform. The 1998 reform, at a minimum, had some impact, as the number of cases increased sharply in 1998 after two years of negative growth.

Figure 2. Number of New and Closed Cases in All District Courts

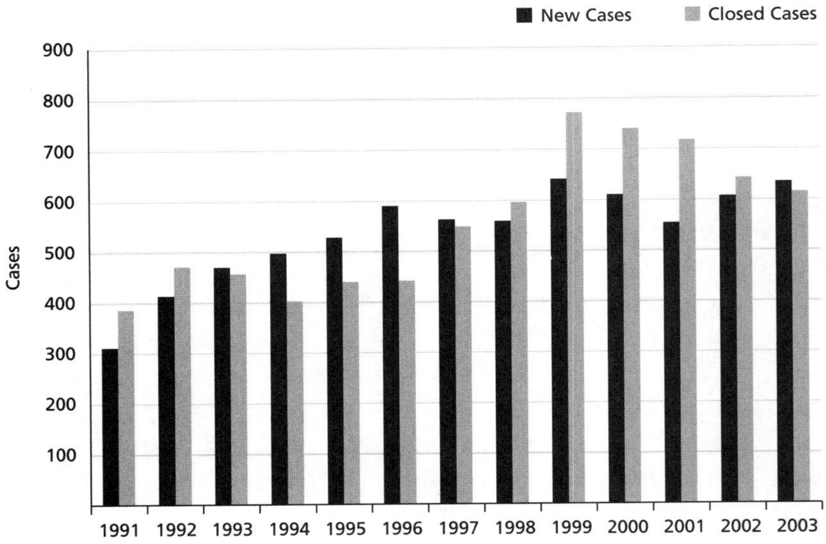

Source: Osaka District Court.

to the already heavy burden on the legal system and further increased the average pendency time for IP cases.

Post reform, however, this statistic seems to have improved significantly; courts are now more efficient in reaching a quick resolution in an IP matter. Since the IPR reform, the number of concluded cases has surpassed the number of new cases in five of the six years for which data are available.

As a direct consequence of the IPR reform, the Tokyo District Court is now handling most new IP cases. Consequently, its caseload has increased from 282 new cases in 1997 to 343 cases in 2003, a 22 percent increase. Figure 3 reflects the number of new cases before the Tokyo, Osaka, and other district courts from 1997 to 2003.

Not reflected in these statistics are more recent high-profile cases that further demonstrate how Japanese companies have become more aggressive in defending their IPR. Among these cases are international disputes relating to flat panel displays between Fujitsu Ltd. and its Korean competitor Samsung SDI. Both firms have urged their respective countries to block the sale of flat panel displays containing the disputed technology by the other party to this lawsuit. Similarly, Matsushita Electric Industrial Co. is

Figure 3. Number of New Cases before District Courts

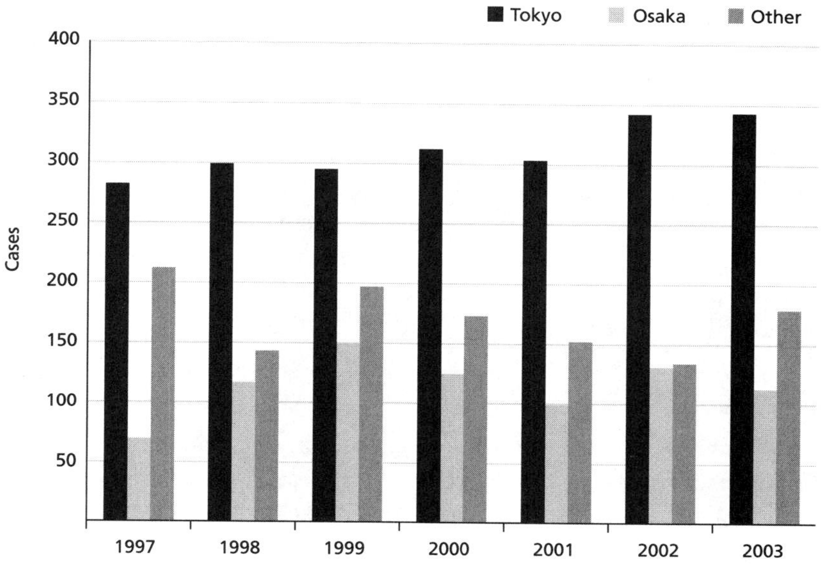

Source: Osaka District Court.

suing LG Electronics of South Korea over patents for plasma display panels. While the case is as yet unresolved, the Tokyo Customs Office has temporarily banned imports of LG Electronics plasma products into Japan. Sharp Corp. is suing TECO Electric and Machinery for patent infringement over LCD technology, and Nichia, a Japanese LED manufacturer, has been and continues to be involved in a string of lawsuits involving its patent relating to LED. Nichia has stated that it vows to continue "to identify infringing LED application products in the market, and enforce its intellectual property rights against any infringers in any part of the world. By doing so, Nichia hopes to contribute to the growth of a fair market, where intellectual property is valued."[13]

There are also a number of patent-related cases filed by Japanese inventors who are seeking a portion of the benefits derived by their employers for their inventions. These lawsuits further illustrate the new Japanese focus on IPR. Most prominent among these types of new IP lawsuits is the case of *Shuji Nakamura v. Nichia Corp.* In 2001,

[13] Nichia press release, at www.nichia.co.jp/domino01/nichia/newsnca_e.nsf/2005/01181, accessed 4 April 2005.

Mr. Nakamura, a former researcher at Nichia, brought legal action against his former employer, a manufacturer of LEDs and laser diodes. Basing his claim on Article 35.3 of the Japanese Patent Law, Mr. Nakamura claimed partial ownership to a patent involving the invention of a blue-light-emitting diode (Blue LED). In January 2004, the Tokyo District Court awarded Mr. Nakamura ¥20 billion (approximately $200 million) for the invention he created while he worked for Nichia. The case received heavy media coverage as it was the largest patent damages award in Japanese history. While it ultimately settled at a small fraction of the court's award, this case set a strong precedent for this type. Subsequent to the Nichia case, similar cases were filed against companies, including Ajinomoto Co., Toshiba, Hitachi Ltd., and Mitsubishi Electric.

Duration

A major component of the IPR reform was an emphasis on speedier trials for IP cases filed in Japan. In 2003, the average pendency time was approximately 15 months, down from a duration of 30 months before the 1998 reform. In fact, the average pendency time of 10.5 months[14] in the Tokyo District Court in 2003 was less than the average pendency time in the U.S. of 13 months.[15] As discussed in more detail below, the disparity between the U.S. and Japanese average pendency times is the result of two factors. First, the difficulty experienced in Japan by plaintiffs in obtaining evidence from defendants traditionally prolonged the amount of time needed to substantiate their claims.[16] Second, Japanese judges usually left the scheduling up to the parties involved in the case, which resulted in further delays.[17] The IPR reform, implemented in 1998 and amended on an annual basis, has addressed the second issue, but there still remain significant hurdles to overcome in regard to the first issue.

---

14 See Tokyo District Court, "Current State of Intellectual Property Litigation in Japan," p. 7, at www.apaaonline.org/data/images/committee_reports/Workshop-Current_State_of_Intellectual_Property_Litigation_in_Japan_(by_Toshiaki_Iimura).doc, accessed 4 April 2005.

15 Authors' analysis of data provided by the Federal Judicial Center. FEDERAL COURT CASES: INTEGRATED DATA BASE, 1970-2000 [PARTS 119-121: APPELLATE DATA, 1998-1999] [computer file]. ICPSR version. Washington, DC: Federal Judicial Center [producer], 2000. Ann Arbor, MI: Inter-University Consortium for Political and Social Research [distributor], 2001.

16 See Tokyo District Court, "Current State of Intellectual Property Litigation in Japan," p. 11, at www.apaaonline.org/data/images/committee_reports/Workshop-Current_State_of_Intellectual_Property_Litigation_in_Japan_(by_Toshiaki_Iimura).doc, accessed 4 April 2005.

17 Id.

Figure 4. Average Duration of Cases in All District Courts

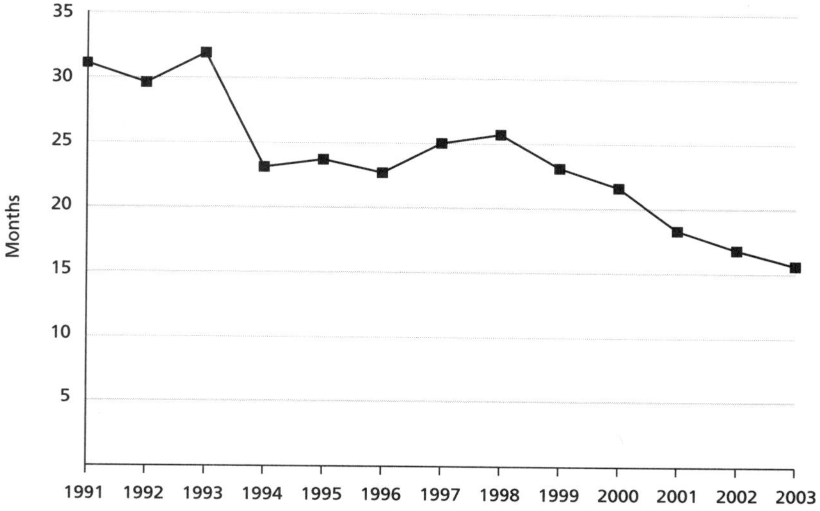

Source: Osaka District Court.

Figure 4 shows the downward trend in the average time needed to resolve an IP case filed in Japanese district courts. Court procedures in patent suits have sped up considerably. What used to take, on average, over 30 months to close in the early 1990s now takes about half that time. Moreover, the average duration has decreased steadily since the beginning of the IPR reform in 1998. This is despite the fact that the number of cases has been steadily increasing over this period, as seen in Figure 2. According to the Osaka District Court, the average duration in the Tokyo and Osaka District Courts is lower than the national average. In 2003, of all the IP cases introduced to the eight district courts in Japan, over 50 percent were resolved within a year and another 32 percent were closed within two years.[18]

Awards

The increase in IPR protection has increased the penalty for firms that infringe. Before the 1998 IPR reform, Japan was known for awarding low compensation for economic damages, if any. The average damages award

---

[18] Osaka District Court.

Figure 5. Average Amount of Damages for Major Lawsuits Regarding Infringement of Patents and Utility Models

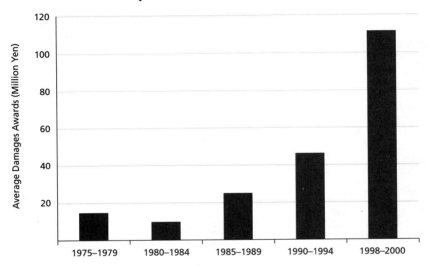

Source: The ABA Section of Intellectual Property Law Newsletter, volume 20, number 4, Summer 2002.

in the U.S. is ¥10 billion (approximately $100 million).[19] The average damages award in Japan—¥46 million (approximately $400,000)—was dramatically lower, less than 1 percent of the U.S. average.[20] As is illustrated in Figure 5, after reform, the average amount of damages for major IP lawsuits in Japan increased by over 150 percent.[21]

This trend suggests that there has been an increase in the probability that the courts will award damages based on lost profits. This, in turn, means that Japanese enterprises will likely face IP damages awards (either as plaintiff or defendant) that are more in line with those in the U.S. This emerging trend can be seen in recent IP related damages awards. For instance, in March 2002, the Tokyo District Court awarded patent owner

---

19 Ryuka Consulting Inc., "The Ryuka Approach to Patent Drafting and Client Servicing," citing a report issued by the Nomura Research Institute, www.ryuka.com/en/about/approach_main.htm, accessed 5 April 2005.

20 Japan Patent Office, "Report Presented by the Intellectual Property Committee of the Industrial Structure Council," December 2001, p. 7, at www.jpo.go.jp/shiryou_e/toushin_e/shingikai_e/pdf/bukai_report_e.pdf, accessed 4 April 2005.

21 Damages awards in Japan generally tend to be lower than in the U.S. as there are no treble or punitive damages in Japan.

Aruze Corp. a record-setting ¥8.4 billion (approximately $63 million). The court based its decision on the revised lost profits model, finding that the plaintiff's profit margin was 56 percent per unit. The previous record for IP damages compensation was *SmithKline v. Fujimoto,* where the Tokyo District Court awarded SmithKline ¥3 billion (approximately $22 million).

Conclusion

Japan's IPR protection has changed dramatically since 1998. Significantly, the Japanese courts now base damages awards more fully on economic principles. In particular, although not explicitly stated, the economic concept of making the plaintiff "whole" now underlies Japanese patent infringement disputes. In addition, the Japanese courts have become more efficient in resolving IP disputes. These changes have important consequences for Japanese firms or firms that have operations in Japan as it increases the likelihood of being involved in a high stakes patent dispute. Businesses are more willing to protect and advance their interests through patent litigation. Moreover, the size of damage awards resulting from such lawsuits has increased. As a consequence, companies doing business in Japan need to be aware of the changes that have taken place. Both plaintiffs and defendants alike must understand how patent infringement damages are now calculated and be prepared to convincingly defend their IPR positions in Japanese courts.

20

Intellectual Property Rights Protection in China: Litigation, Economic Damages, and Case Strategies

Alan Cox and Kristina Sepetys

Intellectual property rights (IPR) have not received strong protection in the People's Republic of China (China).[1] However, as a result of external pressures and internal economic objectives, China is moving closer to the IPR practices and standards found in Western nations. A growing economy, more sophisticated laws, and increased attention to enforcement have led to IPR infringement cases being brought before Chinese authorities in greater numbers.

However, cases are not yet being brought in sufficient numbers nor are fines and damages awards large enough to deter infringement or compensate IPR owners under existing law. The imposition of administrative penalties by enforcement agencies does not provide adequate incentives to infringers to modify or alter their behaviors and practices. Nor do they adequately compensate for the harm done to the owners of the IPR by infringers. In 2003, total fines imposed by Chinese authorities for violations of trademarks, copyrights, and patents collectively amounted to $30 million, only 0.05 percent of the estimated sales rev-

---

[1] See, for example, International Intellectual Property Alliance (IIPA), "2004 Special 301 Report: People's Republic of China"; Graham J. Chynoweth, "Reality Bites: How the Biting Reality of Piracy in China Is Working to Strengthen Its Copyright Laws," *Duke Law & Technology Review* 3 (2003); Charles L. Miller, "A Cultural and Historical Perspective to Trademark Law Enforcement in China," *Buffalo Intellectual Property Law Journal* 2, no. 103 (Summer 2004).

enue losses of over \$60 billion suffered by U.S., European Union, and Japanese companies in the same year.[2]

In addition to the imposition of administrative penalties, China's IPR laws contain provisions for awarding economic damages to individuals and companies in the event their rights have been infringed. Although the laws have been designed to comport with major international agreements, the laws do differ in certain areas from those found in many Western countries. For example, in some instances, the total damages that may be recovered are capped. Even where they are not capped, in most cases, damage awards and fines are low in comparison with those in other countries. Damages are often computed on the basis of the infringer's unjust enrichment. Since infringers usually sell their illegal copies at a small fraction of the price charged by the IPR owner, such unjust enrichment is often modest compared to the lost profits from lost sales. While capping damages can reduce the risk of excessive damage awards unrelated to economic harm, it can also constrain awards to levels well below the actual economic damages incurred. Caps that are too low impose real economic costs on the economy as well as lack sufficient deterrent value.

China has moved in recent years to develop IPR laws and policy that would strengthen the rights of IPR owners and enforce those rights. However, these policies have yet to be fully implemented. Full implementation would likely provide a higher degree of deterrence to potential infringers.

Balancing IPR Protection and Economic Growth in China

Introducing IPR protection in a developing country frequently proceeds through a predictable series of events. Initially, there may be little or no IPR protection and markets characterized by imitation rather than innovation, which may be followed by markets with well-designed and enforced IPR and characterized by higher degrees of domestic innovation. There are, however, conflicts and challenges that may face a country while making the transition to a more mature IPR regime.

Weak Protection: Imitation over Innovation

In the early phases of developing IPR protections, there may or may not be laws governing IPR. If there are laws, they may not be well designed or

---

2   U.S. Department of State Bureau of International Information Programs, "Trade Official Urges China to Punish IPR Violators Forcefully," at usinfo.state.gov/eap/Archive/2005/Apr/14-581627.html.

firmly enforced. In the case of technology, imports exceed exports, and imitation, rather than innovation and invention, prevails. Imitation allows for low-cost production and low prices for goods and services. In the short term, this leads to increased production and consumption of goods and services, which benefits the country's consumers and helps to fuel growth in a developing economy. From an economic point of view, it may be optimal (in a social welfare sense) for a government to provide for only weak IPR early in a country's development, given the substantial consumer surplus costs to IPR protection.

Although a weak IPR regime may support technological growth and development in the short run through imitation, it also serves to discourage domestic innovation, which is a long-run driver of economic growth. There are other drags on economic growth created by IPR violations. For example, uncompensated use of intellectual property through piracy or counterfeiting can effect long-term economic growth since such activities increase the cost of doing business in China. A manufacturer that might consider manufacturing products in China or contributing technology to a joint venture may decide that the risk of patent, trademark, or copyright infringement, and the costs associated with that risk, may be too great and opt to locate in another country. The decision for a manufacturer to produce elsewhere means China will lose a source of taxes, wages, and other revenue contributions. Even if the manufacturer does conduct business, it will do so at a higher cost when IPR protection is weak. Costs will be driven up by restrictions on the use of intellectual property in order to protect the IPR from infringement. The imposition of such constraints will reduce the profitability of using the intellectual property, reducing revenues and tax collections.

Benefits of Domestic Innovation and Invention Prevail

There is an extensive literature examining the broader economic effects of intellectual property protection (or lack thereof) on developing economies.[3] There is a growing consensus that stronger, properly struc-

---

3   See, for example, Carsten Fink and Keith E. Maskus, eds., *Intellectual Property and Development: Lessons from Recent Economic Research* (World Bank and Oxford University Press, http://www.worldbank.org/research/IntellProp_temp.pdf 2005); Robert E. Evenson and Larry E. Westphal, "Technological Change and Technology Strategy," in *Handbook of Development Economics,* vol. 3A, ed. Jere Behrman and T.N. Srinivasan (Amsterdam: North-Holland, 1997); Keith Maskus, "The Role of Intellectual Property Rights in Promoting Foreign Direct Investment and Technology Transfer," *Duke Journal of Comparative and International Law* 9 (1998): 109–161; and Carlos A. Primo Braga, Carsten Fink, and Claudia Paz Sepulveda, "Intellectual Property Rights and Economic Development," discussion paper, Washington, DC, World Bank, 1998.

tured IPR can increase economic growth and improve development processes.[4] The effectiveness of IPR laws and regulations in protecting intellectual property and encouraging growth and development depends upon a number of factors, including their design and implementation. A key objective of IPR laws related to economic growth and development is stimulation of invention and innovation. IPR protection can also deepen markets through improved contract certainty, permitting better monitoring and enforcement of activities at all levels of the supply network, which, in turn, may lead to willingness by innovative firms and their distributors to invest in marketing and brand-name recognition.[5] In addition, effective IPR enforcement may improve the quality of goods over time and facilitate the domestic and international diffusion of knowledge. In a highly developed economy, consumer surplus costs associated with IPR enforcement may be outweighed by the benefits of increased innovation and invention.

China at the Crossroads

It is interesting to consider that perhaps China is at the crossroads in making the transition from an imitative to innovative economy. IPR laws and enforcement procedures are more or less in place, but embracing them fully may present difficult choices. At present, despite strong laws to protect IPR, in some areas and markets the promise of short-term gain is strong and continues to compromise the laws' effectiveness and, by extension, long-run growth.

China has traditionally imported more technology than it exports and has maintained a low level of IPR protection and enforcement compared with other industrialized countries. It now appears to seek the benefits of a strong IPR regime. This, however, may involve incurring short-term costs. These may include the high administrative costs of implementation and enforcement, costs associated with labor shifts from infringing activities to others, and potential for monopoly pricing. These costs may create short-term disincentives for enforcing and upholding IPR laws.

Low-cost imitation of technology and products rather than innovation and invention of new products is common in China. One of the short-term benefits of such practices for a developing country is more production and consumption of goods and services. The country may thus view

---

4 Keith E. Maskus, Sean M. Dougherty, and Andrew Mertha, "Intellectual Property Rights and Economic Development in China," in Fink and Maskus, *Intellectual Property and Development*, 297.
5 Id., 301.

more stringent IPR as having the potential to compromise its economic production and consumption. If better IPR enforcement translates to higher prices in China and the transfer of royalties overseas, the incentive of Chinese authorities to enforce IPR laws and of citizens to observe them may be blunted.

There are other problems associated with partial or weak enforcement and observation of IPR laws. Partial and potentially inefficient work-around solutions may emerge. For example, to safeguard against the risk of infringement, companies that sell into China products with high levels of intellectual property content may need to impose restrictions on the number of people who have access to those products. Similarly, companies may restrict the number of people who can work on a particular component or the conditions under which it may be serviced. To protect against IPR infringement and abuses, Chinese researchers seeking access to foreign technology in some cases may find that it is only possible to gain access to that technology by taking out licenses and through the intermediation of "intellectual property exchanges," organizations established to provide controlled access to intellectual property through licensing from foreign vendors.[6]

Using exchanges, limiting access to technology, and implementing other techniques to manage the potential for infringement may help to address some of the problems with IPR abuses and violations. However, they are an imperfect solution. While these practices may be privately optimal as a means to curb infringement, in the areas of high technology, pharmaceuticals, medical devices, and a host of other sectors, they may be overly restrictive and constrain the dissemination of important technologies and processes, which may be economically inefficient and socially undesirable.

Legislative and Legal Frameworks for IPR Protection in China

Over the past two decades, China has steadily developed an infrastructure to protect IPR, due in some part to pressure from the U.S., the European Union, and other interested parties. China has joined several international agreements to protect intellectual property;[7] drafted and promulgated

---

[6] Mike Clendenin, "Piracy Battle on Silicon Sea," *EE Times*, 23 August 2004.

[7] China has joined nearly all major international IPR conventions, including the World Intellectual Property Organization, in 1980; the Paris Convention, in 1984; the Madrid Protocol and the Washington Convention, in 1989; the Berne Convention and the Universal Copyright Convention, in 1992; the Geneva Phonograms Convention, in 1993; and the Patent Cooperation Treaty, in 1994. China also adheres to several other conventions governing specific industries or disciplines, such as the revised International Convention for the Protection of New Varieties of Plants.

domestic IPR laws; and established specialized courts,[8] registration procedures, enforcement processes, and training programs.[9] (Detailed
descriptions of the patent, copyright, and trademark laws are included in
the Appendix to this chapter.)

In November 2001, China joined the World Trade Organization
(WTO). Since joining the WTO, China has further strengthened its legal
framework and amended its IPR laws and regulations in compliance with
the WTO Agreement on Trade-Related Aspects of Intellectual Property
Rights (TRIPS). The TRIPS Agreement is particularly significant, as it
specifies strong minimum standards for the protection and enforcement
of copyrights, patents, trade secrets, trade and service marks, and indicators or geographic appellation. The result is an extensive, though not
complete, harmonization of national IPR regimes among countries that
are party to the WTO Agreement.[10] Indeed, China's membership in the
WTO may have had a greater impact on IPR enforcement than on any
other business issue.[11] Although the legal framework is not fully developed compared with those of other industrialized nations, these activities
suggest that Chinese IPR institutions and laws may be slowly converging
with international standards.

IPR Law Enforcement

Despite significant progress in developing a comprehensive legal framework, shortcomings in IPR law enforcement in China continue to limit
the law's effectiveness. Various factors serve to compromise enforcement;
for example, the desire to avoid the short-term economic costs described
in previous sections. Corruption and local protectionism can also handi-
cap enforcement efforts, as can limited or insufficient resources and
training available to enforcement officials and lack of public education
regarding the economic and social impact of IPR violations.[12]

---

8   China has established special IPR courts in several provinces and cities to ensure that
    experts familiar with IPR laws and regulations may hear and preside over the cases.
    For more information, see www.chinaiprlaw.com/English/courts/fujian.ht.
9   Training sessions for staff in various IPR-related agencies have been conducted.
    Several major universities have established IPR training programs for judges,
    lawyers, government IPR officials, and business people. See, for example,
    www.sipo.gov.cn/sipo_English/ndbg/nb/ndbg2003/t20041214_37380.htm.
10 La Croix and Konan, "Intellectual Property Rights in China," 20.
11 See, for example, one survey conducted by the U.S.-China Business Council,
    "Membership Priorities WTO Survey, Sept. 7, 2004," at www.uschina.org/public/
    documents/2004/09/wtosurveyfindings.pdf.
12 For further discussion, see Maskus, Dougherty, and Mertha, "Intellectual Property
    Rights and Economic Development in China," 296; and La Croix and Konan,
    "Intellectual Property Rights in China."

Administrative Enforcement

Prosecuting IPR violations and enforcing IPR laws in China can proceed along one of two tracks. The first and most common is the administrative track. In most cases, administrative agencies may not award compensation to an IPR holder. They may, however, fine the infringer, seize goods or equipment used in manufacturing infringing products, and obtain information about the source of goods being distributed.

Administrative fines are generally low and vary from case to case. Information regarding the amount of fines is usually not made public, making it difficult to assess their effectiveness, though it is generally agreed that they are quite ineffective.[13] There are a number of other deficiencies with administrative action. Not only is the IPR owner inadequately compensated, but the fines are too small to deter future infringement or put the offender out of business and an investigation may not be instigated because of local protectionism, lax enforcement, or a lack of resources. A lack of coordination among administrative offices may also make uniform protection of IPR difficult.

Judicial Enforcement

Companies can pursue judicial (civil actions) in the local people's court. Though small companies may continue to prefer to pursue administrative action, the number of IPR cases pursued through the court system is likely to increase as a result of recent changes to the laws designed to strengthen them and provide more guidance and transparency to those pursuing such remedies.[14]

At present there is no U.S. style of discovery; documents and evidence available for building a case are usually quite limited. Reliance upon damages experts—accountants, economists, and other analysts—is permitted by law to both plaintiff and defendant, although it generally does not occur. Damages claimed are typically the result of relatively simple, straightforward calculations. For example, the IPR owner may be awarded the amount of revenue the plaintiff would have earned in the infringement period based on previous sales or the amount the infringer earned

---

[13] IIPA, "2004 Special 301 Report: People's Republic of China," 40.
[14] In its recent report, the International Intellectual Property Alliance remarks upon the growing sophistication and effectiveness of the IPR courts throughout China and the fact that Chinese and U.S. rights holders are using the civil system more frequently. See their "2004 Special 301 Report: People's Republic of China," 43.

as a result of the illegal sale. Generally, courts will award some portion of case-related costs to a successful plaintiff, but it is unlikely that full costs of pursuing the case will be recovered. It is extremely rare for a defendant who is successful in defending his or her action to recover costs.[15]

Both fines and economic damages claimed and awarded, even at the extremes, are low compared to those found in the U.S. and other industrialized countries. In many cases, these damages provide little deterrent and are merely considered a cost of doing business. Table 1 lists several cases and damages awarded that are representative of the damages being awarded in larger cases.

As decided in a notable recent ruling by a Standing Committee of the National People's Congress, beginning in May 2005, lay judges (or juries) may be used in civil and criminal cases, including IPR cases.[16] This ruling gives lay judges, also known as "people's jurors," equal standing with judges in executing their duties in courts. A panel of both professional judges and lay judges (typically on a three-member bench) will determine first instance cases with significant social influence or upon the request of litigants. Lay judge candidates must have a junior college degree or higher, and judges must serve for a term of at least five years. They are entitled to appropriate payment from the courts for attending hearings. People's jurors have been part of China's legal system since 1954. However, before 2005, there were no rules or guidelines explaining their role. Thus, although jurors are not new to China's legal system, their roles and functions until now have not been clearly defined, which inhibited their ability to contribute to the quality of the judicial assessments or decisions.

While criminal prosecutions, including imprisonment, are possible under IPR law, they are not yet commonplace.

Growing Commitment among Chinese Companies to Improving IPR Protection

As more intellectual property owners seek protection for their ideas through the Chinese system and experience the benefits of protection and enforcement firsthand, they may conclude that it is in their interest to have IPR laws strongly enforced and to uphold those laws themselves.

---

15 Alison Wong, "The Life Sciences Patent Battle," *Managing Intellectual Property,*
    February 2004.
16 Alexandra Harney, "Jurors to Judge Copycat Trials," *Financial Times,* 1 March 2005; Liu
    Li and Cao Li, "Jurors to Help Decide Court Verdicts," *China Daily,* 25 April 1995.

Table 1. Examples of Recent Damage Awards in Intellectual Property Cases in China

Type of Case	Companies	Violation Description	Damages Awarded	Source
Copyright	Taiwan-based Fineart Corp. (DEFENDANT) Beijing Hanwang Technology (PLAINTIFF)	Defendant copied Hanwang's software and sold online	US$361,000	"Hanwang's IPR Legal Victory Comes Late," China Daily, 14 March 2005
Copyright	Shanghai Zhongle Film & Television (DEFENDANT) Canadian company Discreet, a division of Autodesk (PLAINTIFF)	Defendant used and exploited software without authorization	US$60,000 (US$120,824 claimed)	Qu, Z, "Protection of Copyright: Another Year of Hard Battle," chinacourt.org, 2 January 2003
Copyright	Beijing Central Press Union Technology and Tianjin Minzu Culture CD (DEFENDANTS) Microsoft (PLAINTIFF)	Defendants, neither of which are underground operations, made 59,000 CDs containing pirated version of Windows XP	Beijing paid $9,600 fine and "illegal turnover" of $1,250. Tianjin paid $1,200 and $70, respectively.	http://www.sipo.gov.cn/ sipo_English/gxfx/zyhd/ t20050205_40166.htm (2004)
Patent	Huaqi and Fuguanghui (DEFENDANTS) Netec Technology Co. (PLAINTIFF)	Defendants infringed Netac's USB flash memory drive patent, resulting in millions of dollars in alleged losses	US$120,000 (US$490,000 in damages claimed)	"Flash Memory Disk Market Under Fire," China Daily, 28 February 2005
Trademark	Beijing JiaYu Wine Co. Ltd. (JiaYu) and JiangXi Happy Wine & Foodstuffs (DEFENDANTS) China National Cereals, Oils & Foodstuffs Corp. (COFCO) (PLAINTIFF)	Defendants used COFCO's trademarked brand and image on their wine products	US$1,876,050 (US$12 million claimed)	"Great Wall Wine Succeeds in Trademark Suit," press release from China National Cereals, Oils & Foodstuffs Corp., 21 April 2005.
Trademark	Bonneterie Garment (Shenzen) Co., Yiwu Xinyipai Garment Co. and Li Zupeng (DEFENDANTS) French firm Bonneterie Cevenole SARL (PLAINTIFF)	Violation involved trademark infringement over the name Montagut	US$93,000	China Daily, 26 April 2005
Trademark	Beijing Metals and Minerals Import and Export Co. (DEFENDANT) Nike (PLAINTIFF)	Defendant attempted to export more than 100,000 imitation Nike clothing items to Russia	US$20,000	"State Firm Sued Over Fakes," China Daily, 21 April 2005

Chinese Companies Challenge Foreign Company Patents

A recent closely watched case involves the pharmaceutical company Pfizer Inc. and the distribution of its drug Viagra in China.[17] In July 2004, the State Intellectual Property Office of the People's Republic of China (SIPO) invalidated Pfizer's Chinese patent for Viagra. The case is significant for several reasons, not least of which is the fact that it marks perhaps the first time that Chinese companies have pursued legal remedies to challenge a Chinese patent owned by a foreign company.

In this case, the competing companies successfully petitioned the regulatory authority to cancel Pfizer's patent for its failure to demonstrate, in accordance with Chinese law, that a particular ingredient was indeed novel and thereby eligible for protection. Pfizer appealed, and the Chinese patent office has not yet released its final decision on this case. The decision will be important as an indicator of the government's willingness to uphold international IPR laws, as well as an indicator of support for imitative, rather than innovative, research. Whatever the final outcome, the case may suggest to Chinese companies that IPR laws may be used to their advantage. Perhaps encouraged by the Viagra case, a number of Chinese companies attacked GlaxoSmithKline PLC's Chinese patent for its diabetes drug Avandia.[18]

In another prominent case, Netec Technology Co., a Chinese company, sued Sony Electronics for USB flash memory disk patent infringement, claiming Sony copied their patented movable storage technology.[19] If successful, this case may also serve to reinforce the value and importance of a strong IPR system to domestic companies in China.

IPR Laws Benefit Companies in Domestic Disputes

In a recent trademark case, China National Cereals, Oils & Foodstuffs Corporation (COFCO), one of China's top 500 companies, initiated judicial proceedings for trademark infringement against two domestic enter-

---

17 Samson G. Yu and Ying Zhang, "Lessons from the Viagra Case," *Managing Intellectual Property,* 2004, supplement, "China IP Focus 2005."

18 Greg Mastel, James B. Altman, and Daniel P. Wendt, "Protecting IP Rights Overseas: Local Courts Are Just One Tool in a Box of Remedies Available to U.S. Companies Seeking to Protect Themselves in Foreign Locations," *IP Law & Business,* September 2004 (www.iplawandbusiness.com).

19 "Flash Memory Disk Market Under Fire," *China Daily,* 28 February 2005.

prises, Beijing JiaYu Wine Co. Ltd. (JiaYu) and JiangXi Happy Wine & Foodstuffs (collectively, the defendants).[20]

In 1974, COFCO registered a series of trademarks, including the words *Chang Cheng* (Great Wall) together with a unique image of the Great Wall. In 2004, Great Wall held an 18.46 percent share of the Chinese wine market, the largest of any one brand.[21] In 2002, COFCO discovered that the defendants had not only used the term *Chang Cheng* as a trademark on their wine products, but they had also copied the plaintiff's registered Great Wall image and were actively selling their product in large volumes throughout China. COFCO requested that all infringement activities be brought to an immediate stop, that a public apology be made, and that damages totaling US$12,106,537 (the exact amount of the illegal revenue generated from sales by JiaYu) and expenses of US$36,320 be paid.[22]

In April 2005, the Beijing Municipal Superior People's Court ruled in favor of COFCO. The court ordered the defendant to immediately cease producing and selling product using this trademark and ordered the defendants to pay COFCO US$1,876,050 in damages.[23] COFCO claimed that the court reasoned that since COFCO has used the Great Wall logo for many years on its wine products and the trademark had become well-known in China's wine market,[24] COFCO's trademark rights were entitled to legal protection. "JiaYu Great Wall" was too similar to "Great Wall," and the defendant therefore had to accept legal responsibility for the trademark infringement. No further information was provided regarding how the damage amount was determined. Although the plaintiffs were awarded significantly less than what they claimed, the amount is still quite significant by Chinese standards. Moreover, as noted, it is important because it indicates a willingness on the part of Chinese companies to rely upon the IPR system.

---

[20] China National Cereals, Oils & Foodstuffs Corp. (COFCO), "Great Wall Wine Succeeds in Trademark Suit," press release, 21 April 2005.

[21] Statistics cited from the China Association of Commerce and China National Commercial Information Center, 3 April 2005, as cited in COFCO, "Great Wall Wine Succeeds in Trademark Suit."

[22] Rouse & Co. International, *China IP Express*, no. 244 (25 February 2005), at www.iprights.com/publications/chinaipexpress/ciex_244.asp#1.

[23] COFCO, "Great Wall Wine Succeeds in Trademark Suit."

[24] COFCO claimed that over the years the Chinese government recognized the brand as a "famous Chinese brand." In November 2000, the China State Administration for Industry and Commerce recognized "Great Wall" as a famous trademark; see COFCO, "Great Wall Wine Succeeds in Trademark Suit."

Preemptive Patenting

China follows a first-to-file system for patents, which means patents are granted to those that file first, even if the filers are not the original inventors. This practice is consistent with activity in other parts of the world, including the European Union, but differs from that in the U.S., which recognizes the first-to-invent rule. Using the first-to-file aspect of the law to their advantage, some Chinese companies are preemptively patenting foreign inventions that have been patented outside of China. Foreign companies will presumably attempt to challenge such patents and will, in the future, take steps to patent in China in a timely manner. In the meantime, these preemptive patenters have developed an interest in maintaining a strong IPR protection regime in China.[25]

At the same time, Chinese firms seeking to export into foreign markets, particularly within the European Union, may find themselves challenged by first-to-file claims. Foreign firms in countries where these rules pertain are also pursuing preemptive patenting, trademarking, and copyrighting to head off the threat of competition from Chinese companies and products in their home markets. European multinational companies have preemptively registered the trademarks of major Chinese enterprises in their respective countries. This can effectively block potential Chinese competitors from using their own brand names when they begin selling in markets outside of China. For example, in a case in German court between the German company Bosch-Siemens and the Chinese company Hinsense, parties settled out of court after Hisense reportedly agreed to pay Bosch-Siemens approximately US$6.5 million to use its own brand name in the European market.[26]

Strategies for IPR Protection in China

Legal Action in China

Despite the difficulty and cost of pursuing legal action in IPR cases in China, many companies, both Chinese and non-Chinese, are choosing to do so. In most cases, fines and damages have not been sufficient to compensate the party being infringed or even to offset the costs of pursuing the case. Nevertheless, although awards are trivial in comparison with those found in the U.S. and other Western nations, many Chinese and

---

[25] Brad Spurgeon, "Pirates File Patents to Beat the System: The New Chinese
Counterfeit Game," *International Herald Tribune*, 15 November 2004.
[26] "Firms Awake to Fact They Must Protect Trademarks," *China Daily*, 7 April 2005.

non-Chinese firms are opting to pursue cases through the Chinese system. Their reasons for doing so are varied. In many cases, the IPR owner may at least obtain an injunction against further infringement. But even if neither an injunction nor damages are available, there may be other strategic reasons for pursuing action.

In a recent example, the U.S. chipmaker Intel sued the Chinese network equipment maker Shenzhen Donjin Communication Technology Co. Ltd in January 2005. Intel accused Donjin of illegally including Intel software in its products. Analysts have speculated that one reason for Intel bringing the suit is to keep Donjin Technology out of the computer technology integration market. Intel said its losses due to Donjin's infringement have reached US$7.96 million and is claiming the same amount in compensation. The sum is equal to Donjin's annual revenue.[27] Donjin countersued, accusing Intel of engaging in illegal monopolistic practices.[28] Donjin alleged that Intel software was so closely tied to its hardware, it prevented customers from using the software in third-party hardware. Donjin's suit seeks a ruling forcing Intel to end allegedly monopolistic practices.

Legal Action Outside China

Given the difficulties in pursuing cases, large companies may be reluctant to file IPR cases in China, where the laws are new, courts may lack experience handling such cases, costs to prosecute are high and unrecoverable, and enforcement is unreliable. As one alternative strategy, non-Chinese companies are filing lawsuits in their home countries. Technology companies and other multinationals are using their own court systems to bring cases against Chinese firms for IPR violations. Presumably, they hope that the desire on the part of the Chinese companies and the Chinese government to export into Western markets will be sufficiently strong that they will be willing to comply with Western standards. As China's export of machinery and products into foreign markets increases, facing an IPR lawsuit in those markets may be an unattractive proposition. It could mean an injunction to stop exporting products to the U.S. and the threat of potentially high damages.

In a recent example of such a case in the U.S., in 2003, Cisco Systems brought suit against Huawei Technologies and its subsidiaries, alleging

---

[27] "Intel Launches Legal Battle Over IPR," *China Daily*, 25 January 2004.
[28] Reuters, "Chinese Firm Sued by Intel Hits Back with Own Suit," 5 April 2005.

that the Chinese telecommunications equipment maker infringed its patents and illegally copied source code.[29] Cisco's suit, filed in the U.S. District Court for the Eastern District of Texas, alleged that Huawei violated several Cisco patents and copied Cisco's source code. The companies settled. Huawei agreed to change its command line interface, user manuals, help screens, and portions of its source code to address Cisco's concerns.[30]

Conclusion

IPR violations may ultimately have negative effects on the broader Chinese economy by discouraging investment and imposing costs upon those companies attempting to offer goods and services. As China becomes a major player in the world economy, it will likely strengthen its commitment to upholding and enforcing international IPR. Chinese laws and regulations are converging with international standards. Patent, trademark, and copyright applications are being filed in growing numbers and damages and fines are increasing. However, violations continue to be widespread.[31] Work remains to be done if China is to accord with other major economic powers in the area of IPR protection, particularly in the area of enforcement and damages.

---

[29] Cisco, "Cisco Files Lawsuit Against Huawei Technologies," news release, 23 January 2003; In the U.S. District Court for the Eastern District of Texas, *Cisco Systems Inc. and Cisco Technology Inc. (Plaintiffs) v. Huawei Technologies Co. Ltd. et al.* Complaint and Jury Demand.

[30] Matt Hines, "Cisco, Huawei Suspend Patent Suit," *C/Net News*, 1 October 2003.

[31] For example, piracy rates remain above 90 percent across copyright industries; IIPA, "2004 Special 301 Report: People's Republic of China," 31.

Appendix: Patent, Trademark, and Copyright Laws in China

In this section we describe the laws that protect patents. We also extend the discussion to trademark and copyright, where there are substantial differences.

1. Patents

a. Laws and Legislation

China's first Patent Law was enacted in 1985 and has been amended twice (in 1992 and 2000) to expand the scope of protection.[32] To comply with TRIPS, the latest amendment extended the duration of patent protection to 20 years from the date of filing a patent application. In 1994, China became a member of the World Intellectual Property Organization Patent Cooperation Treaty (PCT).[33] As a result of this membership, the China Patent Office may now receive international applications filed by entities in any contracting state of the PCT.

b. Application and Registration Procedure

To protect its IPR in China, a company must register its patents and trademarks with the appropriate Chinese agencies and authorities. Patents are filed with China's State Intellectual Property Office (SIPO) in Beijing,[34] while SIPO offices at the provincial and municipal levels are responsible for administrative enforcement.

c. Compensation and Damages

(1) Administrative Action

An injunction or mediation is usually the first course of administrative action in patent disputes. Parties may also pursue cease-and-desist

---

[32] Patent Law of the People's Republic of China, "Adopted at the 4th Meeting of the Standing Committee of the Sixth National People's Congress on March 12, 1984. Amended in accordance with the Decision of the Standing Committee of the Seventh National People's Congress on Amending the Patent Law of the People's Republic of China at its 27th Meeting on September 4, 1992. Amended again in accordance with the Decision of the Standing Committee of the Ninth National People's Congress on Amending the Patent Law of the People's Republic of China adopted at its 17th Meeting on August 25, 2000." See www.sipo.gov.cn/sipo_English/flfg/zlflfg/t20020327_33872.htm.

[33] Full text of the Patent Cooperation Treaty may be found at www.wipo.int/pct/en/texts/pdf/pct.pdf. More information and background is at www.wipo.int/pct/en/.

[34] China State Intellectual Property Office (SIPO), at www.sipo.gov.cn.

orders, product and equipment may be confiscated through raids, and illegal earnings may be confiscated. A penalty may also be imposed. The infringer may be charged a fine of not more than three times illegal earnings or, if there are no illegal earnings, a fine of not more than US$6,000.[35]

(2) Judicial Action

If administrative actions prove insufficient or unsatisfactory, parties may institute legal proceedings in the people's court in accordance with the Civil Procedure Law of the People's Republic of China.[36] Patent holders whose rights have been violated may pursue civil litigation within two years from the date they become aware of infringing activity (or should have become aware).

Compensation for patent infringement damages is based upon the losses suffered by the patentee or the profits which the infringer has earned through the infringement. The patent owner may select either of these two methods. Loss suffered by the patent owner is generally calculated by multiplying the loss in sales of the patent owner's products by the reasonable profit which can be attributed to the sale of each product. If the loss in sales is difficult to calculate, the volume of sales of the infringing products may be used instead. Gains received by an infringer can be calculated by multiplying the infringer's sales volumes by the reasonable profits of each infringing product. The infringer's profit for this calculation should generally be its operating profit, unless the whole of its business is based on the infringement of the patent.

If the patent owner's loss or the infringer's gain is difficult to calculate, one to three times the relevant reasonable patent license fee is one approach that has been considered. If there is no patent license fee for reference or if the patent license fee available is clearly unreasonable, compensation may generally be set between US$605 and US$36,000, but preferably not more than US$60,500, depending upon the situation. Courts may also award compensation for investigation and enforcement costs.[37]

---

35 Patent Law of the People's Republic of China, Article 58 (www.sipo.gov.cn/sipo_
   English/flfg/zlflfg/t20020327_33872.htm).
36 Id., Article 57.
37 Id., Article 60.

2. Trademarks

a. Laws and Legislation

China's Trademark Law was adopted in 1982.[38] The law was revised and expanded in 1993 and again in 2001.[39]

b. Application and Registration Procedure

The State Administration of Industry and Commerce (SAIC) Trademark Office maintains authority over trademark registration, administrative recognition of well-known marks, and enforcement of trademark protection. The Trademark Review and Adjudication Board (TRAB) is responsible for handling trademark registration disputes. A litigation division has been established to represent TRAB in appeal cases. As of 1995, TRAB received approximately 250 cases each year. By 2003, the number of cases had risen to approximately 10,000 a year.[40]

To obtain exclusive rights to the use of a trademark, applicants must file an application with China's Trademark Office. As with patents, China relies upon a first-to-file system that does not require applicants to provide evidence of prior use or ownership. The term of protection is ten years from the date registration is granted.

c. Compensation and Damages

(1) Administrative Action

Trademark disputes generally begin with an administrative investigation. Typically, an administrative investigation will issue an order to the infringer to immediately cease the infringing acts. The authority may also confiscate and destroy the infringing means of production, and fine the infringer. Under the revised Trademark Law, administrative authorities

---

[38] Trademark Law of the People's Republic of China, "Adopted at the 24th Session of the Standing Committee of the Fifth National People's Congress on 23 August 1982." See www.sipo.gov.cn/sipo_English/flfg/xgflfg/t20020416_34755.htm.

[39] Trademark Law of the People's Republic of China, "revised for the first time according to the Decision on the Amendment of the Trademark Law of the People's Republic of China adopted at the 30th Session of the Standing Committee of the Seventh National People's Congress, on 22 February 1993, and revised for the second time according to the Decision on the Amendment of the Trademark Law of the People's Republic of China adopted at the 24th Session of the Standing Committee of the Ninth National People's Congress on 27 October 2001." Id.

[40] Yang Yexuan, "Keeping a Check on Trade Marks in China," *Managing Intellectual Property*, 2005, supplement, "China IP Focus 2005."

may no longer award compensation to the party whose rights have been infringed. Although authorities were able to do so under the old law, in practice, the right was rarely exercised and trademark registrants seeking compensation generally had to go to the people's courts. Administrative authorities now encourage settlement through mediation, though it may be possible for brand owners to obtain compensation from infringers through negotiated settlements.

The Implementing Regulations have increased the maximum fines that may be imposed against infringers. Authorities are now able to levy fines equal to up to three times the infringer's illegal business amount. In addition, regulations provide for discretionary fines up to approximately US$12,000 in cases where it is impossible to ascertain the illegal business amount. There is little guidance to administrative authorities for imposing fines, particularly regarding minimum fines that may be imposed against repeat offenders or infringers involved with counterfeiting.[41]

(2) Judicial Action

Civil litigation against trademark infringers in the people's courts has always been an option, but in the past, trademark owners have avoided pursuing litigation for a variety of reasons. These include the cost of lawyers and investigators, conservative attitudes of courts in compensation calculation, the lack of access to preliminary injunctions, and delays in the issuance of decisions.[42] In recent cases, foreign plaintiffs have had to wait more than a year for Chinese courts to issue a decision, much longer than the six months which is the maximum period for disputes involving domestic litigants.[43] Revisions to the Trademark Law have resulted in provisions that may increase the number of cases filed in the people's courts. Preliminary injunctions are now an option for cases involving infringements of registered trademarks, patents, and copyrights.[44]

According to the Trademark Law, in the event of infringement, damages are calculated as the profit that the infringer has earned during the infringement period; the benefits gained by the infringer or the losses suffered by the party whose rights have been infringed. Plaintiffs may choose the method to calculate compensation for losses, either through assessing the infringer's profits or the plaintiff's own losses. If the

---

41 Baker & McKenzie, "China Intellectual Property Guide," 2004.
42 Id.
43 Id.
44 Id.

infringer's profits are impossible to determine, the profit margin for the plaintiff may be used as a reference. Where the plaintiff elects compensation for its losses, these losses may be calculated by reference to the reduction in sales caused by the infringing product or by multiplying the sales amount of the infringing product by the unit profit of the genuine product. Where neither the plaintiff's damage nor the infringer's profits may be determined, the Trademark Law provides for the payment of statutory damages up to US$60,000. Trademark owners may be compensated for enforcement-related costs.

Under the revisions to China's Criminal Code that took effect in October 1997, certain acts of trademark counterfeiting may be considered criminal, provided that the circumstances are "serious" or involve "relatively large" sales.

3. Copyrights

a. Laws and Legislation

China's Copyright Law was established in 1990 and amended in October 2001.[45] China grants protection to persons from countries belonging to copyright international conventions or bilateral agreements of which China is a member.

b. Application and Registration Procedure

The National Copyright Administration of the People's Republic of China (NCA)[46] has responsibility for copyright administration and enforcement. The NCA also investigates infringement cases, administers foreign-related copyright issues, develops foreign-related arbitration rules, and supervises administrative authorities. Local copyright bureaus are responsible for administering copyrights in their own administrative districts. Unlike patents and trademarks, copyrighted works do not require registration for protection, although it may be helpful as evidence of ownership in enforcement actions.

---

[45] Copyright Law of the People's Republic of China, "Adopted at the Fifteenth Session of the Standing Committee of the Seventh National People's Congress on 7 September 1990, and revised in accordance with the Decision on the Amendment of the Copyright Law of the People's Republic of China adopted at the 24th Session of the Standing Committee of the Ninth National People's Congress on 27 October 2001." See www.sipo.gov.cn/sipo_English/flfg/xgflfg/t20020416_34754.htm.

[46] National Copyright Administration of the People's Republic of China (NCA), at www.ncac.gov.cn.

c. Compensation and Damages

The parties to a copyright infringement suit may request administrative remedies or may institute proceedings directly in a people's court in the absence of a written arbitration agreement between the parties. In addition, the copyright owner may apply to the people's court for an injunction to restrain an infringer or a potential infringer from infringing the owner's rights. Owing to a chronic lack of personnel, the NCA generally encourages complainants to pursue their claims through the people's court system.

Certain copyright activities are considered criminal, and various criminal penalties have been established. These apply in situations where the amounts of illegal income are "relatively large" or constitute a "huge amount" or where other "serious factors" exist. Prosecutors and police have a broad discretion regarding whether or not to pursue criminal actions. Criminal prosecutions are still fairly rare.

(1) Administrative Action

The Implementing Regulations now permit administrative authorities to impose fines of up to three times the illegal gain of an infringer if they determine that the infringement has caused "harm to social and public interests," or up to US$12,000 in those cases where illegal gain cannot be easily determined.[47]

(2) Judicial Action

As with trademark litigation, copyright litigation through the people's court system may be pursued more frequently with the introduction of stronger measures such as preliminary injunctions and the availability of statutory damages.[48] In the event of a copyright infringement, infringers are required to pay damages based upon the actual losses of the copyright owner. Where the actual losses are "difficult to calculate," the damages paid may be based upon the illegal income earned by the infringer. The damages paid to the owner of the rights shall also include the reasonable expenses incurred by the owner of the rights in halting the infringing act, including legal and investigation costs. In cases where the rights owner's damage or the infringer's profits cannot be determined, the current law

---

47 Baker & McKenzie, "China Intellectual Property Guide."
48 Id.

provides for the payment of statutory damages up to US$60,000. Courts may also impose fines against infringers commensurate with those assessed by administrative authorities: up to five times the illegal gain or in cases where it is difficult to determine the amount of illegal gain, up to US$12,000.[49]

---

[49] Copyright Law of the People's Republic of China, Articles 46–48
(www.sipo.gov.cn/sipo_English/flfg/xgflfg/t20020416_34754.htm).

VI

Issues in the Management of Intellectual Property Portfolios

21

Using the Real Option Method to Value Intellectual Property

George G. Korenko

When considering research and development (R&D) investments in intellectual property (IP), companies attempt to make appropriate resource allocation and project evaluation decisions to maximize the future profitability of the company. These decisions are often difficult because of the uncertainty inherent in discovering, developing, and commercializing new products. Economists and finance professionals have long advocated the use of methods such as the discounted cash flow (DCF) method as a rigorous way to make decisions under uncertainty. However, it has been recognized that managers sometimes overrule negative results from a DCF analysis and proceed with an investment in a project that shows a negative present value.[1] Is this behavior rational? Perhaps.

A DCF analysis requires the implicit assumption that once managers decide to pursue an R&D project, they will complete it even if the outlook for the resulting IP becomes unfavorable. In reality, the R&D environment is characterized by technical and market uncertainties that require managers to make decisions about whether to proceed based on the outcome at *each stage* of the process. The optimal path for the project may change substantially from managers' initial expectations. Thus, the DCF method may undervalue projects where substantial uncertainty will be resolved through the R&D process and management can alter the future path of the project based on the outcome of research.

Rather than relying on the DCF method to value R&D projects, it is possible to model a staged decision-making process with management

---

[1] Oliver Gassmann and Maximilian von Zedtwitz, "Innovation Processes in Transnational Corporations," in *International Handbook on Innovation,* ed. Larisa V. Shavinina (Amsterdam: Elsevier Science Ltd., 2003).

flexibility in a financial analysis that more closely mimics real world decision making. Specifically, using the real option method to value R&D projects focuses managers on identifying stages in the R&D process where they will need to make decisions whether to exploit potential opportunities or reduce financial risk. Once managers learn information that will help resolve technical or market uncertainties, they can decide whether to expand, scale back, abandon, or continue a project to develop IP. This managerial flexibility is similar to the flexibility investors enjoy when purchasing financial options.

DCF Method

The DCF method measures the value of developing a technology as the lump sum, net present value (NPV) of the expected revenues of the product embodying the IP less the expenses associated with the R&D process, commercial launch, and manufacturing and marketing of the product over its life cycle. Only future revenues and expenses are relevant; revenues and expenses already realized do not affect the value of the R&D project to investors today. Expected revenues and costs are then converted into present values (PVs) through a discount rate. The discount rate captures both the time value of money and the risk associated with developing and commercializing a product using the IP.[2] Riskier projects receive a higher discount rate to reflect the increased uncertainty associated with the future cash flows. Summing the positive and negative discounted cash flows yields the NPV for the project. Thus, the DCF method considers the amount, timing, and risk of future cash flows from developing and using IP.

The textbook application of the DCF method suggests that managers should only accept projects with positive NPVs and should pursue those projects with the highest NPVs first.[3] The DCF method is widely used because it measures the net contribution of the project to shareholder wealth. Properly applied, it is consistent with the goal of maximizing shareholder wealth.

One weakness of the DCF method is that it assumes that the company will follow a single strategy through the entire project regardless of any new information that may come to light during the R&D and product life

---

[2] These topics are discussed in Chapter 11. See also Richard A. Brealey and Stewart C. Myers, *Principles of Corporate Finance,* 5th ed. (New York: McGraw-Hill, 1996), 226.

[3] See, for example, Brealey and Myers, chapters 5 and 6.

cycles. For example, the DCF method yields an estimate of the NPV of the IP that presupposes technical success.[4] This assumption is unrealistic in a world where managers can use feedback from the R&D process to make decisions regarding production and commercialization.

Real Option Method

Like the DCF method, the real option method values an investment in developing IP based on the expected future cash flows from developing and using the IP. However, the real option method also considers the value of the option to proceed down different, and potentially mutually exclusive, development paths as more information becomes available. These paths may include the option to expand the scope of a project if the outlook becomes more favorable and the option to abandon a project if technical or commercial success appears unlikely. The real option method incorporates this possibility of flexibility as managers gather new information. Thus, it can allow for a more realistic modeling of the R&D process than the DCF method.

The real option method applies financial option theory to investments in real assets such as manufacturing plants and R&D investments. A financial option, such as a call option on a stock, provides the owner with the right, but not the obligation, to purchase shares of the stock at a future date. The decision whether to exercise the option is made only after the owner of the option gathers additional information about the future value of the stock. If the stock is worth more than the agreed future purchase price (the strike price), the owner of the option should exercise the right to purchase the stock at the strike price and sell it at the market price to obtain a profit. If the stock is worth less than the strike price, the option should be allowed to expire at no additional cost to the owner.

Similar to financial options, a real option provides the owner with the right, but not the obligation, to invest in an asset after gathering additional information about the technical and market uncertainties associated with the technology. Companies in a variety of industries (most notably pharmaceuticals and natural resources) have been using the real option method to value investments for over a decade. A primary benefit

---

4 Typically, the cash flows included in a DCF analysis reflect the expected values of the revenues and expenses if the R&D process is successful. The risk of R&D failure is captured in the discount rate.

of the method is that it helps managers evaluate investments as information-gathering efforts rather than as long-term commitments.[5] As a result, managers can add value to projects as information becomes available by reallocating resources from projects more likely to fail to projects more likely to succeed.

The real option method may be most appropriate when

- substantial technical or market uncertainty surrounds the future cash flows associated with the IP, but that uncertainty may be resolved in the future; and
- managers must regularly reevaluate whether or not to continue funding particular research activities and can change the path of the project based on the outcome of additional research.

Since these circumstances are often characteristic of the R&D process, the real option method is well suited to valuing the IP resulting from R&D projects.

Data Requirements

DCF Method

While one of the benefits of the real option method is its more realistic modeling of the R&D process, it comes at the cost of more extensive information gathering than is usually necessary in applying the DCF method. The DCF method can often be applied using forecasts prepared by corporate staff in the ordinary course of business. For example, many companies prepare strategic plans or marketing plans that include forecasts of expected revenues and costs. These data can be fundamental inputs into a valuation using the DCF method. The model may also incorporate appropriate assumptions. For example, the discount rate to use in determining PVs can often be obtained from the company's experience with similar projects or by estimating its cost of capital.[6]

---

5   As Judy Lewent, of Merck, described, "When you make an initial investment in a
    research project, you are paying an entry fee for a right, but you are not obligated to
    continue that research at a later stage." See Nancy A. Nichols, "Scientific Management
    at Merck: An Interview with CFO Judy Lewent," *Harvard Business Review*, January-
    February 1994:90.
6   See Tom Copeland, Tim Koller, and Jack Murrin, *Valuation: Measuring and Managing
    the Value of Companies* (New York: John Wiley & Sons, 1990), chapter 6.

Real Option Method

There are a number of available techniques for implementing the real option method to value and R&D project, including mathematical modeling, simulation, the binomial method, the Black-Scholes option pricing model, and decision trees. The data required for a valuation often depends on the technique that is chosen. I will discuss two of the most commonly applied techniques: the decision tree approach and the Black-Scholes option pricing model.

Decision Trees

A decision tree is a graphical representation of the sequence of decisions that must be made and uncertainties that will be faced during the course of a project. Stages in the process for decisions and resolution of uncertainties are represented by nodes, and the possible outcomes are represented by branches. Thus, a decision tree includes the possible courses of action and the potential outcomes from each action. A useful way to gather the information required to construct a decision tree is to use decision analysis.[7]

Decision analysis is designed to help managers make rational, consistent decisions in an uncertain environment. The first step in applying decision analysis is often to build consensus among the decision makers and knowledgeable functional staff on the problem to be addressed, the decisions that must be made, the objective of the decision-making process, the issues that influence the objective, and the sources of uncertainty. Some of the questions that may be posed include, What decisions and uncertainties are likely to have an economic impact on the company? What uncertainties need to be resolved before managers can make a decision? What are the possible outcomes from resolving these uncertainties, and how likely are they? Answering these questions may require meetings among experts in various functional areas, consensus regarding their projections, and validation of the decision tree model. As a result, this process can be time-consuming. However, it builds consensus and encourages managers to consider the information needed to make future decisions, as well as the future opportunities to alter the project in ways that add value to the project or minimize financial risk.

---

[7] It may also be possible to gather the required information from company documents and interviews with relevant company personnel. This process will likely be less time-consuming than using decision analysis. Nevertheless, decision analysis is used by companies in a variety of industries.

Black-Scholes Option Pricing Model

The Black-Scholes option pricing model can also be used to apply the real option method.[8] However, since this approach involves a formula, it may be less transparent than the decision tree approach. The Black-Scholes formula,[9] which can be used to value either a call option or a real option, depends on five inputs. The following table compares these five inputs for a call option on a stock and a real option:

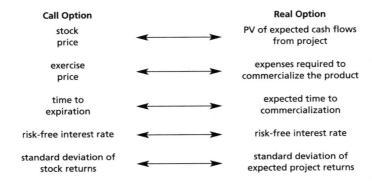

Call Option		Real Option
stock price	→	PV of expected cash flows from project
exercise price	→	expenses required to commercialize the product
time to expiration	→	expected time to commercialization
risk-free interest rate	→	risk-free interest rate
standard deviation of stock returns	→	standard deviation of expected project returns

Obtaining the five data inputs for valuing a real option model involves several steps. First, the expected cash flows from the project after commercialization must be estimated and converted to their PVs. Second, the time and expenses required until commercial launch must be estimated, and the expenses must be capitalized using an appropriate rate of return. Data on the risk-free interest rate are readily available; however, the standard deviation of the project returns must be estimated. An estimate of the standard deviation may be available from the company's experience with similar projects, industry experience, or from a measure of the standard deviation of the stock returns for companies facing risks similar to those inherent in the project to develop and commercialize the IP.

Collecting accurate and reliable data is a crucial step in any valuation. Since the DCF and real option methods rely on estimates of revenues and

---

8 Fisher Black and Myron Scholes, "The Pricing of Options and Corporate Liabilities," *Journal of Political Economy* 81 (May-June): 637-659.
9 The Black-Scholes formula for valuing a call option is $Value = [N(d_1) \times S] - [N(d_2) \times Xe^{-R_f t}]$, where $d_1 = \dfrac{\log [S \sqrt{PV(X)}]}{\sigma\sqrt{t}} + \dfrac{\sigma\sqrt{t}}{2}$, $d_2 = d_1 - \sigma\sqrt{t}$, $N(d)$ represents the cumulative normal probability density function, S is the current stock price, X is the exercise price of the option, t is the time to expiration of the option, R_f is the risk-free interest rate, and σ is the standard deviation of the returns on the stock.

expenses and the risks associated with these cash flows, it is important to understand the source, methodology, and assumptions used to produce these estimates. Interviews with company staff in finance, marketing, and/or other functional areas are often helpful in validating these data. Calculations should begin only after the underlying data are understood and their reliability is confirmed.

Example: Valuing R&D Projects Using the DCF and Real Option (Decision Tree) Methods

To illustrate how to use the DCF and real option methods to value an R&D project, suppose the hypothetical chemical company MegaChem is considering a project to develop a patented lawn care product called GreenAll. The project requires a one-year R&D process that will cost $60 million and will reveal how much it will cost to manufacture the product once it is developed (the cost of goods sold, or COGS). The possible COGS outcomes are $35 per unit and $65 per unit, each with equal (0.50) probability. After the research is complete, the company must decide whether to build a plant to produce GreenAll at a cost of $70 million or

Figure 1. Model of MegaChem's Decision Process Using the Real Option Method (Decision Tree)

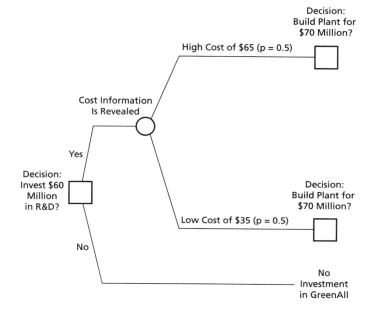

abandon the project. If the company decides to build the plant, it can complete construction quickly and begin selling the product. Figure 1 contains a diagram summarizing the decisions facing MegaChem.

MegaChem's marketing department expects to spend $10 million annually in marketing expenses if the product is commercially launched. The marketing department projects annual unit sales of 10 million and has provided management with three scenarios for the unit price and probabilities associated with each scenario:[10]

- a low scenario assuming consumers perceive the product to be no better than any other lawn care chemical (price equals $4.50 per unit with 0.25 probability);
- a middle scenario assuming some consumers perceive the product to be a substantial advance in lawn care (price equals $8.00 per unit with 0.50 probability); and
- a high scenario, assuming consumers perceive the product to be a breakthrough in lawn care (price equals $10.00 per unit with 0.25 probability).

Note that there are two sources of uncertainty in this example: 1) the COGS required to manufacture the final product and, 2) the price of the product. The DCF method and the real option method incorporate these types of uncertainties in different ways and, as a result, often yield different results. Given the data collected for this hypothetical example, it is possible to apply the DCF method and the real option method using the decision tree technique and compare the results.

Using the DCF Method

To apply the DCF method, the first step is to determine the expected costs and revenues. The marketing expenses equal $10 million annually. However, the expected COGS depends on the outcome of the R&D. The DCF method incorporates uncertainty about the R&D outcome by using the expected value of the COGS. There is a 50 percent probability that the COGS will equal $35 per unit and a 50 percent probability that the COGS will equal $65 per unit. Thus, the expected COGS equals the sum of each possible COGS multiplied by its associated probability. In this case, the expected COGS equals $50 per unit ($35 x 0.5 + $65 x 0.5 = $50). Similarly, uncertainty about the future price of GreenAll is captured by calculating

---

[10] These scenarios assume the company has decided to commercialize GreenAll.

Table 1. Valuation of MegaChem's Product GreenAll Using the DCF Method

Year	Expected Sales ($Millions)	R&D and Production Investments ($Millions)	Expected COGS ($Millions)	Expected Marketing Expenses ($Millions)	Expected Net Income ($Millions) (1)-(2)-(3)-(4)	Discount Factor ($Millions) at 10%	Expected NPV of Net Income ($Millions) (5) x (6)
	(1)	(2)	(3)	(4)	(5)	(6)	(7)
2005	–	60	–	–	(60)	1.0000	(60)
2006	76	70	50	10	(54)	0.9091	(49)
2007	76	–	50	10	16	0.8265	13
2008	76	–	50	10	16	0.7514	12
2009	76	–	50	10	16	0.6831	11
2010	76	–	50	10	16	0.6210	10
2011	76	–	50	10	16	0.5645	9
2012	76	–	50	10	16	0.5132	8
2013	76	–	50	10	16	0.4665	7
2014	76	–	50	10	16	0.4241	7
2015	76	–	50	10	16	0.3855	6
2016	76	–	50	10	16	0.3505	6
							(20)

the expected sales. Expected sales are calculated as the sum of each possible value for the price multiplied by its associated probability and the total volume. The expected sales for GreenAll equal $76 million [($4.50 x 0.25 + $8.00 x 0.50 + $10.00 x 0.25) x 10 million units = $76.25 million].

To calculate the value of the project using the DCF method, MegaChem must first subtract the expected costs from the expected sales. The expected costs include the one-time R&D investment of $60 million, the one-time production investment of $70 million, the annual expected COGS of $50 million, and the annual marketing expenses of $10 million. Subtracting these expenses from the expected sales yields the expected annual net income from the project, as shown in Table 1. The annual net income in each year is converted to PV using the company's discount rate for such investments of 10 percent. Based on this information, the value of the project is −$20 million. Since the value of the project is negative, the DCF method suggests that MegaChem should not invest in the R&D for GreenAll.

Using the Real Option Method—Decision Tree

To calculate the value of the GreenAll project using the real option method, the company can construct a decision tree to model its investment decisions. A decision tree provides a way of representing alternative sequential decisions and the possible outcomes when future uncertainties are resolved. The decisions and uncertainties are ordered from left to right in the tree with all possible final outcomes represented by the endpoints of the tree. Points at which managers must make decisions, or decision nodes, are represented by square boxes, and uncertainties, or chance nodes, are represented by circles. If a chance node appears before a decision node, the associated uncertainty is assumed to be resolved before the decision is made; that is, the outcome of the uncertainty represented by the chance node is known to the decision maker. The decision and chance nodes are connected by branches representing the potential outcomes. The decision tree also incorporates branches for the choices of not investing in the project at all or undertaking the initial investment but abandoning the project before commercialization.

Uncertainties are represented in a decision tree through the chance nodes. Specifically, a probability is associated with each possible outcome from a given chance node. Once all the potential outcomes for the decision and chance nodes are arrayed in the decision tree, we can weigh each final outcome by the probability that it will occur and evaluate whether the expected outcome of the project is positive or negative. A primary difference between the real option method and the DCF method is that the real option method accounts for the option to abandon the project before it is completed.

The solved decision tree for MegaChem's investment problem is in Figure 2. The decision nodes represent points where MegaChem managers must decide how to proceed with the project. The decisions to be made are whether to invest in the R&D process and, assuming the R&D is completed, whether to build the plant and commercialize the product. Chance nodes represent uncertainties that will be resolved at a later date. The uncertainties facing MegaChem are the cost of production and the selling price for GreenAll. To arrive at the solved decision tree, the company must first determine the values of the endpoints and the optimal decisions given those endpoint values.

The company's initial decision is whether to invest in the R&D project. Once it learns the outcome of the R&D, MegaChem must then make a decision whether to continue the project. To determine whether these

Figure 2. Valuation of MegaChem's Product GreenAll Using the Real Option Method (Decision Tree)

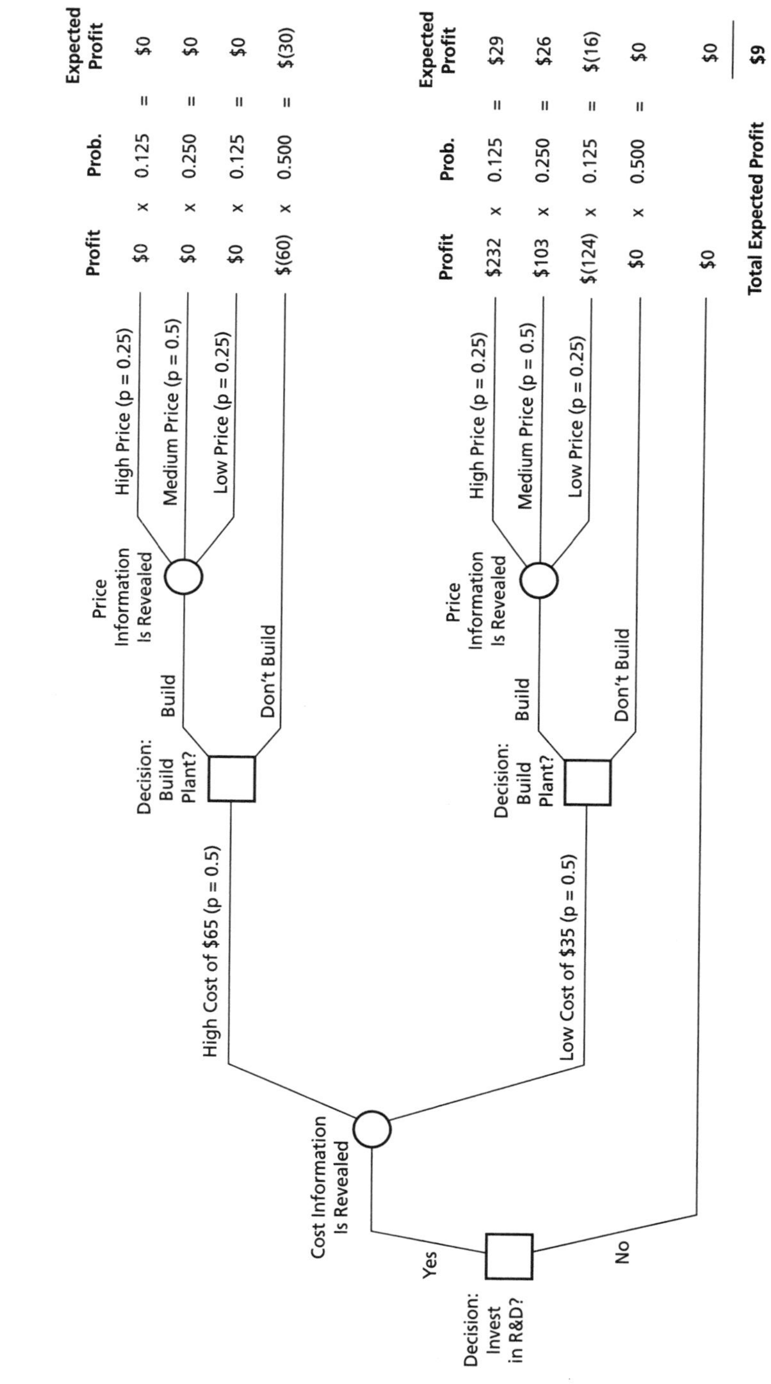

Table 2. Endpoint Values for MegaChem Decision Tree for GreenAll

Cost Scenario	Build/Price Scenario	Profit	Probability	Expected Value of Profit
		($Millions)		($Millions) (3) x (4)
(1)	(2)	(3)	(4)	(5)
High Cost Outcome	Build			
	High Price	41	0.25	10
	Medium Price	(91)	0.50	(46)
	Low Price	(320)	0.25	(80)
	Expected Value			(116)
	Don't Build	(60)	–	(60)
Low Cost Outcome	Build			
	High Price	232	0.25	58
	Medium Price	103	0.50	52
	Low Price	(124)	0.25	(31)
	Expected Value			79
	Don't Build	(60)	–	(60)

investments are likely to be profitable, the decision tree is solved backward (i.e., from right to left). Specifically, the value at each endpoint was solved using the DCF model in Table 1, but the inputs used were the decisions and information collected in arriving at each endpoint instead of expected values. Table 2 contains the final profit outcomes at each endpoint. Given the resulting values, the company can work backward to determine the optimal decision.

If the outcome of the R&D is the high COGS and MegaChem builds the plant, it will only realize positive profit if it can charge the high price. See Table 2, column 3. Given the profit for the three possible price outcomes and their associated probabilities, commercializing GreenAll with a high COGS is expected to result in a loss of $116 million. See Table 2, column 5. In contrast, if the high COGS outcome is realized, MegaChem can choose to abandon the project and lose only $60 million. Thus, the optimal decision if the R&D outcome is a high COGS is to abandon the project and avoid future losses. A similar analysis of the low COGS R&D outcome reveals that the expected profit from building the plant and commercializing GreenAll equals $79 million, while abandoning the project results in a $60 million loss. See Table 2, column 5. Thus, the optimal decision if the COGS turns out to be low is to continue the project and commercialize GreenAll.

Looking at the solved decision tree in Figure 2, we can see these results reflected in the Profit and Expected Profit columns. Given that MegaChem should choose the "Don't Build" path if the high-cost R&D outcome is realized, the expected profit is equal to the profit from choosing this option (−$60) multiplied by the probability that the high-cost outcome is realized (0.50), or −$30. Since the "Build" decision is not optimal on this branch of the tree, the associated profits for the endpoint branches equal $0. Similarly, if the low-cost R&D outcome is realized, MegaChem should choose to build the plant and commercialize the product for an expected profit of $39 ($29 + $26 − $16). For the low-cost R&D outcome, the "Don't Build" decision is not optimal and the endpoint equals $0 since MegaChem should not follow that path. Adding the values of the positive and negative values for Expected Profit yields a total expected profit for the project of $9 million.

Comparing the Results from the DCF and Real Option Methods

In the MegaChem example, using the DCF method resulted in a negative valuation for the project and the conclusion that the project should be rejected. However, the DCF framework did not allow for a realistic assessment of MegaChem's R&D process. It assumed that MegaChem would proceed with building the plant and commercializing the product regardless of the outcome of the research. This one-strategy, one-path model did not allow for managers' flexibility in making decisions to minimize MegaChem's financial risk if the COGS turns out to be high and exploit the favorable opportunity if the COGS turns out to be low.

Unlike the DCF method, the real option method allows for the possibility that MegaChem will abandon the project after gathering information and thereby avoid some of the worst possible outcomes. The real option method treats the $60 million R&D investment as an investment in learning rather than a commitment to the entire project. Compared to the DCF method, the real option method reduces the fixed costs associated with initiating the project from $130 million to only $60 million. It also avoids the unrealistic assumption that MegaChem would pursue a project that is likely to result in losses if the COGS outcome is high.

Example: Using the Real Option Method—Black-Scholes Option Pricing Model

The Black-Scholes option pricing model can also be useful for valuing R&D projects. As an illustration, suppose the company SmallPharma has completed the R&D process for its first product, Zees, an innovative new treatment for insomnia. SmallPharma is considering whether to apply for regulatory approval and commercialize Zees. This decision is particularly important because the company also has a follow-on treatment for insomnia, named BigZees, which is in the late stages of development. The company anticipates it may obtain regulatory approval for commercial sale in four years. However, there is substantial uncertainty regarding the competitive and regulatory environment that the company may face in four years.

SmallPharma staff has prepared a financial analysis for Zees assuming the product will have a commercial life of four years. Table 3 shows the sales, remaining R&D and production investments, COGS, and marketing expenses for the product. Based on its risk assessment for Zees, SmallPharma uses a discount factor of 20 percent to convert the resulting annual net income into PV terms. According to the textbook DCF decision rule, SmallPharma should not pursue approval of Zees because the resulting NPV is −$13 million. In this case, the launch costs associated with learning to manufacture the product (production investments) and educate physicians and patients about this new mode of treatment (marketing expenses) are relatively high. Given the risk of the project, these start-up costs overwhelm the subsequent profits. However, if SmallPharma does not launch Zees, it does not expect to be able to launch BigZees later. As a result, SmallPharma's finance staff suggests supplementing this analysis by valuing the option to commercialize BigZees.

Table 4 contains a summary of the valuation of SmallPharma's option to commercialize BigZees. SmallPharma projects that it will spend an additional $50 million annually for four years to complete development,

Table 3. Valuation of SmallPharma's Product Zees Using the DCF Method

Year	Expected Sales ($Millions)	R&D and Production Investments ($Millions)	Expected COGS ($Millions)	Expected Marketing Expenses ($Millions)	Expected Net Income ($Millions) (1)-(2)-(3)-(4)	Discount Factor ($Millions) at 20%	Expected NPV of Net Income ($Millions) (5) x (6)
	(1)	(2)	(3)	(4)	(5)	(6)	(7)
2005	–	350	–	50	(400)	1.0000	(400)
2006	175	–	18	80	77	0.8333	64
2007	200	–	20	100	80	0.6944	56
2008	300	–	30	100	170	0.5787	98
2009	500	–	50	100	350	0.4823	169
							(13)

apply for regulatory approval, and prepare the manufacturing facility for production. Capitalizing these costs at the discount rate of 20 percent yields a PV of $323 million. The PV of the expected net income from selling BigZees equals $251 million. Based on the standard deviation of the stock returns for small pharmaceutical companies, SmallPharma estimates that the appropriate standard deviation is 40 percent. Thus, the inputs into the Black–Scholes model are

expenses required to commercialize the product	=	$323 million;
PV of expected cash flows from project	=	$251 million;
expected time to commercialization	=	4 years;
risk-free interest rate	=	3 percent; and
standard deviation of expected project returns	=	40 percent.

Using these values in the Black–Scholes formula shown above, the value of the option to commercialize BigZees is $67 million. The value of this

Table 4. Valuation of SmallPharma's Option to Commercialize BigZees Using the Real Option Method and the Black–Scholes Option Pricing Model

	Precommercialization Expenses for BigZees ($Millions)			
	2005	2006	2007	2008
A. Expenses	50	50	50	50
B. Capitalization Factor (20%)	2.08	1.73	1.44	1.20
C. Expenses in 2009 dollars (A x B)	104	87	72	60
D. Total	323			

	Postcommercialization Cash Flows for BigZees ($Millions)						
	2009	2010	2011	2012	2013	2014	2015
E. Net Income	(80)	(50)	70	105	315	473	591
F. Discount Factor (20%)	0.48	0.40	0.33	0.28	0.23	0.19	0.16
G. Net Income in 2005 dollars (E x F)	(38)	(20)	23	29	72	90	95
H. Total	251						

Inputs to Black-Scholes Option Valuation Model

I. Precommercialization Expenses	$ 323 million
J. PV of Expected Cash Flows	$ 251 million
K. Expected Time to Commercialization	4 years
L. Risk-Free Interest Rate	3 %
M. Standard Deviation of Returns	40 %
N. Black-Scholes Value of Option to Commercialize BigZees	$ 67 million

option more than offsets the $13 million expected loss from obtaining approval and commercializing Zees. Thus, SmallPharma should commercialize Zees to enhance its experience and reputation in the market while maintaining the option to commercialize BigZees. Of course, if the market appears unfavorable when the company must decide whether to commercialize BigZees, SmallPharma can choose to abandon the technology. Given this flexibility and the uncertainty regarding the competitive and regulatory environment, the expected return from SmallPharma's strategy is $54 million ($67 − $13).

Conclusion

Companies in the pharmaceutical industry have used the real option method to value R&D projects and make investment decisions for over a decade. However, the real option method can be useful to companies in a wide variety of industries, including biotechnology, chemicals, computers, consumer products, electronics, media and entertainment, medical devices, software, and telecommunications. Companies in these industries increasingly rely on their IP to generate growth. As a result, it is more important than ever for them to manage and value their investments in researching and developing IP.

In some cases, the real option method provides a more realistic estimate of the value of an R&D project than the DCF method. Using DCF analysis, we implicitly assume that companies manage projects passively and complete them even if the outlook becomes unfavorable. Since the R&D environment is characterized by technical and market uncertainties, the optimal path for the project may change substantially from managers' initial expectations. The real option method is a useful technique for addressing these issues.

The focus of the real option method is to encourage managers to consider decisions that must be made in the future and the information required to make them. Using information from experts in the relevant functional areas, this forward-looking focus can help uncover opportunities to add value to the IP during the R&D process or mitigate financial risk. Thus, the real option method may be most useful for valuing IP when managers have the ability to expand, contract, continue, or abandon an R&D project. By modeling this flexibility, the real option method can help managers to minimize the financial risk associated with R&D projects and maximize the value of the IP they produce, if successful, by making incremental investments in information gathering. In gathering information and making decisions at each stage of the R&D process, the company can determine whether to continue to manage a project when positive information is revealed or abandon a project when adverse information arises.

22

Transfer Pricing Issues Affecting the Value of Intangible Property in Multinational Companies

It's Not How Much You Earn, It's How Much You Keep

George G. Korenko

Intangible property is emerging as an important income-producing asset for many companies.[1] Multinational companies often expend substantial resources across various countries identifying, developing, managing, and using their intangible property. For these companies, international use of their intangible property may result in transfers between affiliates in different countries. These transfers are likely to give rise to taxable transactions. For example, a multinational company that develops a patented technology in the U.S. may need to transfer patent rights[2] to a manufacturing entity in another country such as Ireland or Singapore.[3] In each case, the respective national tax authorities require that the transfer of patent rights between related entities in different countries be priced to ensure that appropriate taxes are paid. The price in such a transaction is called a transfer price, and if it is representative of the outcome of a transaction between unrelated parties, the transfer price is said to be arm's length.

---

[1] Intangible property includes primarily intellectual property, but it also includes other intangible assets such as customer lists and employment contracts.

[2] Transfers of patent rights may also involve transfers of other forms of intangible property such as technical information and know-how. In this chapter, I refer to such transfers collectively as transfers of patent rights.

[3] Corporate tax rates may differ substantially between countries. For example, the corporate tax rate in the U.S. is higher than those in Ireland and Singapore.

Multinational companies cannot pursue appropriate transfer pricing policies by merely filing the appropriate tax returns.[4] Companies must use appropriate methods and data when determining transfer prices for intangible property. To evaluate whether a company's transfer prices are arm's length, tax authorities may review the functions each party performs, the risks they assume, the costs they bear, and the associated returns. If they determine that the transfer price is not arm's length or it is inconsistent with the company's valuations of the same or similar intangible property for other forums (e.g., accounting standards), the company may be subject to tax adjustments, interest, and penalties. Thus, the costs associated with inappropriate transfer prices can potentially be very high. According to a report released by the Treasury Inspector General for Tax Administration in 2003, the Internal Revenue Service (IRS) proposed almost $500 billion in adjustments to the taxable income for large and midsized companies' returns in 2002—not including interest and penalties.[5] Double taxation is also a real possibility.[6]

In addition to the potential costs associated with inappropriate transfer prices, there may be substantial financial and strategic consequences if the company ignores the costs and benefits of different transaction structures. For example, to transfer patent rights between affiliates, companies can decide whether to license or sell the patent from one affiliate to another or to have the affiliates develop the technology jointly through a cost-sharing agreement.[7] While this decision will likely depend on several factors, it can affect the company's effective tax rate and, thus, its after-tax income. For

---

4   Transfer pricing policies actually begin in the corporate boardroom, where the audit committee may be required to approve a transfer pricing service provider. The Sarbanes-Oxley Act of 2002 bars a company's auditors from providing certain nonaudit services, including valuation, legal, and expert services. An auditor must be pre-approved by the company's audit committee to provide tax services.

5   This information is based on the most recent data available. See Treasury Inspector General for Tax Administration, *Current Trends in the Administration of International Transfer Pricing by the Internal Revenue Service,* ref. no. 2003-30-174, 15 September 2003.

6   Double taxation refers to a company paying taxes to two tax authorities on the same income stream. GlaxoSmithKline faces possible double taxation that could result in a $5.4 billion payment for taxes and interest relating to transactions between 1989 and 1996. See Tamu N. Wright, "Glaxo Sees Global Scrutiny for Transfer Pricing of Popular Drugs," *Transfer Pricing Report* 12, no. 22 (31 March 2004): 1041. The IRS subsequently issued a deficiency notice for $1.9 billion for the period 1997 to 2000. See "Glaxo Gets Second Deficiency Notice, Will Seek to Consolidate with Pending Case," *Transfer Pricing Report* 13, no. 18 (2 February 2005): 949.

7   A cost-sharing agreement allows affiliates in different countries to share the costs and benefits, including use rights, of developing the intangible property.

example, a 1 percent decrease in the effective tax rates for some of the largest pharmaceutical firms in the U.S. in 2002 and 2003 could have yielded additional after-tax profits of as much as $90 million to $125 million.[8]

Addressing proactively the appropriate price and structure for intercompany transfers of intangible property can reduce the likelihood of tax controversies, ensure that transfer prices for intangible property are consistent with valuations of the same property in various other forums, and help companies assess the tax consequences of these transactions. Companies that pursue appropriate, well-conceived transfer pricing policies may be able to keep more of what they earn.

What Is a Transfer Price?

Consider a hypothetical multinational pharmaceutical company named Pharm Inc. Suppose PharmHigh, Pharm Inc.'s research and development (R&D) laboratory in the U.S., develops and patents a compound used in the product Cureit. PharmLow, Pharm Inc.'s Irish affiliate, has the capability to manufacture, market, and distribute Cureit in non-U.S. territories.[9] The functions PharmLow actually performs will depend on the structure of the intercompany transactions between PharmHigh and PharmLow.

PharmLow could license patent rights from PharmHigh to use the technology to manufacture, market, and distribute the product outside the U.S. The transfer price in this transaction is the amount that PharmHigh charges PharmLow for the non-U.S. patent rights. This hypothetical structure is illustrated in Figure 1.

Figure 1. Licensing Transaction

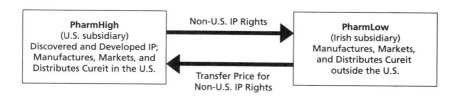

---

8   The largest firms were identified from "Fortune 1,000 Ranked Within Industries," *Fortune,* 5 April 2004: F-59. The effect of a lower effective tax rate was estimated based on company financial reports in years where there were no extraordinary items (e.g., mergers or substantial write-downs). The mean increase in after-tax profits for all 10 companies would have been $46 million.

9   For U.S. sales, assume PharmHigh arranges for the manufacturing and marketing of Cureit through other affiliates or third parties.

Figure 2. Sale of Goods Transaction

Alternatively, PharmHigh could manufacture Cureit and sell the finished product to PharmLow for marketing and distribution outside the U.S. Since this is a transaction involving the sale of goods, assume that PharmLow does not require a patent license. The transfer price in this transaction is the amount that PharmHigh charges PharmLow for the finished product.[10] This hypothetical structure is illustrated in Figure 2.

In this case, assume that Pharm Inc. chooses to have PharmHigh license the technology to PharmLow. Transactions between related entities are called *controlled transactions*. Tax authorities review companies' transfer prices for controlled transactions to ensure that appropriate taxes are paid.

Valuing Intercompany Transactions Involving Intangible Property

In the U.S. and the Organisation for Economic Co-operation and Development (OECD), transfer prices are required to comply with the arm's length standard.[11] The arm's length standard requires the transfer price to reflect the outcome that would have occurred if independent entities had negotiated a transaction for the same property or services under the same circumstances. Given the functions performed and risks assumed by the affiliates involved in an intercompany transaction, companies generally determine the appropriate transfer price based on data from transactions between unrelated parties (uncontrolled transactions) or based on the profitability of independent parties. The allowable meth-

---

10 There may be several additional ways to structure intercompany transactions that facilitate sales of Cureit outside the U.S.

11 See *Internal Revenue Service Section 482 Regulations (TD 8552)*, issued 1 July 1994 (section 482 regulations), and *OECD Transfer Pricing Guidelines for Multinational Enterprises and Tax Administrations* (OECD guidelines), respectively.

ods for applying the arm's length standard are generally similar under the IRS section 482 regulations and OECD guidelines, but tax authorities in some countries express a preference for certain methods over others. In the hypothetical example discussed above, PharmHigh is a U.S. entity. Thus, I will discuss the methods specified in the section 482 regulations.

Methods for Determining Transfer Prices for Intangible Property in the U.S.

The IRS section 482 regulations specify three methods for determining the arm's length result for the transfer of intangible property: (1) comparable uncontrolled transaction (CUT) method, (2) comparable profits method (CPM), and (3) profit split method—either comparable profit split method (CPSM) or residual profit split method (RPSM).[12] Rather than specifying a preferred method, the section 482 regulations require taxpayers to use a method selected under the best method rule.[13] The taxpayer should determine the best method based on the facts and circumstances of the controlled transaction, the degree of comparability between the controlled and uncontrolled transactions, the completeness and accuracy of the underlying data, the reliability of the assumptions, the sensitivity of the results to deficiencies in the data and assumptions, and the confirmation of the results by another method.[14]

CUT Method

The CUT method "evaluates whether the amount charged for a controlled transfer of intangible property was arm's length by reference to the amount charged in a comparable uncontrolled transaction."[15] To be considered comparable under the CUT method, the intangibles involved in the controlled and uncontrolled transactions must be used in connection with similar products or processes within the same general industry and must demonstrate similar profit potential.[16] Profit potential is most reliably measured by calculating the net present value (NPV) of the benefits to be realized as a result of the transfer.[17] In addition, the circumstances

---

[12] The regulations also permit the use of an unspecified method.
[13] Reg. Sec. 1.482–1(c).
[14] Reg. Sec. 1.482–1(c)(2).
[15] Reg. Sec. 1.482–4(c)(1).
[16] Reg. Sec. 1.482–4(c)(2)(iii)(B)(1).
[17] Reg. Sec. 1.482–4(c)(2)(iii)(B)(1)(ii). The benefits measured in the NPV calculation may include, for example, profits or cost savings from using the technology.

of the controlled and uncontrolled transactions must be comparable.[18] The best comparable uncontrolled transaction is a transfer of the same intangible property under the same circumstances (e.g., profit potential, sharing of risks, stage of development, etc.). While such comparables are rarely (if ever) available, it may be possible to apply the CUT method using comparables from the company's own transactions with third parties in the market for similar intangible property.[19]

CPM

The second method specified in the section 482 regulations is the CPM, which establishes an arm's length operating profit by comparison to the profitability of comparable third party companies engaged in similar business activities under similar circumstances.[20] Under this method, an appropriate measure of profitability[21] is calculated from comparable firms' data and applied to the tested party.[22] Thus, the profitability from using the intangible is compared to the overall profitability of a set of companies in the same industry that own similar intangible property. The reliability of the method depends upon the degree of comparability between the tested party and the uncontrolled entities. However, the standard of comparability required is less stringent than that for the CUT and profit split methods and the "CPM generally would be considered a method of last resort" if sufficient data were available to apply another method.[23]

Profit Split Method

The final specified method for pricing intangibles under the section 482 regulations is the profit split method.[24] Under this method, an arm's

---

[18] Reg. Sec. 1.482-4(c)(2)(iii)(B)(2).
[19] See Richard P. Rozek, "Applying the Best Method Rule When Reliable Internal Comparable Intangibles Exist," *Tax Notes International* 8 April 1996: 1191-1204.
[20] Reg. Sec. 1.482-5(a).
[21] The section 482 regulations refer to these measures of profitability as "profit level indicators." Reg. Sec. 1.482-5(b)(4) defines appropriate profit level indicators as the rate of return on capital employed, financial ratios such as the ratio of operating profit to sales or the ratio of gross profit to operating expenses, and other profit level indicators.
[22] Reg. Sec. 1.482-5(b)(2)(i) defines the tested party as the participant in the controlled transaction for which the most reliable data are available and for which reliable data regarding uncontrolled comparables can be located.
[23] Preamble to Reg. Sec. 1.482.
[24] Reg. Sec. 1.482-6(a).

length result is determined by comparing the relative contributions made by each of the controlled participants to the overall operating income of a transaction and allocating returns based on the relative value of these contributions. The relative value assigned to these contributions must take into consideration functions performed, risks assumed, and resources employed by the controlled taxpayer in relation to any activity involving the transfer of the intangible property.[25] The regulations specify that an arm's length allocation of profits or losses can be determined using either the CPSM or the RPSM.[26]

CPSM

The CPSM may be applied when there exist reliable income and cost data for uncontrolled firms with similar transactions and activities to those exhibited by the controlled taxpayer in the relevant business activity.[27] Therefore, factors that could affect prices or profits must be evaluated in establishing the comparability of transactions under the CPSM. These factors are functions performed, contractual terms, risks assumed, economic conditions, and property or services transferred.[28] Once comparable uncontrolled transactions are identified, an arm's length result is determined by applying the relevant profit split for the uncontrolled transactions to the combined operating profit of the controlled transaction. As with the CUT method, the CPSM can be successfully applied using the taxpayer's own transactions with third parties.[29]

RPSM

The RPSM uses a two-step approach to determine an arm's length allocation of operating profit or loss for both routine contributions and non-routine intangible property. First, RPSM requires an allocation of "operating income to each party to the controlled transactions to provide a market return for its routine contributions to the relevant business activity."[30] This allocation is typically based on a CPM approach. Second, the RPSM requires that the resulting residual profits attributable to non-

---

[25] Reg. Sec. 1.482–6(b).
[26] Reg. Sec. 1.482–6(c)(1).
[27] Reg. Sec. 1.482–6(c)(2).
[28] Reg. Sec. 1.482–1(d)(1).
[29] See Richard P. Rozek and George G. Korenko, "Transfer Prices for the Intangible Property Embodied in Products with Extraordinary Profit Potentials," *Tax Notes International* 18 October 1999: 1553-1565.
[30] Reg. Sec. 1.482–6(c)(3)(i)(A).

routine intangibles be allocated among the controlled taxpayers based upon the relative value of contributions of nonroutine intangible property to the overall enterprise.[31]

Example: Using a Company's Third-Party Transactions and the CUT Method to Derive an Arm's Length Transfer Price

To illustrate the application of the arm's length standard under the section 482 regulations to a transfer of intangible property, consider the transfer of patent rights from PharmHigh to PharmLow. Specifically, suppose PharmHigh transfers the non-U.S. patent rights to the technology that it developed to PharmLow through a license agreement. In this case, Pharm Inc. must determine the arm's length price (e.g., a royalty rate) for the patent rights transferred.

Identifying Data

The section 482 regulations require Pharm Inc. to identify the best method for analyzing the controlled transaction between PharmHigh and PharmLow. To determine the best method, the section 482 regulations require an evaluation of both the degree of comparability between the controlled and uncontrolled transactions and the quality of the data and underlying assumptions. Thus, the choice of the best method often depends on the data available on the controlled and uncontrolled transactions. The available data for analyzing a transfer of patent rights typically include the following:

- **Company License Agreements with Third Parties:** Many multinational companies that transfer patent rights between affiliates are also active in the external market for patented technologies. If available, data on a company's agreements with third parties may be useful in modeling its behavior in the market for patent rights. However, a license agreement by itself does not provide sufficient information to determine how the licensor and licensee envisioned sharing the profit associated with the underlying technology. This information can often be obtained from financial or commercial analyses for management to review in assessing whether to approve entering into an agreement. These financial analyses reflect the

---

[31] See Harlow Higinbotham, "The Profit Split Method: Effective Application for Precision and Administrability," *Tax Management Transfer Pricing Special Report*, (NERA, 2 October 1996: 1–23).

Table 1. Summary Information on Pharm Inc. License Agreements with Third Parties

Licensor (1)	Licensee (2)	Product (3)	Type of IP Transferred (4)
Pain Co.	Pharm Inc.	Pain Drain	patent rights
Big Knee	Pharm Inc.	Swell Down	patent rights
Cold Inc.	Pharm Inc.	Flu Brew	patent rights
Cardio	Pharm Inc.	Heart Help	patent rights

expected revenues and costs from using the patent rights based on the specific facts and circumstances for the transaction.

• **Public Data on License Agreements:** There are numerous public sources of information on license agreements. These include subscription databases such as *Windhover* and *Recombinant Capital* (Recap), as well as freely available sources such as U.S. Securities and Exchange Commission filings, court cases, and trade press.

• **Public Data on Comparable Firms:** The section 482 regulations allow use of financial data from firms identified as comparable to the relevant entity involved in the controlled transaction. These data are used to compare the profitability of comparable companies to the profitability of the controlled transaction.

Assume that a review of the available data reveals that Pharm Inc. negotiated four agreements with other companies for the patent rights to technology embodied in a pharmaceutical product and prepared financial analyses of the agreements for management to review in deciding whether to enter into the transactions. Specifically, Pharm Inc. signed agreements with Pain Co. for Pain Drain, Big Knee for Swell Down, Cold Inc. for Flu Brew, and Cardio for Heart Help. Table 1 contains information on the licensor, licensee, product, and type of intangible property transferred.

Evaluating the Available Data

Pharm Inc. License Agreements

The four agreements between Pharm Inc. and third parties represent arm's length transactions for patent rights in the same general industry as the controlled transactions (pharmaceuticals) and under similar conditions.[32] The agreements also contain detailed information on the functions performed and risks borne by each party. This information and the associated financial analyses are useful for comparing the functions performed and risks borne to those for the controlled transaction. If there are any material differences, the taxpayer must be able to make accurate quantitative adjustments to account for such differences. Comparing the Pharm Inc. license agreements to the controlled transaction, the company concluded that it performs similar functions and bears similar risks associated with the development and commercialization of Pain Drain, Swell Down, Flu Brew, and Heart Help as for the controlled transaction for Cureit. According to the section 482 regulations, "[d]ata based on the results of transactions between unrelated parties provides the most objective basis for determining whether the results of a controlled transaction are arm's length."[33]

The financial analyses prepared for Pharm Inc. management to review when deciding whether to enter into each transaction reflect the criteria the company uses when determining whether to enter into license agreements with third parties in the normal course of business. The licensor owns the patent rights and expects to earn profits from payments for transferring use rights to the licensee. The licensee expects to realize profits by exploiting the licensed technology. The total NPV of a license agreement is the sum of the NPVs of the expected profit streams of both the licensor and the licensee. Due to the strategic nature of license negotiations between unrelated parties, the licensor does not have access to the expected revenues and costs of the licensee. However, a licensee has the ability to calculate the expected royalty income to be received by the licensor based on its own sales projections. Thus, it is possible to calculate NPVs for both the licensor and licensee using data that would have been available to a licensee in an arm's length negotiation.[34]

These data capture the most reliable information available about the profit potential of the associated intangible property. In addition, they reflect Pharm Inc.'s own behavior in the market for patented technologies. As a result, if such agreements and associated financial analyses are avail-

---

[32] These conditions include functions performed, contractual terms, risk borne, economic conditions, and products transferred. See Reg. Sec. 1.482-4(c)(2)(iii) and Reg. Sec. 1.482-1(d).

[33] Reg. Sec. 1.482-1(c)(2).

[34] Calculating the NPVs for the uncontrolled transactions and for Cureit is discussed below.

able, they often provide the most complete and accurate data for determining an arm's length price for intercompany transfers of patent rights.

Public Data

While they may be useful in some cases, public data on license agreements and public financial data on companies do not contain the same level of detail as a company's own license agreements with third parties and associated financial analyses. Public data on license agreements typically include summaries of the financial terms but do not include information on the size, timing, or risk associated with the cash flows. In addition, these sources often lack detailed information on the transferred intangible property or the terms of the agreement. Public data on comparable companies reflects financial information on these companies' overall activities rather than the use of specific patent rights. Thus, neither public data source is as comprehensive and reliable as Pharm Inc.'s agreements and associated financial data.

Choosing the Best Method

The section 482 regulations require the transfer price for intangible property to conform to the arm's length standard and to be commensurate with the income attributable to the intangible property. Given the license agreements negotiated at arm's length and financial analyses prepared by Pharm Inc. personnel in the normal course of business at the time of the transaction, the CUT method and CPSM emerge as viable candidates for the best method for determining an arm's length transfer price.[35] The CPM and RPSM rely in whole and in part, respectively, on the profitability of comparable companies in determining a transfer price for an individual transaction. In contrast, the CUT and CPSM utilize Pharm Inc.'s data on its license agreements with third parties. In this case, Pharm Inc.'s internal data are more reliable and accurate reflections of how the company would have negotiated a license for Cureit at arm's length. I will apply the CUT method to the hypothetical Cureit transaction to demonstrate how an arm's length price can be determined using these data.[36]

---

[35] The CPSM relies on similar data to those used for the CUT method. However, the CPSM relies on all of the uncontrolled transactions with a range of profit potentials and circumstances, whereas the CUT method relies only on the uncontrolled transaction or transactions that most closely satisfy the comparability criteria.

[36] For a discussion of how to apply the CPSM using data from a company's transactions with third parties, see Rozek, "Applying the Best Method Rule," and Rozek and Korenko, "Transfer Prices for the Intangible Property."

In applying the CUT method, the section 482 regulations require the taxpayer to identify uncontrolled transactions that are comparable to the controlled transaction based on the following factors:

Comparable intangible property[37]
- similar products or processes within the same general industry or market
- similar profit potential

Comparable circumstances[38]
- terms of transfer
- stage of development
- rights to receive updates, revisions, or modifications
- duration of license
- uniqueness of property and degree and duration of protection
- economic and product liability risks assumed by transferee
- existence of collateral transactions
- functions performed by licensor and licensee

Each of these factors should be considered when determining possible adjustments to the financial analyses of the controlled and uncontrolled transactions. However, using the company's own license agreements and applying NPV analysis mitigates the need for additional adjustments.

Based on the comparability criteria listed above, Pharm Inc.'s license agreements with third parties and the associated financial analyses are potential comparable uncontrolled transactions. These license agreements and the Cureit transaction are for similar products (patented technologies embodied in pharmaceutical products) in the same industry. The financial data associated with these controlled and uncontrolled transactions are sufficiently detailed to allow comparison of the profit potentials and circumstances for the transactions. Moreover, the NPV analyses the company prepared for the license agreements and for Cureit capture any differences in the comparable circumstances. Each of the circumstances listed above affects the revenues, costs, risks, or timing of the cash flows associated with the using the patented technology. For example, consider two license agreements for the same technology that are similar in every respect except one provides exclusive rights and the other provides nonexclusive rights. Under the nonexclusive license, if there is a possibil-

---

[37] Reg. Sec. 1.482–4(c)(2)(iii)(B)(1).
[38] Reg. Sec. 1.482–4(c)(2)(iii)(B)(2).

ity that another company may license and commercialize the product, then the projected price and quantity sold will likely be lower for the licensee than it would have expected under an exclusive agreement. This results in lower revenue and profit streams and a lower NPV for the nonexclusive agreement. Based on similar reasoning, NPV analysis considers each of the comparability factors and adjusts for any differences between the controlled and uncontrolled transactions.[39] Thus, the license agreements and NPV analyses for Pharm Inc.'s license agreements and for Cureit allow for comparison of profit potentials and satisfy the remaining comparability criteria under the CUT method.

Calculating the Arm's Length Transfer Price

Pharm Inc. can use the financial analyses it prepared for the uncontrolled transactions to develop a standardized approach for an NPV calculation.[40] Table 2 contains the NPV analysis for the product Heart Help that Pharm Inc. licensed from Cardio.[41] Net income for Pharm Inc. is calculated by subtracting from net sales the projected costs, including cost of goods sold (COGS), royalty expenses, marketing expenses, and R&D expenses, and applying an appropriate tax rate (in this case, 35 percent). Pharm Inc. can estimate income for Cardio by applying the royalty rate to the net sales projections, adding any lump sum or milestone payments made to the licensor, and applying the appropriate tax rate to the results. The derived net income for Pharm Inc. and Cardio is then discounted to the year in which the parties signed the agreement, or 1997. The NPVs are then adjusted for inflation to express the results using common dollars. In this case, all NPVs are expressed in 2003 dollars. Adding the resulting NPVs for Pharm Inc. and Cardio together yields a total NPV for each agreement of $844.8 million. The share of the total NPV to Pharm Inc. and Cardio equals 76 percent and 24 percent, respectively.

By preparing similar financial analyses for the other three uncontrolled transactions, Pharm Inc. can determine the profit potential and

---

39 See Rozek, "Applying the Best Method Rule," for a discussion of how NPV analysis captures and adjusts for differences in each comparability factor.
40 Of course, the taxpayer's method should be consistent with standard valuation principles.
41 NPV analysis is a standard financial tool that business managers use to value specific projects. It restates all expected positive and negative cash flows over the life of an investment in present dollars and adds these present values to determine if the investment is likely to yield a profit. Future values are expressed as present values through use of a discount rate, which measures the opportunity cost of capital for the investment's level of risk.

Table 2. NPV Analysis of Pharm Inc. Agreement with Cardio for Heart Help

Year	Net Sales ($ Millions) (1)	COGS ($ Millions) (2)	Royalties ($ Millions) (1)x0.18 (3)	Marketing ($ Millions) (4)	R&D Expenses ($ Millions) (5)	Net Income before Taxes ($ Millions) (1)-(2)-(3)-(4)-(5) (6)	Net Income ($ Millions) (6)x0.65 (7)	NPV of Net Income Received by Pharm Inc.	
								Discount Factor 10% (8)	NPV of Net Income ($ Millions) (7)x(8) (9)
1997	0.0	0.0	0.0	0.0	20.0	(20.0)	(13.0)	1.0000	(13.0)
1998	0.0	0.0	0.0	0.0	20.0	(20.0)	(13.0)	0.9091	(11.8)
1999	0.0	0.0	0.0	0.0	18.0	(18.0)	(11.7)	0.8264	(9.7)
2000	0.0	0.0	0.0	0.0	15.0	(15.0)	(9.8)	0.7513	(7.4)
2001	39.0	3.9	7.0	24.0	15.0	(10.9)	(7.1)	0.6830	(4.8)
2002	136.5	13.7	24.6	40.0	0.0	58.2	37.8	0.6209	23.5
2003	243.8	24.4	43.9	40.0	0.0	135.5	88.0	0.5645	49.7
2004	380.3	38.0	68.4	35.0	0.0	238.9	155.3	0.5132	79.7
2005	487.5	48.8	87.8	30.0	0.0	320.9	208.6	0.4665	97.3
2006	541.1	54.1	97.4	25.0	0.0	364.6	237.0	0.4241	100.5
2007	560.6	56.1	100.9	25.0	0.0	378.6	246.1	0.3855	94.9
2008	585.0	58.5	105.3	20.0	0.0	401.2	260.8	0.3505	91.4
								Total in 1997 dollars	490.3
								Total in 2003 dollars	642.3

(continued)

Table 2. (continued)

NPV of Net Income Received by Cardio

Year	Net Sales ($ Millions) (1)	Royalty Rate (%) (2)	Royalty Income ($ Millions) (1)x(2) (3)	Net Income before Taxes ($ Millions) (4)	Net Income ($ Millions) (4)x0.65 (5)	Discount Factor 10% (6)	NPV of Net Income ($ Millions) (5)x(6) (7)
1997	0.0	18.0	0.0	0.0	0.0	1.0000	0.0
1998	0.0	18.0	0.0	0.0	0.0	0.9091	0.0
1999	0.0	18.0	0.0	0.0	0.0	0.8264	0.0
2000	0.0	18.0	0.0	0.0	0.0	0.7513	0.0
2001	39.0	18.0	7.0	7.0	4.6	0.6830	3.1
2002	136.5	18.0	24.6	24.6	16.0	0.6209	9.9
2003	243.8	18.0	43.9	43.9	28.5	0.5645	16.1
2004	380.3	18.0	68.4	68.4	44.5	0.5132	22.8
2005	487.5	18.0	87.8	87.8	57.1	0.4665	26.6
2006	541.1	18.0	97.4	97.4	63.3	0.4241	26.8
2007	560.6	18.0	100.9	100.9	65.6	0.3855	25.3
2008	585.0	18.0	105.3	105.3	68.4	0.3505	24.0
						Total in 1997 dollars	154.6
						Total in 2003 dollars	202.5

Total NPV of Net Income for Heart Help Agreement ($642.3+$202.5) = $844.8

Share of Total NPV of Net Income to Pharm Inc. ($642.3/$844.8) = 76.0%

Share of Total NPV of Net Income to Cardio ($202.5/$844.8) = 24.0%

Table 3. Database of Pharm Inc.'s License Agreements with Third Parties

Product	Licensor	Total NPV of Net Income ($ Millions)	Share of Total NPV	
			Licensor %	Licensee %
(1)	(2)	(3)	(4)	(5)
Pain Drain	Pain Co.	188.2	20.0	80.0
Swell Down	Big Knee	418.1	30.0	70.0
Flu Brew	Cold Inc.	501.6	17.5	82.5
Heart Help	Cardio	844.8	24.0	76.0

licensor/licensee profit shares for each third-party agreement. These data establish a database of potentially comparable uncontrolled transactions. Table 3 shows the total NPV for the licensed technology in each of Pharm Inc.'s uncontrolled transactions and the share of the NPV received by the licensor and licensee. The share of the total NPV to the licensor represents the amount paid for the technology.

To apply the CUT method, the NPV analysis for the controlled transaction should be based on the standardized method developed from the uncontrolled transactions.[42] Table 4 contains the financial analysis for Cureit using the standardized process described above for Heart Help. Specifically, to determine the profit potential for Cureit, Pharm Inc. calculates the total NPV of profits from the product using the same revenue and expense categories, discount rate assumptions, and inflation adjustments applied to the uncontrolled transactions. Using this standardized approach, the NPV of profits for Cureit equals $843.1 million.

To identify the appropriate CUT given these data, the section 482 regulations suggest matching the controlled and uncontrolled transactions based on profit potential.[43] In this case, the profit potential for Cureit is most similar to that for the Heart Help transaction. Thus, the arm's length price for the intellectual property embodied in Cureit equals the share of the NPV of profits to the licensor in the Heart Help transaction of 24 percent. Using the financial analysis for Cureit, it is straightforward to calculate the royalty rate that provides the 24 percent arm's length share of the total NPV of net income to PharmHigh.[44] Table 5 shows the

---

[42] See Table 2 for the analysis of Heart Help.

[43] Reg. Sec. 1.482-4(c)(2)(iii)(B)(1)(ii). Other comparability factors have already been met or adjustments have been incorporated into the financial analyses.

[44] The royalty rate can be calculated using the Solver function in Excel.

Table 4. Total NPV of Net Income Earned by Pharma Inc. from Non-U.S. Sales of Cureit

Year	Net Sales ($ Millions) (1)	COGS ($ Millions) (2)	Production Margin ($ Millions) (1)-(2) (3)	Marketing ($ Millions) (4)	R&D Expenses ($ Millions) (5)	Net Income before Taxes ($ Millions) (3)-(4)-(5) (6)	Net Income ($ Millions) (6)x0.65 (7)	Discount Factor to 1998 at 10% (8)	NPV of Net Income ($ Millions) (7)x(8) (9)
1998	0.0	0.0	0.0	12.0	20.0	(32.0)	(20.8)	1.0000	(20.8)
1999	0.0	0.0	0.0	33.0	20.0	(53.0)	(34.5)	0.9091	(31.4)
2000	92.0	13.8	78.2	50.0	20.0	8.2	5.3	0.8264	4.4
2001	165.0	24.8	140.3	50.0	20.0	70.3	45.7	0.7513	34.3
2002	255.0	38.3	216.8	50.0	15.0	151.8	98.6	0.6830	67.3
2003	347.0	52.1	295.0	50.0	15.0	230.0	149.5	0.6209	92.8
2004	443.0	66.5	376.6	50.0	15.0	311.6	202.5	0.5645	114.3
2005	579.0	86.9	492.2	50.0	15.0	427.2	277.6	0.5132	142.5
2006	601.0	90.2	510.9	35.0	15.0	460.9	299.6	0.4665	139.8
2007	590.0	88.5	501.5	20.0	5.0	476.5	309.7	0.4241	131.3
								Total in 1998 dollars	674.5
								Total in 2003 dollars	843.1

351

NPV analyses for PharmHigh and PharmLow in the controlled transaction including the arm's length royalty rate. In this case, PharmLow should pay PharmHigh a royalty rate equal to approximately 14.9 percent of net sales to provide it with 24 percent of the expected NPV of net income. This royalty rate is derived using the data and valuation methodology from the company's own license agreements with third parties and provides an arm's length transfer price. Moreover, the underlying valuation is consistent with internal valuations from licensing transactions that are used as inputs. Since they do not rely on the same data as the CUT method, the CPM and the RPSM may provide different results.

Interaction of Transfer Pricing and Other Valuations

Determining transfer prices for intangible property is not necessarily an isolated activity. In addition to transfer pricing, companies prepare valuations of intangible property for several forums, including business decisions, financial reporting (SFAS 141 and 142), venture capital financing, licensing, litigation, and patent donations. Rigorous transfer pricing valuations are important because they may be reviewed in other forums. For example, tax authorities may request valuations prepared for internal business decisions. Similarly, transfer pricing valuations have been reviewed for damage analyses in some patent infringement matters. In each case, an inappropriate transfer price could result in unnecessary controversies.

Companies can take steps to reduce the potential for inconsistent transfer pricing valuations. For example, when preparing a transfer pricing analysis a company should consider its policies for internal valuations in light of the applicable tax regulations. Such policies might specify the time period to use for forecasting cash flows, inflation rate assumptions, and the discount rate or rates to be used for various types of projects. These valuation principles can provide a standard set of assumptions for valuations prepared across forums, including transfer pricing.

Structuring Intercompany Transactions

When considering an intercompany transaction, companies should determine the functions performed and risks assumed by each entity. In the hypothetical controlled transaction, if PharmHigh agrees to perform and fund additional clinical trials after signing a license agreement, it should actually perform these functions and bear the associated risks. Similarly, if PharmLow agrees to bear product liability risks, it must actually incur

Table 5. NPV Analysis of PharmLow License from PharmHigh for Cureit

NPV of Net Income Received by PharmLow

Year	Net Sales ($ Millions) (1)	COGS ($ Millions) (2)	Royalties ($ Millions) (1)x0.149 (3)	Marketing ($ Millions) (4)	R&D Expenses ($ Millions) (5)	Net Income before Taxes ($ Millions) (1)-(2)-(3)-(4)-(5) (6)	Net Income ($ Millions) (6)x0.65 (7)	Discount Factor 10% (8)	NPV of Net Income ($ Millions) (7)x(8) (9)
1998	0.0	0.0	0.0	12.0	20.0	(32.0)	(20.8)	1.0000	(20.8)
1999	0.0	0.0	0.0	33.0	20.0	(53.0)	(34.5)	0.9091	(31.4)
2000	92.0	13.8	13.7	50.0	20.0	(5.5)	(3.6)	0.8264	(3.0)
2001	165.0	24.8	24.6	50.0	20.0	45.7	29.7	0.7513	22.3
2002	255.0	38.3	38.0	50.0	15.0	113.8	73.9	0.6830	50.5
2003	347.0	52.1	51.7	50.0	15.0	178.3	115.9	0.6209	72.0
2004	443.0	66.5	66.0	50.0	15.0	245.6	159.6	0.5645	90.1
2005	579.0	86.9	86.3	50.0	15.0	340.9	221.6	0.5132	113.7
2006	601.0	90.2	89.5	35.0	15.0	371.4	241.4	0.4665	112.6
2007	590.0	88.5	87.9	20.0	5.0	388.6	252.6	0.4241	107.1

Total in 1997 dollars 513.1

Total in 2003 dollars 641.4

(continued)

Table 5. (continued)

NPV of Net Income Received by PharmHigh

Year	Net Sales ($ Millions) (1)	Royalty Rate (%) (2)	Royalty Income ($ Millions) (1)x(2) (3)	Net Income before Taxes ($ Millions) (4)	Net Income ($ Millions) (4)x0.65 (5)	Discount Factor 10% (6)	NPV of Net Income ($ Millions) (5)x(6) (7)
1998	0.0	14.9	0.0	0.0	0.0	1.0000	0.0
1999	0.0	14.9	0.0	0.0	0.0	0.9091	0.0
2000	92.0	14.9	13.7	13.7	8.9	0.8264	7.4
2001	165.0	14.9	24.6	24.6	16.0	0.7513	12.0
2002	255.0	14.9	38.0	38.0	24.7	0.6830	16.9
2003	347.0	14.9	51.7	51.7	33.6	0.6209	20.9
2004	443.0	14.9	66.0	66.0	42.9	0.5645	24.2
2005	579.0	14.9	86.3	86.3	56.1	0.5132	28.8
2006	601.0	14.9	89.5	89.5	58.2	0.4665	27.2
2007	590.0	14.9	87.9	87.9	57.1	0.4241	24.2
						Total in 1997 dollars	161.6
						Total in 2003 dollars	202.0

Total NPV of Net Income for Heart Help Agreement ($641.4+$202.0) = $843.4

Share of Total NPV of Net Income to Pharm Inc. ($641.4/$843.4) = 76.0%

Share of Total NPV of Net Income to Cardio ($202.0/$843.4) = 24.0%

Note: Detail may not add to total due to rounding.

the relevant expenses and bear these risks. However, companies still have the flexibility to assess the costs and benefits of different structures for the intercompany transaction including license or sale of the technology, sharing of R&D costs, or using affiliates to perform only marketing and distribution functions (i.e., no manufacturing).[45] While some costs and benefits may relate to corporate goals and thus be difficult to quantify, one factor that can be quantified using financial data is the effective tax rate for the transaction.[46]

To illustrate the effect of different transaction structures on a company's effective tax rate, consider two alternative structures having PharmLow sell Cureit outside the U.S.[47]

- **Sale of Goods:** PharmHigh funds all R&D and owns the resulting intangible property embodied in Cureit. PharmHigh arranges for manufacturing and marketing of Cureit in the U.S. PharmLow purchases Cureit from PharmHigh and markets and distributes the product outside the U.S. In this case, there is no transfer of patent rights from PharmHigh to PharmLow.

- **Licensing:** PharmHigh funds all R&D, owns the resulting patented technology, and licenses the rights to that technology to PharmLow for manufacturing, marketing, and distributing Cureit outside the U.S. Based on the previous calculation of the arm's length price for the technology, PharmHigh receives a 24 percent share of profits or a royalty rate of 14.9 percent.

In addition, suppose the tax rate for PharmHigh is 35 percent, while the tax rate for PharmLow is 10 percent. Assume PharmHigh can arrange to have Cureit manufactured, marketed, and distributed in the U.S., while PharmLow can manufacture, market, and distribute the product outside of the U.S.[48] Using the financial data in Tables 4 and 5, it is possible to simulate the before-tax income and the tax payments for PharmHigh and PharmLow under these two scenarios. As is illustrated in Table 6, for the purpose of this analysis, assume that there are two types of transactions: sale of goods and licensing.

---

[45] Other arrangements may also be possible.

[46] Other considerations may include administrative ease, allocation of risks between affiliates, and efficiently funding the cash needs of affiliates subject to repatriation taxes in different countries.

[47] Steven Hannes, a partner at McDermott, Will & Emery in Washington, DC, provided assistance in defining the structure of these arrangements.

[48] PharmHigh may require assistance from other affiliates or third parties.

Table 6. Tax Consequences of Sale of Goods vs. Licensing for Cureit

Type of Arrangement	PharmHigh				PharmLow			
	NPV of Income before Tax ($ Millions)	NPV of Royalty Payments from PharmLow ($ Millions) 14.9% Royalty Rate	Total NPV of Income for PharmHigh ($ Millions)	NPV of PharmHigh's Tax Payments ($ Millions) 35% Tax Rate	NPV of Income before Tax ($ Millions)	NPV of PharmLow's Tax Payment ($ Millions) 10% Tax Rate	Total NPV of Tax Payments ($ Millions)	Effective Tax Rate %
	(1)	(2)	(1)+(2) (3)	(4)	(5)	(6)	(4)+(6) (7)	(7)/[(3)+(5)] (8)
Sale of Goods	1,011	–	1,011	354	26	3	357	34
Licensing	487	124	611	214	427	43	257	25

Sale of Goods: PharmHigh reimburses PharmLow for its costs and provides an arm's length return to PharmLow for performing marketing and distribution functions outside the U.S.

Licensing: PharmHigh licenses to PharmLow the rights to use the Cureit IP to manufacture, market, and distribute the product outside the U.S. Assumes the PharmHigh receives a 24 percent share of the total NPV of net income after taxes.

Assumptions: All R&D is performed by PharmHigh.

PharmHigh's tax rate equals 35 percent.

PharmLow's tax rate equals 10 percent.

Marketing and distribution expenses receive a markup of 20 percent.

PharmHigh and PharmLow incur equal marketing and distribution expenses.

PharmLow makes 60 percent of unit sales but only 50 percent of revenues due to lower prices in PharmLow's territory.

Does not consider possible repatriation of profits or withholding tax.

In the sale of goods transaction structure, PharmHigh performs R&D and manufacturing functions for worldwide sales of Cureit, and performs marketing and distribution functions in the U.S. PharmLow is only responsible for non-U.S. marketing and distribution functions. PharmHigh performs more functions and bears more risk than PharmLow and receives the returns associated with these functions and risks. As a result, PharmHigh earns an NPV of income before tax of $1,011 million, which is substantially higher than PharmLow's NPV of income before tax of $26 million (Table 6, columns 1 and 5). Using the assumed tax rates for each entity, the NPV of tax payments for PharmHigh and PharmLow equal $354 million and $3 million, respectively, for a total of $357 million (Table 6, columns 4, 6, and 7). The effective tax rate can be calculated by dividing the total NPV of tax payments by the total NPV of income before tax for both affiliates. The effective tax rate for the sale of goods transaction structure equals 34 percent (Table 6, column 8).

For the licensing transaction structure, PharmHigh still performs the R&D function, but each affiliate performs manufacturing, marketing, and distribution functions and bears the associated risks for its respective territory. Since PharmLow performs additional functions and bears more risks than in the sale of goods transaction structure, its share of the NPV of income before tax is higher under a licensing transaction structure. Specifically, under the licensing structure PharmHigh and PharmLow earn NPV of income before tax of $611 million (including royalties) and $427 million, respectively (Table 6, columns 3 and 5). Using the assumed tax rates for each entity, the NPV of tax payments for PharmHigh and PharmLow equal $214 million and $43 million, respectively, for a total of $257 million (Table 6, columns 4, 6, and 7). The effective tax rate for the sale of goods transaction structure equals 25 percent (Table 6, column 8).

The structure of the arrangement for funding R&D can affect substantially a company's after-tax profits.[49] Given the data and assumptions for Pharm Inc.'s intercompany transactions for Cureit, there is a substantial tax savings from using a licensing transaction structure compared to the sale of goods transaction structure. Specifically, the total NPV of tax payments is $100 million less than under the sale of goods transaction structure. The difference in the effective tax rates for the two transaction structures is 9 percentage points. This represents substantial

---

[49] Companies may only realize the projected tax savings if the product is successful and market, regulatory, and other conditions unfold consistent with the underlying assumptions in the simulation.

profit that Pharm Inc. can keep and reinvest in its business or distribute to shareholders.

Conclusion

Given the increasing importance of intangible property in generating returns for multinational companies, it is not surprising that intercompany transfers of intangible property across national boundaries are also increasing. As a result, transfer pricing issues are an important consideration for multinational companies when they identify, develop, manage, and use their intangible property. These issues include using appropriate data and methods to determine arm's length transfer prices and evaluating the costs and benefits of different structures for transactions between affiliates. Proactively evaluating the appropriate price and structure for these intercompany transactions involving intangible property can reduce the likelihood of tax controversies, provide a view of the value of the intangible property at issue that is consistent with its value in other forums, and assist companies in assessing the tax effects of different transaction structures. Ultimately, intercompany transactions that are appropriately priced and structured may allow companies to keep more of what they earn.

23

Finding Patent Litigation Strategies That Make Economic Sense
When Should Firms License?
When Should They Litigate?

Phillip A. Beutel

How should you advise your client about the best way to proceed if it is charged with infringing another company's intellectual property (IP), or if it discovers that a rival is using its protected IP? When this first occurs, your client may be emotional, or may feel wronged or wrongly accused.

It is at this early point in the life of a case that your client should be thinking about the ultimate objective of litigation. Your client may want you to file suit to put a stop to the infringement and perhaps push for a quick preliminary injunction, but then caution you to keep legal costs to a minimum. At this early stage, particularly when emotions might be running high, it is important to focus on the only win that matters—a win in the marketplace.

To explore the litigation strategies facing your client and to simplify the discussion that follows, consider the following hypothetical situation: Assume that your client, ABC Co., owns some IP and it believes that an infringing competitor, ReplicaCorp (RC), has stolen that property.[1] After a review of its patent claims and an examination of the allegedly infringing product, ABC asks you to send a letter to RC asking that the copycat product be immediately pulled from the market. Suppose that the infringer does not stop and, ultimately, ABC asks you to prepare and file a complaint.

ABC is in business to make money from selling products and not in the business of making (or spending) money in litigation. While RC's

---

[1]   For the sake of simplicity, the text describes a situation in which the IP at issue is a patent. Unless noted otherwise, the economic factors affecting the license-or-litigate decision are the same for other forms of IP.

supposed infringement may be emotionally distressing, ABC's problem really boils down to a threat to its market position and, therefore, to its ability to make money. Unfortunately, at the early stages of the litigation, many companies forget this basic fact and may need guidance.

Of course, you can follow ABC's wishes, select a venue, and file a complaint. But, to best serve ABC's interests, you also need to help ABC figure out what is really at stake. What does management want to accomplish in the marketplace? It may be helpful at this stage to remind ABC that it faces a decision: It must choose whether to litigate and, if so, whether to file for a preliminary injunction. Ultimately, it must choose whether to settle the case or go to trial in the hopes of being awarded damages, being aware, of course, that each path has its own set of costs and its own uncertainty about ABC's likelihood of prevailing.[2] Of course, the strength of ABC's liability case (e.g., the likelihood that the court will broadly construe the patent claims and there will be convincing evidence that RC chose to infringe willfully) will also importantly influence which litigation strategy is best. For the remainder of this chapter, however, these factors are taken as a given, allowing us to focus solely on the *economic* factors that are sometimes given too little weight in strategic decision making.

The path your client should choose depends on the expected payoff from each possible outcome: winning, losing, or settling. As a practical matter, for the litigation to make economic sense, ABC should understand what is at stake before filing its complaint. The relevant question is: What is the ultimate goal?

No doubt, ABC wants to protect its investment in the product embodying its IP. How should it do that? Does it ultimately want to exclude RC completely, or now that the infringement has occurred, might ABC be better off with a licensing arrangement? The answer lies in the economics underlying the choice between licensing and litigating.

ABC's Strategic Options: Eliminating the Infringer Versus Licensing

Factors Favoring Exclusion

To organize your thinking about these issues, begin by asking the following question: When should ABC pursue a litigation strategy in which the

---

[2] If roles were reversed, and ABC was the defendant, it would have to decide how hard to fight the case and come to terms with the fact that the litigation is going to cost money—both as ongoing litigation expenses and, ultimately, at settlement or perhaps as an unfavorable judgment at trial.

goal is to keep RC out of the market entirely?[3] The answer is straightforward: It should pursue this strategy if allowing RC to remain in the market would cause ABC to lose more money than if it were to grant RC a license. To see this, recognize that the cost of licensing can be measured as the reduction in ABC's profits caused by sales lost to its own licensee. If ABC cannot recover at least these costs in the form of a royalty from RC, it will be better off by choosing not to license the technology.

This is the first principle of licensing: No willing licensor will license its technology if it expects to earn lower profits after licensing than it would by using the patent to entirely exclude others. How do *you* know, before the fact, if ABC is better off excluding RC in its entirety? There are a number of economic factors to consider to help answer that question.

ABC's Ability to Make the Infringer's Sales

Assume ABC has sufficient manufacturing and marketing capacity to capture both its own and RC's sales. Also assume (a) ABC can actually reach every customer that is buying RC's infringing product (i.e., RC does not operate in a particular geographic area or in a field of use that ABC is unable to reach), and (b) RC's customers do not have a meaningful degree of loyalty to RC, and therefore, ABC would be likely to persuade all of RC's customers to buy its own product instead.

Under these circumstances, all else being equal, allowing RC to stay in the marketplace will cause a relatively large decrease in ABC's profits. ABC would demand a royalty that would at least compensate it for the profits it would expect to lose on sales lost to RC.[4] If the royalty did not cover those expected losses, then ABC should eliminate RC from the

---

3   *Exclusion,* in this context, means withholding the patented technology from rivals, including RC. RC may still compete with ABC, but may do so only with noninfringing economic alternatives.

4   The extent to which ABC is able to obtain a royalty from RC that is at least sufficient to cover those lost profits may also depend on other factors, such as asymmetric information between the parties. For example, one or the other party may have more (or better) information about the costs of producing the patented product or about the likelihood that consumers will demand the patented product or certain ancillary items. This information asymmetry may affect each party's relative bargaining position and may, therefore, affect the royalty rate to which the parties might agree. It may even make it impossible for the parties to reach agreement. Indeed, no agreement would be reached if ABC has a (perceived) cost advantage compared with RC or if ABC expects to sell more ancillary items with the patented product than does RC. In these situations, the profits RC expects to gain from licensing may be less than the profits ABC views as at risk from granting a license to a competitor.

market by refusing to grant the license. By following this elimination strategy, ABC would forego royalty income from RC, but its overall profits would be higher than if it were to grant a license.

Availability of Economic Alternatives

What happens when ABC eliminates RC from the market? Since this is the same as reducing the number of sellers, economic theory predicts that prices will likely go up (ABC will also gain sales, but for the moment, consider the effects only of the price increase).[5] ABC's profit per unit will go up as a result of the higher prices (although, as prices go up, the law of demand tells us that people will buy less, so take this offsetting factor into account as well). Other things being equal, a higher profit per unit would make an exclusion strategy more attractive.

This raises a question: Is there any easy way to tell if eliminating RC is likely to result in a meaningful increase in price? The answer is yes. The market information you need is the extent to which there are noninfringing *economic* alternatives available both to consumers and to RC.[6] If the patented feature contributes substantially to consumer demand, and there are few, if any, noninfringing economic alternatives to which consumers would turn if RC's infringing products were not available, then ABC can reasonably be expected to have substantial profits at risk from granting a license to a rival. All other things being equal, this circumstance supports an exclusion strategy.

As an economic matter, the *elasticity of demand* provides the information you need to discern the availability of acceptable economic alternatives.[7] A small elasticity of demand is associated with a demand curve that is fairly steep. This means that if (equilibrium) quantity changes, even just a little—say, because an infringer enters the market—then price will change more.

---

5   It may be that lost sales are extensive but price erosion is small. Indeed, in certain circumstances, it may be difficult to identify the degree of price erosion incrementally caused by the infringement.
6   If the IP at issue is a trademark, the corollary is: To what extent are there alternative trademarks to which the alleged infringer could turn, and what would be the cost to that rival of creating and promoting that trademark so that mark had equivalent "value"?
7   Again, the elasticity of demand refers to the sensitivity of sales to a change in price. More precisely, the own-price elasticity of demand is the percentage decrease (increase) in sales that would result from a 1 percent increase (decrease) in price. The elasticity at issue here is the elasticity for the product group consisting of the patent owner's and infringer's products.

The implication is that, all other things being equal, if the elasticity of demand for the patented product is relatively small, then the infringement itself will likely have a relatively large depressing effect on price and, therefore, on ABC's profits. Consequently, as above, ABC would demand a royalty that would at least compensate for the price-depressing effect of granting a license to a competing rival. If circumstances make it unlikely that RC would agree to pay at least that amount, then ABC would pursue an elimination strategy. All other things being equal, if you see that the market is characterized by a small elasticity of demand, you could support a litigation goal of driving RC from the marketplace.[8]

While it is easy for an economist to refer to the elasticity of demand as the primary marketplace evidence that can support this strategy, there are several economic factors you can observe that may suggest that the elasticity is small. The most important of these are the number and quality of alternatives available to consumers.

If there were *no* noninfringing alternatives, consumers would probably be unresponsive to price changes; they would have no place to turn. Put differently, the elasticity of demand would be small. However, what happens when that assumption is relaxed? In particular, what if there are no products that have the same *technical* specifications, but, in practice,

---

[8] Of course, if the patent owner can easily convert the infringer's customers to its own product and can make all of those sales, then, even if the elasticity of demand were relatively large, it may still have an incentive to file for an injunction and, if successful, keep output unchanged. The text merely describes the market signals corresponding with the patent owner's relative incentive to pursue a licensing versus injunction strategy.

Moreover, and on the other hand, if the elasticity of demand is small, the patent owner can reasonably expect substantial price erosion if it permits a licensee to enter the market (or if injunctive relief is denied, allowing an infringer to continue competing). Even in that situation, the parties might still be able to reach agreement on licensing terms if, but only if, the licensing fee fully compensates the patent owner not only for lost profits on sales it expects to lose to its licensee but, also, for lost profits from this expected price erosion. The discussion in the text is simplified to clarify the choices facing the patent owner and is based on the implicit assumption that, at the very least, it would be uncertain about whether the infringer would agree to such license terms.

In general, the discussion in the text relating to the role of the elasticity of demand is based on an underlying assumption that the patent owner and the accused infringer behave, in practice, as Cournot competitors. That is, they produce homogenous products, do not cooperate, have some degree of market power (due to the presence of some barriers to entry), and compete by choosing output levels simultaneously, taking the prior output of their rivals as a given.

there are alternatives to the patented product to which consumers can and do turn—i.e., so-called *economic* alternatives.[9]

If such alternatives exist and the patented invention is only a minor improvement over them, the elasticity of demand will probably be large. Accordingly, you need to look for the degree to which consumers find other products to be acceptable economic alternatives to the patented product, even if they do not have all of the same technical features. Again, all other things being equal, when the elasticity of demand is small, an exclusion strategy makes economic sense.

Infringer Behavior

Of course, elasticities are not the only piece of marketplace evidence relevant to determining an economically rational strategy. The way RC typically competes in the marketplace may also play a role in this decision.

For example, if RC is a price leader—or particularly aggressive in its selling practices or promotional policies—then, all else being equal, allowing it to stay in the marketplace will cause a relatively large decrease in ABC's profits. ABC would be better off eliminating RC from the market as long as any royalty to which RC might agree did not at least offset the expected decrease in ABC's profits from RC's price-leading or other aggressively competitive behavior.[10]

Convoyed or Ancillary Sales

Last, the extent to which the patent owner and prospective licensee make convoyed, or ancillary sales, can also influence ABC's choice of litigation strategy. Consider the case in which ABC believes that infringement will cause it to lose substantial sales of, and profits from, ancillary items.[11]

ABC could properly claim that those losses support a relatively higher royalty—i.e., enough to compensate not just for the lost sales of the patented product but also for lost ancillary sales. All other things being

---

9 For example, consider an invention for a bracket made out of a new type of ceramic material that can be used to hold auto mufflers in place. While there may not be anything that is *technically* comparable, the old types of metal bracket and even a metal coat hanger might be used in practice. These are clearly *economic* alternatives for the invention.

10 As a matter of economics, this example is one in which the infringer is "more" competitive than Cournot (see note 8). Any analysis of the parties' relative negotiating positions and optimal litigation strategies requires a careful assessment of the underlying economic behavior of the parties.

11 These are sometimes called convoyed sales, follow-on sales, or ancillary sales.

equal, substantial expected losses on ancillary items would support an exclusion strategy.[12]

Factors Favoring Licensing

When would you favor litigation as a strategy to bring RC to the bargaining table and get a licensing agreement? Here, relaxing the assumptions from the previous section, the answer is straightforward: Try to use litigation to force a licensing agreement if the royalty stream ABC will likely earn is more than it would lose from coexisting with RC. What are the market conditions that favor this strategy?

Large Elasticity of Demand

Following the same logic as described above, a licensing strategy makes economic sense when the elasticity of demand is large. This may occur, for example, when there are many acceptable noninfringing economic alternatives. This means that entry by an infringing competitor—or the forced exit of an infringing competitor—will not cause much of a price change.

But, again, elasticity is not the only marketplace factor that you can observe that informs this decision. You should also consider RC's relative costs and the extent to which RC can expand the market.

Infringer's Costs

What would happen if RC's incremental costs of making and selling the product are lower than ABC's?[13] In this situation, RC would be able to reduce the price below that offered by ABC and, all else being equal, be able to capture a relatively larger share of overall sales. Of course, this could have a severe impact on ABC's profits. Indeed, if RC's costs are low enough, it may even be able to drive ABC out of the marketplace entirely.

---

12 However, if those ancillary items are not *functionally* related to the patented product, then, under Rite-Hite, ABC would not be able to argue that it was entitled to those losses as part of a lost profits damages claim (*Rite-Hite Corp. v. Kelley Co. Inc.*, 56 F.3d 1538, 1544-45 [Fed. Cir. 1995]). Indeed, if much of ABC's losses are likely to result from lost ancillary sales (especially if those sales are not functionally related to the patented item), then, other things being equal, this distinction may tip the balance toward a decision to claim royalty rather than lost profits damages.

13 The appropriate costs for determining price are always *incremental* costs. These represent the additional costs that the firm would incur in order to make and sell one more item. Put another way, they represent the costs the firm would avoid if it makes and sells one fewer item.

While it is true that this price and profit reduction can be prevented by eliminating RC, that may not be the profit-maximizing litigation strategy. Since RC has a cost advantage, all else being equal, it can earn more money than ABC on each item it sells. This means that RC is better able to pay royalties than if it had no particular cost advantage.

In this situation, ABC could view the litigation as an opportunity to get a share of this larger profit base in the form of relatively high royalty payments.[14] In fact, whenever market conditions allow RC to make more money than ABC on any particular sale, ABC's strategy should be to find a way to let RC make those sales and then give over a share of its profits as royalty payments.

Can the Infringer "Expand the Market"?

A licensing strategy also makes sense if there are certain customers that only the infringer can reach or who only the infringer is likely to persuade. If the infringer can expand the market in this way, then it certainly is going to be able to make more money on those particular sales than would the patent owner.[15] Accordingly, it would be in ABC's interest to try to get a share of the profits RC earns on those sales.

Again, to the extent that the patent owner does not have the manufacturing capacity, selling ability, market reach, or ability to persuade the infringer's customers, then, other things being equal, the infringer is probably able to expand the market and the litigation strategy should focus on bringing the infringer to the bargaining table.

---

[14] More precisely, depending on the extent to which RC has a relative cost advantage, it may be that the royalty income ABC might earn would exceed its own profits from making and selling the product. In the extreme, this situation suggests ABC should forego participating in the market and instead earn royalty income from the low-cost infringer. ABC may then also consider granting an exclusive license to RC.

[15] Alternatively, consider the situation in which the patent owner is a relatively small unknown firm while the infringer sells large well-known brands. Here, the infringement may result in the patented product becoming more well-known more quickly than if the patent owner kept the market entirely to itself. In this situation, the market is expanded such that the patent owner's own sales are greater more quickly than would otherwise have been the case. Its profits on this (incrementally) larger volume of sales may exceed its losses from the infringement—either in sales lost to the infringer or from price erosion. Faced with this type of infringement, a licensing strategy would appear to be the economically sound litigation strategy.

The Importance of History

There is one other group of factors that can be fairly easily observed that may affect whether licensing makes economic sense:

- ABC's historical licensing and marketing policy;
- historical royalty rates ABC received for the patent itself or for related or similar inventions; and
- historical royalty rates paid by RC for comparable inventions.

In a nutshell, the parties' historical behavior may provide very useful information on the amount of money ABC can reasonably expect to get from a licensing agreement relative to the avoided lost profits from keeping the market entirely to itself.[16] If ABC has a history of licensing the patent, then the share of RC's sales that it would get (if RC is excluded from the market) would, all other things being equal, be small relative to the size of the royalty payments. This is because ABC would get a royalty on all of RC's sales but would only be likely to recover a small share of additional sales if RC were entirely excluded from the market.

An Aside: The Infringer's Perspective

Thus far, I have focused primarily on the patent owner's perspective. The underlying economics, however, are the same for defendants. That is, the accused infringer would benefit from going to the bargaining table, sooner rather than later, if it is likely to earn more under a licensing agreement than the expected value of any award that the court might impose.

As a general matter, defendants must come to the realization that a consequence of being served with a complaint is that litigation *will* cost it some amount of money in litigation expenses, a settlement payment, or damages. How much money, of course, depends on the probability that the patent owner prevails at trial. It also depends on precisely the same economic factors that were explored above.

If the infringer's product is better, if it can reach customers the patent owner cannot, if it has a meaningful cost advantage, and if the elasticity

---

[16] In this connection, if there are a number of infringing competitors, there is the additional strategic question of who to sue first. Once you have determined that the proper strategy is to license the infringers, then which firm ABC sues first—depending, of course, on those competitors' relative cost advantages and abilities to expand the market—may establish a royalty rate that your client may have to live with in subsequent negotiations.

of demand is large because there are many acceptable noninfringing economic alternatives, then the infringer may be better off, sooner rather than later, agreeing to settle the case with a licensing arrangement.

Conclusion

For your patent infringement litigation strategy to make economic sense, you need to know at the outset of a case, and perhaps before filing the complaint, a few basic economic facts. Most important among those facts are the availability of economic alternatives and the relative cost advantage, or disadvantage, held by the patent owner.

By looking at these economic factors at the outset of the case, and not at the end in connection with damages, the litigation will more likely result in the only win that matters to your client—a win in the marketplace.

Contributors

Phillip A. Beutel, *Senior Vice President, NERA*

Dr. Beutel specializes in intellectual property economics, the evaluation of commercial damages, and antitrust analysis. In his intellectual property practice, Dr. Beutel has conducted research and prepared expert reports for patent, trademark, and copyright infringement disputes, false and misleading advertising cases, and matters requiring the valuation of intangible assets for business dissolution proceedings, compliance with the Financial Accounting Standards Board, or determining intracompany transfer prices. He has also assessed the commercial success of patented innovations in connection with invalidity claims and has experience critiquing damage models, applying econometric and statistical methods, and designing and providing economic analysis of consumer surveys. Dr. Beutel has testified in court and has appeared before antitrust enforcement agencies. He has published articles in economics journals and in course handbooks for the Practising Law Institute and has been a guest lecturer on antitrust economics at Fordham Law School and the Chicago-Kent School of Law.

Sarah M. Butler, *Consultant, NERA*

Ms. Butler has managed a wide range of consulting projects in the areas of intellectual property, antitrust, and false advertising. Her work has primarily focused on the use of survey data to assess consumer confusion in trademark and trade dress cases, determine the impact of false advertising claims, and estimate market share in antitrust matters. She also has extensive experience with the creation of original surveys and the critique of surveys submitted by opposing counsel and has worked on a number of probability and estimation sampling projects. In intellectual property, her industry experience includes food products, clothing, and health insurance. She has also managed surveys of consumers, physicians, and IT professionals and has designed samples using insurance records, legal documents, real estate transactions, and radio play lists.

Joseph P. Cook, *Vice President, NERA*

Dr. Cook specializes in law and economics, industrial organization, and behavioral game theory. He has engaged in research and prepared reports on a variety of issues, including those relating to intellectual property, economic damages, antitrust and competition policy, and auctions. He has analyzed the competitive consequences of various settlements of intellectual property litigation and has contributed to antitrust projects involving monopolization, boycotting, predatory pricing, tying and bundling, price fixing, patent settlements, and price discrimination. Dr. Cook has testified on economic matters both in deposition and at trial. He has been published in a number of journals, including the *Journal of Political Economy* and the *Journal of Economic Behavior and Organization* and has served as a referee for the *Journal of Economic Behavior and Organization* and the *Journal of Risk Research.* He has presented his work and lectured on economics both in Europe and the U.S.

Alan Cox, *Senior Vice President, NERA*

Based in San Francisco, Dr. Cox participates in NERA's Intellectual Property, Antitrust, and Securities and Finance Practices. He has extensive testimonial experience, particularly in the semiconductor, biotechnology, retailing, telecommunications, and energy industries. He has estimated damages in intellectual property matters involving semiconductor process and design patents, biotechnology patents, golf ball trade secrets, disputes over technology sharing agreements, and patent fraud. He has also testified on antitrust allegations arising from licensing practices, and on antitrust issues in Robinson-Patman Act matters, matters involving allegations of price fixing, and attempts to monopolize. In securities and finance matters, he has filed reports in class action securities fraud cases and affidavits on class certification, the impact of allegedly disparaging statements on securities prices, and a wide array of financial damages. Dr. Cox has previously held positions as a Senior Vice President at LECG and as a Visiting Economist at the Massachusetts Institute of Technology's Energy Laboratory.

Jesse David, *Vice President, NERA*

Dr. David provides research and testimony for projects associated with intellectual property matters and other business disputes. He has developed testimony for cases involving patent infringement, trademark and trade dress violations, theft of trade secrets, and other disputes associated with technology agreements. These cases have included the determination of economic damages related to technologies such as electronic funds transfer, heart-surgery devices, hand-held diagnostic instruments, remote thermometers, semiconductors, and printed circuit board manufacturing. He has also conducted valuation analyses for intangible assets in the context of due diligence, insurance purchases, and litigation risk assessments. As part of his role at NERA, Dr. David researches and tracks recent trends in patent litigation and the effects of litigation on patent value. He also writes and speaks frequently on intellectual property issues and other topics.

Christian Dippon, *Vice President, NERA*

Mr. Dippon specializes in the evaluation of economic damages in intellectual property disputes and is also an expert in the economics, business, and regulation of the telecommunications industry. In intellectual property and commercial litigation matters, he advises his clients on calculating economic damages in cases of intellectual property infringement, allegations of breach of contract, fraud, misrepresentation, and other commercial damages claims. He has also conducted market research studies in a number of industries, employing qualitative choice models and marketing surveying tools. Mr. Dippon has extensive testimonial experience and has consulted to clients in the U.S., Japan, Hong Kong, UK, China, Brazil, Singapore, Dominican Republic, Korea, and Australia. He is a frequent lecturer on the application of rigorous economic techniques for intellectual property damages estimation and on telecommunications issues. He has also published several papers on a range of competition issues and has authored a chapter in an Internet marketing textbook.

Eugene P. Ericksen, *Special Consultant, NERA*

In addition to designing statistical samples and directing surveys for clients, Dr. Ericksen's fields of expertise include survey research and demographic methods. In his current role at NERA, he frequently testifies and consults as an expert on questionnaire design, statistical sampling, and demography. In addition to his consulting work, Dr. Ericksen is a

Professor of Sociology and Statistics at Temple University, where he teaches courses in statistics, research methods, sampling, and census data usage. In the past, he has served as a member of the 2000 Census Monitoring Board and, in 2001, provided expert testimony on the 2000 Census before the U.S. Senate Committee on Commerce, Science, and Transportation. He was also appointed as Co-Chair of the Special Advisory Committee on the 1990 Census by the Secretary of Commerce, where he advised on possible methods of adjusting for differential under-count. Dr. Ericksen's articles have appeared in the *Journal of the American Statistical Association, Demography, American Sociological Review,* and *Population Studies.* He is a Fellow of the American Statistical Association and was Associate Editor of the *Journal of the American Statistical Association* from 1989 to 1991.

John H. Johnson, *Senior Consultant, NERA*
Dr. Johnson's work at NERA focuses on the use of econometric methods in litigation. He has extensive experience with intellectual property, antitrust, and labor matters involving estimation of damages, allegations of price fixing, and economic analyses with large transaction and demo-graphic data sets, including volume of commerce calculations, pricing analyses, and econometric damages modeling. He has also developed economic arguments in class certification matters and has worked on a variety of merger and competition policy issues. Prior to joining NERA, Dr. Johnson was an Assistant Professor of Economics and Labor and Industrial Relations at the University of Illinois at Urbana-Champaign, where he taught courses in labor economics, with a special focus on discrimination in the labor market.

Vinita M. Juneja, *Senior Vice President, NERA*
Dr. Juneja directs projects chiefly in the areas of finance, securities economics, and valuation. She has been retained on hundreds of securities and financial valuation matters involving securities fraud claims, valuation of restricted or illiquid stock, derivative actions, stock repurchases, insider trading, manipulation, churning and suitability, ERISA related claims, market timing, fund advisor fee structures, and valuation of businesses and financial assets. Many of these projects have involved the measurement of the impact of an event on a security's value, such as the impact of a patent infringement claim on a company's stock price. Dr. Juneja has testified and submitted affidavit and expert report testimony in federal

district court proceedings and in hearings including arbitrations. She is also an arbitrator for the NASD. While completing her doctorate in economics at Harvard University, she participated in teaching courses in microeconomics and the economics of business and government.

Noriko Kakihara, *Associate Analyst, NERA*
Ms. Kakihara has extensive experience analyzing damages in intellectual property litigation. She received her BA in economics and BS in computer science from Stanford University. Prior to joining NERA, Ms. Kakihara was a research assistant in the Stanford Economics Department and at the Stanford Law School. She has also served as a consultant in the information technology field.

George G. Korenko, *Senior Consultant, NERA*
Dr. Korenko has valued intellectual property and businesses, conducted transfer pricing analyses, evaluated and prepared damages calculations in intellectual property, antitrust, and contract disputes, prepared public policy studies, and analyzed competitive issues. He has valued intellectual property and prepared damage estimates for companies in numerous industries including pharmaceuticals, chemicals, computers, industrial equipment, health care services, and consumer goods. His transfer pricing work has used economic, accounting, financial, and statistical analyses to identify arm's-length prices consistent with U.S. and foreign tax guidelines for intangible property, tangible property, and services. Prior to joining NERA, Dr. Korenko was an Assistant Professor of Business and Economics at Meredith College and an Instructor at the University of North Carolina at Chapel Hill. He has published articles in the *Journal of World Intellectual Property, Tax Notes International, International Transfer Pricing Journal,* and *Transfer Pricing Report* and has served as a referee for *The Energy Journal.*

Susan C. S. Lee, *Consultant, NERA*
Dr. Lee's areas of expertise include intellectual property, antitrust and competition policy, and market design. She provides litigation support related to the competitive effects of mergers, price fixing conspiracies, price discrimination, attempted monopolization, and commercial disputes. She has conducted economic analyses for a range of industries, including pharmaceuticals, health insurance, gas and oil distribution, and financial products. Before joining NERA, Dr. Lee served as an Assistant

Professor of Economics at Florida State University, where she taught undergraduate and doctoral-level courses in microeconomic theory and mathematical economics and spoke frequently on game theory and computational economics topics.

Gregory K. Leonard, *Vice President, NERA*
Dr. Leonard specializes in applied microeconomics and econometrics. He has provided expert analysis, as well as written and oral testimony, in the areas of intellectual property, antitrust, damages estimation, statistics and econometrics, and labor market discrimination. Dr. Leonard was one of the developers of the merger simulation technique that is now widely used to analyze the competitive effects of mergers. He has published in the *RAND Journal of Economics,* the *Journal of Industrial Economics,* the *Journal of Public Economics,* the *Journal of Labor Economics, Antitrust Law Journal,* and the *George Mason Law Review.*

Alyssa Lutz, *Partner, EconFocus, LLC*
Dr. Lutz's work has focused on intellectual property and antitrust issues in the airline/aerospace and healthcare industries. In intellectual property matters, she has evaluated antitrust counterclaims and calculated economic damages from patent and trademark infringement and theft of trade secrets. She has also assessed the competitive effects of mergers and other business combinations and has evaluated both liability and damages issues in cases involving a wide range of antitrust issues. She previously served as a Visiting Scholar in the Department of Finance and Business Economics at University of Southern California's School of Business and Administration and has spoken frequently on appropriate methods of calculating intellectual property damages, as well as on antitrust issues in an intellectual property context.

Thomas R. McCarthy, *Senior Vice President, NERA*
Dr. McCarthy leads NERA's U.S. Health Care Practice. He specializes in the economic analysis of regulatory, public policy, and litigation matters in health care markets, including the economics of intellectual property protection and the estimation of contract, trade dress, trade secret, and patent damages. Often these intellectual property issues involve medical equipment and devices, though Dr. McCarthy has worked in a wide variety of other industries as well, including supermarket equipment, computer hardware, greeting cards, and CD-Rs. Before joining NERA, Dr.

McCarthy taught at Oakland University, served as a graduate instructor at the University of Maryland, and was a staff economist with the Federal Trade Commission. He has published several papers on antitrust damages and health care issues in the *Journal of Health Economics* and in American Bar Association publications. He is also co-editor and principal author of a year-long, two-volume study of health care financing reform in 12 industrialized countries, published by Kluwer.

Christine Meyer, *Senior Consultant, NERA*
Dr. Meyer conducts economic research and analysis in the areas of intellectual property, commercial damages, business valuation, antitrust, and labor economics. She has written expert reports on economic damages arising from patent infringement, calculated economic damages from the misappropriation of trade secrets and breaches of contract, and analyzed the value of patents, licenses, and potential business acquisitions. She has also estimated the competitive effects of mergers and acquisitions and has evaluated damages in cases involving alleged resale price maintenance and price discrimination. Her work frequently incorporates various econometric techniques such as demand modeling and the design and analysis of discrete choice consumer surveys. Prior to joining NERA, Dr. Meyer served as an Assistant Professor of Economics at Bentley College and as a Visiting Assistant Professor at Colgate University. She also worked as a Consultant for Data Resources, Inc. and was a contributing author to the U.S. Department of Commerce's *U.S. Industry and Trade Outlook.*

Rika Onishi Mortimer, *Senior Consultant, NERA*
Dr. Mortimer specializes in applied econometrics, industrial organization, and health economics. Her work has included analysis of mergers, monopolization, bundling, discrimination, damages, and other antitrust matters in a variety of industries. Dr. Mortimer began her career as an economist at the Antitrust Division of the United States Department of Justice, where she evaluated the competitive effects of proposed mergers and agreements. In this role, she specialized in empirical studies and econometric analyses, including the estimation of demand elasticities for various products using scanner data, as well as the assessment of consumer harm resulting from proposed mergers. At both NERA and the Antitrust Division, she has used her Japanese language skills to contribute to foreign antitrust and trade investigations involving the Japan Fair Trade Commission and Japanese and multinational firms.

Richard T. Rapp, *President, NERA*

Dr. Rapp has been President of NERA since 1988. He specializes in intellectual property, antitrust, and international economics and advises clients in the computer, semiconductor, pharmaceutical, newspaper, book, and music industries on antitrust and intellectual property economics. His work includes pricing, licensing, standards, and royalty rate determination, intangible asset valuation, estimation of damages, market power analysis, and high technology antitrust. Dr. Rapp has presented studies and testified before the Federal Trade Commission, the Federal Energy Regulatory Commission, the Federal Communications Commission, the United States International Trade Commission, and numerous federal district courts. Prior to joining NERA, he was an Associate Professor at the State University of New York at Stony Brook.

Bryan Ray, *Senior Consultant, NERA*

Mr. Ray has contributed to a variety of consulting assignments in the areas of intellectual property economics, antitrust and trade regulation, and the calculation of economic damages in commercial disputes. His research in these areas spans many industries and has been incorporated into both expert testimony and presentations to mediators and regulatory agencies. In matters involving intellectual property, Mr. Ray has consulted on the estimation of damages for cases involving patent, trademark, and copyright infringement, the theft of trade secrets, and Lanham Act violations. He has also valued intellectual property for purposes of SFAS 141/142 compliance, transfer pricing, and asset sales and analyzed various claims related to the alleged anticompetitive use of patents and copyrights. Mr. Ray has published articles in the *International Tax Journal* and *Managing Intellectual Property*.

Kristina Sepetys, *Senior Consultant, NERA*

Ms. Sepetys specializes in economic policy and analysis consulting across various practice areas and industry sectors. She has worked with governments, utilities, associations, and regulatory bodies to develop and implement restructuring programs designed to introduce greater levels of competition in the electric and gas sectors in the U.S. and abroad. Ms. Sepetys is the co-author of *Restructuring Electricity Markets: A World Perspective* and has published many articles addressing related topics. She has lived in Hong Kong and Taiwan and has studied classical, literary, and modern vernacular Mandarin Chinese at Harvard University.

Ramsey Shehadeh, *Senior Vice President, NERA*
Dr. Shehadeh specializes in the economics of intellectual property and antitrust, economic design, and the application of statistical modeling and econometrics to these areas. He has extensive experience analyzing the valuation and pricing of intellectual property, including the calculation of economic damages from patent, copyright, and trademark infringement, as well as the calculation of economic damages in breach of contract and other commercial disputes. He has also conducted research and prepared reports on the competitive effects of mergers, joint ventures, and other business combinations and has addressed a broad range of market power issues in civil antitrust cases. Dr. Shehadeh's work has been incorporated into expert testimony presented in litigation, as well as before the Federal Trade Commission and the United States Department of Justice. In addition, while completing his doctorate in economics at Cornell University, he taught graduate-level courses in mathematical economics.

Marion B. Stewart, *Senior Vice President, NERA*
Dr. Stewart is the Chair of NERA's Intellectual Property Practice, which focuses on the valuation of patents, trademarks, and other intellectual property, the calculation of economic damages resulting from infringement, and other issues related to intellectual property economics. His interest in the economics of intellectual property ranges from fundamental economic research on "preemptive innovation" to practical calculation of the value of intellectual property and the evaluation of such issues as the commercial success of patented inventions. In this role, he has testified in U.S. federal and state courts on numerous intellectual property issues. Dr. Stewart's other areas of interest include the economics of antitrust and energy economics. Before joining NERA, Dr. Stewart was Associate Professor of Economics at Rutgers University. He has edited one book, *Energy Deregulation and Economic Growth,* and is the author of more than 30 articles published in *The Quarterly Journal of Economics, The American Economic Review, Journal of the Patent and Trademark Office Society, Canadian Journal of Economics, Resources and Energy,* and elsewhere.

Lauren J. Stiroh, *Senior Vice President, NERA*
Dr. Stiroh specializes in the economics of intellectual property, commercial damages, and antitrust. Much of her work and research has focused on the intersection of intellectual property and antitrust litigation. She

has conducted studies of patent value and assessed damages from patent infringement in a number of sectors. In high technology industries, in particular, she has analyzed the impact of standard setting on patent value and issues related to market power. In addition, she has conducted research and prepared expert reports on a variety of issues arising from antitrust allegations, has created and critiqued damages models in a variety of contexts, and is experienced in survey design and the econometric analysis of consumer survey data. Dr. Stiroh has presented her research before the Federal Trade Commission (FTC), the United States Department of Justice (DOJ), the Canadian Competition Bureau, and in expert testimony. She has also written articles and given speeches for the American Bar Association, Law Seminars International, the Practising Law Institute, and the 2002 FTC and DOJ joint hearings on "Competition and Intellectual Property Law and Policy in the Knowledge-Based Economy."

Paola Maria Valenti, *Senior Consultant, NERA*
Dr. Valenti specializes in the economics of intellectual property, the economics of antitrust, and the economics of commercial disputes. Her intellectual property practice focuses on the valuation of patents and the calculation of damages resulting from patent infringement. Her work in antitrust includes assessing the competitive effects of mergers and joint ventures in several industries, as well as analyzing market power issues such as price fixing, price discrimination, predatory pricing, and standard setting. In addition, as part of her commercial disputes practice, Dr. Valenti conducts research on liability and damages in disputes related to breach of contract and business interference. Prior to joining NERA, Dr. Valenti worked as a consultant at the World Bank. She has written papers on topics including literacy, child health, poverty, and inequality in developing countries.

Lawrence Wu, *Senior Vice President, NERA*
Dr. Wu specializes in intellectual property, antitrust, and health care economics. He is an expert in the application of econometrics and statistical methods and in the use of consumer surveys in litigation. He also has experience assessing antitrust issues related to the licensing of intellectual property, including patent pools. His areas of specialization include health care services and medical devices. Dr. Wu has provided written and oral expert testimony on numerous occasions, including testimony in U.S.

district courts and presentations before the Federal Trade Commission (FTC), the United States Department of Justice, and the European Commission. He also has been retained as an economic expert in price fixing and other antitrust litigation to assess issues related to liability and damages. In addition, he has published articles in *The Antitrust Bulletin, Antitrust Report, European Competition Law Review, Journal of Business Venturing,* and *Medical Care,* and he is the editor of a book, *Economics of Antitrust: New Issues, Questions, and Insights.* Prior to joining NERA, Dr. Wu was a staff economist in the FTC's Bureau of Economics.

Jason Zeitler, *Consultant, NERA*

Mr. Zeitler specializes in the economics of intellectual property and has in-depth knowledge of general financial analysis and asset valuation techniques. His work ranges from the valuation of copyrights, patents, or trademarks to the calculation of economic damages resulting from infringement. He has managed numerous patent-infringement cases for clients in the biotechnology, computer, financial services, medical supplies, pharmaceutical, and telecommunications industries. In the past, he has also worked on cases involving securities fraud and regulation of the telecommunications industry.

Index

25 percent rule
50−51, 85−88, 104

A

abbreviated new
drug application
(ANDA) 212, 215,
217, 220, 252−254
AC Nielsen 113
accounting alloca-
tion rules 192
distortions in 193
Addanki, Sumanth
268
*Advertising and
Competition:
Theory, Measure-
ment and Fact* 103
*Advertising and
Market Power* 103
Aghion, Phillipe 6
Agreement on
Trade-Related
Aspects of
Intellectual
Property Rights
(TRIPS) 278−279,
298, 307
Agribusiness 145
*Ajinomoto Co. Inc. v.
Archer-Daniels-
Midland Co.* 57, 84

*Alden W. Hanson v.
Alpine Valley Ski
Area Inc.* 84
allocated cost
measure 193
*Amazon.com Inc. v.
Barnesandnoble.
com Inc.* 210
American
Association for
Public Opinion
Research 139
*American Journal of
Agricultural
Economics* 145
ancillary sales
364−365
*Annales d'Economie
et de Statistique* 111
Anstine, Jeff 145
*Antitrust Bulletin,
The* 256, 379
*Antitrust Guidelines
for the Licensing of
Intellectual
Property* 233, 245
Antitrust Law Journal
114, 256, 374
antitrust policy 3,
6−7, 256
Applied Economics
145
*Applied Economics
Letters* 145

arm's length 14, 48,
60, 62, 66, 99,
104, 335, 338−345,
356, 373
licenses 345, 355
negotiation 344
royalty 352
transfer price
335−336, 338,
342, 345, 347,
350, 352, 358
*Aro Manufacturing
Co. v. Convertible
Top Replacement
Co.* 70
*Asking Questions: A
Practical Guide to
Questionnaire
Design* 128
asymmetric infor-
mation 361
attorneys' fees 175

B

backward citation 22
balance of hardships
210
Bands, Bruce A. 18
bargain 48, 52, 228
bargaining power 52,
59−60, 62−65, 70
bargaining range
52−54, 57, 59−60,
63−66

Baumol, William J.
178, 192
Beeney, Garrard R.
233, 245
before-after
approach 43
Berndt, Ernst R. 10,
145
beta of the stock
price 157
Beutel, Phillip A. xv,
69, 95, 359, 369
*BIC Leisure Prods.
Inc. v. Windsurfing
Intl. Inc.* 42, 115
BIC Leisure Products
79
Bigelow, J. 256, 264
*Binghamton Masonic
Temple Inc. v. City
of Binghamton*
179–180
*Bio-Rad Laboratories
Inc. v. Nicolet
Instrument Corp.*
73, 91, 211
*Bio-Technology
General Corp. v.
Genentech Inc.* 210
bioequivalence 252
Black, Fisher 322
Black-Scholes
Option Pricing
Model 321–322,
329, 331
Blinder, Alan 178
blocking 65, 233
patent 65, 237, 245

positions 233–234,
248
Bloomberg 181
Board of Patent
Appeals and
Interferences 202
Bose Corp. v. JBL Inc.
89
Bowers, Christopher
179
Bowman, Kenneth R.
145
Bradburn, Norman
128–129, 135
brand equity 103
branded drug manu-
facturers 251–252
breach of contract
97, 153, 177, 371,
377–378
Brealey, Richard
178–179, 181, 318
Bresnahan, T. 113
Bristol-Myers
254–255, 265
Brorsen, B. Wade 145
Bulow, J. 256
Bureau of Economic
Analysis (BEA) 7
Bureau of Labor
Statistics 6, 144
BuSpar 254
but-for 27, 33,
35–38, 45, 73, 75,
78, 80–81,
119–120, 171, 173,
185–186,
189–190, 194, 216,
280

cost 28
investment 171
price 28–29, 37,
73, 123, 155
quantity 28
world 27–29,
31–39, 41, 43,
45–47, 112–113,
115, 117–124,
141, 158, 186,
189, 241, 267
Butler, Sarah M. 125,
369

C

*Cable Electric
Products Inc. v.
Genmork Inc.*
197–198
Cabral, Luis 8
Canon Kabushiki
Kaisha 277
capacity constraints
39, 190
Carlson, Steven C.
234
causation 37, 46, 73,
77, 104, 186, 204
*Cayuga Indian Nation
of New York v.
Pataki* 170
*Cede & Co. v.
Techicolor Inc.* 181
*Cement Division,
Natl. Gypsum Co.,
et al. v. City of
Milwaukee* 170
Cervero, Robert 145

China ix, xiii, 285,
293–309, 311, 313
Code-Alarm 92
Code-Alarm Inc. v.
Electromotive
Technologies Corp.
92
Comanor, William S.
103
Combris, Pierre 145
comparable profit
split method
(CPSM) 339, 341,
345
comparable profits
method (CPM)
339–341, 345, 352
comparable
uncontrolled
transaction (CUT)
method 339–342,
345–347, 350, 352
comparables 48, 61,
74, 90, 340
method 49
transaction 91
compatibility 77–78,
229, 232
competitive effects
44, 111–112, 235,
244, 246–247,
249, 265, 373–375,
377–378
complementarity 40,
77–78, 236, 240
complements 40,
77–78, 236
complementary
goods 77

Computer Assisted
Telephone Inter-
viewing (CATI) 127
confidence interval
128, 164–165, 166
constant mean
return model 158,
160
Consumer Price
Index (CPI) 144
consumer surplus
257–261, 264,
295–296
consumer welfare 4,
7–9, 237, 243, 251,
259, 264
Converse, Jean 135
convoyed sales 34,
40–41, 46, 90, 112,
364
Cook, Joseph P. 141,
267, 370
Copeland, Tom 320
copying 195
copyrights ix, xii, 21,
95, 106, 293, 298,
310–311, 376, 379
Corfam 12
corrective
advertising 106
Cost Allocation
Rules 192
cost method 102
cost-saving
invention 64
costs 9, 12, 14, 19, 28,
32–33, 35, 39, 44,
48, 52–58, 66,
73–74, 83, 87–91,

96, 98–100, 103,
105, 123, 144, 171,
173–174, 180–182,
186–193, 196,
199–203, 207,
212–214, 216, 220,
225–228,
230–232, 234,
237–238, 245, 247,
282–283,
294–296, 298,
300, 304–306,
308, 312, 318, 320,
324–325, 330–331,
336, 343–344,
346–347,
355–356, 358–361,
365
administrative 186,
296
compliance 226
debt 170–171, 174
direct 186, 231
direct labor 186
fixed 33, 74, 186,
190, 193,
282–283, 329
incremental
40–41, 83,
85–86, 93, 106,
144, 147,
185–191, 193, 365
labor 186, 296
linear transporta-
tion 272
litigation 257,
261–262,
264–265, 277,
280

lumpy 193
nonlinear 190
opportunity 82,
  99, 102, 106, 231
product 186
sunk 57—58, 240,
  248
transaction 226,
  233—234, 237
transportation
  190, 272
variable 186,
  191—193
variable overhead
  186
Cotter, T. 256
counterfeiting 295,
  310—311
Cox, Alan 293, 370
Crane, D. 252, 256
cross-licensing 233,
  256
  discounts 241
*Crystal
  Semiconductor
  Corp. v. Tritech
  Microelectronics
  Intl. Inc.* 42—43,
  79, 115—116, 268
Cunningham, M. A.
  217
*Current Issues in
  Economics and
  Finance* 8
customer lists 46,
  95, 335

D

daily excess returns
  156
damages xi—xii,
  27—28, 34, 40, 45,
  47—49, 52, 65—66,
  69—78, 80—81, 83,
  89—91, 95—96,
  104—107, 111—112,
  115, 117, 119—120,
  123—125, 136, 144,
  149, 151, 153,
  155—156, 162,
  166—167,
  169—170, 172—180,
  182—183, 185—186,
  191, 193, 209—212,
  216, 219, 252,
  267—268,
  271—272, 274,
  277—285, 288,
  290—291,
  293—294,
  299—301,
  303—313, 360, 365,
  367—379
  calculating 82
  compensatory xii
  economic 66, 104,
    106, 144, 278,
    280, 282, 284,
    289, 293—294,
    300, 370—371,
    374—377, 379
  noneconomic
    methods xii
  speculative 211
  treble 175, 284, 290

*Datascope Corp. v.
  SMEC Inc.* 175
Daubert challenge
  107
David, Jesse xv, 169,
  195, 371
Davidson, C. 111
Davidson, Sidney
  186
dead-weight loss 231
debt rate 172—174
  defendant's 172
decision tree
  321—324, 326—329
Defense Department
  3
*Del Mar Avionics v.
  Quinton Instrument
  Co.* 74
*Demaco Corp. v. Fl.
  Von Langsdorff
  Licensing Ltd.* 197
demand curve
  29—33, 36—39, 362
demand elasticity 39
demand-enhancing
  invention 64
Deneckere, R. 111
Department of
  Justice (DOJ) 111,
  233, 235, 245—246,
  378
Diamond, Shari 127
differentiated
  products 28, 111, 124
Digital Equipment
  Corporation 10
DiMasi, Joseph A.
  214

diminution of a
patent owner's
brand value 95
Dippon, Christian
xv, 277, 371
disclosure rules
224–226, 232
discount rate 40,
101, 169, 177–183,
318–320, 325, 331,
347, 350, 352
discounted cash flow
(DCF) 101, 218,
317–320, 322, 326,
328–330, 332
discounted net
present value 202
*Discrete Choice
Methods with
Simulation* 142, 147
discrete choice mod-
els xii, 147–148
discriminatory
licensing 242,
246–248
diseconomies of
scale 190
distribution
agreements 95
DOJ and FTC Joint
Hearings on
Competition and
Intellectual
Property Law and
Policy in the
Knowledge-Based
Economy 233
double-blind 130, 137
double counting 54,

106
*Dow Chemical Co. v.
Mee Industries Inc.*
60
Dow Jones Industrial
Average 159
Dunbar, Frederick
144, 153, 156
Duncan, Michael 145
DuPont 12

E

*Ecolochem Inc. v.
Southern California
Edison Co.* 197
econometric models
17, 142
discrete consumer
choice 142
Econometrica 6, 14,
113
*Economic Analysis of
Law* 199
Economic Inquiry 215
Economic Journal
14–15, 272
economic principles
xi, 27–28, 34, 41,
47, 69, 73, 81–82,
105, 112, 124, 195,
211, 278, 281, 291
economic rationality
58, 69, 72, 77, 79
*Economics of
Advertising, The*
103
*Economics of New
Goods, The* 113

*Economics: Principles
and Policy* 178
economies of scale
54, 190, 248
elasticity of demand
36, 38–39, 41, 80,
114, 119, 362–365
See also demand
elasticity
cross–price
36–37, 44–45,
118–119,
121–123
own-price 36–37,
39, 43, 118, 362
electronics industry
15
Elfakhani, Said 176
Eli Lilly 217–219
*Eli Lilly and Co. v.
American
Cyanamid Co.* 217
Energy Capital
Corporation 182
entire market value
rule 76
Epstein, R. 114
Ericksen, Eugene P.
125, 371
Escher, Susan 172
Espinosa, Juan A. 145
Esquibel, A. K. 174
established royalty
47, 60–61, 66, 90,
92
estimation window
157–161, 165
Ethridge, Don E. 145
Evans, David S. 268

eve of first infringe-
ment 48, 57–58, 65
event study 153–158,
166–167
See also event
studies
methodology xii,
153, 155–156,
165, 167
misuse of 166
event window
156–157, 162–163,
165, 167
explanatory variables
142, 147

F

fair market value
97–98
false advertising 125,
134–135, 139, 369
false infringement
claims 167
Federal Reserve
Board 180
Federal Rule of
Evidence 703 127
Federal Trade
Commission (FTC)
111, 233, 245,
251–255, 265,
378–379
Ferguson, James M.
103
Financial Accounting
Standards Board
(FASB) 96–97, 369

Financial Accounting:
An Introduction to
Concepts, Methods,
and Uses, 6th ed.
186
financial options
318, 319
first infringement
48, 57–58, 65,
70–71, 81
First National Bank v.
Standard Bank 170
Fisher, Franklin M.
170, 172–175
five-channel audio
technology 242
Florida Law Review
252
Fogarty, Michael S.
18
follow-on sales 364
Fonar Corp. and Dr.
Raymond V.
Damadian v.
General Electric
Co., and Drucker &
Genuth, MDS, P.C.,
d/b/a South Shore
Imaging Associates
89
forward citation 22
forward payment
252, 256, 259, 261
forward self-citation
22
four-factor standard
209
Frank, Peter B. 91,
153

Frank, Richard G. 215
free of unfair
discrimination
condition 230
Frey v. Smith & Sons
180
Froeb, L. 111, 113
FTC v. Bristol-Myers
Squibb Corp.
254–255, 265
FTC v. Schering-
Plough Corp. 254
Fuji Photo File Co.
Ltd. 277
Full Draw Productions
v. Easton Sports Inc.
269
functionally related
77, 365

G

Gallini, Nancy T. 19
Gambardella,
Alfonso 207
gamma (γ) 160
Gassmann, Oliver
317
generic drugs 212,
251–252
Genzyme 7–8
geographic markets
269
George Mason Law
Review 111, 374

Georgia-Pacific Corp. v. United States Plywood Corp. 48, 57, 60, 69–71, 74, 83, 86, 90, 151

Georgia-Pacific Factors 60–61, 65, 70, 86, 89–90

Gilbert, Richard J. 234

Goldscheider, Robert 50, 85–88

goods market transactions 49

goodwill 97, 103, 211

Goodwin, Barry K. 145

Gordan, R. 113

Grabowski, Henry G. 214

Graham v. John Deere Co. 196

Grain Processing Corp. v. American Maize-Products Co. 27, 35, 53, 79, 80–85

Grant, Warren R. 145

grantback provisions 242, 245–246, 248

Griliches, Zvi 9, 142, 145

Grossman, Gene M. 6

H

H.H. Robertson Co. v. United Steel Deck Inc. 210

Hagy, Alison P. 145

Hall, Bronwyn H. 19–21

handheld personal digital assistant devices 21

Hannes, Steven 355

Hansen, Phillip 145

Hansen, Ronald W. 214

Harvard Business Review 320

Hausman, J. 111–114

Health Affairs 214

health industries 21

hedonic models 98, 144

hedonic price regressions 142–145, 147

Heineken 42

Helpman, Elhanan 6

Hensher, David A. 148

Higinbotham, Harlow 342

Hitachi Ltd. 277, 288

Ho, Mun S. 8

Hotelling model 272

Hotelling, H. 272

Howard A. Fromson v. Western Lithoplate and Supply Co. and Bemis Co. Inc. 89

Howitt, Peter 6

Hybritech Inc. 197–198, 210–211

Hybritech Inc. v. Abbott Laboratories 210

Hybritech Inc. v. Monoclonal Antibodies Inc. 197

hypothetical 28, 44, 73, 84, 88, 95, 97, 112, 117, 126, 146, 154, 156–157, 160–162, 166, 269, 281, 323–324, 337–339, 345, 352, 359

license 49, 92–93, 151

negotiation 48–49, 52, 54, 57, 60–62, 64–66, 70–71, 83, 85–93, 141, 281, 283–284

I

Ibbotson Associates 181

IBM 10

IDEA: The Journal of Law and Technology 217

Illinois Tool Works Inc. v. Grip-Pak Inc. 210–211, 219

IMS Health 113

In re Ben Huang 199, 202

In re Denis Rouffet,
Yannick Tanguy,
and Frederic
Berthault 195
In re Mahurkar
Double Lumen
Hemodialysis
Catheter Patent
Litigation 79
In the matter of
Genzyme Corp./
Novazyme Pharma-
ceuticals Inc. 7–8
In the Matter of
Rambus Inc. 6–7
incremental costs
xii, 40–41, 83,
85–86, 93, 106,
144, 147, 185–191,
193, 365
analysis 185, 188,
194
multiproduct
setting 191
incremental
revenues 185
incremental sales 63,
186–187, 190, 194
Industrial
Organization,
Economics, and the
Law: Collected
Papers of Franklin
M. Fisher 170
industry averages
48–51, 62, 92, 212
method 49–50
industry price index
188

information
asymmetries 177
Information
Resources, Inc.
(IRI) 113
infringement xi, xiii,
14, 19, 21, 27–31,
33–35, 37–38,
40–41, 43–45,
47–48, 53, 57,
65–67, 69–73,
75–84, 90–91, 95,
105–106, 112,
125–126, 136, 139,
144, 149, 151,
153–155, 157, 167,
170, 175, 177, 179,
185–186, 189, 201,
209–211, 215–217,
220, 233–234, 239,
251–254, 267–270,
272, 278, 280–282,
284, 287, 290–291,
293, 295, 297, 299,
301–303, 305, 308,
310–312, 352,
359–360,
362–364, 366, 368
injunctive relief
209–212, 217–218,
363
innovation ix–xii,
3–11, 13, 16–20,
22–23, 78, 207,
212, 214, 233,
237–238, 242,
245–246, 256,
294–296, 317

economically
efficient 9
market 3–4, 6,
8–9
Innovation and
Growth in the
Global Economy 6
Innovation and Its
Discontents: How
Our Broken Patent
System Is
Endangering
Innovation and
Progress, and What
to Do About It 9
Innovation Policy and
the Economy 237,
256
intangible 95
assets ix, 95–97,
101, 106, 143,
335, 369
property 335–346,
350, 352, 355,
358, 373
intellectual property
ix, xii, 3–4, 6–8,
12–13, 17, 21, 27,
44, 47, 69, 75, 91,
95, 98, 111–112,
114, 118, 125–128,
130, 136, 139, 141,
143–144, 147, 151,
153–154, 167, 169,
179, 185, 223–224,
226–227, 233–234,
237, 244–247, 265,
268, 277–278, 281,
285, 287–288, 290,

293, 295–302, 307,
309–310, 312, 317,
335, 359, 369–379
economics 6, 12
litigation 111,
153–154, 167,
268, 288, 370,
373
policy 21
surveys 126–128,
136
*Intellectual Property
Infringement
Damages: A
Litigation Support
Handbook, 2003
Cumulative
Supplement* 179
interest rate xii,
169–172, 176,
179–180, 182–183,
200, 322, 331
internal rate of
return 173
Internal Revenue
Service (IRS) 336,
339
*International
Handbook on
Innovation* 317
*International Journal
of the Economics of
Business* 113
International Patent
Classification 22
intracompany
royalty 95
trademark
licensing 96

IP Litigator 268
irreparable harm xii,
209–212, 215–220
IRS section 482 reg-
ulations 339

J

*J.T. Eaton and Co. v.
Atlantic Paste and
Glue Co.* 197
Jaffe, Adam B. 9,
17–18, 237
James, Charles A. 233
Japan ix, xiii, 22,
277–278,
280–285,
287–291, 294
Japanese Patent law
278, 280, 288
Jarosz, John 50, 86,
88
*Jeffrey Gilbert v.
MPM Enterprises
Inc.* 181
Jensen, Gail A. 145
Johnson, John H. xv,
13, 153, 372
joint licensing 233,
239–240, 243, 246
arrangements 233,
245
*Joint Licensing of
Multiple Patents*
240
joint profit maxi-
mization 114
*Jones & Laughlin Steel
Corp. v. Pfeifer* 177

Jones, Charles I. 6
Jones, Derek C. 8
Jorgenson, Dale W. 8
*Journal of
Accounting,
Auditing and
Finance* 174
*Journal of Cultural
Economics* 145
*Journal of Economic
Behavior and
Organization* 8, 370
*Journal of Economic
Literature* 156
*Journal of Economics
& Management
Strategy* 215
*Journal of Health
Economics* 214, 375
*Journal of Human
Resources* 145
*Journal of Industrial
Economics, The*
17–18, 103, 112,
145, 374
*Journal of Law and
Economics* 192
*Journal of Law,
Economics, &
Organization* 111
*Journal of Legal
Studies, The* 172
*Journal of Political
Economy* 6, 142,
322, 370
*Journal of Proprietary
Rights* 90
Judge Easterbrook 80

*Juicy Whip Inc. v.
Orange Bang Inc.* 78
Juneja, Vinita M. 153,
372

K

Kakihara, Noriko
277, 373
Kalos, Stephen H. 90
*King Instrument
Corp. v. Luciano
Perego et al.* 78
Kish, Leslie 137
Klein, Joel I. 233, 245
Kodak 20, 89
Koehn, Michael F.
192
Koller, Tim 320
Korenko, George G.
317, 335, 341, 345, 373
Kruger, Kurt 172

L

*Laitram Corp. v. NEC
Corp.* 173
*Lam Inc. v. Johns-
Manville Corp.* 47,
73, 211
Landes, Elisabeth M.
103
Lanham Act 125
See also Lanham
Trademark Act
*Lanham Trademark
Act* 106, 134, 376
Lanjouw, Jean Olson
14–17, 21–22
Lanzillotti, R. F. 174

leader-follower
model 114
Lecocq, Sebastien
145
Lee, Susan C.S. 267,
373
Lee, William
Marshall 87
Leonard, Gregory K.
xiii, 27, 111–112,
251, 374
Lerner, Joshua 9,
236–237
les Nouvelles 50,
85–88
*Lesona Corp. v.
United States* 76
Lewent, Judy 320
license fee 225, 308
licensing 13–14, 49,
52–55, 59, 62, 71,
78, 83, 85, 88, 90,
92–93, 95–97, 99,
104, 106, 112, 141,
144, 149, 151, 153,
166–167, 195, 197,
224–226, 228,
231–233, 239–248,
256, 281, 297, 337,
352, 355–357,
360–361, 363,
365–368
agreement 13, 52,
149, 153,
166–167, 239,
247, 281, 365,
367
negotiations 112,
144, 240, 281

linear cost function
191
litigation xi–xii, 14,
21–23, 27, 60, 65,
69, 73, 79, 91, 93,
95–96, 111,
124–125, 136, 139,
141, 149, 151,
153–154, 167,
172–174, 177, 179,
210–211, 216,
233–234, 251–252,
254–265, 267–268,
277–280, 285, 288,
291, 293, 308–310,
312, 352, 359–360,
364–368
costs 257, 261–262,
264–265, 277,
280
patent xii, 21–22,
69, 79, 124, 195,
210, 217,
251–252,
255–256, 259,
261, 265, 279,
291, 359, 371
strategy 360, 364,
366, 368
*Litigation Economics
Review* 172
*Litigation Services
Handbook: The
Role of the
Financial Expert* 153
*Lleco Holdings Inc. v.
Otto Candies Inc.*
179

Locatelli-Biey, Marilena 145

Logistics and Transportation Review 145

long-felt but unsolved need 195

lost profits xii—xiii, 27, 32—35, 37, 40—41, 45—48, 53—55, 66, 71—81, 99, 105, 111—112, 115, 117, 119—120, 124, 153, 166—167, 177—178, 180—181, 183, 185, 212, 216, 267—274, 278—280, 282—284, 290—291, 294, 361, 363, 365, 367

  calculation xii, 54, 74

  convoyed sales 34, 41, 46

lost sales 32—34, 39—43, 45—46, 54, 71, 73, 76—78, 82, 105, 112, 115—116, 119—120, 122, 149, 187, 191—192, 216, 268, 272, 280, 294, 362, 364

Louviere, Jordan J. 148

lump-sum payments 231

Lutz, Alyssa 185, 268, 374

M

MacKinlay, A. Craig 156

Mahurkar Double Lumen Hemodialysis Catheter Patent Litigation 79

make-whole 66, 74, 76—77, 173, 175, 280

Maness, Robert 215

Manual for Complex Litigation 125, 139

Manual of Patent Examining Procedure 198

marginal cost 30—31, 33, 44, 73, 114, 118, 244, 247—248

marginal revenue curve 30, 33

market xiii, 4, 8—10, 12, 14, 28, 31—32, 34—39, 41—43, 45, 48—54, 56, 70—71, 73—76, 79—81, 86, 90, 92—93, 96—99, 101—102, 104, 106, 112—113, 115—123, 126—127, 130—131, 141—142, 146, 148—151, 153—154, 157—162, 164, 167, 174—175, 177, 182—183, 189, 194—198, 200—201, 203—206, 211—212, 214—215, 217, 219, 223—224, 226, 228—231, 234—235, 237—238, 240—242, 246—248, 252—260, 262, 267—274, 287, 317—320, 332, 337, 340—342, 344, 346, 355—357, 359—367

  definition 115, 268, 269

  expansion effect 122

  factors 48, 142, 238, 240

  models 158, 160, 165, 215

  segment rule 115

  share approach 41—43

  transaction method 102

market power xii, 72, 75, 103, 113, 223, 229, 232, 239, 242, 268, 270—271, 274, 363

market-based evidence 13, 69, 74—75

market-based method 49—50

market-based negotiation 52, 65

market-based
  royalty range 52
Matsushita Electric
  Industrial Co. Ltd.
  277
McCarthy, Thomas
  R. 233, 374–375
McDermott, Will &
  Emery 355
meaningful context
  197, 202
mechanical indus-
  tries 15
Medicare
  Prescription Drug,
  Improvement, and
  Modernization Act
  of 2003, The 253
Medicare reform bill
  265
Mehring, Joyce S. 145
Merck 320
Merck & Co. Inc. v.
  Teva
  Pharmaceuticals
  USA Inc. 149
Merck and Co. v.
  Danbury Pharmacal
  Inc. 198
merger simulation
  44, 111, 114
merger-induced
  price effects 111
mergers xii, 44, 111,
  236, 337
Meyer, Christine 83,
  169, 375
Micro Chemical Inc. v.
  Lextron Inc. 81

Miles Laboratories
  Inc. v. Shandon Inc.
  199
Minnesota Mining
  and Manufacturing
  Co. v. Alphapharm
  Pty. Ltd. 218
Minnesota Mining
  and Manufacturing
  Co. v. Johnson &
  Johnson
  Orthopaedics Inc.
  211
misappropriation of
  trade secrets 177
misrepresentations
  of technology 167
Mobil Oil
  Corporation v.
  Amoco Chemicals
  Corp. 84
model of strategic
  interaction 114
monopoly profits
  239, 255
Monz, John 170
Morrisey, Michael A.
  145
Mortimer, Rika
  Onishi 251, 375
Mulhern, Carla 50,
  86, 88
multivariate
  regression model
  158, 160
Murrin, Jack 320
Myers, Stewart C.
  178–179, 181, 318

N

NASA 18
Nash bargaining
  solution 261
Nash-Bertrand equi-
  librium 114, 118
National Science
  Foundation 5
Neibergs, J. Shannon
  145
NERA Economic
  Consulting ix, xi,
  xv, 112, 210, 268,
  342
net present value
  (NPV) 202,
  318–319, 325, 330,
  339, 344,
  346–354, 356–357
network industries
  248
Neupak Inc. v. Ideal
  Manufacturing and
  Sales Corp. 197,
  202
Nevo, A. 111, 113
New Economy
  Handbook 8
nexus 195, 198, 200,
  202, 204–205
Nichols, Nancy A.
  320
Nikon 78
noncompete/non-
  solicitation clauses
  in employment
  agreements
  95–96, 105–106

noneconomic methods xii, 83, 278

nonleading question 129

nonobviousness claim 198

nonpatent intellectual property 95

nonprobability sample 136–137

Nordhaus, William 178

normative analysis 199

Northern Helix Co. v. The United States 180

novel 22, 52, 223, 302

Novo Nordisk of North America Inc. v. Genentech Inc. 210

NTP Inc. 21

O

O'Brien, Vincent E. 91

obviousness 195

Organisation for Economic Co-operation and Development (OECD) 338–339

P

Pakes, Ariel 14–15, 17

Panduit Corp. v. Stahlin Bros. Fibre Works Inc. 35, 69, 185

Panduit factor 35, 38–39, 41

Paper Converting Machine Co. v. Magna-Graphics Corp. 74

Parr, Russell L. 143, 179

Patell, James M. 172

patent in suit 60, 65, 90

patent litigation xii, 21, 24, 27, 69, 79, 124, 195, 210, 251–252, 255–256, 259, 261, 265, 279, 291, 359, 371

patents xi, 4, 7–9, 13–23, 49–50, 61–63, 70, 74, 86, 90–91, 95, 136, 142, 196, 212, 223–226, 230, 232–237, 239–246, 248–249, 252–253, 256, 277–278, 281, 283, 285, 287, 290, 293, 298, 302, 304, 306–307, 309–311, 337
comparable 61
duration 61, 63, 170, 307
essential 234–236, 239–246, 248

infringement xi, xiii, 21, 27–28, 37–38, 41, 45, 69–70, 80, 82–83, 105, 112, 125, 136, 139, 144, 149, 153–154, 157, 175, 177, 185, 209–210, 217, 220, 234, 251–252, 254, 267–268, 278, 280, 284, 287, 302, 308, 352, 368, 371–372, 375, 378–379
nonessential 242–244
survey 126

per-patent valuation 244

pharmaceutical ix, xii, 8, 15, 21, 38, 113, 123, 135, 201, 205–206, 209, 212–215, 217–220, 251–253, 259, 302, 331–332, 337, 343, 346

Pharmaceutical Research and Manufacturers of America 207, 212–213

Pharmacia 211, 219–220

Pharmacia & Upjohn Co. (Pharmacia) 211, 219–220

Polaroid 20, 89, 92

Polaroid Corp. v. Eastman Kodak Co. 89

Polymer Technologies Inc. v. P. Bridwell 210

Posner, Richard A. 199, 201

prejudgment interest rate 169–170, 172, 183

preliminary injunction xii, 157, 209–211, 217–219, 359–360

Presser, Stanley 135

price discrimination 230–231, 246–248

price erosion 33–34, 38, 41, 43, 45, 54, 71, 73, 80, 105, 119–120, 122–124, 220, 268, 272, 280, 362–363, 366

Price Indexes and Quality Change 142

price-cost margins 80, 114

price-sensitivity 29–30, 32, 36, 38–39

prime rate 170

Principles of Corporate Finance 178–179, 181, 318

prior art 35, 63, 195, 279

product bundling 235

product characteristic 141–142, 144, 146–148

methods for measuring the value of 141

profit split methods 89, 340

profit-maximizing quantity 30

property rights ix, 4, 21, 185, 224, 265, 278, 287, 293, 295–296, 298

public interest 210

Public Utilities Fortnightly 192

Purdue Pharma L.P. v. Boehringer Ingelheim GMBH 210

Putman, Jonathan D. 17

Q

quality-adjusted price index 144

quantity index 188

Quarterly Journal of Economics 6, 377

R

Rambus 6–7

Ramos, Carey R. 233

RAND Journal of Economics 14, 16, 19, 21, 111, 227, 256

Rapp, Richard T. xv, 69, 223, 376

Ray, Bryan 69, 83, 376

real and nominal price increases 80

real option method 317–324, 326–327, 329, 331–332

reasonable and non-discriminatory (RAND) 226, 228–229, 246

reasonable royalty 27, 47–48, 50, 52–54, 56, 59–60, 62, 64–66, 69–72, 74, 76, 81–85, 87–93, 106, 112, 141, 209, 228, 244, 280

calculations 185, 283

reasonably foreseeable 76–77

reduced form model 144

Reebok Intl., Ltd. v. J. Baker Inc. 210–211

Reference Manual on Scientific Evidence 127

regression analysis 22, 142, 187–188, 191

relevant product 137, 269

relief-from-royalty 104

replacement cost
approach 101
research and
development
(R&D) ix, xii, 3–4,
6–10, 12, 15,
18–20, 154,
200–201, 205,
211–220, 227, 246,
277, 317–321,
323–330, 332–333,
337, 347–348, 351,
353, 355–357
Research in Motion
21
residual profit split
method (RPSM)
339, 341–345, 352
retail scanner data
113
reverse payments
xiii, 251–252,
255–256,
260–261,
264–265
*Review of Economic
Studies* 6, 14
*Review of Economics
and Statistics* 145
right to exclude
209–210, 216
right to practice the
patent 62–63
risk 86, 96, 99, 101,
105, 169, 172–175,
178, 181–183, 199,
214, 226–227, 231,
234, 237, 257,
294–295, 297,

318–319, 321,
329–330, 332,
344–345, 347, 357,
361, 362
free rate 170,
173–177, 180,
182
aversion 261–262,
265
premium 262
Rister, M. Edward
145
*Rite-Hite Corp. v.
Kelley Co. Inc.* 40,
55, 76, 78, 365
RJ Reynolds' smoke-
less cigarette 12
Robbins, Richard L.
196
robustness 158, 166
Romaine, R. Craig
170, 172–175
Romer, Paul M. 6
*Roper Corp. v. Litton
Systems Inc.* 210
Rosen, Sherwin 142
Rosenberg, Nathan
8, 11
Rosenfield, Andrew
M. 103
royalty 47–66,
70–71, 74–76,
85–92, 95–96, 99,
104–105, 224–225,
228–231, 234, 241,
244, 247, 255, 259,
279, 283, 344, 347,
354, 356, 361–367
arm's length 60, 352

bargain 48, 52, 228
calculations 69,
74, 83, 185, 283
damage calcula-
tions 66
determination
48–51, 54–55,
71, 228
measure of
damages 85
negotiations 66, 93
opportunistic
224–225
royalty rate 14, 61, 63,
87, 89, 91–92, 223,
231, 238, 240–242,
244–245, 248, 281,
342, 347, 349–350,
352, 354–355, 361,
367
royalty rates 50, 70,
74, 85–87, 91–93,
228, 235–242, 244,
246–248, 281, 367
Rozek, Richard P.
340–341, 345, 347
Rubinfeld, D. 114
rule of thumb
48–50, 85, 89, 104

S

Salkever, David S.
215
sample sizes 137
sampling methods
44
Samuelson, Paul 178
Sarbanes-Oxley Act

of 2002 336
Schankerman, Mark
 14–16, 21–22, 227
Schein 254
Scherer, F. M. 214
Schildkraut, M. 256
Schmalensee,
 Richard 103
Scholes, Myron 322
Schwarz, Norbert 135
Science and Inno-
 vation: The U.S.
 Pharmaceutical
 Industry During the
 1980s 207
secondary 157, 220
 considerations
 195, 197
 meaning 130–131,
 133
segment share
 approach 42–43
Segway 10–11
semi-conductor
 industry 19
Semiconductor Corp.
 v. Tritech Micro-
 electronics Intl. Inc.
 et al. 42, 79, 115,
 268
Sepetys, Kristina xv,
 293, 376
Serwin, Ken xv
SFAS No. 141,
 Business
 Combinations 97
SFAS No. 142,
 Goodwill and Other
 Intangible Assets

97
Shapiro, Carl 237,
 256
Shehadeh, Ramsey
 210, 267, 377
Shelper, Nicole 144
Simmons, Phil 145
simple interest 171
simulation model
 124
Smith International
 Inc. v. Hughes Tool
 Co. 210
Smith, Gordon V. 143
social welfare xi, 10,
 231, 264–265, 295
 losses 231
Sony Corp. 277
SSNIP 269
Standard Havens
 Products Inc. v.
 Gencor Industries
 Inc. 211
Standard Manufac-
 turing Co. Inc. v.
 United States 89
standard setting
 223–231, 235, 237
standard-setting
 organization (SSO)
 xii, 224, 227, 230, 232
Stanley, Linda R. 145
State Industries Inc. v.
 Mor-Flo Industries
 Inc. 41, 75, 115
State Industries' 75
state of mind of the
 respondent 139
Stated Choice

Methods: Analysis
 and Application
 148
Statement of
 Financial
 Accounting
 Standard (SFAS)
 97
statistical analysis
 128, 160, 186–187
statistically signifi-
 cant 128, 137, 146,
 156, 165
statutory fixed rates
 170
Stern, Scott 237
Stewart, Marion B.
 xv, 195, 210, 268,
 377
Stickney, Clyde P.
 186
Stiroh, Kevin 8
Stiroh, Lauren J. xiii,
 3, 27, 223, 268, 377
stock market index
 model 158, 160
stock market model
 160
Stocks, Bonds, Bills
 and Inflation:
 Valuation Edition:
 2003 Yearbook 181
strategic response
 hypothesis 19–20
structure of demand
 45
substitutability 30,
 79, 236
substitutes 30,

36–37, 41–43,
50–51, 72, 74–75,
79, 82, 118, 123,
223, 235–236, 244,
267–271
noninfringing 35,
72–75, 267
Sudman, Seymour
128–129, 135
sunk investments
58, 225
Super Audio CD
[SACD] 242
Supreme Court of
the United States
70, 177, 196
*Survey Questions:
Handcrafting the
Standardized
Questionnaire* 135
surveys 18, 44,
104–105, 125,
127–130, 132–134,
136, 139
questions 128–135
sampling 44, 137
secondary
meaning
130–131, 133
telephone
127–129, 133,
136, 139
validation
128–129, 321
Suzumara, Kotar 9
Swait, Joffre D. 148

T

Tabak, David 153, 156
Takenaka, Toshiko
280–281
tangible asset 97,
102
*Tax Notes
International*
340–341
technical substitutes
72, 75
technological
progress 3–4,
7–10, 55, 63
*Technology and
Growth* 8
*Technology
Management
Handbook* 50
technology market 4,
9, 49, 223, 226,
228, 231–232
Texas Instruments
20
*The Practice of
Econometrics:
Classic and
Contemporary* 10
*The Procter & Gamble
Co. v. Paragon
Trade Brands Inc.*
89, 92
theft of trade secrets
95–96, 153, 178
*Thinking About
Answers* 135
Thompson, R. S. 145
Tights Inc. v. Kayser-

Roth Corp. 84
time value of money
169, 175, 178–179,
181–183, 216, 284,
318
*Timing of the
Negotiation* 57–58
Tirole, Jean 236
Toshiba Corp. 277,
288
trade dress 95, 104,
125, 130, 139
trade secrets ix,
95–96, 153,
177–178, 284, 298
trademarks ix, xii, 21,
95, 99, 103, 106,
293, 303–304,
307, 309–311, 362
Train, Kenneth E.
142, 147
Trajtenberg, Manuel
18
transactional sales
data 146
*Transco Prods. Inc. v.
Performance
Contracting Inc.* 175
transfer prices 96,
336–339, 341, 345,
352, 358
Treasury Inspector
General for Tax
Administration
336
Treasury-bill rate
170
*Trell v. Marlee Elecs.
Corp.* 91

triopoly 272–273
TSC Industries Inc. v. Northway Inc. 156
Tschirhart, John 145
TWM Manufacturing Co. Inc. v. Dura Corp. and Kidde Inc. 73
tying 235, 242–244, 247–248

U

U.S. Department of Labor 6, 144
U.S. Department of Labor, Bureau of Labor Statistics 144
U.S. District Courts 21, 277
U.S. Securities and Exchange Commission 343
unbiased signal 262
uncertainty xii, 3–4, 7–12, 66, 158, 172, 178, 180, 200–201, 234, 236, 317–318, 320–321, 324, 326, 330, 332, 360
unfair discrimination 230–231
United States Court of Appeals for the Eleventh Circuit 255

United States Court of Appeals for the Federal Circuit (CAFC) 19, 60, 73, 89, 149, 182, 210
United States Court of Appeals for the Sixth Circuit 69
United States Department of Justice 111, 223, 233, 375, 377–379
United States District Court for the District of New Jersey 219–220
United States International Trade Commission (ITC) 277, 376
United States Patent and Trademark Office 4, 19, 134, 149, 198, 209, 277
United States Patent and Trademark Office Annual Reports 4–5
University of Chicago Law Review 179
University of Houston Law Center 217
University of Pennsylvania Law Review 196–197
unjust enrichment 106, 294

Urban Studies 145
Utah Medical Products Inc. v. Graphic Controls Corp. 92

V

Valenti, Paola Maria xv, 185, 378
valuation 14, 17, 47, 74, 95–97, 99–105, 107, 113, 141–142, 147, 167, 180, 244–245, 320–322, 336, 347, 352
Valuation of Intellectual Property and Intangible Assets 143
value-in-use 97–99
Visser, Michael 145
Volkswagen 130–132
von Zedtwitz, Maximilian 317

W

W.L. Gore & Associates Inc. and Gore Enterprise Holdings Inc. v. International Medical Prosthetics Research Associates Inc. 89

Wagner, Michael J. 91, 153

walk-away points 112, 257

Wang, Z. 145

weighted average cost of capital (WACC) 174, 181

Weil, Roman L. 153, 172, 186

Werden, G. 111, 113–114

Western Journal of Agricultural Economics 145

Wiggins, Steven 215

Willig, R. 192, 256, 264

willingness to accept 53, 59, 63, 66, 74

willingness to pay 44, 53, 55–56, 59, 62–65, 100, 144, 147–148, 238

Wilson, Thomas A. 103

Windhover and Recombinant Capital (Recap) 343

Wolfson, Mark A. 172

Wu, Lawrence xv, 233, 378–379

X

Xerox 133

Y

Yale Journal on Regulation 234

Yarway Corp. v. EUR Control USA Inc. et al. 73

Yin, Xiangkang 8

Z

Zanola, Roberto 145

Zeitler, Jason xv, 209, 379

Ziedonis, Rosemarie Ham 19–20

Zona, J.D. 111–114

Zuscovitch, Ehud 8